BAYEUX IN THE LATE EIGHTEENTH CENTURY

A plan of Bayeux after a plan of *c.* 1767

To Caen

St Nicolas de la Chêsnée

St. Exupère Par.

et Manufacture des Pauvres

le-Petit Bureau

St. Jean Par.

Hôpital Général

les Capucins

la Madeleine Par.

Halle au blé

le Collège

Séminaire

St. Vigor Hôtel Dieu

le Petit Par.

AURE

St. Laurent Par.

St. Ouen Par.

St. Martin Par.

Evêché

les Augustins

St. Sauveur P. r.

St. Malo Par.

la Cathédrale

Doyenné

Abreuvoir

AURE

St. Patrice Par.

la Charité

le Marché

St. André Par.

St. Ouen du Château Par.

la Poterie Par.

la Barrière

To Port en Bessin

les Ursulines

les Bénédictines

les Cordeliers

To Balleroy

To Cherbourg

BAYEUX IN THE LATE EIGHTEENTH CENTURY

A Social Study

BY

OLWEN H. HUFTON

OXFORD
AT THE CLARENDON PRESS
1967

Oxford University Press, Ely House, London W. 1

GLASGOW NEW YORK TORONTO MELBOURNE WELLINGTON
CAPE TOWN SALISBURY IBADAN NAIROBI LUSAKA ADDIS ABABA
BOMBAY CALCUTTA MADRAS KARACHI LAHORE DACCA
KUALA LUMPUR HONG KONG TOKYO

PRINTED IN GREAT BRITAIN

PREFACE

THIS study reflects some of the current preoccupation of students of eighteenth-century France with urban social structure and its relevance to the Revolution of 1789. It was undertaken with the purpose of examining the careers and fortunes of the individuals composing a particular society in the hope of lending a greater actuality and precision of meaning to the over-generalized class terms—*noblesse*, *bourgeoisie*, clergy, artisan --in which historians are accustomed to deal and which are often too vague to reveal anything of the essential nature of society.

The use of detailed case histories can introduce the immediate truth of personal experience into social analysis and throw a different light on the human consequences of political and economic change. They have been used extensively in this study to find out how the people of Bayeux lived under the old régime and what effects the Revolution had on their livelihood. Bayeux before 1789 leant on wealth drawn from the countryside in the form of rents or tithe by an affluent bishop and rich higher clergy and on the anachronistic administrative establishments of the old régime, but it had no economic vitality of its own. Nor by mere parasitism could it provide for a rapidly increasing population. Poverty emerges as the main theme of the book and the bulk of those living in the town were a social group to which this study gives just predominance, the poor—those out of work or unable to work, or most commonly those for whom the rewards of a hard day's toil were insufficient for the maintenance of themselves and their families. Even more numerous than the adult males, who were at least potential earners of an adequate personal income, were the women whose labour society estimated at a value far below the meagre amount it allowed the working man and for whom child-bearing engendered further economic problems. These and the children, wanted and unwanted, but proliferating beyond any means which eighteenth-century Bayeux commanded for their support, occupy a special place in the study. The means by which they eked out a miserable livelihood, on ecclesiastical alms or private charity, were no less intrinsically bound up with the old régime than the princely income of the bishop and chapter or the sums the law-court judges and tax collectors managed to wrest from an unwilling populace.

During the Revolution, Bayeux had its artificial buttresses removed by the destruction of the wealth of the church and the modernization of the country's administration, and with its pinions removed, was forced to attempt to live of its own—an attempt which enjoyed no shadow of success, given the slender resources of most of its inhabitants. The history of Bayeux during the Revolution is largely a history of that failure. To a declining town with insurmountable economic problems at the end of the old régime, the Revolution itself dealt a blow from which the town did not, until after 1944, recover; for only then, in the graves of the dead of the D-Day landings, did it find any substitute for the alms and largesse of the church of the old régime.

My grateful acknowledgements are due to Professor A. Cobban for his continual encouragement, guidance, and endless patience throughout the writing of this book from its inception to the final manuscript. I am indebted also to Professor Alun Davies of the University of Swansea for his interest and well-informed advice, to M. Marc Bouloiseau of the Sorbonne for suggestions on source material, to Mr. Richard Cobb whose extensive knowledge of the revolutionary archives was of invaluable assistance, to Dr. Winifred Edington for placing at my disposal much of the material she collected on the Civil Constitution of the Clergy in the diocese of Lisieux, and to Professor Jack Simmons of the University of Leicester for reading and criticizing the manuscript.

My research during protracted periods in France was made possible by the generosity of the Central Research Fund of the University of London, the Eileen Power Memorial Fellowship, the Research Fund of the University of Leicester, the 27 Foundation, and the Centre National de la Recherche Scientifique. My acknowledgements are also due to the staffs of many libraries and archives, notably those of the Archives Nationales, the Archives Départementales du Calvados, and the Bibliothèque de Bayeux who afforded me every help.

Finally, I want to thank my friends in the seminar of French History at the University of London who discussed with me many of the themes treated here and to whom my debt is great.

O. H.

Leicester, 27 October 1965

CONTENTS

LIST OF ABBREVIATIONS

A.N.   Archives Nationales
A.D.C.   Archives Départementales du Calvados
A.M.B.   Archives Municipales de Bayeux
B.V.B.   Bibliothèque de la Ville de Bayeux
B.C.   Bibliothèque du Chapitre
A.C.   Archives Communales

PART ONE

Bayeux before the Revolution

I

BAYEUX IN THE EIGHTEENTH CENTURY

Une ville ancienne et considérable, capitale du Bessin, en Normandie, parlement de Rouen, intendance de Caen, avec un riche évêché suffragant de Rouen; chef lieu d'une élection de son nom. Outre le tribunal de l'élection, il y a plusieurs autres jurisdictions, sçavoir, la vicomté, le bailliage, le grenier à sel, la maîtrise des eaux et forêts. Il y a aussi une amirauté, et une maréchaussée. On y compte 17 paroisses (dont trois réunies), tant dans la ville que dans les faubourgs. 1640 feux et environ 10,000 âmes. Cette ville est située dans une contrée extrêmement fertile, surtout en pâturages, sur la rivière d'Aure ... pendant longtemps cette ville a été fort considérable; mais celle de Caen, qui est dans son voisinage, lui a enlevé presque tout son commerce. Néanmoins la ville de Bayeux continue de se soutenir avec quelque éclat, à cause de la bonté de son terroir.[1]

So wrote the Abbé Expilly on the subject of Bayeux in his detailed topographical dictionary, published in 1762. He went on to list the names of the parishes, the villages falling under the jurisdiction of the *élection* court, and to tell the story of St. Exupère who had lived there in the fourth century. On industry and commerce, which he was so quick to note elsewhere, he is silent; and the entry is concerned rather with memories of the past than with the actualities of 1762, with the prestige of antiquity, rather than present activity.

In appearance Bayeux in the eighteenth century was essentially little different from the town of the present day. If brick houses earned for Toulouse the name of *ville rose* the local stone of the Bessin gave Bayeux a prevailing grey-cream colour. The surrounding villages of St. Martin des Entrées and St. Vigor merged into it, and the fields within the town and the long vegetable gardens attached to most sizeable houses combined to give the impression of a number of small villages clustered around an immense and extremely fine Gothic cathedral rather than of a considerable

---

[1] Abbé Expilly, *Dictionnaire géographique, historique et politique des Gaules et de la France* (Paris, 1762), vol. i, p. 487.

urban concentration. The episcopal palace and the deanery adjoined the cathedral; whilst scattered throughout the town lay the large religious houses, the Benedictines, the Ursulines, the newly built house of the Sisters of Charity, the ancient priory of St. Nicolas des Coustils. The seminary for the training of priests had been repaired and partly rebuilt in 1754, and the *bailliage* court some years later. In short, the impression to the casual onlooker was one of opulence, especially if he stayed on the residential side of the river. The Aure, at this point a mere few feet wide, trickled through the centre of the town but was a hindrance rather than an asset since it made the nearby houses miserably damp. It separated the *haute ville* where lived the rich, the nobles, and the higher ecclesiastics, from the *basse ville*, the parishes of St. Jean and St. Exupère, where the poorer population lived in small, overcrowded houses. The wet climate of the Bessin and the heavy clay soil ensured that many of the town roads were often waterlogged —as it still does—whilst the stagnant water which gathered in the market square was as much a problem for the municipal council then as in recent times.

When one thought of Bayeux in the eighteenth century, as now, it was as the centre of a large and important bishopric, the oldest of the seven sees of Normandy. The bishopric of Bayeux dated its origins to the fourth century and counted St. Exupère as its first bishop. Fifteen of the holders of the title, between St. Exupère and Joseph Dominique de Cheylus who was bishop in 1789, had been beatified, and several honoured with the purple. His jurisdiction extending over some 611 parishes, the bishop of Bayeux was first suffragan of the archbishop of Rouen, and, as such, had the right to consecrate him. It is doubtful if any other town in Normandy, with the exception of Rouen, had an ecclesiastical importance superior to that of Bayeux, or if any at all could count such a high proportion of ecclesiastics amongst its population. The cathedral had a chapter of twelve great dignitaries, some forty-nine canons and a *bas chœur* of eighty-seven. There were seventeen parish priests and fifty others, eight chaplains of the collegiate church of St. Nicolas des Coustils, a large seminary which fluctuated in size according to the time of year, three small male religious communities—the Augustinians, Cordeliers, and Capucins of some ten members each—and four large female communities—the Ursulines with fifty nuns, the Sisters of Charity with some forty-six, the Benedictines of the Holy Sacrament with some thirty-six, and finally a hardworked community of forty Sisters of Providence. All these combined to make the presence of the church much felt within the town. In a town of 10,000 a clerical population numbering between 500 and 600 formed about 6 per cent. of the total. Orléans, also centre of a bishopric, had a similar number of clergy, but in that town of some 41,000 inhabitants they constituted less than 2 per cent. of the population.[1] It was impossible to set foot in Bayeux and be unaware that this was a clerical city.

The Abbé Expilly also stressed the importance of Bayeux as an administrative centre. The presence there of five courts, employing over a hundred men, meant that approximately one man in thirty, or one in every hundred inhabitants, if asked his profession, would define himself in terms of some office or post concerned with the administration of justice. There is nothing to suggest that the number was extraordinarily high: one little *bourg*, of a mere 3,000 inhabitants, in the seventeenth century had a *bailli*, a *prévôt*, a *lieutenant*, a *procureur fiscal*, six notaries, four *sergeants*, twelve *procureurs*, and fourteen *greffiers*.[2] Bayeux was more than a mere *bourg*. France under the *ancien régime* was marked by a plethora of jurisdictional bodies which had come gradually into being and whose powers extended over areas varying as greatly in extent as the courts did themselves in importance. Most, by 1789, possessed a mere fraction of their original power and recent administrative changes had challenged, abolished, or rendered precarious the mere existence of some.

Briefly, Bayeux was the point of convergence for several channels of administration branching from the central government. The *bailliage* court was the most important, originating in the twelfth century when the Paris government had sent out *baillis* for the administration of justice in the king's name, the *bailli* being the representative of royal power within a specified area. The system was institutionalized, the individual *bailli* being replaced by a *bailliage* court centred in the most important town of the area. The *bailliage* was further divided in Normandy into *vicomtés* which judged the affairs of those townsfolk who were neither noble nor ecclesiastic before reference to the *bailliage*.

---

[1] G. Lefebvre, 'Urban Society in the Orléanais', *Past and Present* (April 1961), p. 48.
[2] A. Babeau, *Le Village sous l'ancien régime* (5th ed. 1915), p. 218.

The *élection* as an administrative unit had been created during the late Middle Ages for purposes of taxation, in all areas where there were no effective provincial estates to debate the amount of taxes with the *contrôleur général*. The jurisdiction of the *élection* court of Bayeux extended over some 172 parishes,[1] and the court was responsible for the division and collection of taxes such as the *taille, aides,* and *octrois,* and passed judgement on disputes arising therefrom. Appeal was to the *cour des aides* of the provincial *parlement*.[2]

Again, the *maîtrise des eaux et forêts* established at Bayeux was a small part of a once important administrative organization both for the royal domain and for forests belonging to other individuals. There were some twenty *grandes maîtrises* in France in the eighteenth century of which three were in Normandy, at Alençon, Caen, and Rouen. These were further broken down into *maîtrises,* five of which composed the *grande maîtrise* of Caen. Each *maîtrise* had a *maître particulier* who every six months made a tour of the forests and navigable rivers of the *maîtrise*. Offenders were brought before the court, which had sovereign judgement over minor matters, while major cases had to be referred to the *grande maîtrise*.[3]

The *grenier à sel* was responsible for the administration of the *gabelle*. Its officials assessed the individual levy, were present at all distributions and sales of salt, and had jurisdiction over offenders. Appeal from the court of the *grenier à sel* was to the *cour des aides,* as for the *élection* court.

Lastly, the *amirauté de France* exercised its powers by tribunals called *amirautés* established in Paris and in the provincial *parlements*. Minor cases relating to some aspects of maritime commerce, fishing, rights of wreck, and offences committed in the ports were transacted by *amirautés particulières* established within the jurisdiction of the various *parlements*—there were some seventeen within that of Rouen, of which one was at Bayeux.

The list of the courts present in Bayeux is impressive, but their heyday was past and their decline had begun long before the eighteenth century. The need of the royal government for money

---

[1] F. Mourlot, *La Fin de l'ancien régime dans la généralité de Caen* (1913), p. 6.
[2] M. Marion, *Dictionnaire des Institutions de la France au XVIIᵉ et XVIIIᵉ siècles* (Paris, 1923), pp. 198–201.
[3] Ibid., pp. 193–4.

in the late seventeenth and early eighteenth centuries gave them a new and artificial lease of life, continuing their existence by the constant creation of petty officials. Courts which had been destroyed were re-created : offices were abolished and re-established —always at a price, and France was covered for the purposes of the royal treasury with a proliferation of petty and often conflicting jurisdictions. The inevitable result was that justice and administration were costly, slow, and defective. Moreover, there was not enough business to justify their existence, and the central government accentuated their decline by choosing to bypass them for administrative purposes, leaving them with no more than their judicial functions, using for the former the *intendant* and his personnel. It was to the *intendant*, for example, that the division and collection of all new taxes, such as the *capitation* and the *vingtième*, were given, instead of to the *élection*, and his control was extended over the allocation of the *gabelle*. In addition, he had control over the police and his agent of information, the *sub-délégué*, who had all the effectiveness of the man on the spot, could see that justice was rendered impartially, and be an effective menace to the power of the courts.

In the late 1740s this paradoxical and deceptive policy of increasing the courts and their personnel whilst simultaneously diminishing their authority was abruptly terminated and the situation faced more squarely. In 1749 all *vicomté* and *prévôté* courts were suppressed in towns where there existed *bailliages*. Bayeux counted amongst this number. Similarly a movement was directed towards suppressing the *bailliages* in towns which had a *présidial* court. In the seventeenth century Bayeux had 'vingt-deux juges de capacité et suffisance, la plupart gentilshommes et de qualité et les autres bourgeois'.[1] In 1728 the total number of the high officials of the *bailliage* and the *vicomté* was about fifteen.[2] In April 1761 an edict for the reorganization of the *bailliage* reduced the number of officials to twelve, the number still existing in 1789. In 1788 the entire suppression of the *bailliage* court at Bayeux and the transference of its powers to the *présidial* at Caen was mooted as part of Lamoignon's plan to eliminate the superfluous courts which clogged the effective working of the

---

[1] E. Michel, *Études statistiques, économiques, financières et agricoles. Un canton type* (Nancy, 1910), vol. iii, p. 319.
[2] A.D.C. C6070.

French administration, but more weight seems to have been given to the idea of uniting the courts of St. Lô and Thorigny to the *bailliage* of Bayeux.[1]

At least the *bailliage* court managed to keep alive. The *élection* was less successful. In the seventeenth century the *élection* court of Bayeux had had twelve judges, but these had diminished by the mid eighteenth century to a *président*, a *lieutenant*, and a *procureur du roi* with some two or three *élus*.[2] An edict of September 1772 suppressed the *jurisdictions des traites et du quart bouillon* of the province of Normandy and transferred their powers to the *élection* courts where one existed as at Bayeux.[3] Even this increased business failed to keep the court of Bayeux active. The *vingtième* lists of 1781 declared that the court was much fallen into discredit.[4] It was temporarily abolished early in 1788 and did not meet after that date.

The *maîtrise des eaux et forêts* and the *grenier à sel* shared the fate of the *élection* court. It is difficult to find mention of the first in the records of the eighteenth century, beyond its attempts to assert its superiority over the *élection* court in public processions[5] and the bankruptcy of its high officials. In 1788 the *maîtrise* of Bayeux together with those of Caen, Valognes, and Vire in the *généralité* of Caen were officially suppressed, though they were temporarily and ineffectively reopened for a few brief months by Necker.[6] The *grenier à sel* had, in the course of the century, most of its powers transferred to that at Caen. It very rarely met. As for the *amirauté* of Bayeux, it continued its shaky existence until the outbreak of the Revolution. Little by little its powers had been sapped. The jurisdiction over the River Aure had been given to the *intendant*. In 1757, when the *amirautés* of Carentan, Isigny, and Grandcamp were united, it managed to survive but the business it transacted was hardly extensive.

Initially, Bayeux had been the seat of the *intendance*, but the choice had been based on the prestige and antiquity of the cathedral city, reasons which Chamillart readily set aside in 1690 when he

---

[1] A.D.C. C6074. *Correspondance avec tous les bailliages relativement à l'enregistrement de l'ordonnance concernant l'administration de la justice, 1788.*

[2] Michel, op. cit., vol. iii, p. 319.

[3] A.D.C. C6257. *Suppression des Jurisdictions des Traites et du Quart Bouillon de la Province de Normandie, septembre 1772.*

[4] A.D.C. C5467. *Vingtième d'offices et droits, 1781.*

[5] A.D.C. C266.   [6] A.D.C. C6290.

made the larger and more important town of Caen the centre of the *généralité*. It was, however, still centre of a *subdélégation* and was considered the second most important town of the *généralité*.

The lack of mention by the Abbé Expilly of any industry at Bayeux was not entirely due to negligence, for the name of Bayeux did not evoke the idea of a manufacturing centre. Nor for that matter did those of most towns of the *généralité* of Caen. Even so their manufactures, if small in comparison with those of more industrial towns like Rouen or Lille, were more considerable than those of most French towns. Bayeux in the second half of the seventeenth century had been the beneficiary of a programme of industrial development introduced by the central government for areas with an unemployment problem. Bayeux and the neighbouring towns of Valognes, St. Lô, Coutances, Granville, and Vire had become centres of a small but prosperous woollen stocking industry, copied from an English model, employing at Bayeux alone by the end of the seventeenth century over four hundred workers.[1] Attempts had also been made to extend the production of woollen cloth in the area. The nascent French industry enjoyed protection from foreign competition by a high tariff, whilst within France the small urban industries were buttressed by laws limiting textile production to the towns and their suburbs, thus cutting off any competition from rural industry. The small-scale nature of these industries cannot be overstressed. Apart from the stocking workers, those employed in textile production in Bayeux did not exceed a hundred at the beginning of the century and there was nothing in the town which even remotely resembled a factory. The stocking makers, carders of wool, and weavers were gathered in little workshops, each containing no more than one or a handful of men;[2] and each trade was organized into separate gilds which had a monopoly of a particular branch of industry within the town, applied their own conditions and fees for elevation to mastership and full membership of the gild and laid down regulations relating to the size and quality of finished products. The gilds of Bayeux were not over-demanding in their entrance requirements; anyone who had served an apprenticeship and could pay a minimal sum was allowed entry. Indeed the entry rates to the textile workers' gilds of a small town like Bayeux

[1] E. Levasseur, *Histoire des classes ouvrières en France* (1859), vol. ii, p. 213.
[2] A.D.C. C2796. *Arts et métiers, Bayeux, 1750.*

or Valognes could hardly have been lower.[1] The masters were
very far from being rich men; the bulk of them earned scarcely
sufficient for a bare subsistence. In fact, the *subdélégué* of Bayeux
complained that the major fault of most of these gilds was that
they were prepared to admit almost indiscriminately any of their
apprentices and that hence most of the masters were very poor
men.[2] Their poverty meant, he went on, that they could not think
of improvement or expansion or new inventions or indeed alter
in any way their traditional methods of production. Too many
produced for a restricted market goods which could not in
cheapness and quality compete with the textiles of Rouen and
Elbeuf, even before foreign competition had to be faced. The
masters of the small gilds could expect to do nothing except
supply some of the clothing needs of the town and surrounding
villages. For small non-capitalist manufacturers the gilds were
regarded as important because by himself the individual manufacturer had no means at his disposal to withstand oppression.
The carders of wool and the stocking manufacturers during the
1760s exhausted the funds of their gilds in a long lawsuit against
the municipal council because the latter, hard pressed for funds,
had chosen to step up the *octrois*. These duties, levied on goods
entering the town, were the chief source of municipal revenue and
the town was attempting to augment those imposed on raw wool
by demanding the same sum on the pound that other towns like
Caen demanded for the fleece. In the local law-courts they could
get no justice because the judges were members of the town council
and a costly transfer had to take place to the *cours des aides* at
Rouen.[3] Protection against injustice was perhaps the most cogent
reason why the gilds exercised such a strong hold over their
members, but there was also an emotional element involved. Each
gild had its own patron saint and was tied to a particular church.
Each had a special place in public processions, with its own banners
and symbols. It held its own ceremonies to honour deceased
members. Though officially abolished in 1793, many of these
practices still continued on the eve of the First World War.[4]

    These customs dated back in many cases to the fifteenth century.
They had become an essential feature of everyday life. Indeed the
town was packed with medieval remains from its impressive

[1] A.D.C. C2796. *Arts et métiers, Bayeux, 1750.*   [2] Ibid.
[3] A.D.C. C2861.   [4] Michel, op. cit., vol. iii, p. 210.

cathedral to its crumbling courts and antique craft gilds. In 1770 its resources were not much greater than they had been three or four centuries before, when its population was smaller. Wednesday and Saturday were market-days when the small town came momentarily to life and did most of its trade. It furnished the peasants who came to sell their grain and livestock with clothing, shoes, cooking pots, and pans. It repaired their tools. The apothecaries' shops sold them cures for their ailments which they could not obtain in an isolated village. These were the days upon which the tradesmen of Bayeux depended for their livelihood.

A town of such limited resources was singularly ill equipped to cope with the sudden upward movement of population which was such a general feature of eighteenth-century Europe and which became apparent in France during the second quarter of the century. The population growth still remains a largely unexplained phenomenon, nor in a pre-census age is it easy to offer precise figures. There is no real information on the size of Bayeux in the early part of the century when administrators were unconcerned with population statistics. A rough estimate made in 1741 placed the population between 6,000 and 7,000.[1] By 1774 an estimate based on information afforded by the *gabelle* lists arrived at the figure of 9,198[2] and by 1791 it stood very approximately at 10,320.[3] The *élection* of Bayeux showed a surplus of births over deaths throughout the forties, fifties, sixties, and seventies. Indeed the *subdélégué* remarked with surprise that, in spite of the death toll from the outbreak of miliary fever, in 1774, the *élection* showed a slight rise in the number of births and no increase in the number of deaths on the preceding year.[4] The increase was not sustained throughout the eighties, but among the *élections* within the *généralité* of Caen, Bayeux was in this respect unique.[5] However, parish registers indicate over the century a marked decrease in the rate of infant mortality. From 1700 to 1789 the number of babies per hundred born in the overcrowded parish of St. Jean who could expect to die before they reached their fifth year fell from thirty-five to twenty-six.[6] Mortality rates in the town, it would seem, continued to be much higher than those of the countryside;

[1] Ibid., vol. i, pp. 12–13.   [2] A.D.C. C176. See Appendix I.
[3] A.D.C. Lx. *Assistance, Bayeux, 1791.*
[4] A.D.C. C242.
[5] A.D.C. C153–7, 160. *Mouvement de la population 1782–1787.*
[6] A.D.C. *Registres paroissiaux, Bayeux 5–9, St. Jean.*

but against this, the town population grew because of a rural influx whose full extent, especially in the early part of the century, is virtually impossible to estimate but which is rendered readily explicable by the situation arising from the population explosion.

A larger population demanded increased food supplies and new opportunities for employment. But the consumption of grain was rapidly, by the third quarter of the eighteenth century, outstripping its production. The result was a rise in the price of food commodities, the necessities of life, of some 65 per cent., as against a general increase of 22 per cent. in nominal wages.[1] The effects of the agrarian crisis were experienced by town and country alike. Indeed, to attempt to study social conditions in the town without taking into consideration the changing conditions in the country would be to distort the picture. In the countryside the peasant who had produce to sell was able to prosper, because of the heightened prices his goods could command. But the farm labourer or the peasant whose holding was inadequate for the proper support of his family was not in the same happy position. He was constantly subjected to economic difficulties. His ideal was, of course, to liberate himself from the pressure of rising costs by the acquisition of a piece of land sufficient to keep his family so that he did not have to worry about increasing prices. He aimed at subsistence farming. On the other hand, land can rarely have attracted the capitalist exploiter more. The end of the old régime was marked by a scramble for land on the part of poor peasant and capitalist exploiter alike. Forests and marshes were drained and put under cultivation, but still there was not enough. The bulk of the peasant proprietors of Lower Normandy owned only a few *perches* of land attached to a cottage and a small kitchen garden; the whole of which was not assessed for tax purposes at more than ten *livres* and which was quite insufficient for the maintenance of a family.[2] There is also evidence of a marked increase in the number of landless peasants in the area: men who were dependent on being hired by larger farmers and who as wage-earners were constantly subjected to the pressure of rising

[1] C. E. Labrousse, *Esquisse du mouvement des prix et des revenus en France au XVIIIe siècle*, 2 vols. (1933), and *La Crise de l'économie française à la fin de l'ancien régime et au début de la Révolution* (1944).

[2] A. Davies, 'The Origins of the French Peasant Revolution of 1789', *History*, xlix (1964), p. 27.

costs. But at the other end of the scale, large landowners were effecting changes which were to be of consequence to the economy of the whole region and it is impossible to describe Bayeux in the eighteenth century without reference to these changes, whose impact on the town was almost as great as on the country.

The tendency of the provinces of France had been, from time immemorial, to be virtually self-supporting; no region could depend on another for supplies. Wherever possible grain had been grown to provide bread for the immediate area and this sometimes on land totally unsuited to arable farming, a practice perpetuated by the small farmer intent above all upon feeding himself and his family. The climate of the Normandy Bessin was far too wet for wheat. On the other hand, as pasture land it was some of the richest in France and its potentialities in this respect were becoming obvious to the large landowner intent on profit.[1] The period 1749–90 saw a clear movement amongst large landowners and large-scale tenant farmers away from arable and towards pasture farming.[2] The movement was even more clearly marked in the nearby *élection* of Carentan.[3] The subsistence farmer continued to grow grain to feed his family, but at the upper end of the scale the capitalist farmer was rapidly moving over to pasture. His profits were encouraging. To the west of Bayeux, in the region of Isigny, the production of butter was expanding greatly. It was shipped from this small port along the Channel and up the Seine to feed the great towns of Rouen and Paris.

The results of this incipient agrarian revolution were twofold: at the one end of the scale greater wealth for the large landowners and those who traded in dairy produce, and at the other a large number of rural day labourers thrown out of work because pastoral farming demanded less hands than arable. This in turn could not fail to make an impact upon the town. Situated as it was in the midst of a rural area whose nature was rapidly changing, it would have been strange had Bayeux escaped a strong influx of immigrants from the countryside. In fact some 46 per cent. of those living in Bayeux in 1796 were drawn from outside, mostly

---

[1] A. J. Bourde, *The Influence of England on the French Agronomes* (1953), p. 214.

[2] F. Duterque, 'Modes d'exploitation et d'amélioration du sol dans la région de Bayeux au XVIIIe siècle', *Actes du 81e Congrès National des Sociétés Savantes* (Rouen–Caen, 1956), pp. 177 ff.

[3] M. Duval, *L'Élection de Carentan du milieu du XVIIe au milieu du XVIIIe siècles* (Caen, 1963), p. 193.

from a twenty-mile radius to the south and west.[1] The bulk of those who came were day labourers or single women seeking employment either as domestic servants or as lacemakers. The fact that the town had only scanty resources did not deter them. In Rouen or Elbeuf before the 1780s they might have found work in the expanding textile industries, but this was not the sort of work for which the men at least were searching. They were not, in the country areas, accustomed to such work. They were used to the open air and to casual if hard manual labour, often being employed successively for the hay harvest and then the corn harvest and during the winter months perhaps as part-time labourers in the town. It was this last sort of labour which the surplus rural population sought. The town of Bayeux had by the end of the eighteenth century a surfeit of bricklayers, roof-builders, sabot-makers, and above all casual labourers, ready to navvy and earn their living as best they could. Their wives, or single women, who came from the country districts because their families could not support them, were more accustomed to domestic industry which confined them to the house. The lace industry absorbed some, but female labour was plentiful and poorly paid. Those who came were not seeking their fortunes : word did not go round that the muddy streets of Bayeux were paved with gold. Rather was the step one of despair : of recognition that a livelihood was no longer to be made in the countryside and that even if they joined the ranks of the urban beggars, as such they would belong to a large community and would not pass unnoticed in the town as they might well in the countryside. Hardly a room in the cramped parish of St. Jean was not packed to overflowing. The immigrants did not all come at once : their arrival was in handfuls and over a long period. Had it been on a smaller scale there would have been nothing really unusual in a country town absorbing some of the surplus of the countryside. But the town simply did not have the means at its disposal to employ all those who came.

For Bayeux the agrarian crisis meant an increase in the price of food and a steady influx of labourers seeking employment. The first consequence was in turn to have an impact upon the small-scale industries of the town. Industry in Bayeux consisted mainly of the manufacture of woollen stockings, using raw wool partly

[1] A.M.B. *États de la population, an IV.* These registers state the date of entry of each citizen into the town and place of birth.

from the Cotentin nearby and partly from Spain, of a coarse linen cloth used mainly for sails in the fishing villages of the Channel coast and of a slightly finer linen used for shirts, petticoats, and bed-clothes, and lastly of woollen cloth. None of the products appears to have been of a high quality, though the flax fibre used in the linen production was excellent and grew well in the rich soil of the Normandy Bessin. These local industries were perhaps less dependent on supplies of raw material from abroad than were those in the rest of northern France. On the other hand, they were not well placed for marketing their goods. They were distant from a port of any size and continued petitions of the people of Bayeux for the construction of a new harbour at Port en Bessin met with no response. Normandy possessed the second largest trade fair of France, the Foire de Guibray, where the products of the stocking *manufacture* were sold during the early part of the century and had some popularity with Paris, Brittany, and occasionally Dutch wholesale merchants. But for the rest, a town like Bayeux, which was the marketing centre for the surrounding district, found its main market in its clothing demands.

Small-scale industry of this nature is an extremely sensitive plant: a blow from which a large concern can emerge can threaten it with entire extinction. Dependence on a local market meant exposure to the fluctuations of local economy. In the aftermath of a bad harvest, when the expense of food commodities led to an increase in the cost of living, a small non-capitalist manufacturer could be ruined, partly because his own increased outlay on food robbed him of the wherewithal to buy the raw material and partly because his customers had to cut down on other commodities as they too spent more on food. At a time of steeply rising prices, when the number of landless in the area was increasing and the purchasing power of standard wages diminishing, the demand for consumer goods necessarily fell.

The Bayeux stocking industry never recovered from the great depression of the 1740s which began with the failure of the harvest in 1739. In 1741 the *faiseurs de bas au métier* represented a community of 100 masters and 480 employees already in debt.[1] In 1750 there were only some 17 masters working mainly without journeymen.[2] They were not alone in their hardship. At Cherbourg in 1745 it was stated that out of 565 persons employed in the

[1] A.D.C. C2821.   [2] A.D.C. C2796.

making of cloth, 355 alone had work.[1] At Valognes nearby, the
subdélégué wrote, also in 1745, that three-quarters of the industrial
workers languished in poverty and the masters made barely
enough to live.[2] Caen and Vire made similar complaints. Bayeux
never faced a higher unemployment rate than in the 1740s.
Weavers ceased to take cloth to the fair at Caen and the name of
Bayeux was erased from the accounts.[3]

The improved harvests of 1754–6 had done little to restore
the situation when the Seven Years War broke out. Prolonged
British bombarding of the Normandy coast and attempts to cut
off French convoys from the Indies and to destroy French coastal
trade severely hampered the industry of northern France. Spanish
wool, cotton from French America, the West Indies, and
Salonica, the Picardy flax boats, were spasmodic in their arrival.
Since the last war, wrote the *inspecteur des manufactures* of the
généralité of Caen in 1763, very little raw material had arrived and
he fervently hoped that with the peace and the freedom of the
seas, plenty would return.[4] More especially the war cut off from
the *généralité* the Breton stocking market. These difficulties were
accompanied at Bayeux by attempts on the part of an impoverished
municipal council to augment municipal funds by increasing the
octrois on raw materials entering the town. Coming at a time when
they could least afford it, the carders of wool and the stocking-
makers were badly hit and tried if possible to find alternative
employment.

But this was not easy to find. By the mid 1760s unemployment
and under-employment were grave problems for Bayeux. Attempts
were made to provide further employment with charitable funds
by inviting British spinners from Sens to give instruction on the
latest methods.[5] The town, however, already produced more than
its markets could absorb and the attempts at expansion were not
accompanied by the discovery of new markets. The municipal
government's proposal to abolish the *octrois* on raw materials
intended for the charitable *manufacture* produced an indignant
outcry from the existing manufacturers, for they claimed the cloth

---

[1] C. Gaillardon, 'L'Industrie et les industriels de Normandie au moment de la
convocation des États Généraux de 1789', *Revue de Cherbourg* (1907–8), p. 139.

[2] Ibid.

[3] A.D.C. C2965. *Toileries, Foire Royale de Caen.*

[4] A.D.C. C6411.

[5] A.D.C. C2955. *Toileries.*

produced in this way would undersell their own products and hence would aggravate, not alleviate, the situation of the town.

The government measures of 7 September 1762 which removed the ban on textile production outside towns delivered another blow. The manufacturers of Bayeux claimed, in 1766, that the country people made an inferior cloth which they could sell to the merchants at a lower price, because the country manufacturers did not have to pay the *octroi* on raw material which added to the costs of production for the town. Hence they might very well, with cheaper goods, capture the market.[1]

The immediate results did not bear out the fears of the Bayeux weavers. If anything, business showed a slight rise by the early 1770s. The next sharp fall in production only occurred somewhere between late 1777 and 1780, but in 1785 the name of Bayeux disappeared entirely from the records of textile production in the *généralité*.[2]

The decline of these years cannot be attributed to any one isolated factor. The town had to submit not only to increased competition but to a marked rise in the cost of bread, which was sustained throughout the late seventies and aggravated in the eighties. After thirteen years of peace England and France went to war again in 1776, which meant increased expenditure by the central government and hence increased taxation and economic insecurity. By this time, too, a general weariness characterized the Bayeux manufacturers which spelled death to any project either on the part of the government or of local enterprise.

The government was by no means unaware of the decline of these small-scale industries or, by the 1770s, of the serious lack of employment occasioned by their collapse. It believed that above all France needed markets abroad for her manufactured goods. But here she met the constant opposition and competition of cheaper English goods, manufactured in uniform lengths and of a superior quality. It pursued a policy, albeit spasmodic, of finding out English methods and attempting to seize English markets. As early as 1749 Marc Morel, *inspecteur des manufactures* of the *généralité* at Caen, was sent to England to study methods of production and to see what could be done to save the dwindling industries of the *généralité*.[3] But the conditions of English industry

[1] Ibid.   [2] A.D.C. C2966-9. *Toileries.*
[3] A.D.C. C2852.

could not be imposed on the impoverished masters of a town like Bayeux. They had none of the advantages of the English: neither ready supplies of raw material, nor ample markets, nor the capital of men who could feel confident that industry was a paying concern. When the government, hopeful of capturing English markets abroad, circulated samples of English cloth to the town to inquire whether something similar could be produced at the same cost, the manufacturers always gave the same reply: that they simply did not have the means at their disposal.[1] The unpalatable truth was that French fabrics could not sustain British competition and the fact was proved to the little masters of Bayeux by putting actual samples of English cloth into their hands and asking if they could make it at the same price.

Bayeux, in fact, was devoid of any solution to its unemployment problem. The administration, central and local, repeatedly expressed the belief that salvation would lie in the introduction of machines, new industries, and the adoption of English methods.[2] From the actual manufacturers, however, one hears nothing either of machines or of improvement, only of their poverty, of the decline in production and above all, fear and resentment of British competition. Their concern was not with industrial expansion, for they feared that any increase or extension of industry at home would rob them of the few markets they had. Hence they maintained a rigidly protectionist attitude of mistrust, which, the Provincial Assembly held, was ultimately destructive of any new enterprise.[3]

The only industries in the town which in any way held their own throughout the century were the tanning industry, the pottery *manufacture*, and the production of lace. The first employed about a dozen men, who were all gathered in the parish of St. Vigor where the water supply was good. Some of them had succeeded in doing very well and alone among the manufacturers of the town they could afford to purchase land and comfortable houses. They complained of their poverty, but this is not borne out by an examination of their resources. They were, they said, more than overtaxed: the *marque des cuirs* was an extra charge they could not afford and the high quality goods they produced could not withstand the competition of cheaper

---

[1] A.D.C. C2853. Letters of 25 May and 26 August 1762.
[2] A.D.C. C7651. *Commission Intermédiaire 1788.*   [3] Ibid.

products.[1] The potters, who used the coarse clay of the Bessin as raw material for a thick, brown earthenware which was used for household pottery and for bottling *eau de vie*, could be counted on one hand. The lace industry had originally been established for purposes of charity, to employ women and young girls who otherwise had no means of support. It was introduced by a canon of the cathedral, who advanced a sum to start a school at the end of the seventeenth century, invited Dutch workers to Bayeux to teach the craft, and left the business of direction to the Sisters of Providence. By the early 1780s it occupied some 600 women and girls, and in 1788, 1,200 in Bayeux and district.[2] Many of the girls who were employed were either orphans or destitute and the wages paid were either exceptionally low or non-existent, since the nuns provided the homeless children with food and shelter. The market was excellent, for lace made up into *fichus Marie Antoinette* was high fashion. Moreover, amongst the buyers were counted the English. The profits went mostly into the hands of the religious orders and into those of the few merchants who carried out the business side of the trade. Humanitarianism can rarely have assumed a more profitable form.[3]

Bayeux by the end of the old régime was a declining town whose crumbling courts and dwindling industries could not support its growing population. Only in the pastureland that surrounded it lay any obvious sign of economic strength and here, as the Abbé Expilly suggested, was the source of such prosperity as sections of the town population possessed. Into the town came the rents, dues, tithes, and all the proceeds of landownership which gave the upper clergy, the wealthier *noblesse*, some of the *bourgeoisie*, and even, indirectly, the poor who depended on ecclesiastical charity the means on which to live. Ancient and dignified, its cathedral spires dwarfing the town and towering over the flat green meadows for miles around, Bayeux was economically dependent on the Bessin.

[1] A.D.C. C2926. *Tanneurs.*
[2] L. A. Lefebure, *Histoire de la dentelle à Bayeux de 1696 à 1900* (Bayeux, 1913), p. 7.
[3] J. C. Perrot, 'L'Industrie et le commerce de la dentelle dans la généralité de Caen à la fin de l'ancien régime', *Actes du 81ᵉ Congrès des Sociétés Savantes* (1956), pp. 215–37.

II

THE CLERGY

A STUDY of society in Bayeux begins logically with a study of the church and ecclesiastical society, for the church was the backbone of the town and the part it played in the lives of the townspeople was far from being confined to purely spiritual matters. Bayeux was not only an important diocesan centre, the oldest of the seven sees of Normandy, but its bishop was the tenth richest prelate in France and its cathedral chapter one of the most ancient, wealthy, and, to the bishop's discomfiture, most assertive in the country. No single individual and no single institution in the town was as well endowed as the bishop and chapter and none enjoyed either the same prestige, privileges, or authority or affected to such an extent the lives of the townspeople.

The bishopric of Bayeux extended over 611 parishes and was worth at least 90,000 *livres* annually to the bishop. This revenue was based largely upon the income from seven *baronnies*—St. Vigor, Neuilly l'Évêque, Airel, Crépon, Boisdelle, Douvres, and Cambremer—and eighty fiefs. The bishop of Bayeux was, moreover, *seigneur tréfoncier* of Port en Bessin, Commes, Surrain, St. Laurent sur Mer, Sommervieu, Carcagny, Juaye, and Ellon. Fairs and markets held in Bayeux added to the profits of the bishop.[1] He possessed a delightful country palace at Sommervieu in the midst of superb lands and in good hunting country and an elegant town house in Bayeux itself. To become bishop of Bayeux was the near acme of the aspirations of an ambitious cleric and, once attained, was rarely followed by further preferment. The right of presentation to dioceses in France lay in the hands of the monarch and noble families with the right influence at court had, by 1789, secured a monopoly. A key position, such as the bishopric of Bayeux, demanded both influential social connexions and assiduous attendance at court from those who aspired to hold it.

[1] A.D.C. C275.

De Luynes was the son of the Duc de Chevreuse Montfort. Nominated in 1727 to the position of *abbé commandataire* of Cérisy, by 1729, at the age of twenty-five, he was bishop of Bayeux.[1] Rochechouart, his successor, was related to the Duc de Montmart, peer of France. Born in 1693, he was bishop of Evreux in 1734 and bishop of Bayeux in 1753.[2] His successor, de Cheylus, had had a far more chequered career and had passed from being *abbé* of Cormeilles to dean of the cathedral chapter of Lisieux in 1754 and thence to the position of bishop of Tréguier in 1762. Then by astute attendance at court he secured the patronage of the Comtesse d'Artois who made him her first almoner and obtained for him the bishopric of Cahors in 1766. Ten years later, at the age of fifty-nine, he became bishop of Bayeux.[3]

The bishop was rarely in residence and great though his wealth and dignity were, his effective authority over the diocese was narrowly circumscribed. He presented to a mere eleven benefices out of 611. Moreover, such administrative authority as he possessed was challenged at every point by the cathedral chapter, with whom he was in constant conflict. The chapter had the virtue of permanence, whereas bishops died or departed, leaving the running of the diocese to the chapter during the vacancy. Furthermore, there was an organized system for the complete administration of the diocese by the chapter even when a bishop was in office; the unit was divided into archdeaconries over which archdeacons had the right of visitation and the *grands vicaires*, who were often numerous, had gradually acquired a large share of diocesan government.[4] Any bishop of Bayeux could choose between two alternatives, either of seeing that these officials carried out their duties efficiently, or of slipping into the position of a dignified figurehead, withdrawing with his princely income to Paris or Sommervieu and leaving the diocese to run itself—or rather leaving it to the canons. The greater the authority that devolved upon this august body, the less the friction between bishop and capitular clergy.

The influence of the chapter of the cathedral church of Bayeux cannot be overstressed. A large, though loosely knit community

---

[1] J. Laffetay, *Le Diocèse de Bayeux au XVIIIe siècle* (Bayeux, 1876), p. 24.
[2] Ibid., p. 78.
[3] Ibid., p. 192.
[4] E. Sévèstre, *Les Problèmes religieux de la Révolution et de l'Empire en Normandie* (Paris, 1924), vol. ii, p. 7.

of sixty-two—a dean, twelve dignitaries, and forty-nine canons—
corporately, it was no less rich than the bishop, was always on the
spot to maintain its rights, was often better versed in local affairs,
and was ready constantly to assert its privileges at the bishop's
expense. Its right of jurisdiction over the priests and inhabitants
of a hundred parishes had been cut by the government, at the
bishop's instigation, to nineteen by 1789,[1] but the bishop remained severely restricted by the chapter. It was there when he
arrived and at the installation ceremony he was forced to swear to
maintain its rights; he could claim a say in succeeding appoint-
ments within the chapter, but vacancies did not occur often, for
once in office, a canon did not on the whole move and a bishop
not infrequently found that the very men he chose forsook his
interests for those of the body to which they now belonged. The
grands vicaires held the key positions in running the diocese and
any bishop, whether more interested in the effective administration of the diocese or merely in collecting his revenues without
challenge, would try to see that as soon as possible these positions
were filled by men he could trust. This was most frequently
done by installing personal friends in a vacant canonry and then
elevating them to higher ranks as soon as a vacancy occurred,
which could take time; but herein lay another source of discord
between bishop and chapter. The new men were invariably outsiders, whilst the bulk of the canons were of the region and knew
one another well. Even more friction occurred if the bishop chose
to concentrate power in the hands of the members of the chapter
he considered most worthy of it. When de Luynes singled out the
Abbé Hugon to be *de facto* administrator of the diocese during his
frequent absences in Paris, the canon was faced with the unconcealed hostility of the rest of the chapter. In the circumscribed
community of a small town, petty jealousies were a constant feature
of life and the venerable canons were far from immune to them.
They had plenty of time on their hands in which to contemplate
their position *vis-à-vis* the bishop and the most effective ways of
asserting their independence. Little or nothing attached the
canons to the bishop as an individual. When in late 1790
the episcopal palace at Bayeux and its effects were auctioned,
the canons were prominent amongst those bidding.

---

[1] M. Béziers, *Mémoires pour servir à l'état historique et géographique du diocèse de
Bayeux* (Rouen, 1896), vol. i, p. 331.

The corporate revenues of the chapter assured the canons of a comfortable income. They were drawn from estates, dues, rents, tithes, and privileges. In addition, each canonry was attached to a prebend—land from which the holder drew the revenue—which varied in value from 10 *livres* to 2,400 *livres* annually.[1] Moreover, the dignitaries held, in addition to their prebend, rich benefices with extra revenues. Twenty-seven of the prebends included fine houses in Bayeux itself.[2] Even if one entered the chapter in possession of no more than the poorest prebend, rapid elevation to a better one invariably followed. It was rare for a canon of Bayeux to have to live on less than 8,000 *livres* a year. The income was attractive and the duties demanded of the canons in exchange were far from onerous. The church of the old régime has been described as a 'luxurious system of outdoor relief for the nobility'[3] and at Bayeux this was particularly true of the canonries. The chapter was not quite the monopoly of the local *noblesse* but an overwhelming proportion of it did originate from wealthy noble families of the region. A Beaumont, a Dastignac, a Voisvenal, a d'Anferville, a d'Audibert, a de Boisjugan, a de Carles, a des Fresnes, a de Landes, a de Marguerie, a de Norant, a de Subtil, a d'Etreham—noble names of long standing in the Bessin—were included, with many others, amongst the canons and dignitaries of the cathedral of Bayeux. Nepotism was not infrequent and some of the canonries of Bayeux appear to have had as much an hereditary character as many positions in the law-courts. The capitular clergy were an exclusive little community and did their best to see that men of their own kind filled any vacancies that occurred.

Theoretically at least, the chapter was highly organized: its twelve dignitaries had carefully outlined duties and each was endowed with an impressive list of privileges. The most important member was undoubtedly the dean, who presided over all the deliberations of the chapter and acted as *curé* for all the cathedral clergy. By virtue of his position he was *seigneur* and *baron* of La Ferrière au Doyen and presented to the cures of this parish, La Ferrière Harenc, La Ferrière du Val, Castilly, du Fresne, Thaon, Surrain, and St. Loup of Bayeux. He had the right to collect the

---

[1] B.V.B. MS. 48. *État des bénéfices de l'ancien diocèse de Bayeux.*

[2] Béziers, op. cit., vol. i, p. 339.

[3] J. McManners, 'France', in *The European Nobility in the Eighteenth Century*, ed. by A. Goodwin (London, 1953), p. 26.

déport—the first year's revenues of a newly installed priest—in all these parishes. He presented as well to the cures of St. Malo, St. André, and St. Jean at Bayeux. His benefice gave him revenues of 4,500 *livres* per year exclusive of his share in the corporate revenues of the cathedral and of any prebends he might hold.[1] He owed his position to election by the other members of the chapter.

Two of the four deans of Bayeux in the period 1730–89 were local men. The first was from Rouen, son of a *conseiller au parlement* who had been *abbé* of Loc Dieu in 1726, canon of Tours, then Meaux, and lastly St. Germain at Bayeux before he was elected dean in 1734. He resigned to become abbot of Barbelles in the diocese of Sens and in 1746 became bishop of Avranches. De Cristot, who succeeded him as dean, was a local man who had been canon of the cathedral of Bayeux since 1719. Made dean in 1736, his ability became known to Cardinal Fleury and the latter nominated him to the bishopric of Séez. The third, de Beaudois, was of Dax in Provence but had begun his ecclesiastical career by holding a prebend at Rouen, then at Bayeux where he was elected dean in 1741.[2] He resigned the position in 1764 and became abbot of Nöé in the diocese of Evreux where he died in 1780. He was succeeded by de Marguerie, a local man who still held office in 1789.

The second dignitary of the cathedral was the *grand chantre* who, in theory, was chosen by the bishop for this position, which brought with it a benefice of 1,100 *livres* and made the holder *seigneur* and *patron* of the parishes of Neuilly l'Évêque and des Oubeaux.[3] In practice the bishop was rarely able to assert his right to choose the *grand chantre* because the chapter claimed that the bishop's privilege only applied if the *grand chantre* died in office without nominating his successor. This assertion allowed the *grands chantres* of Bayeux to dispose of their office in the most casual fashion imaginable. The first, Bernard Campagne, came from Bayonne and became canon at Bayeux in 1693 and *grand chantre* in 1729, resigning from the position in 1742 when he was about to die, in favour of a relative, Pierre Campagne who was also from Bayonne. The latter found the wet climate of the Normandy Bessin little suited to his taste. He was also tone deaf,

[1] Béziers, op. cit., vol. i, p. 333.   [2] Ibid., p. 376.
[3] Ibid., p. 377.

a fact that seemed to worry him more than the other canons, though it caused the choir boys much merriment when as chanter he failed to hit the right note. He decided to opt out of his exalted position and readily exchanged the grand chantership of the cathedral of Bayeux for the cure of Tartas, a little parish in Gascony, where he died some years later. The parish priest of Tartas, who must have been impressed with the bargain he had struck, died two months after assuming office. The bishop then stepped in and chose des Fresnes, son of a local noble and connected to several of the best families of the area. In his early twenties when given the position, he still held it in 1789.[1]

The chancellor, originally keeper of the seals, was the third dignitary. By the eighteenth century he had no extra duties for the 1,530 *livres* which he received from his benefice.[2] De l'Espinay, who held the position in 1749, was of a noble Breton family and had previously served in the army. He secured his position through the influence of a relative, but found the peaceful life of a capitular cleric little suited to his taste and he quarrelled with the rest of his colleagues. He returned to Paris where he died in the 1760s having abandoned, but not resigned, his office several years before—though he still drew his revenues. His successor, de Nicolay, was of a noble family of Montpellier and was called to Bayeux by Bishop Rochechouart, who made him vicar general and gave him the prebends of Feuguerolles and Gavray. When l'Espinay died he became chancellor.[3]

The treasurer ranked next in dignity after the chancellor and his office gave him a further 3,000 *livres* per year. As administrator of the chapter's corporate revenues, however, the position was indeed important and a treasurer devoted to philanthropy and public works could do much for the town at the chapter's expense. But for the presence of the Abbé Hugon, a native of Limoges, brought to Bayeux by de Luynes in 1729, as treasurer, Bayeux might have lost much in the way of charity. His work for the poor was indefatigable but the popularity of this outsider, both with the townspeople and the bishop who allowed him to make all decisions relating to the diocese in his name while he was absent in Paris, caused the canons to prevail upon de Luynes's successor, Rochechouart, to reduce his influence; they persuaded him that it

---

[1] Ibid., pp. 388–9. [2] Ibid., p. 390.
[3] Ibid., p. 405.

was greater than that of the bishop himself. He was forced to
evacuate the episcopal palace where he had been living and no
longer served as confessor to the bishop. His successor, de
Loucelles, a local man who had been canon for almost thirty
years when he became treasurer, followed his example and continued much of his work.[1]

The four archdeacons followed the treasurer in the canonical
hierarchy and all of them in 1789 were drawn from the local
noblesse; so were a *chantre*, *scholastique*, and *pénitencier* who completed
the high cathedral dignitaries. The *grands vicaires* were chosen out
of the twelve dignitaries; at any one time the diocese was likely
to have about four.

The position of a canon of the cathedral was entirely what its
occupier chose to make it. It could be a comfortable sinecure for
the man who wanted a dignified position, high income, and his
family close at hand, a niche rather than a rut which was too
pleasant to abandon; it could be a stepping-stone to a higher
position; at its best, it could be an unrivalled opportunity for
philanthropy and good works. The first was certainly the most
prevalent attitude. Whilst deans frequently became bishops, for
many to be a high dignitary of the cathedral was an end in itself,
a very comfortable position for which the exertions of dancing
attendance in Paris to seek a bishopric were by no means adequate
compensation. How many must have echoed the envious tones of
the Marquis de Franchon:

Je suis bien aise pour mes enfants d'avoir pris le parti des armes;
mais quelle différence pour moi si j'avais pris celui de l'église. Que de
peines, que de travaux n'ai-je pas essuyés. Que cette vie est différente
de celle d'un chanoine.[2]

True, there were minimal duties to be performed: the chanting
of the office, the ceremonies of the cathedral. If the archdeacons
were in any way assiduous they could be kept hard at work. They
were supposed to visit the parishes of the archdeaconry regularly,
examine the condition of the church and the cemetery, inquire into
the conduct of the parish priest and his *vicaire* and *habitués* and the
state of church funds. In addition they were supposed to inspect
the schoolteacher and see if the midwife was sufficiently devoted

---

[1] Béziers, op. cit., vol. i, pp. 423–4.
[2] P. de Vaissière, *Gentilshommes campagnards de l'ancienne France* (Paris, 1903), p. 372.

to duty and if any abuses had crept into religious practice.[1] But such visitations were indeed rare. De Rochechouart was clearly dissatisfied with the way they discharged their obligations. In any case, many of the duties were phrased too nebulously to be executed with any degree of efficacy. If the church of the parish in question was falling apart, the chapter was not going to take steps to remedy it out of its funds. The parish priest did not need to fear interruption from the archdeacons in the day to day management of his cure. Nor did the midwife, for her devotion to duty was measured by her rapidity to christen children at birth lest they died before the priest reached them and to report all births, living or dead, for registration.

The chapter of Bayeux produced no theologian in the eighteenth century and only one scholar, Béziers, whose elevation was pure accident. It frequently quarrelled with the seminary which was directed by the Lazarists, whose ultramontanism during the early part of the century had aroused the suspicion of the chapter that the young priests were being inculcated with heresy.[2] The chapter's assertions on these matters could not, however, be proven and the bishop discounted them. Indeed, the bishop was far more concerned about the persistence of at least four of the canons in attending masonic assemblies; but he could not prevail upon them to renounce their interest in freemasonry, nor could they be persuaded to look upon its doctrines as in any way incompatible with the teachings of the church.[3]

The chapter of Bayeux was a self-willed little community, intensely proud of its rights and defensive of its position, unprogressive and in size out of all proportion to its duties and revenues. Idleness indeed was the main enemy for the canons of Bayeux. With comfortable houses and an ample income, the temptation to do nothing was clearly too great for many of them. On the other hand, if they had any particular interests, they could indulge them to the full. De Loucelles spent his mornings in devotions and spiritual exercise and his afternoons either at the meetings of the *bureau de charité* or preparing reports on its activities. Determined to find a remedy for the town's unemploy-

[1] Béziers, op. cit., vol. i, p. 425.
[2] G. Bonnenfant, *Les Séminaires normands du XVIe au XVIIIe siècle* (Caen, 1915), p. 198.
[3] E. Sévèstre, *La Vie religieuse dans les principales villes normandes pendant la Révolution* (Paris, 1945), pp. 74–75.

ment problem, he was persuaded that the answer lay in industrial development. The manufacturers of the town found him a perpetual busybody, constantly intervening and asking questions on the manufacture of raw materials and the tricks of business in order that he might help the *manufacture des pauvres*. They closed their doors to him, jealous for their trade, but this only led the canon to start an active correspondence with foreign manufacturers and to invite distinguished businessmen to his house. The post brought him samples of foreign cloth whose quality he scrutinized in relation to its costs and methods of production and which he then carefully put away for future reference. Feret Dulongbois participated actively both at masonic meetings and the town's literary society. He was an avid, if not a wide reader and particularly interested in history and archaeology, a taste he was able to indulge—though he was perhaps considered rash by his fellow canons in his proneness to question the authenticity of many of the cathedral's most treasured relics. Dulongbois had a leaning towards controversy at an academic level and was always willing to welcome at his house those with similar interests. Others had a taste for litigation and ample opportunity to exercise it. D'Audibert once a month tried to summon the canons to spend an afternoon discussing the interminable law-suits in which the chapter was involved. The longest concerned the absorption of the revenues of the disused leper house, St. Nicolas de la Chêsnée, into those of the chapter—a claim which the town hospital, the *hôtel Dieu*, was anxious to contest.[1] The canons declared that they were ready to use the money for the poor but that the question at issue was not how the money was spent but who could consider themselves fully entitled to the income. At the same time they took the bishop to law over a small payment to the poor which his distant predecessors had allowed to lapse. Strife with the bishop was usually of a highly academic nature. The issues involved were almost always trivial and often concerned minimal sums of money or minor infringements of authority, but the canons were anxious to keep the bishop in what they considered his rightful place and never wasted an opportunity for asserting themselves.

On the whole, the canons were not shrewd businessmen when it came to managing their estates. They were more interested in maintaining their revenues intact than in enhanced profits.

[1] A.D.C. H. Suppl. 1009.

Ecclesiastical rents did not soar to the same extent as others in the area. But a few of the canons were actively concerned with their estates and the extra profits a canon could make to increase his income. Voisvenal kept careful accounts, became an *abbé in commendam*, and had a keen appreciation of economic realities. Others were perhaps harassed by impecunious families, anxious for a subsidy, and were not allowed to forget economic considerations. De Boisjugan found his early career marred by an over-demanding family which was never far from the bankruptcy courts and which expected financial help from the one son it was deemed could afford to give it. Not until his father went to the guillotine and his sisters fled to England did the unfortunate canon secure any peace and the chance to use his ability in the service of the church.

La Cauve interested himself in the organization of special services in the cathedral and rarely wasted an opportunity for a ceremony. Few royal births or French victories in the field went unmarked by a *te deum* in the cathedral of Bayeux. Dastignac was a popular preacher selected for Lenten and Advent addresses and to make funeral orations for the more notable dead of the town. The municipal council sought his services for important occasions and the Benedictine sisters to celebrate any special anniversary.

The nuns at the *hôpital général* and the *hôtel Dieu* had the canons quite shrewdly assessed and knew which were likely to be swayed by a worthy cause, which would give if harassed and which were content to leave charity to the cathedral treasurer and the more formalized methods of according relief. The canons rarely won a dispute with the Sisters of Charity or the Sisters of Providence, whose continual struggle for the poor of the town made them opponents too formidable for any canon intent on an easy existence to counter. Indeed, perhaps some of the intensity with which the canons fought the issue of the property of St. Nicolas de la Chênsée with the *hôtel Dieu* stemmed from a deep rooted desire to score a triumph over the reverend mother, Mère Angélique, whose immediate recourse when the house fell into difficulties was to the cathedral chapter. Many of the canons had a strong sense of social obligation which took the form of a benevolent paternalism towards the least fortunate members of society.

Besides the canons, the cathedral employed a *bas chœur* of

eighty-seven, including chaplains, sacristans, choir-masters, and
musicians, all of whom earned very little from their positions but
who usually supplemented them by small benefices or other posts.
In matters of music and ceremonial, Bayeux, considering the
wealth of the diocese, was extremely economical. Angers, whose
bishop and chapter were less rich, imported foreign musicians
and spent lavishly on improving the musical standards of the
cathedral,[1] but the canons of Bayeux were unswayed by such
considerations. Their attitude perhaps reflects the traditional
Norman parsimony and general reluctance to spend more than was
strictly necessary. True, the chapter of Bayeux maintained a
choir school for eight chosen choristers, but the children were
selected not on the basis of who had the finest voice but on the
poverty of the family from which they came. A careful inquiry was
made when a position fell vacant into which families would profit
from discharging a small boy on to the church and if this would
help them to bring up other small children.[2] The boys who
secured entry to the choir school were indeed fortunate. The
canons spared nothing for their well-being. They were well
taught, fed, clothed, and housed at the expense of the chapter and
when they left school were given 200 *livres* to pay for an apprenticeship and to help to maintain themselves during the training period.
Many of them found their way into the church.

The presence of men like Hugon and de Loucelles as chapter
treasurer was also the guarantee that the chapter of Bayeux would
not undertake any lavish building schemes in the eighteenth
century. They kept the cathedral in good repair and sanctioned
the installation of a new pulpit—Bayeux prided itself on the quality
of its preaching—but beyond this, the cathedral escaped any
major embellishment. Extravagance was never a criticism levelled
against the canons as it was against the bishop—especially de
Cheylus whose hunting parties were known far and wide for their
lavishness.

The canons were the only wealthy clerics with whom the
townspeople were in close contact, for the bishop was usually
absent and there were no wealthy religious houses in the town.
The three male communities of the town, the Augustinians, the

---

[1] J. McManners, *French Ecclesiastical Society under the Ancien Régime* (Manchester,
1961), pp. 26–32.
[2] A.D.C. Q. *Biens du Chapitre.*

Cordeliers, and the Capucins, were small and dwindling. At no stage in the century did any of them include more than a dozen men and their revenues were all under 5,000 *livres*—a sum sufficient for mendicants and nothing more. Occasionally they appeared in the streets to collect alms but this practice was strongly condemned by the chapter, who held that the monks were depriving the truly poor of their income. Only the Cordeliers carried out any function beyond the purely religious by serving as a retreat for the mentally sick ecclesiastics of the diocese who were sent there to rest at the order of the bishop, and occasionally they accepted mentally deficient children whose families could afford to keep them there. In contrast, the female communities were large and active, if no richer. The Benedictines of the Holy Sacrament kept their house going by running a *pension* for retired ladies of gentle condition, who took up residence—usually accompanied by a personal servant—behind the high walls of the community. They also ran a school for the children of good families. The Benedictines were a relatively backward-looking order; those who took its vows were usually the children of the minor *noblesse* and higher officials of the area, and many of them had received their primary education with the order.

Poorer girls were educated by the Ursulines, a house of seventeenth-century endowment and a highly respected community of some fifty nuns. Neither the Benedictines nor the Ursulines, however, rivalled in importance to the town the newly installed Sisters of Charity of St. Vincent de Paul or the Sisters of Providence, who alone administered to the aged, crippled, sick, and orphaned of Bayeux in the eighteenth century. The social origins of these women were diverse. The dowry their families were obliged to pay for their entry was 140 *livres*, which excluded the poorest members of society, but the hardness of the life deterred many more. Some of the Sisters of Providence were barely literate and their medical knowledge negligible but nevertheless, with limited means and slight capacities, they did what they could.

If the regular clergy of Bayeux were not numerous, the same could not be said of the lower secular clergy of the town. Bayeux was divided into fourteen parishes—an extraordinarily high number for a town of its size—of very uneven proportions ranging from 60 to 2,000 communicants. The necessary qualifications for holding such a benefice were a theological degree from the

university and a few months spent in the seminary at Bayeux
preceding ordination or a longer training period of up to two
years with the seminary. Then, it was hoped, one would obtain
a benefice with cure of souls, or failing this, would become a
vicaire and assist a parish priest. The latter selected his *vicaire* at
will and paid him out of the income he received from his benefice
so that if this was small he was unable to give his subordinate
very much; the *vicaire* on the other hand might reasonably expect
that when the *curé* resigned his benefice, for reasons of old age or
to accept another, he would do so in favour of his assistant, a
practice which was permitted only if the *patron* of the parish did
not have a candidate he was anxious to promote. But it was not
unknown for the incoming priest even to turn out the old *vicaire*[1]
and not every newly ordained priest was fortunate enough to find
a parish priest to employ him as an assistant. A diocesan centre
like Bayeux had large numbers of these unemployed ecclesiastics,
known as *habitués*, who lingered in the town hoping to find a
patron and who were in very poor circumstances.

The cures of Bayeux offered very little income to their priests.
St. Jean, the largest, including income from property and the
casuel (church offerings and collections), was worth about 500
livres which the *curé* and *vicaire* had to share; St. Laurent was worth
about 400 *livres* in property and *casuel*; St. Malo, La Madeleine, and
St. Martin were worth less than 300 *livres*; St. Patrice, Notre Dame
de la Pothérie, St. Exupère, and St. Loup were better endowed
but the incumbent had to live on the *portion congrue* since the parish
tithe was in the hands of the chapter; St. Ouen and St. Sauveur
had no revenues at all but the *curé* could claim a pittance out of the
revenues of St. Nicolas de la Chêsnée. Even less fortunate than
these were the priests of St. André and St. Vigor le Petit which
though rated benefices with cure of souls offered the *curé* so little
that unless he managed to combine the position with a benefice
without cure or a small job, he could not manage to survive.[2]

The parish priests of Bayeux were amongst the poorest of the
diocese for they fell, for the most part, even below the *curés à
portion congrue*. To qualify for the *congrue*—a fixed stipend payable
by the tithe owner to the holder of the benefice—the tithe and
church endowments had to be in hands other than those of the

[1] Sévèstre, *Les Problèmes religieux . . .*, vol. ii, p. 12.
[2] Béziers, op. cit., vol. ii, pp. 66–122. See Appendix II.

parish priest. Most of the priests of Bayeux, however, themselves received the revenues of their parishes, their poverty being a consequence of the inadequacy of these. Government attempts in 1786 to raise the *portion congrue* to a minimum of 700 *livres* brought relief only to four parishes of the town; for the rest, nothing was done. The parish priests of the town were committed to an unremitting struggle to secure for themselves a living wage. They had, obviously, to obtain another benefice without cure of souls or some other additional source of income and preferably one which did not absorb too much time. The teachers of the choir school, for example, were drawn exclusively from the priests and *vicaires* of the town. Teaching, however, was a demanding task, whereas chaplaincies attached to the cathedral and small religious houses were not. The chaplaincy attached to the *hôtel Dieu* was an important one. The priest who administered the sacraments and gave spiritual comfort to the sick did not receive a stipend for his services but he did receive good meals on the days he attended the hospital. However small the revenues of this establishment, it fed its priests on fresh fish, duckling, or good beef, depending on the day of his visit, vegetables, butter, and the best cider—the nuns did not economize on spiritual services. To serve as chaplain to the old ladies at the Benedictines was an even more enviable position, which added an extra 200 *livres* to the income of the holder, but it was rarely given to a young man and even if the old ladies were not numerous they liked a lot of individual attention, which took time.

Hence the parish priest of St. Laurent who derived less than 400 *livres* from his benefice made at least half that amount again as a teacher at the choir school. The priest of St. Malo drew the income simultaneously from a chaplaincy and ate twice a week at the hospital. The hardship lay in waiting for these extra sources of income for chaplaincies and teaching positions were not always readily available. Unless the parish priests were fortunate enough to own a little property in their own right, they could look forward to much effort and years of waiting before they secured for themselves a tolerable personal existence. The church merely demanded that the aspirant to the priesthood should have 150 *livres* of independent revenue a year, so that it lay open to all but the poorest sections of society. Most of the *curés* of Bayeux were of quite humble origins, the sons of petty tradesmen or small landowners[1] with only slight personal resources to ease their situation.

The clergy of other towns of the diocese were not as poor as those of Bayeux. At Caen, for example, the priest of St. Pierre had 3,000 *livres* per year, of St. Gilles 1,600, and even the poorest 600 *livres*.[2] Even so, the cures of Bayeux were not vacant: but they did change hands rapidly. Some of the parish priests of the town were like the unemployed *habitués* and hoped that in due course something would come their way. With good fortune one might attract the attention of the right people and secure a better appointment. Of the 611 cures of the diocese of Bayeux, the bishop presented to eleven, the chapter to seventy, and the rest were in the hands of religious orders, of *seigneurs*, and a few in those of the king.[3] The chapter had obviously the greatest influence; no individual religious community or noble could compete with it. The patronage of an influential canon was the most valuable asset a priest could have.

Promotion to a position higher than that of parish priest was extremely rare even for the most able. But it was not unknown. Michel Béziers, son of a poor shoemaker, was born in 1721. The poverty of his parents secured his entrance as a child to the choir school of the cathedral. He took holy orders and by 1748 was *vicaire* of the parish of Vaux and in 1754 parish priest of St. André at Bayeux. He had long since embarked upon the studies which were to make him the outstanding antiquary of Normandy of the eighteenth century, and even as a humble priest at Bayeux he was well known. Promotion, however, in spite of his fame, was long in coming and when it did come it was under extraordinary circumstances. In 1764 a canon of the Holy Sepulchre of Caen, in possession of the prebend of Moult in the chapter of Bayeux, resigned his benefice to a Sieur Autin, a boy of fourteen years. His parents put him in the monastery of the Cordeliers at Bayeux. The boy, however, denied that he had any clerical vocation and frequently took unauthorized leave. One day he signed on as a soldier in a company being formed by the Marquis de Faudoas—he was then seventeen years old. He thought he would

[1] B.C. MSS. 232–301. *Insinuations Ecclésiastiques.*

[2] B.V.B. MS. 48. *État des bénéfices de l'ancien diocèse de Bayeux. XVIIIe siècle.*

[3] B.V.B. MS. 27. *État des officialités, archidiaconés, doyennés et paroisses du diocèse de Bayeux au XVIIIe siècle.*

pass on his canonry to a cousin. Another canon of the cathedral, Jahiet, however, heard of the plan and spoke to the Marquis. Faudoas, indignant at Autin's conduct, ordered the boy before him together with Jahiet and Béziers, whom Faudoas deemed worthy of promotion, and two notaries. Autin resigned his canonry and prebend to Béziers, who obtained from Rome the necessary letters of provision and assumed office. A few years later he successfully resisted the attempts of the young man, disillusioned with army life, to retrieve his surrendered canonry, and died in office in 1782.[1]

Guillaume Moussard as parish priest of La Pothérie attracted the attention of the bishop, who engaged him as his secretary. In 1711 he became canon of the cathedral and received the prebend of Merville. In 1729 he became grand vicar of De Luynes, who was never afraid of promoting an able man. He died in 1756, widely recognized as a man of keen intellect.[2]

These two men were of exceptional ability. The parish priest who achieved a reasonable rural living, or a position in Caen, could count himself fortunate. Merit was rarely rewarded; noble birth, connexion, and patronage were the keys to advancement.

The general poverty of the parish priests was perhaps an effective deterrent to securing a high standard of capable entrants to the lower clergy. De Rochechouart was disturbed about the low intellectual level of the priests of the diocese and insisted upon their presence at annual conferences held in the seminary to draw their attention to their duties as spiritual directors, but many in outlying districts neglected to attend.[3] They pleaded that in their absence there was no one to carry out their duties or that they were physically incapable of undertaking a long journey. Nevertheless, the bishop felt he had achieved something and the practice was not wholly abandoned by his successor, de Cheylus. If standards were not high, the diocese of Bayeux was rarely shaken by any major scandal. The bishop was disturbed to learn in 1774 that a priest in an outlying parish had engaged a housekeeper of doubtful reputation whom he stubbornly refused to dismiss and was prepared to defy even the bishop.[4] But this was

[1] Béziers, op. cit., vol. i, pp. xiii–xiv.
[2] Ibid., vol. ii, pp. 103–4.
[3] Laffetay, op. cit., p. 128.   [4] A.D.C. H. Suppl. 1308.

an isolated case. Cases of neglect of duty and drunkenness were perhaps more common, but in the main the parish clergy of the diocese, if uninformed, did what was required of them.

The poverty of the parish priests, the *vicaires* and *habitués* of Bayeux, and the slowness of promotion, assured the presence of a core of dissatisfaction within the ecclesiastical framework. The parish priests and those without any sort of living together formed a left wing in permanent opposition to all other sections of the church—bishop, chapter, and religious order. On the occasions when they came into contact with the upper branches of the ecclesiastical hierarchy friction ensued. At two stages in the century deadlock occurred in the administration of charity because the parish priests could not agree with the chapter on how alms should be collected and to whom they should be distributed, and declared themselves more competent to judge these questions than the chapter.[1] The *habitués* who had little regular work and too much time on their hands were a particularly disruptive element in ecclesiastical society and very ready to criticize their superiors. They hung about the streets, the canons claimed, and sometimes brought disgrace upon the church by begging. Drunken scenes occasionally occurred and such incidents were used by the canons to lend support to their grievances against a seminary which had presented for ordination young men totally unfitted for service in the church.

There was little contact between the upper and lower clergy and certainly no understanding. The personal struggle against poverty of the majority of young priests in the area when they were faced with the apparent wealth of the bishop and chapter and the ease of the life of a capitular cleric led to embittered relationships. When at last a priest ceased to be a *vicaire* and was presented to a benefice with cure of souls, he was forced to sacrifice his first year's revenue to the bishop and chapter who owned the *déport*. Sometimes a part or even a whole of the tithe which should have been his main support found itself in the hands of the over-wealthy ecclesiastic and the parish priest was left to claim the *portion congrue* and to take from his parishioners fees for services which the tithe should have covered and which they paid with great reluctance. In addition, the amount of time the priests of Bayeux had to spend in school teaching and supplementary

1 Laffetay, op. cit., p. 193.

posts was time they should have spent on their pastoral duties, and they were quick to stress this aspect of the situation when an opportunity arose for airing their grievances in 1789.

The extremes of wealth and poverty between the upper and lower clergy were particularly striking at Bayeux. They did not, however, conceal the collective wealth of the institution from lay society, and ecclesiastical revenues were the object of widespread rancour. The income of the clergy of Bayeux was based almost entirely on land, and during a period of intense land hunger the vast ecclesiastical estates could not fail to attract covetous glances from poor peasant and speculator alike. The bulk of the property of the bishop and chapter was held on lease by large tenant farmers whose main complaint was that the church was an unprogressive landlord. Indeed, it had a vested interest in retarding the development of capitalist agriculture which in the Bessin was increasingly taking the form of pasture farming—by ancient prescription immune from tithe.

When the widespread conversion of arable land to pasture occurred in Normandy in the eighteenth century, the clergy were anxious in their own interests that lands should be taxed as they had been when they were arable. The *parlement* of Rouen backed their demands by an *arrêt* of 16 July 1749 which declared that in the *bailliages* of Coutances and Bayeux tithe could be collected on pasture land, provided it was of less than forty years' conversion from arable and was used for the pasture of beasts raised for sale and not merely kept for domestic purposes. This second clause provided a loophole which lesser jurisdictions were able to use to give decisions in favour of the farmer, decisions which the *cour des aides* regularly declared invalid.[1]

Then the policy of the *parlement* changed abruptly. An *arrêt* of 19 May 1784 declared that in Normandy only wheat, maize, rye, and hay were permanently subject to tithe; tithe on anything else could only be levied if it had been so over the previous forty years.[2] The rubric recognized, if tacitly, the principle that tithe could not be levied on newly converted land. This complete reversal of policy might well have arisen from an increasing awareness on the part of the *parlementaires* of their interests as

[1] H. Marion, *La Dîme ecclésiastique en France au XVIIIe siècle et sa suppression* (Bordeaux, 1912), pp. 46–47.
[2] Ibid., pp. 140–1.

landowners. After this date, it became common for the bishop,
chapter, and landowning religious houses to write into the leases
they made to new tenants express prohibition of any agricultural
change. They were instructed to plant the fields with the traditional
crops and to see that the land on the expiration of the lease was
in exactly the same condition as it had been when the lease was
undertaken.[1] But they could only apply these rules to land they
owned and not to the property of others. By the end of the old
régime the higher clergy were complaining bitterly of a marked
diminution of revenues. The situation also reacted upon the poor
curés à portion congrue, because, invariably, the tithe owner leased
out the tithe to the highest bidder who naturally ceased to pay the
owner and the *congrue* when the tithe could not be collected. The
chapter at Bayeux wrote to the *chef de l'agence générale du clergé
de·France* complaining that throughout the diocese after 1784
there was a general refusal to pay the tithe on anything but corn.[2]
Finally the clergy succeeded in obtaining from the king a royal
declaration in May 1786 suspending the *arrêt* of 1784. The *parlement*
of Rouen refused to register it. Stalemate was reached and it had
not been broken by 1789. On the eve of the Revolution, bad
harvests and the refusal to pay tithe on pasture meant that the
wealth of the church in Lower Normandy was not what it had
been. Some, however, could afford to lose more than others, and,
as usual, the simple priest felt the hardship most.

The situation of the lower clergy was clearly growing worse
not better. Benefices in the Bessin were undergoing a marked
depreciation in value because of this widespread change from
arable to pasture. The situation in the diocese of Bayeux was
perhaps not so difficult as in the neighbouring dioceses of
Coutances and Lisieux, where benefices were lying empty because
they no longer afforded the titulary sufficient to live on. The
pinch was felt more immediately by the rural clergy than the
town priests, but the endowments of the latter of Bayeux were in
any case inadequate, and the new developments menaced still
further their prospects of ever doing any better. Even the bishop
and chapter were directly hit and the relationship between the
bishop and the local law-courts became difficult in the extreme.
The bishop complained that he could never get a local court to
pass a judgement in his favour on the subject of levying tithe on

---

[1] Duterque, op. cit., p. 181.   [2] A.N. G⁸ 623.

pasture land; he spoke angrily of the ingratitude and high-handedness of the officials of the courts who were out to rob the church and never failed to criticize it. The same men, he held, were found at masonic meetings hard at work undermining the position of the church.[1] In reply, the *cahier* of the third estate of Bayeux, drafted in 1789, was to begin with a severe indictment of the wealth of the upper clergy and to terminate with the words: 'their kingdom is not of this world'.[2]

If the wealth of the upper clergy in this area was not what it had been, it was still considerable. Ecclesiastical revenues were obviously inequitably distributed and the largest part placed in the hands of the least active members of the secular clergy. Clerical income was also the object of keen resentment by sections of the town population, but if the officials of the courts spoke bitterly, such criticism was a luxury the bulk of the towns-people could not afford. Clerical income was drawn from the country, not from the town. Moreover it brought money into a town with few other resources. If the bishop spent some of his money in Paris the canons rarely left the town. The church was the most considerable employer of Bayeux. At least 120 servants, male and female, were employed by the bishop, chapter, and small religious houses. In addition, several hundred women and girls had been trained and continued to work at the lace *manufacture* of the Sisters of Providence. The diocese had two apostolic notaries, an archivist, an architect for counsel on repairs and building, a *greffier des insinuations ecclésiastiques*; the bishop's court employed two *baillis*, a *greffier*, and a bailiff. Both bishop and chapter had to employ a *feudiste*—a lawyer with a specialized knowledge of feudal dues, indispensable when the church was on the defensive for rights it had possessed from time immemorial. Again, they employed at least eight tax collectors in the town who were sent to work in the country after the harvest and two auditors of accounts. Someone was needed to ring the cathedral bell and set the clock, clean the churches, collect pennies for the hire of chairs in the cathedral. There were bookbinders, makers of credence tables and *prie-Dieu*, craftsmen who could repair chalices and ornaments, jewellers and makers of crucifixes, decorators, carvers, sacristans, and grave-diggers. The church was as important

[1] Sévèstre, *La Vie religieuse* . . . , p. 75.
[2] E. Anquétil, *Cahier du Tiers État de Bayeux* (Bayeux, 1886).

to the town as a consumer as it was as an employer. If the bishop
only appeared in the town during the hunting season, he did not
come alone and he spent lavishly; diocesan conferences held in the
seminary brought more trade into the town. The purveyor of
candles for use in the cathedral did a good business, as did the
maker of clerical habits. In hard cash, the church represented to
the people of Bayeux about 400,000 *livres* dispensed as wages, to
purchase consumer goods, and as charity.[1] It was a large sum of
money and Bayeux's most considerable source of income. The
way in which it was spent was of consequence, directly or indirectly, to a large proportion of the artisan class of the town and
to some of the *bourgeoisie*. Bayeux was economically dependent
upon its church and the extent of that dependence will become
more fully apparent when the resources of the rest of the urban
population, and in particular the poorest sections of society, are
examined.

[1] A.D.C. Lx. *États d'assistance, Bayeux.*

III

THE *NOBLESSE*

THE term *noblesse* in the eighteenth century was used to designate widely differing sorts of people. It comprehended dukes and peers and marshals of France along with illustrious national and provincial figures and innumerable small and unimportant local nobles. In Bayeux alone, though it was very far from being a busy provincial centre, some eighty noble families were in almost permanent residence and another twenty maintained a house there although absent on military service or employed in an office elsewhere, perhaps at Rouen or Caen. The number is large[1] and the men and women who enjoyed social pre-eminence within the highly restricted framework of the Bayeux community were indeed a very diverse collection of individuals. They included a few large landowners and many more urban officials, a handful of army officers, a large assembly of cathedral canons, younger sons whose incomes contrasted un-favourably with those of their elder brothers who lived on their estates nearby, several widows and spinsters of all ages, some of whom were in religion, and a few very poor men and women. Less than a sixth of these eighty noble households had been ennobled before the end of the fifteenth century; a handful had been ennobled as a recognition of their espousal of the cause of Henry IV at the end of the religious wars; the majority, at least a third, had become nobles during the seventeenth or early eigh-teenth centuries and are representatives of the *noblesse de robe* of that day. The last had attained *noblesse* gradually and according to a well-marked pattern. It had often begun with a purchase of an office in the local law-courts in the latter half of the seventeenth century and later, with the profits derived from that office, one in the *parlements* or that of *secrétaire du roi* which secured personal *noblesse* and the promise of hereditary *noblesse* to come. The rest of

[1] Toulouse was ten times larger than Bayeux and had a *parlement* but only twice as many nobles resident. R. Forster, *The Nobility of Toulouse in the Eighteenth Century* (Baltimore, 1960), p. 102.

the *noblesse* of Bayeux had been ennobled at some stage of the preceding two centuries, or had married heiresses of the region and had come to Bayeux from outside or had been granted posts in the area conferring *noblesse*.[1]

Amongst those families of the area which counted a companion of the first dukes of Normandy or a crusader as an ancestor, those of the Marquis de Campigny, de Toulouse Lautrec, de la Rivière, and de Pierrepont were the most influential in the town. The Marquis de Campigny was the most detested noble in the town, for Bayeux fell within the *seigneurie* of Campigny and its elevation in the late eighteenth century into a marquisate had involved a long and expensive lawsuit, which the town lost, in an effort to prevent the creation of a marquisate and the ensuing augmentation of de Campigny's privileges at the expense of the town. The others maintained a house in Bayeux while possessing within the Bessin large and attractive estates where they usually lived. The Marquis de Faudoas, on the other hand, rivalled in wealth only by Campigny and the Sieur de Vidouville, although frequently absent in Caen where he held a position in the municipal government, and less frequently on his estates at Castilly, chose the town as his principal residence. The Marquis de St. Vast, *maréchal de camp*, and holder of the *cordon rouge*, was the occupier of another house in the parish of St. Malo at Bayeux. A near neighbour was the Comte d'Albignac, *colonel des dragons de la reine*. The military governorship of the town had since the seventeenth century lain in the hands of the wealthy de Coulons family. The outstanding military personality of the town was without doubt the Baron de Wimpffen. Of Alsatian origin, he had married a wealthy heiress of Bayeux, and after distinguishing himself in the American War of Independence had returned to the area. New-comer though he was, he was to represent the nobles of the *généralité* of Caen in the Estates General.

These were the wealthiest nobles of the town. They paid between 300 and 500 *livres* of *capitation* tax, which was twice as much as that paid by the wealthiest *roturier* of the town and far more than the sum demanded of those of more recent ennoblement. There was one exception to this, however: the noble Sieur Durel,

---

[1] These conclusions are based on: (1) G. Chamillart, *Recherche de la noblesse en la généralité de Caen en 1666 et années suivantes* (Caen, 1887); (2) G. du Boscq de Beaumont, 'Les Anoblissements et les maintenues de noblesse dans la généralité de Caen', *Annuaire du Conseil Héraldique de France* (1907), pp. 76–164.

seigneur of Vidouville, *contrôleur de la maison du roi*, who was the
richest man, with the exception of the bishop, in the town of
Bayeux, though he only resided there in winter. His wealth was
founded on astute investments in offices by his ancestors during
the early seventeenth century, selling out before the depreciation
of the mid eighteenth century set in, and unscrupulous management of his estates. Not surprisingly, he was the first noble of the
area to have his property attacked by his tenants in 1789.

For the most part, the wealthiest nobles of Bayeux, the Marquis
de Campigny, de Pierrepont, de la Rivière, the Baron de la Tour
du Pin, and the military governor of the town, Couvert de
Coulons, lived solely on their income from property. The military
governorship of the town was a purely titular position. De Coulons
declared that he made nothing from it and that, in fact, the repair
of the *château* had to be met from his own purse.[1] Very few of
the great nobles of the town seem to have been absentee. The
Marquis de Balleroy had been in constant attendance at Versailles
until exiled to his *château* after a quarrel with the Duchess of
Châteauroux, but the bulk of the Norman nobles stayed at home.
The true-born Norman is the Scot of France, famous above all
for his economical living. But they were also not without their
pride. When, in 1778, some of the greatest nobles of France,
headed by the Duc de Broglie and the Duc de Coigny, spent
months in Bayeux preparing the invasion of Britain, the Marquis
de la Rivière went to great lengths to surpass all others in the
magnificence of his dinner parties. The expense entailed and the
gambling debts he incurred on these occasions forced him to part
with portions of his family lands.[2] But such extravagance is the
more remarkable for its very rarity.

Little information exists upon these men as landlords and on
the relationship between them and their tenants. The parish *cahiers*
of the *bailliage* of Bayeux have never been found. Such scanty
evidence as remains, however, points to the existence of much the
same sort of conflict as that which was taking place in other
parts of France. At a time of rising costs and in an area whose
potentialities as rich pasture land were being quickly recognized,

[1] A.D.C. C4261. *Château de Bayeux*. De Coulons complained that 'pendant vingt
ans qu'il a été gouverneur et commandant pour le roi à Bayeux, il n'a eu ni gages ni
appointements, ni gratifications bien qu'il ait été obligé de faire d'autant plus de
dépenses qu'il a eu pendant tout ce temps des garnisons dans la ville'.

[2] M. Pezet, *Les Seigneurs de Ryes en Bessin*, p. 188.

the large landowners of the Bessin were out to realize all they could. Enclosure was widespread and conflict with the *seigneur* over the question of the common land frequent. Meuvaines in 1772 undertook a lengthy lawsuit in an attempt to counter the Marquis de la Rivière's claims to the common lands.[1] Neuilly la Forêt took its *seigneur* to court on a similar issue.[2] The parish of Banville opposed its *seigneur* on his claims to *triage*, which was the right claimed by the *seigneur* to take back two-thirds of the common land, which, he held, had been conceded by his ancestors to the parish.[3] This was the most acute sort of quarrel in Lower Normandy and far exceeded in bitterness any relating to the payment of seigneurial dues. The common lands were an important part of the economy of the peasant: they meant the possibility of pasturing cattle, keeping his own lands free for grain, and it was vital to fight for them. Villages were prepared to struggle for years to hold on to them, impeded always by the expense of a long lawsuit and the partiality of French justice.

This handful of illustrious houses were the drones *par excellence* of the area. They intermarried, entertained one another, joined the bishop's hunting parties, and sought each other's company in a highly exclusive masonic lodge which met in Bayeux, where they staunchly refused the qualification 'brother' to anyone who was not quite of their kind, and this included the petty *noblesse* who were less wealthy than themselves.[4] They were distant figures to most of the townsfolk, but the latter had less cause to feel resentment towards them than their tenants in the country. Indeed, these wealthy houses created work for many of the townspeople. However rarely they used them, their houses had no less than a dozen servants each—cooks, valets, footmen, laundry and scullery maids—before coachmen and postilions and stable-boys were taken into account. In addition, they were considerable purchasers. The lace manufacturers of the town could count on regular purchases of their finer lace for ruffles and petticoats and of the heavier lace for table and bed linen. Their patronage was important to innumerable shoemakers and wigmakers, seamstresses, and craftsmen.[5] They were not remarkable

[1] A.C. *Meuvaines, Biens Communaux: Procès contre M. de la Rivière, 1772–1777.*
[2] A.C. *Neuilly la Forêt, Biens Communaux.*
[3] A.C. *Banville, Propriété Communale: Triage avec le seigneur, 1769.*
[4] De Loucelles, *Histoire générale de la franc maçonnerie en Normandie* (Dieppe, 1875), p. 33.   [5] A.D.C. Lx. *États d'assistance, Bayeux.*

for their generosity to the poor, but the leavings from their tables were regularly collected by the paupers of the *hôpital général* and used to enrich the poor-house soup.

Far more numerous than these wealthy nobles and much more familiar figures to the bulk of the townspeople were the fifty or so families whose tax levy was somewhere between 20 and 150 *livres*, a sum roughly equivalent to that paid by the wealthiest *bourgeois* families of the town. The bulk of these were of robe origins, but by the middle of the eighteenth century the old divisions of robe and sword were essentially derivative and amongst the *noblesse* of middling means intermarriage and interchange of occupation made any such distinction impossible to apply. The Anfrye family, for example, had been ennobled in the mid seventeenth century when the Sieur d'Anfrye had bought the office of *procureur général du grand conseil* and later that of *secrétaire du roi*; but if the next two generations had remained in the law, by 1789 the only Sieur d'Anfrye left in the area was a retired army officer living comfortably, if not luxuriously, as a *pensionnaire du roi*.[1] The Le Brethon family had become noble in the person of Jean Baptiste Le Brethon, *conseiller du roi au bailliage et siège présidial de Coutances* in 1700.[2] His children came to live at Bayeux but the evidence is that they lived on income from property and that they no longer owned any office in the courts. The same is true of the Dumanoir family. The head of the Dumanoir family in 1758 was *président* of the *élection* court of Bayeux and of the *grenier à sel*. He was also the third generation of the family to be holder of the office of *secrétaire du roi*.[3] By the end of the old régime his son had sold the offices and lived on the revenues from the *seigneurie* of Juaye. Again, the Suhard's robe derivations were buried deep in the sixteenth century when Pierre Suhard was *lieutenant général du bailliage*.[4] His son became a *conseiller* in the *parlement* of Rouen, but by 1789 the family was represented by Nicolas Suhard living on the revenue from the family lands at Grandcamp, a canon of the cathedral of Bayeux, and a spinster sister living as a *pensionnaire* at the Benedictines. Similarly in reverse, the Genas Duhomme family had been ennobled before the end of the fifteenth century but the family had been quick to appreciate the profits to be made from justice

---

[1] Du Boscq de Beaumont, op. cit., p. 79.   [2] Ibid., pp. 92–93.
[3] Ibid., p. 97.   [4] Chamillart, op. cit., pp. 252–6.

and throughout the second half of the seventeenth century onwards they were closely involved in the high offices of the *bailliage* and *vicomté* courts. The Adam family, of equally ancient derivation, had one branch which maintained itself by positions in the *grenier à sel* of Caen and Bayeux.

Nothing creates a more false impression than de Tocqueville's statement that the *noblesse* despised administrative posts.[1] On the contrary, in this part of Normandy at least, all the administrative positions of any importance were filled by nobles. Those who were in provincial and local office were not drawn from the wealthiest and most distinguished families, though there were exceptions to this. The highest positions in the municipal government of a large city like Caen, for example, carried with them great prestige. The mayor and the four important *échevins* of the town from 1766 to the end of the old régime were all nobles of ancient extraction and great wealth. The Comte de Vendoeuvre was mayor, the Marquis de Faudoas his first *échevin*, and St. Manvieu and d'Argouges, two names with lengthy histories in Chamillart, were next in rank.[2] The prestige attached to the position of mayor or *échevin* of Bayeux was doubtless distinctly less. Nevertheless, throughout the century, it was customary for the mayor of Bayeux and usually one *échevin* to belong to the *noblesse*, though not the *haute noblesse*, of the town.

Positions in municipal government were not sinecures. They demanded constant attendance. Men who had a career to maintain as well not infrequently resigned from office at Bayeux. Moreover, the state of municipal funds did not permit anything but the most slender remuneration for the mayor and *échevins*. Dignity and hard work were the main attributes of the offices.

In this part of Normandy the *subdélégué* was also drawn from one of the families of the urban *noblesse*. This, like the position of mayor, was one demanding much work and providing very little remuneration. Indeed the wealthier the *subdélégué*, the less he need be paid by the *intendant* and hence the less the drain on the taxes of the province. Some refused any remuneration at all. The office at Bayeux passed from Genas Duhomme to his nephew. The

[1] A. de Tocqueville, *L'Ancien régime et la Révolution*, vol. ii, p. 103.
[2] J. Yver, 'Une administration municipale "orageuse" à Caen à la fin de l'ancien régime. La mairie de M. de Vendoeuvre', *Mémoires de l'Académie des Sciences, Arts et Belles Lettres de Caen*, vi (1931), p. 251.

family had a long tradition of public service. Possessing 12,000 *livres* of revenue from his land at Rubercy, Genas received, on average, 600 *livres* per year as *gratification* for the work he did as *subdélégué* and the burden of the work was such that he needed a secretary to whom he paid 250 *livres* per year out of that sum. But for his income from land, continuance in office would have been impossible.

On the other hand, while Genas Duhomme and the mayor de la Londe worked hard for little or nothing, some of the nobles at Bayeux were bound up with perhaps the most profitable money-making expedient of the old régime, the collection of taxes. A du Bosq de Beaumont was *receveur des tailles*. An Adam, one of the oldest names of the Bessin, was *receveur des gabelles* at Bayeux and Caen. The Sieur de Charlemont was *directeur des aides*. In 1715 the Sieur du Bosq de Beaumont had his newly acquired noble status withdrawn because he had only 2,000 *livres* of revenue.[1] His son, however, made sufficient from collection of the *taille* to permit the family in 1761 to re-acquire the status, and the Sieur du Bosq who received the *taille* collection of the *élection* of Bayeux in the 1780s was possessor of an income estimated at about 40,000 *livres*.[2]

All the judges and high officials of the *bailliage* court were nobles and the positions were jealously handed on from one member of a family to another. They were the best-paid positions in the courts of Bayeux and the monopoly of them by a scarcely changing group of nobles meant that promotion in the courts of Bayeux was clearly blocked at the top. Conscription into the ranks of the *noblesse* via an office in a minor court had certainly ceased in Bayeux by the mid eighteenth century. The current office-holders who held fairly important positions had closed their ranks and the rest had diminished in value with the importance of the courts.

The urban nobles of comfortable rather than great means formed a group which partly monopolized the government of the town and the surrounding district, helped the canons run the *bureau de charité*, and directed civic functions. They were big fishes in a very small pond and commanded the respect of the towns-people. They intermarried, sent their daughters to the Benedictine

[1] A.D.C. C6433. *État de nouveaux anoblis revoqués, 1715.*
[2] A.D.C. C4639.

school, and sometimes their sons shared tutors. Some of their
wives ran an association known as *les dames de la marmite*, which
was intended to help needy families with food; but it functioned
very irregularly and was not popular with the poor of the town,
who claimed that as long as a cooking pot or stick of furniture
remained in their houses *les dames de la marmite* were unlikely
to give any aid.

There were seventeen noble households in Bayeux which paid
less than twenty *livres* of *capitation* and among these were nine
widows or spinsters of very moderate or slender means, three
very poor noble families, and five lesser army officers. Two of
these families touch the lowest level of all on the tax lists—the
level of the poor tradesmen and wool carders. Only three of them
were represented at the election of representatives by the nobles
of the *bailliage* in 1789. For the most part they lived very humbly
on the income from a small patch of land or a few houses and
none of them had more than one servant. They could be distinguished from the officials, professional men, and merchants of the
town in that they lived on the income from property alone and
were much poorer. Their position was made more difficult, on the
one hand, by the laws of *dérogeance* and, on the other, by the laws
relating to inheritance.

Dérogeance, or loss of *noblesse*, could come about only through
treason or the exercise of a profession which was not regarded
as compatible with noble rank, and by the end of the old régime
these were very few in number. At the beginning of the seventeenth century the exercise of any form of commerce was forbidden to anyone who wished to remain noble, but this ban was
lifted from wholesale trade in 1645 and the *noblesse* of Normandy
were, according to the jurist Houard, fully free to speculate, be
concerned with wholesale trade, practise the law or medicine, and
indulge in the creative arts. Only retail trading and manual work
were totally condemned.[1]

What was theoretically permitted was not always practised,
especially by the poorest nobles who feared that once they had
embarked upon an occupation, little would distinguish them from
the third estate. A stigma remained attached to many occupations,
especially to trade in any form. The minor nobles of Bayeux had

---

[1] D. Houard, *Dictionnaire géographique, historique, étymologique, critique et interprétatif
de la coutûme de Normandie* (Rouen, 1780–2), vol. i, p. 481.

their pride. *Noblesse* gave something more than exemption from the *aides* and the *octrois*; it singled a man out from the rest of the population by according him a position of prestige in the community. He had a special place in church and received communion first at mass. He had a pre-eminent place in public processions. If he wished to continue to enjoy these marks of deference, he must keep up appearances and avoid doing anything which might detract from his claims to *noblesse*. Besides, some of the poorer nobles were related to wealthy and important names and had not always been in straitened circumstances. To write in terms of families is always misleading. A study of the *noblesse* of Bayeux reveals great contrasts in the fortunes of different sections of the same family. Whilst one member of the de Pierrepont family paid 417 *livres* yearly in *capitation* tax, another paid 51 *livres*. Whilst the Marquis de Briqueville lived sumptuously on vast estates, *seigneur* of Isigny and omnipotent in a town whose wealth was rapidly growing, a relative lived quite simply in a very modest house at Bayeux.

Such inequalities in noble wealth were partly due to the laws of inheritance. The *coutûme de Normandie* declared that noble fiefs were indivisible and should pass in their entirety to one heir. Each of the male children of a deceased noble had the right of choosing, in order of seniority, the fief that he preferred. In the event of a deceased noble having only one fief to bequeath, it passed undivided to the eldest male heir, who had to concede to his brothers some form of compensation, under no circumstances exceeding a third of the total value of the fief. The *cadets* of Normandy were legendary for their poverty resulting from this ruling. Women could expect nothing in the way of land in the dowry, nor in the testament, if there were any male heirs. If the father died leaving unmarried daughters they were assigned to the wardship of the eldest brother. His duty was to find each sister a husband or to pay her a sum of money (*mariage avenant*) which should be decided upon by the family.[1] Women were regarded as taking money out of the family, an attitude which would appear to have been common throughout France.[2] On the

---

[1] C. Lefebvre, 'L'Ancien droit successoral en Normandie', *Nouvelle Revue historique de droit français et étranger* (1917), pp. 73–124.

[2] One or two daughters per generation married at Toulouse. Forster, op. cit., p. 129.

other hand, an heiress with money, even of a newly ennobled
family, could expect to make an excellent marriage.

At a time of increasing costs and when more children were
surviving infancy, fathers of large families could look forward to
much effort if they were to conserve for their names any sort of
wealth. No matter how rich the family, children in large quantities
were a very mixed blessing. The eldest son was usually the only
one in the family who could feel really secure. The others were
dependent upon parental skill and ingenuity in finding them a
position independent of the family fief, in the church, the army, to
a lesser extent the navy, and the law-courts. The head of the
family who had to undertake this task was dependent on his
contacts and his good fortune. He was limited on the one hand
by the laws relating to *dérogeance* but he was aided on the other by
several opportunities which lay open exclusively to children of
noble birth. These included admission to some cathedral chapters
and to certain posts in the church, the army, and the administration. As their need to find an income for their sons independent
of the family lands grew with rising costs and larger families, the
noblesse became increasingly defensive of their monopoly of these
positions.

Daughters did not, on the whole, create many problems. They
could be consigned to convents and, after the payment of a
dowry, often quite small, the strain of their upkeep taken from
the family budget. It was rare to find more than two daughters
per generation marrying at Bayeux. The *noblesse* of the town did
not expect their daughters to undertake the hard life of a Sister
of Providence or a Sister of Charity, but that of a Benedictine
was not over-demanding. The order drew the distinction between
the *religieuse de chœur* who entered the order for spiritual con-
templation and the rest who came to carry out more menial
tasks. The former were drawn exclusively at Bayeux from the
daughters of the petty *noblesse*. They retired behind the high walls
of the community and were unconcerned with the rest of society.

For sons, the church could mean a promising career. The
wealthiest families, with good connexions at court, might secure
a bishopric for one of their sons, but for those who lacked
connexion with such names as the Artois, there might be a position
in the nearest cathedral chapter. For the one bishop at Bayeux
there were forty-nine canons, some of whom were very wealthy.

Even if the family could not secure a prebend which carried with it a residence in the town, and had to provide one out of the family revenues, since celibacy was a condition of entering the church, the property of a noble canon would on his death revert to the family and nothing would be lost permanently. Nor did one have to pay anything to secure the position. The de Beaumonts, d'Albignacs, the des Fresnes, and other notable families inevitably succeeded in getting a son well placed in the church.[1] The life of a canon was infinitely to be preferred to that of a monk, for beyond nominal celibacy no real renunciation was involved and one did not have to go far afield and leave one's relatives.

A military career, in comparison, was a much more hazardous business. One needed both money and influence if one was to make one's way with any success. The son of a Normandy noble of moderate means was unlikely to reach the rank of general, though his noble status raised him automatically to that of *lieutenant*. The nobles of Bayeux who found their way into the lower ranks of the army were far from rich. Thus the brother of the Sieur de Malherbe, who was *seigneur* of Juvigny and an extensive landowner at Commes, described himself as *major du régiment de Bourgogne*. At the *vingtième* assessment of 1783 he wrote a cogent note to the *subdélégué* urging that his house assessment be reduced from 400 to 300 *livres*. He was, he said, very hard pressed. He had done some forty years' service, had nothing but the income from his military career, and had two sons to educate. The *subdélégué* investigated and confirmed the appeal.[2] A similar note came from Dumesnil de Bigardière and the official added to the tax list the note : 'vouloir bien considérer qu'il est sans fortune et qu'il ne subsiste que par son état de lieutenant'.[3] The younger sons of the de Rampant, de Valois, and de Varennes families— all of them *lieutenants d'infanterie*—were in a similarly poor financial position.

The situation in which a father of a large family found himself and what he did to secure careers for his children are best illustrated by specific examples. François Claude Godard du Bosq, *seigneur* of Bussy, Condeville, and Donville, had eleven children, six daughters and five sons. Of the daughters, two married, one

[1] *La France Ecclésiastique, 1783* (Paris, 1783), pp. 63–64.
[2] A.D.C. C5310. *Vingtième de la ville de Bayeux, Rue de St. Sauveur.*
[3] Ibid. *Rue de la Pothérie.*

became a nun, another died a spinster at the age of seventy-four, and two died while young. One of the sons inherited the fiefs of Bussy and Condeville and married, the second became a canon of the cathedral, the third inherited the small fief of Donville and married, one entered the army and died soon afterwards, and one died as a child.[1]

The Chevalier de Patry had four sons and only one fief. The projected invasion of England by France and Spain in 1778 provided him with a solution. Troops in impressive numbers were drawn together near Bayeux at the Camp de Vaussieux. The Duc de Broglie and the Duc de Coigny were in frequent attendance and the delays the enterprise occasioned afforded an opportunity for the petty *noblesse* of Bayeux to throw open their houses, welcome the visiting high nobles, and hope that their hospitality might be rewarded. Their energy was remarkable. By the time the enterprise was abandoned, the Chevalier de Patry, remorseless in his assiduous entertaining of the Duc de Coigny, had secured suitable military careers for three of his sons.[2]

De Wimpffen himself came from an Alsatian family of eighteen children of whom seven were sons. One became chamberlain to the Duc de Deux Ponts, a second canon of Wissembourg, a third colonel in the service of the Emperor and the other four went into the French Army. Several of the daughters entered convents.[3]

The recurring need of the petty nobles of the town for an income independent of the family fief perhaps in part explains why some of the nobles who were certainly not of robe origins bought positions in the local courts. Those they acquired were usually those conferring the most prestige and the greatest remuneration.

Adroitly managed, the situation of a noble family could be exploited very successfully and sometimes the *cadets* emerged wealthier than their brothers who were mere landowners. An examination of the Subtil family, for example, reveals three sons, one of whom inherited the family lands at Barbeville. The second was a *lieutenant des vaisseaux du roi*, the third became a canon of the cathedral. Yet the second is found paying a *capitation* tax

---

[1] E. Angérard, *Notes sur une famille Bayeusaine du XVIIIe siècle* (Caen, 1907), pp. 16–18.
[2] Pezet, *Bayeux à la fin de l'ancien régime* . . . , p. 46.
[3] Ibid., p. 5.

almost twice that of his brother;[1] while the third lived very comfortably on his ecclesiastical revenues.

A similar story can be told of the Deslongparts family which was ennobled in the late seventeenth century. The main inheritor, Richard Louis Néel Deslongparts, *écuyer*, *seigneur* of Belzaize, and *ancien officier des mousquetaires gris et colonel de cavalerie en retraite*, paid a mere 99 *livres* of *capitation* in comparison with a brother who was judge of the *bailliage* and who paid 144 *livres*. Other families by various methods succeeded in securing satisfactory incomes for all their sons. None of the Gosset brothers was left landless. If the eldest was solely a landowner, one brother was *chanoine de Mathieu* and vicar general of the cathedral of Bayeux, the last brother was an official of the *bailliage*. The Jahiet family exhibits a similar pattern. These families, however, belong to the middle strata of the *noblesse*. For the poorest nobles the situation was more difficult.

Whereas younger sons of the English gentry had an outlet in commerce and industry, no parallel opportunity existed in France. True, the noble did have the freedom to invest in commerce if he so wished, or, which is more to the point, if he had the money. But for those without spare capital the future was bleak. They could not enter the workshops of industry without *dérogeance*, and indeed there was little to encourage them so to do. The industrial experiments at Bayeux had met with failure, one after another. The nobles who wished for profitable commercial speculation had to look further afield. No isolated example was the young noble for whom the *intendant* of Caen solicited a *sauf conduit* in 1776. Hard pressed for money, he had joined forces with a grocer, who had some spare capital, in commercial speculation, and the two had promptly gone bankrupt with debts at Dunkirk, Le Havre, and La Rochelle.[2]

The bankruptcy of poor noble families was indeed common. The most notorious case resulting from commercial enterprise at Bayeux was that afforded by the Sieur de Boisjugan in 1776. A man of very adequate means who had at least 12,000 *livres* of *rentes*, he was unfortunate enough to be the father of fourteen

---

[1] Offices in the navy would appear during this period to have conferred greater wealth than many in the army, but the navy did not offer the same social prestige as the army. Naval officers were not included in the regulations of 1750 creating the *noblesse militaire*. M. Reinhard, 'Élite et Noblesse', *Revue d'histoire moderne et contemporaine*, iii (1956), pp. 8–11.   [2] A.D.C. C251. *Sauf Conduit*. 17 July 1776.

living children of whom, even worse, nine were sons. He had to
secure incomes for his numerous sons—the daughters he relegated
to convents as soon as they were old enough. Even though he had
recourse to all the usual ways of finding employment for one's
children—one he made a canon, one an army officer, one an
official of the *bailliage*—several remained. He decided, fatally, to
speculate in the increasingly lucrative apothecary trade by
exploiting markets as yet untapped. He bought drugs from an
apothecary of Bayeux, hired a ship, and sent off two of his sons
to San Domingo. The inhabitants of the island did not share the
French enthusiasm for patent medicines and the enterprise failed.
The debts incurred rose to 30,000 *livres*; the family was faced with
bankruptcy and the wrath of the merchant apothecaries.[1]

The *intendant* tended to show a sympathy towards destitute
nobles which was rarely shared by the townspeople or the
subdélégué. Only very occasionally was a bankrupt noble refused a
sauf conduit on the terms he demanded. The Hüé family of Cussy,
near Bayeux, came almost to expect an annual subsidy from the
intendant to help them to subsist. Both husband and wife were
aged and their income a mere 250 *livres* annually, but, Genas
the *subdélégué* claimed, they managed during three successive years
to get their debts paid by the *intendant* Fontette, and add a further
300 *livres* to their income. Genas was of the opinion that the practice
should be terminated. Divining a lack of sympathy on the part of
the *subdélégué*, Hüé wrote directly to the *intendant*:

Car vous êtes un homme très charitable pour la pauvre noblesse
qui sont hors d'état de pouvoir vivre pour le présent. C'est pourquoi,
Monseigneur, j'ai recours à votre aimable charité . . . M. de Fontette
qui était ci-devant intendant dans la généralité avait bien des bontés
pour moi, et il m'accordait tous les ans une somme de 300 livres comme
représentant l'aimable personne de Sa Majesté, et vous, Monseigneur
qui la représentez aujourd'hui en sa place, je vous prie de m'accorder
cette même grâce.[2]

Such direct begging letters were rare. Far more common was
the *sauf conduit* solicited by a bankrupt young noble whose commercial speculations had met with failure or who had overspent
in the army, or who had inherited debts from his father. Towards
these, the *intendant* generally urged special leniency in his recommendations to the *contrôleur général*.

[1] A.D.C. C256. *Sauf Conduit.* 24 April 1776.   [2] A.D.C. C955.

Indeed, on occasion the *intendant*'s mercy would appear to have been limitless. A request for a *sauf conduit* of 1782 illustrates the type of case which always received lenient treatment. The Sieur de Troismonts wrote:

La situation dans laquelle je me trouve n'est point venue de ma faute. Fait pour jouir d'une fortune considérable pour un particulier, j'ai été élevé dans une honnête opulence. A vingt ans, j'ai épousé une femme respectable, nièce de Montaigu, maréchal de camp . . . Deux ans après mon mariage, j'ai perdu mon père. Voulant faire honneur à sa mémoire je me suis rendu héritier. Les charges de cette succession excédaient de plus de 3,000 livres ce qu'elle me rapportait.[1]

The *intendant* gave his support to the granting of a *sauf conduit*. Such clemency rarely characterized his attitude towards those of lowlier origins.

The poverty of some of the old families of the Normandy Bessin and of many of the younger sons or relatives of many rich families offers a marked contrast to the wealth of the newly ennobled families of the area. Only three families in Bayeux received ennoblement after 1750. Of these, two were of the *noblesse militaire*. Michel Le Courtois de Surlaville, son of Thomas Le Courtois, *avocat au bailliage*, was captain and *chevalier de St. Louis* in 1745 and ennobled in the capacity of *maréchal de camp* in 1762.[2] Another, Bailleul, *mousquetaire*, who was ennobled about the same time, was a man of great wealth.[3] Apart from these, one man had received noble status as a *conseiller* of the *conseil supérieur*. Maupeou decided, when he dissolved the *parlements* and created the *conseils supérieurs* in their stead, that the high officials of the new courts, if they were not nobles, must be ennobled to give status to his administrative experiment.

The *anobli* was accorded a social status less elevated than the rest of the nobles. In public processions he was placed behind the *noblesse de race*. His relations with the *noblesse* depended, it would seem, on the extent to which he tried to assert his newly acquired status, and upon how wealthy he was. The noble mayor of Caen and his *échevins* refused to accept an *anobli* as first *échevin*.[4] This is hardly surprising in light of the wealth and antiquity of the Vendoeuvre family and of the *échevins*. The former might very well have hesitated before associating on familiar terms with the

[1] A.D.C. C491.   [2] Du Boscq de Beaumont, op. cit., p. 103.
[3] Ibid., p. 82.   [4] Reinhard, op. cit., p. 30.

noble mayor of Bayeux. Le Courtois remains an obscure figure at
Bayeux, but Bailleul, who had three daughters and no male heirs,
found as husbands for his daughters the Baron de Wimpffen, the
Marquis de Saffray, and the Comte d'Albignac, who were the
best of the current marriage market.[1] Money, it would seem,
removed all barriers between the *anobli* and the *noblesse de race*.

A study of the *noblesse* of Bayeux is a study of a complex group
of people, large landowners, urban officials, widows and spinsters,
younger sons, army officers, cathedral canons, and a few poor
families who could barely make ends meet. The bulk were not
concentrated either at the top or the bottom of the scale. Most
lived simply in a house of moderate size, simply furnished, with
two or three servants—nearer the wealthy *bourgeoisie* in their way
of living than either the great houses who topped the noble scale
of wealth, or the poorest nobles who could only be equated in
wealth with the artisan class.

These groups only occasionally met and never associated.
Nothing cemented them together to form a caste. The ancient
and wealthy *noblesse*, the Marquis de Campigny, de la Rivière, de
Pierrepont, enjoyed a position of isolation from the moderately
wealthy urban nobility carrying out useful public functions in the
company of the professional sections of the *bourgeoisie* from whom
some of them had originally been recruited. This nucleus of
urban nobles was equally severed from the type of noble which
this study does not include, the small parish *seigneur*, who had no
connexion with the town and who was cut off by his small means
from association with the great noble families and by distance and
difference of function from the urban nobles engaged in local
administration. For these more isolated parish *seigneurs*, exemption
from the *taille* and seigneurial dues was a more considerable part
of their income than for the urban nobles or the great families,
and *noblesse* gave something more than social prestige, it gave
economic advantages. Their difference in outlook—they were
essentially more conservative than the great nobles for whom
pecuniary privileges meant relatively less, or the urban nobles
who were in more direct relationship with sections of the
bourgeoisie and hence were more aware of the hostility of public
opinion—was to be eloquently illustrated in the events leading to
the elections for the Estates General.

[1] Pezet, op. cit., p. 46.

IV

THE *BOURGEOISIE*

F OR official purposes, such as the drawing up of tax lists, there were resident in Bayeux in 1789 some 1,200 adult males either exercising an occupation or possessing some means of livelihood. Of these, 130 boasted professional status, over a hundred being lawyers or officials of the courts and the rest doctors, surgeons, and apothecaries. Suppliers of food, grocers, bakers, butchers, fishmongers, and fruiterers made up a further hundred members of the population. Forty termed themselves merchants either of cattle, dairy produce, or lace. Another score of men qualified themselves as tax collectors, royal or seigneurial. As one might expect from the nature of the town, the industrial workers formed a relatively small proportion of the male population, some 130 men in all. The rest were crammed into the building trades or were shoemakers, tailors, barbers, wig-makers, candlemakers, or carried out the thousand and one small jobs that could be found in any town : hotel and innkeepers, cutlers, saddlers, soap-makers, coopers, haberdashers, locksmiths, tinsmiths, goldsmiths, clock-makers, mirror glaziers, clerical workers, policemen, pin-makers, keepers of cafés, ironmongers, drapers, glovemakers, and so on.[1]

To draw a hard and fast line and call some members of this society *bourgeois* and others merely artisan is a virtually impossible task, easy perhaps only at the extreme ends of the economic scale. The term *bourgeois* was used very loosely in the eighteenth century and in no way denoted a precise economic level or position of social standing in the urban community. It was used indiscriminately to describe all those who belonged neither to the privileged orders on the one hand nor to the poorest sections of the artisan class on the other. Predominantly the population of the town was composed of shopkeepers and petty

[1] A.D.C. C4542–7. *Capitation des bourgeois et des arts et métiers, 1781–1787*; C4645. *Capitation des offices de judicature, 1787*; C4665. *Capitation des exempts et privilégiés, 1789*.

tradesmen and those involved in the administration of the town and the surrounding area. Over half those rated on the tax lists hovered dangerously on the fringe of destitution. Little new wealth was apparently being created in the town and its industrial resources were negligible. Nevertheless, it was possible to live in Bayeux in the eighteenth century and make money. Some occupations paid very well and others kept those who practised them well above the ranks of the destitute.

In terms of relative wealth the collectors of seigneurial rights, receivers of taxes, merchants dealing in cattle, dairy produce, and lace, innkeepers, the highest officials of the law-courts, and the apothecaries fall almost entirely into the higher income group whilst the number of manufacturers in this group is small. The professional men, lawyers, doctors, and surgeons, are scattered from the top to the very bottom of the scale, the surgeons especially comprehending one very wealthy and one or two who are described by the *subdélégué* as reduced to the bare necessities of existence.[1] The bailiffs and *procureurs* of the courts fit, for the most part, into the middle income groups though occasionally one rises to the top of the scale. The wealth of certain suppliers of food, notably the grocers, is clearly remarkable, but others—butchers, fruit and vegetable sellers, fishmongers, and some bakers—are equally remarkable for their poverty and together with the textile and manual workers form the bulk of the urban artisan class. The artistic occupations—sculptors, painters, and architects —along with the school teachers, public servants, police, and clerical workers, also belong to the lowest income groups. Further generalizations based on the scale of relative wealth is difficult. One find drapers, candlemakers, wig-makers, tanners, even clock-makers, appearing in both the higher and lower income groups. But by itself a division based on wealth does not reveal very much since it does not take into consideration many other factors essential to any study of society. At any given time a society includes young and old, those at the peak of their careers and those in the middle, perhaps rising, perhaps stuck, and those at the very beginning whose prospects might be excellent but whose immediate returns are negligible. It does not take into account the motives behind the adoption of a particular occupation. Above all it does not indicate how far the professional

[1] A.D.C. C2796. *Arts et métiers, Bayeux, 1750.*

qualification was merely nominal and used to sum up a host of different sources of income. It ignores in fact many of the basic premisses upon which society is based and, most important, the way in which people live. To understand the *bourgeoisie* of Bayeux and arrive at something deeper than a superficial division of the population in rather meaningless economic terms, each of these considerations must perforce be examined.

The courts of Bayeux, most of which met so rarely and whose business yearly diminished, would seem at first glance to have offered little in the way of remunerative employment. Yet many of the varied occupations they afforded attracted widely differing sorts of people. The highest venal positions of judge of the *bailliage* court and those of *avocat* and *procureur du roi* in the same court and of judge and some of the *élus* in the *élection* court were the most important judicial posts in the area. All in 1789 were filled by nobles. Secondly, there were the high officials of the smaller courts, the *maîtrise des eaux et forêts*, the *amirauté*, and the *grenier à sel*, offices which were the creation of a king in need of money and which were held in courts which rarely met: these offices are always described as bringing more honour than profit to those who exercised them.[1] Thirdly, there were the numerous lawyers whose positions were not venal and whose income from the law depended upon acquiring a large and important clientele, which could be secured only by a reputation for ability and success. Fourthly, there were those concerned with the business side of the courts—the *procureurs*, bailiffs, notaries, and the *contrôleur des actes*, whose income was based on fees paid for the registration of notarial acts. Lastly, the courts afforded small and even menial positions—clerks of the police, *archers gardes de la connétablie*, who conducted the prisoners into the court, *jurés crieurs* who made announcements—positions which perhaps offered a few extra *livres* yearly to the income of those who owned them. Obviously positions differing so greatly in scope were acquired for different reasons. The high judges of the *bailliage* and *élection* courts were drawn from the *noblesse* of the area. These were the key positions in the courts and time had bestowed upon them great dignity. Those who held them were men of great wealth and at Bayeux, as at Orléans, they were all in the possession of nobles.[2]

---

[1] A.D.C. C5467. *Vingtième d'offices et droits, 1781.*
[2] Lefebvre, 'Urban Society in the Orléanais . . . ', pp. 50–51.

These positions were not sinecures and demanded much more constant attention than other positions in the courts. The burden of duties was such that in some areas of France there was a serious under-staffing of these posts. One *intendant* at least complained that the only offices which were avoided were those concerned with the day to day administration of civil justice.[1]

The law and the administration of France under the old régime were surrounded by an aura of prestige to which no other profession or pursuit could aspire. The origin of the respect for those who sat in judgement is too deep rooted to trace. The courts had once been the sole means by which the royal will had been conveyed to the provinces of France. The supreme law-courts, the *parlements*, were still the only institution of sufficient strength in France to dare to question the will of the monarch. Some of the gloss of the greatest courts had rubbed off on to the smaller; indeed, the petty jurisdictional bodies of the *amirauté*, *eaux et forêts*, *grenier à sel* and in some cases the *élection*, only survived into the eighteenth century at all because although administratively redundant, their officials continued to command respect, and the monarchy in its efforts to raise money in the seventeenth and eighteenth centuries had chosen to exploit the accepted way of rising in the social scale. The answer to the question what, in this society, gave social standing, seems to have been quite simply to make one's way into the administration by way of the law-courts. In this way one could be assured of a place in the public eye and a measure of authority, however small.

Whereas in the *bailliage* court the judges were kept fairly busy, and the profession of *avocat* and the positions of *procureur*, notary, and bailiff usually presupposed an active career in the law, the offices of the minor courts, which so seldom met, were much less onerous. However financially unremunerative they were, they had been and were still, on occasion, in demand by men who had made their money in trade and wanted to increase their personal prestige in the public eye. To be a judge in a minor court one needed money, not legal training. Sometimes this was the expedient of an elderly man who retired from commerce, lived on his property, and attended the court on the few occasions it met.

[1] L. E. Everat, *La Sénéchaussée d'Auvergne et le siège présidial de Riom au XVIIIe siècle*, p. 54.

Tillard des Acres, for example, had been an apothecary of some wealth, owning considerable property. In 1787 he passed on his trade to his son and bought the position of *greffier* in the *élection* court, a position which brought him a mere 200 *livres* a year[1] compared with 1,200 *livres* he drew yearly from his property in Bayeux alone. With plenty of property acquired during a successful career, he settled down to a comfortable old age, assured of a respectable status in the town and describing himself now by his new title of *greffier en élection*.

Again, Phillipe Vallerend was an important wholesale trader in cattle and owner of extensive properties at Bayeux and Monceaux. In 1786 he bought the office of *procureur du roi* at the *grenier à sel*. By this date the work of the *grenier à sel* at Bayeux was negligible and it would seem that the only man making anything out of the *grenier* was the *receveur des gabelles*, who combined the position with *receveur* at the *grenier* of Caen. Vallerend did not desert his occupation of *marchand de bœufs*, the main source of his wealth, but thereafter styled himself *procureur du roi au grenier à sel*.[2]

In such positions one had very little to do, one could mix with the *noblesse* who held positions in the court, and take a prominent place in public ceremonies. The importance of such considerations during the mid century led to a protracted struggle between the smaller courts, wherein the officials of one court attempted to assert precedence in public ceremonies over those of another in a veritable battle for social prestige.[3] The *maîtrise des eaux et forêts*, which so rarely met, tried on several occasions to assert its authority over the *élection*. Its judges occupied the seats of the *élection* court at mass in the cathedral, since they were in a more elevated position than those assigned to the *maîtrise*. The humiliated officials of the *élection* could retaliate only by slipping into the chapter stalls, to be turned out by the indignant canons. Again, at the inception of a new municipal council the *maîtrise* tried to assert precedence over the other courts by proclaiming its loyalty first and out of turn. The aim of those who bought these positions was not to find a career in the law but to gain social prestige in the community. With a safe income from other sources, they were relatively indifferent to the return in money from the office, if the

---

[1] A.D.C. C5467. *Vingtième d'offices et droits, 1781.*
[2] A.D.C. C9263. *Registre du Contrôle.* Entry no. 126, 27 May 1786.
[3] A.D.C. C266.

return in admiring glances at their flowing robes and judicial
caps was high. Virtually alone in the courts, they were unconcerned with the profits of justice.

They were indeed in an enviable position, for the law represented
their social aspirations and not their livelihood. Far less fortunate
were the thirty or so lawyers of the town who shared the dignity of
the judges and officials. The word *avocat* was a nebulous qualification in France in the eighteenth century. It simply meant that
one had taken a degree in civil or canon law, sworn on oath, and
had been inscribed in a court register; it did not necessarily mean
that one practised or made a living from the law.[1] A man went
into the law sometimes to prepare himself for an office if one was
owned by his family, but far more often on the slim hope of
making a name for himself. He needed no capital to start a
practice and there was the faint hope that if he proved brilliant
he might make his way to the top, perhaps as far as the *parlements*.
The multiplicity of income groups to which the *avocats* of Bayeux
belonged is largely to be accounted for by the fact that many were
young men waiting to inherit an office if one was in the family, or
else the clientele and business of an older *avocat*. Many an *avocat*,
well into his twenties, was forced to admit that he was without
work and his tax form bore the inscription 'fils de famille qui ne
fait rien'.[2] The amount a mere *avocat* made from the law was
bound to be dependent on the clientele he could command and
this in turn was inevitably conditioned by his experience and reputation in the law. If those at the top were doing well and
moving in exalted circles, those at the bottom were waiting for
better things to come, a period of waiting which could be indefinitely protracted, more especially if one's connexions were
limited. Any aspiring *avocat* would try to marry himself into a
family concerned with the administration of justice. Indeed,
from 1750 to the end of the old régime the only example of an
avocat of Bayeux who did not marry a woman from a family with
similar interests in the law was one who married a doctor's
daughter. Intermarriage doubtless helped one's professional
connexions and strengthened the chances of getting business.

The bulk of legal business transacted in the eighteenth century
was indeed extensive. The multiplicity of taxes, direct and indirect,

---

[1] Marion, *Dictionnaire* . . . , p. 30.
[2] A.D.C. C4679. *Requêtes en décharge et modération, 1773.*

demanded by the royal treasury, dues extorted by *seigneurs* lay and ecclesiastical, brought even the most humble landowner or tenant farmer up against endless injustices, which might well terminate in the courts if he refused to pay. In spite of this, the amount of work in the courts alone was not sufficient to employ the thirty lawyers Bayeux possessed. They were in a difficult position, for in choosing their profession they had cut off several channels of profit. However poor, exploitation of land or another privilege or office was the only means by which an *avocat* might supplement his income from the law. Commerce, denied in some of its aspects to the *noblesse*, was denied in its entirety to the *avocats*.[1] For many the prospect was wholly bleak even if they inherited an office, unless they had a commensurate backing in land and wealth. Indeed, a mere legal qualification and the inheritance of an office which brought in nothing could be the quickest way to bankruptcy, and this was not infrequent.[2] A real difference in wealth is often apparent between those who had inherited an office for long in the family and those who bought one. In 1773 the Sieur Fontaine, *procureur du roi au grenier à sel*, paid 20 *livres* of *capitation*: in 1786 Vallerend, the cattle merchant, acquired the office and paid 90 *livres* in tax.[3] The Sieur Marie, new acquirer of the office of *maître particulier des eaux et forêts*, showed a marked superiority in wealth over Bobé, the former holder, whose bankruptcy had caused him to take flight.[4] On the other hand, those who, like Philippe Delleville, had inherited both land and office, succeeded to an elevated status both in respect of wealth and prestige.

No one can live, many of the *avocats* of Bayeux learnt, on honour alone. But there was one direction at least in which a solution could be found and solvency achieved.

The increase in the price of agricultural produce encouraged *seigneurs* to claim their dues more diligently and this meant in kind rather than money. Dues which had been commuted into money payments in the Middle Ages for sums which meant nothing in eighteenth-century terms were re-examined and turned back into

[1] Houard, op. cit., vol. iii, p. 192.
[2] In the 1780s a *maître particulier des eaux et forêts*, the *garde marteau* of the same court, and a *receveur des tailles* at Bayeux all went bankrupt. All had inherited their offices. A.D.C. C5467, C577, C251.
[3] A.D.C. C4645. *Capitation des offices de judicature, 1787.*
[4] A.D.C. C5467.

their original payment in kind. Some *seigneurs* urged their officials
to make discoveries of new or lapsed payments and promised them
a percentage of any increase in revenue.[1] Done assiduously the
results could be impressive, and obviously those best fitted to
carry out the work were those with a legal training who knew how
much or how little could be done without violating the letter of
the law. The bishop and chapter each employed a lawyer concerned exclusively with the defence of the feudal rights they
enjoyed. A further half-dozen lawyers had part-time employment
with noble landowners. The peasant had few means by which to
gain justice. Any extensive *seigneurie* had its own court to which
his grievances had to be referred in the first instance and the
judge of that court, the *bailli*, was, in at least four instances in the
élection of Bayeux, an *avocat* of the *bailliage*. Hence the same man
who had recommended changes in old seigneurial taxes might, if
the peasant objected, be judge of the legality of his claims. Moreover, his very income might well be dependent upon upholding
the claims of the *seigneur*. Even if the *seigneurie* did not have its own
court and the case was referred to the *bailliage*, the chances of
justice for the peasant were slight. To secure success in the courts
one had to pay one's way. It followed that the legal profession
was bitterly resented in the countryside. But the lawyers were not
the only vultures preying on the pickings of the malversation of
justice. The *procureurs*, bailiffs, and notaries were each in their way
dependent on what they could mulct by fair means or foul from
the rest of the population, the only difference being that far less
pretence was involved. In examining these professions we leave
behind us the glory of rhetoric and the *éclat* of the magistrature,
the traditions proclaiming nobility of status and the laws for-
bidding participation in commerce. Nor does one hear these
positions talked of as bringing more honour than profit.

An examination of the income from the office of *procureur* or
bailiff immediately poses the question, just how did their possessors
manage to survive? *Procureurs* averaged between 200 and 300
livres annually, bailiffs between 50 and 222 *livres* according to the
court.[2] At a time when an annual income of some 250 *livres*
would allow only bare subsistence to one man alone, these offices
would hardly seem to offer much, particularly if one had an outlay

[1] Davies, op. cit., p. 36.
[2] A.D.C. C5467. *Vingtième d'offices et droits, 1781.*

of at least twenty times, and often more, the annual income from the office.[1] The *capitation* lists, however, place these office-holders well above the lowest income groups, and none of the offices of bailiffs, *procureurs*, and notaries were vacant at the drawing up of the *vingtième d'offices* in 1781.[2]

For what reasons were these offices purchased if they were so unremunerative? There are various answers. For some the lower offices represented a transitional stage on the way to a superior position. Amongst the bailiffs, *procureurs*, and notaries of the courts of Bayeux a very marked progression is obvious from position to position and court to court. The cheapest position to buy, usually, was that of bailiff in one of the lesser courts. Of all the officials in the law-courts the bailiffs were probably the most unpopular, for they derived the bulk of their income as bailiffs from the seizure of property to pay debts. The office carried with it in some respects the antithesis of social prestige as well as not offering a steady income. The *intendant* remarked of them that profit for the owner depended entirely on good luck and on the confidence reposed in him by the public.[3] A holder of the office of bailiff had therefore to find another source of income on which to live, and to move on as soon as the opportunity presented itself to the office of *procureur*, first in the lesser courts and then in the *bailliage*. The pattern is consistently repeated by the new acquirers of the position. J. B. Le Romain, for example, was, in 1779, bailiff of the *amirauté*, in 1781 *procureur* in the *élection*, by 1787 *procureur* in the *bailliage*.[4] Richard Hardouin began his career as a wholesale draper, bought the office of bailiff, and moved several years later to the position of *procureur* of the *bailliage*. Michel Vautier was a bailiff in 1773 and ten years later notary.

With the position of *procureur* a tendency manifests itself which holds equally true of the notaries. The *procureurs* of Bayeux present a picture of men who use their positions not to supply the bulk of their income but as the basis of a business career. They are estate agents, rent collectors, and ultimately moneylenders. Their position in the courts seemed to fit them with the necessary qualifications to attract this kind of business, at which some were

[1] Ibid.   [2] Ibid.   [3] Ibid.
[4] A.D.C. C4639. *Capitation des offices de judicature, 1779*; C5467. *Vingtième d'offices et droits, 1781*; C4645. *Capitation des offices de judicature, 1787*.

obviously more successful than others. Hence the same Richard Hardouin, who began life as a draper and never abandoned the drapery trade, having been successful as a bailiff and a *procureur*, was by 1788 manager of the property of the Sieur Dumanoir, a noble absent in Cayenne, and rent collector for the *hôpital général* of Bayeux. Le Pelletier, *agent de Monsieur*, brother of the king, was a former *procureur* of the *élection* of Bayeux. Le Paulmier, the most important *receveur* of seigneurial rights for the bishop of Bayeux, had the same early training in the courts. Duhamel de Vailly, notary of Bayeux, carried out the notarial work connected with the bishopric and the tax farming of the diocese was put into his willing and none too scrupulous hands, as were the affairs of the Comtesse de Gramont. Michel Vautier, who had been first bailiff and later notary, was one of his main agents. Obviously not everyone did as well as Vailly or Le Pelletier. Everything depended on business acumen and this perhaps only a fraction possessed, but the way to a successful business career through the courts was a clearly possible path and many took it.

Those who never moved from the position of bailiff or *procureur* had to find another expedient for raising money. There lay open to the bailiffs of Normandy the exploitation of the office of *sergent* in the noble fiefs known as *sergenteries*. Within the area of the *sergenterie* the exploiter might carry out the duties of bailiff to the exclusion of the bailiffs of the royal courts. Very often the *sergenterie* afforded the exploiter a larger income than he could make from royal justice. The position of *sergent* was as attractive to the royal bailiff as the position of *bailli* was to the *avocat*. The bailiff rented the right from the *seigneur* and was not himself the possessor.[1] At least six of the bailiffs of Bayeux owed a substantial proportion of their incomes to the exploitation of a *sergenterie*.[2]

The *procureurs* and bailiffs were everywhere the subject of criticism. The latter especially were greatly mistrusted. Nevertheless, they were often sought out by the peasantry for consultation. A peasant who considered himself the victim of an injustice by a landlord who was overcharging him or attempting to deprive him of his rights would look not to an *avocat* to whom he would have to pay heavy fees and who in any case was considered partial in his need to secure business, but to a bailiff who

[1] A.D.C. C5467. *Vingtième d'offices et droits, 1781.*
[2] See Appendix III.

charged much less and who was regarded as relatively dis-interested. In fact, his qualifications as adviser might be negligible and since he also was likely ultimately to profit from business in the courts, he was all too ready to advise his client to resort to the law. The most likely result was yet more expense for his victim.[1]

The opportunities which lay open to the unscrupulous bailiff were the basis of at least one fortune in the town of Bayeux. The third richest non-noble of the town had made his money as chief bailiff of the *élection* court in the 1760s from the seizure of the effects of those who had not paid their taxes. True, a certain amount had gone into the coffers of the court to meet the deficit of their failure to pay, but sufficient had lined Douesnel's purse first. The experience gained in exerting pressure on the peasantry made him an efficient tithe collector and his fortune did not cease to grow at the expense of the peasants and landowners of the diocese. His will is almost a catalogue of his acquisitions in silver, *objets d'art*, and fine furniture. Hence tradesmen like Hardouin the draper or Liégard the tinsmith or Duclos, a former clock-maker,[2] all invested in the office of bailiff or *procureur* hoping to make a profit from it.

The bailiffs were not the lowest in popularity amongst the country people and sections of the town population who were their victims. No one surpassed the *commis des aides* in unpopularity. Instituted to collect the taxes on drinks entering the town and to measure the alcoholic content of the cider and *eau de vie* made by the peasantry, their professional perquisite was the seizure of any alcohol smuggled into the town, for which they had the right of search. They were poorly paid and their very poverty made them utterly dependent on their confiscations.

The hatred felt by the exploited towards these petty officials was strongly tempered by envy. However parasitically the latter might exploit the anomalies of the administrative system at the expense of the rest of the population and live in effect off the labours of others, the *cahiers* of the gilds and parishes show that their position was looked upon by many in both town and country as a desirable one. It was after all the easiest way to make one's living: others toiled and the official reaped the reward. It was always easy

---

[1] P. Bernier, *Essai sur le tiers état rural ou les paysans de Basse Normandie au XVIIIe siècle* (Mayenne, 1892), p. 166.
[2] A.D.C. C138.

to find applicants to fill a vacancy: some operated on a part-time basis and raided houses and cellars when least expected, after normal working hours when illicit alcohol was most likely to be in circulation.

If the legal profession was overcrowded the reverse was true of the different branches of the medical profession. Of all occupations the practice of medicine was, in the eighteenth century, the one perhaps subject to the most inner dissensions and debate. Over western Europe as a whole in the course of the century there are many signs indicative of a new and general consciousness of the power of medical science, of which the mere names of Jenner, Quesnay, and Chirac are sufficient indication. But to be set against this there were time-honoured traditions, applicable only in the conditions of a medieval society, which were responsible for endless conflict and served as a real barrier to progress. Tradition marked off the doctors from the surgeons by according them a far greater degree of social prestige. They, like the *avocats*, were gathered not into a gild of tradesmen but into a *collège* of professional men. The origin of this difference lay in the early medieval period when clerics alone were men of learning and yet were forbidden by the church to spill blood. Hence, while they could be physicians and diagnose cures, any work involving the knife had to be left to the surgeons who were regarded as grossly inferior and were associated in a corporation with the barbers of the town. The association was thrown off in 1743 but the surgeons did not achieve professional status without a long and bitter struggle with the doctors, a struggle which manifested itself repeatedly in the course of the century. The conflict was intensified in Bayeux because the best surgeons of the town were qualified doctors who had studied medicine at university and hence could more than compete with the doctors of the town. The surgeons were the progressive element, but it was becoming increasingly difficult to judge where the one profession ended and the other began. In some cases doctors were entering spheres previously left to surgeons. It was, for example, a doctor not a surgeon who represented Bayeux at the courses in midwifery sponsored and subsidized by the government in 1776 in Caen.[1] The doctors were in fact becoming very defensive about their rights. They consistently tried to assert their traditional superiority over the

[1] A.D.C. C985. These were the famous courses given by Madame Du Coudray.

surgeons in Bayeux and went so far as to side with the church against the establishment of a surgical school by the Le Tual family, the cleverest surgeons of the town.[1]

At its lowest level, the medical profession included the worst kind of quacks. In Granville it was declared that the only previous experience most of its surgeons had had on going into practice was gutting fish.[2] The country districts were much worse off in this respect than the towns, where the presence of a few good doctors and surgeons could do something to lift the general level. It is difficult in Bayeux, for example, not to be impressed by the repeated exertions of the Le Tual family for the benefit of medical science: their continued presence, for which they were largely unpaid, at the hospital, their attempts to form a surgical school, the younger Le Tual's addresses to the literary society upon exercise and fresh air as a means to good health.[3] The countryside certainly felt itself badly treated in respect of medical services and complained of the lack of good doctors to come to its aid.[4] But the question was always who would pay the doctor or surgeon if he set up a practice outside the town. Certainly the poor peasantry would have been unable to do so. Whatever the reiterated demands of the countryside for good doctors and surgeons, the number of truly remunerative posts was very limited. This perhaps partially explains the fear of the doctors that the surgeons were taking over their work. Not infrequently the best positions were passed from one member of a family to another. Indeed it was impossible to become a doctor in Bayeux unless one had the right family connexions. The same was true of the most qualified surgeons. Hence the elder Le Tual passed on his position of *premier chirurgien du roi* at the *hôtel Dieu* to his young son. The surgeons of Bayeux tried to contest the bestowal of the key surgical position of the town upon the young man on the grounds of his youth and lack of experience in comparison with older surgeons. The Le Tual monopoly, however, was long established and was maintained.[5]

[1] A.D.C. C629.
[2] Doubtless this was in part an exaggeration but it was apparently common in the port of Granville for men to set themselves up as surgeons falsely declaring they had been ships' doctors. A.D.C. C2812.
[3] F. Pluquet, *Notice sur les établissements littéraires et scientifiques de la ville de Bayeux* (Bayeux, 1834), p. 15.　　　　　　　　　　　　　　　[4] Bernier, op. cit., p. 46.
[5] A.D.C. H. Suppl. 1082. F18. *Chirurgiens de l'hôtel Dieu, 1774.*

The corresponding position of *premier médecin du roi* at the *hôtel Dieu* had been held by an old man who took the title and left the work to a younger doctor who had the promise of the position after him but gained nothing from the work.[1] After the death of the old man the younger took on the title but in turn left the work to others and his attendance was rare.[2] These positions in themselves did not pay well but they picked out the titulary as the foremost doctor or surgeon of the town and they were a fiercely contested honour.

Hence it would appear that the medical profession had much in common with the *avocats*. For both it was necessary to wait for dead men's shoes, and in some cases this period of waiting could continue well into middle age. In the meanwhile the practitioner remained quite poor. Moreover, it was virtually impossible, it would seem, at Bayeux, for an unknown man whose family had not been long connected with medicine to get anywhere. Those at the top had been there for many years.

The poorest surgeons of the town were forced to find some means of implementing a minute income. Those who were in this position were not always the uninformed nor those without hope of a future succession. The Sieur Mortier du Gravier was accorded in 1775 a *sauf conduit* after bankruptcy. Since he could make very little from his work as surgeon, his wife opened a café and hoped to make ends meet from the sale of alcohol.[3] Another surgeon of the town simultaneously maintained the position of brigadier of the *maréchaussée*.[4] At nearby Coutances at least one surgeon maintained a shaky existence by keeping a draper's shop.[5] These expedients were necessary where the professional income was not sufficient for a livelihood, but though a poor surgeon could stoop to practise them a poor doctor could not.

The professions gave prestige but little else. Nor did those of doctor and surgeon open up the same opportunities for profit on the side as did that of *avocat*. Neither branch of the medical profession was able in fact to make anything which approached the profits of a simple apothecary. The wealth of the latter has two explanations: the growth in the use of medicaments in the eighteenth century and, arising from this, the decision of the

---

[1] A.D.C. C629.   [2] Ibid.   [3] A.D.C. C588.
[4] He is qualified by both titles on the capitation lists.
[5] 'Chirurgiens de l'ancien régime', *Annales de Normandie* (1953), p. 91.

central government which was anxious to diminish or alleviate the effects of certain diseases—notably syphilis, a widespread problem by the mid century—by distributing medicine and medicaments, oil and dressings for sores to the country districts from the centre of the *généralité* or the *élection*.[1] Eyewitnesses were doubtful of the beneficial qualities of these free distributions and spoke of an ignorant *curé* giving out medicine without instruction as to its use to an even more ignorant peasant who in good faith swallowed dangerous ointments intended for external applica-tion.[2] The most disastrous consequences, however, did not destroy a pathetic faith in the power of medicine. Nothing could hide the fortunes the apothecaries were making even in a small town like Bayeux. They had profited as well from shaking off their gild association with the grocers in 1776 and the latter were no longer allowed to sell drugs. The original union of the two in a gild had been due to the extensive trading activities of the grocers and to the ignorance which regarded certain foods, notably sugar, as possessing medicinal qualities.[3] The increase in knowledge which proclaimed these ideas fallacious received concrete expression in 1776, but the actual division had been effected long before. A decision of the *bailliage* of Caen in 1753 expressly forbade the grocers to dabble in medicine and concluded that though two hundred years ago, when the grocers and apothecaries had been joined, there had been justification for belief in such a union, this was no longer the case.[4] The grocers were prepared to fight, the more so because the trade of the apothecaries was becoming so lucrative and extensive, but they lost the battle. The doctors too were thrown on the defensive. The apothecaries' trade in a marketing centre was especially good, for the country people when they came to market would patronize them. Moreover, until 1776 a visit to the apothecary might often be a way of by-passing the doctor, for the apothecary memorized the cure for ailments advised by the doctor and was often as capable as the doctor of diagnosing minor complaints. Hence he could save the patient the time and, more important, the money involved in visiting the doctor. The only person to complain was the doctor

[1] A.D.C. C953.
[2] P. Bernier, op. cit., p. 46. Compounds of mercury were used for the treatment of syphilis and these were particularly dangerous in the hands of the uninformed.
[3] Marion, *Dictionnaire* . . ., p. 20.
[4] A.D.C. C2808.

who resented these encroachments upon his business. The practice was forbidden in 1776.

Most of the branches of the medical profession were split by conflict within. Always there were the informed and the less informed. The apothecaries' gild at Bayeux argued for years over what the *chef d'œuvre* should be. They were divided between those who thought it should be a standard examination demanding a uniform knowledge of certain drugs and those who thought it should demand no more than a knowledge of the drugs most commonly in use. The argument terminated in the courts.[1] Those making the more difficult demands won. Wherever there were gilds of apothecaries their entrance rates seem to have been high in comparison with those of other gilds. They were intent on keeping the profit in the hands of the few. But the demands they made at least avoided the worst abuses of towns where no apothecaries' gild existed. Cherbourg, also in the *généralité* of Caen, in a plea to the *intendant* to establish a gild of apothecaries in the town, revealed that at present those who sold drugs and medicaments in the town were two former surgeons, one of whom left the running of the business to his servant together with a small drapery concern. Another was a former tinsmith who had done a little barbering before deciding to open an apothecary's store and the other was the wife of a barber who sold medicine and candles.[2] None had any knowledge of medicine. Bayeux could at least feel sure that its apothecaries had served a three years' apprenticeship, and in many cases much more, for on occasion even the entrance of a master's son, whose three years' apprenticeship had appeared to teach him little, met the opposition of the community.[3]

The apothecaries straggled the boundary between the professional and commercial elements in the population. Tradition accorded the judges, officials of the courts, lawyers, and doctors a prominence in society which was not derived from their personal wealth. The *procureurs* and notaries followed the lawyers and doctors, then the *négociants en gros*, the surgeons and those in the artistic occupations with finally the artisans and those who worked on the land last in the scale of descent.[4] Thus a professional man,

[1] B.V.B. MSS. 205–11. *Pièces relatives aux apothicaires.*
[2] A.D.C. C2800. *État des particuliers vendant drogues et médicaments dans la ville de Cherbourg, 1787.*
[3] B.V.B. MSS. 205–11.
[4] This was the order of priority in public processions and ceremonies and the

however poor, had a higher social standing than one whose wealth was derived from commerce. If the latter wished to raise himself in the social scale his best recourse was to buy an office. In some towns this partial divorce between prestige and economic strength led to direct conflict, as at Rouen, where an affluent merchant group took over the municipal government and was at loggerheads with the officials of the courts.[1] In Bayeux the commercial interests, if wealthy, were small and less assertive and to all appearances deferred to the professional groups on questions of precedence.

The most affluent sections of the commercial elements of the population of Bayeux were undoubtedly the cattle and dairy produce wholesale merchants and the lace manufacturers, because they were dealing with goods constantly in demand. There were only perhaps a dozen involved exclusively in the cattle trade, nor was the rearing of cattle for beef as common in this part of Normandy as in the Cherbourg peninsula whence cattle were sent regularly, via Bayeux and Caen, to the markets of Paris and Rouen. Nevertheless the trade of the cattle merchants of Bayeux paid well. So did that of the handful involved in the sale of butter to the same markets, though again the main centre of this trade was not Bayeux but Isigny, which was rapidly ousting Bayeux as the business centre of the region. The town boasted only four lace merchants or manufacturers, all of whom were doing extremely well, who arranged for the distribution of the raw material, silk or linen, to women working at home and who negotiated the sale of the finished product at Guibray or Caen. Alone of the manufacturers of Bayeux they could show a substantial profit.

The well-to-do artisan was not absent in Bayeux in the eighteenth century if he practised some highly skilled craft. Pillet Desjardins the potter had a substantial business, so had the wealthy goldsmith of the town and the maker of ecclesiastical hats. These were the sort of men who were chosen to represent the

municipal edict of 1776, for example, decreed that notables should be elected by each of the following groups in line of descent: (1) the clergy, (2) the *noblesse*, (3) the officials of the *bailliage*, (4) the officials of other courts, (5) the *avocats*, (6) the doctors and *bourgeois vivant noblement*, (7) notaries and *procureurs*, (8) *négociants en gros*, (9) surgeons and those practising the liberal arts, (10) the artisans. F. Mourlot, *La Fin de l'ancien régime dans la généralité de Caen* (1911).

[1] Bouloiseau. *Cahiers de doléances du tiers état du bailliage de Rouen* (Paris, 1957), pp. lxxxiv–lxxxv.

artisan on the town council and to mix there with the professional classes.

For the rest, of the host of petty tradesmen the grocers were clearly the wealthiest and were accorded pride of place over any other body of merchants. The other suppliers of food-stuffs were not well off. The butchers were the poorest, largely because meat was only in demand by the relatively rich. It was out of the reach of the artisan. The bakers belonged to several income groups. The poorest merely baked the loaves prepared by the poorest sections of the community. The wealthier purchased corn in their own right. Again, however, in the case of all these commercial pursuits occupational income has to be set against many other sources and considered in relation to the whole income. An astute investment in land or property of some kind, at a time when the price of property was rising, might well make the occupational income merely a fraction of the whole. Living in a country town in the midst of some of the most fertile land in France, the citizens of Bayeux were as anxious as anybody else to profit from land speculation. It was after all the most obvious way of making money. The economy of a successful businessman was likely to be as complex as that of a professional man. Many a small grocer or candlemaker managed by investment to triple or quadruple the income he made from trade. It was also the safest type of investment. No lace manufacturer knew how long lace would be in fashion and the market large: no apothecary knew how long he could maintain the profits of his trade; but what both could well know was that the price of property would not fall. Above the ten *livres* level of the *capitation* assessment which included about a quarter of the taxpayers of the town, it becomes practically the rule for the *bourgeois* to have property outside Bayeux. These property interests obviously varied greatly in size and value. Sometimes the holdings were concentrated within one area. Sometimes they were scattered across districts miles apart. Sometimes men acted in conjunction to buy them. Business partners like Le Gambier and Le Bas, cattle traders of steadily increasing means, who never hesitated to invest in the wealth-yielding lands of the Bessin, were sometimes associated in the buying of land with de la Mare, the grocer, the three together forming a wealthy triumvirate.[1] Herils Laval, the hatter, and Hippolite Guérin, the

[1] A.D.C. C9264. *Registre du contrôle.* Entry nos. 50, 121.

lawyer, made similar investments together. Sometimes one is astonished at the smallness of the strip of land which would interest a buyer. De la Mare, the grocer, whose property in and around Bayeux brought him in at least 1,500 *livres* a year, was interested in land offering no more than 15 *livres* annual income at Port en Bessin.[1] The poor artisan wanted land he might himself work, but the wealthier sections of the *bourgeoisie* let their property and drew the income. A clear distinction can be made between those who inherited the wealth they possessed in land and those who acquired it. Generally speaking, of the inhabitants of Bayeux who were rated highest on the tax lists, those of the professional classes, lawyers, doctors, and surgeons who were wealthy and also landowners had inherited both the wealth and the property. The active new acquirers of land belonged to the wealthy commercial classes—traders, apothecaries, grocers, and the occasional manufacturer whose goods were in demand—men whose occupations were in themselves becoming increasingly remunerative. Hence the economy of the first, those with professional occupations, tends to present a picture of a far more static nature than that of the second, the commercial classes, those sections of the population concerned with active economic expansion and investment.

They all clung to their property above everything else. They would struggle along under financial embarrassment which might easily have been relieved by the capital raised from the sale of their land rather than have recourse to this. Land was the best source of income: it was the guarantee of a comfortable old age. Many of the testaments of the *bourgeois* of Bayeux reveal attics stocked with sacks of grain, the profit from property in the country which maintained them during the year. This, together with the long vegetable gardens their houses possessed, kept them safe from shortage and procured them a relative immunity from the pressure of rising prices. The purchase of land was the best one could do for oneself and one's posterity.

House ownership too, in a town whose population was expanding, was an investment almost as attractive as the possession of land. One grocer made 1,600 *livres* annually from houses he owned and let in Bayeux. Again, Tillard des Acres, an apothecary, made 1,000 *livres* a year by letting rooms in the parish of St. Jean.

[1] A.D.C. C3080.

Investments made on this scale are relatively rare. Sections of the legal profession, the *procureurs* and bailiffs and, to a less extent, the *avocats*, were remarkable for having several houses and portions of houses which they owned and leased out throughout the town. Doubtless this was due to their very professions, in the course of which they might come across the property of people in debt which they could acquire for a very little.[1]

There were profits to be made as well from the exploitation of what the peasant regarded as the main social abuses of the old régime. At the very top of the scale of wealth some of the *bourgeoisie* of Bayeux were owners of seigneurial rights. Most of these were members of families which had been wealthy and of importance in the town throughout the eighteenth century and perhaps earlier. Most of them were as well important office-holders. They were not newly rich men. The Dozevilles, *avocats* and *seigneurs* of Tracy, the de Vailly, notaries and *seigneurs* of Tracy, the Dellevilles of St. Pierre du Mont, were all men of long-standing wealth. Merchants and manufacturers were not as frequently owners of *seigneuries* at Bayeux as in the *élection* of Rouen, but even in Rouen mercantile wealth was of too recent creation for merchants and manufacturers to be extensive owners of seigneurial rights in 1789.[2] On the other hand, at Bayeux the commercial and businessmen frequently farmed seigneurial rights. The bishop and chapter of Bayeux were the most important *seigneurs* of the region. Their vast estates were leased out over periods of nine years to whoever could afford to take them on. The bishop's register for 1763 shows, as three consecutive entries, Laurens Le Boucher, apothecary, in enjoyment of the *seigneurie* of Surrain and St. Laurent sur Mer; Louis le Pelletier, *procureur* of the *élection* and *agent* of Monsieur, brother of the king, in enjoyment of the *seigneurie* of Carcagny and Duey; whilst Alexandre Le Paulmier, recipient of dues for part of the bishop's estates, exploits the rights of the *baronnie* of Boisdelles.[3] The farmer had to pay nine years' anticipated revenue in advance but was left a wide margin of profit.

Collection of the tithe provided a similar opportunity to increase one's income, though on a much smaller scale than by the

---

[1] A.D.C. C5310. *Vingtième de la ville de Bayeux.*
[2] Bouloiseau, op. cit., p. xxix.
[3] B.C. MSS. 210. *État des revenus de l'évêché de Bayeux en 1763.*

exploitation of seigneurial rights. The cathedral chapter was the largest single tithe-owner of the diocese, though it was run a close second by the bishop. Even the tithe of some of the meagre cures of Bayeux fell into the hands of the canons. The tithe was leased out for a nine-year period in exchange for a lump sum. Thus Robert Douesnel, chief bailiff of the *élection* court, made over 1,000 *livres* yearly from the collection of the tithe of St. Patrice. Gabriel Robert, a tenant farmer on the fringes of the town, made about half as much from that of St. André. A third of the tithe of La Pothérie added 200 *livres* to the income of Julien Marie, one of the potters, while another part of that of St. Patrice earned for Claude Gouze, a candlemaker, some 500 *livres*.[1] If the individual renting a parish tithe was also a landowner in the same parish he was in a particularly strong position for its effective collection. Robert Le Parfait for example, owner of the inn L'Image St. Martin, at Bayeux, and an extensive landowner at Monceaux, went to great lengths to collect the scattered tithe rights of the same parish.[2]

The collection of taxes was the basis of more than one fortune in the town of Bayeux. The most striking example was the career of Gabriel Cahier. Son of a joiner who could barely make ends meet, as a boy he was employed on the estate of the Marquis of Balleroy. He was quick to learn. It took him fifteen years to become chief agent of the marquis and under twenty to become the fourth richest man in the town of Bayeux. His son became an *avocat* in the *parlement* of Rouen, scorning the impoverished courts of Bayeux, but the basis of the family fortunes was the profit made from the peasants of Balleroy.[3] Some of the wealthiest men of the town were middle-men for the great *noblesse*, the church, or the government, and as money passed through their hands in the form of dues and taxes en route to the ultimate owner, some stuck. It was they rather than the great nobles, ecclesiastics, or government, whose agents they were, who were in direct contact with the people. The Marquis de Balleroy, the bishop of Bayeux, or the *intendant* in Caen was only concerned with getting his revenues in: if M. Cahier, agent of the first, or M. Vailly, agent of the second, or

---

[1] A.D.C. C4543–7. Lists of *faisant valoir* are annexed to each separate parish in the capitation lists.
[2] A.D.C. C9263. *Registre du Contrôle*. Entry no. 132, 1 June 1786.
[3] Pezet, op. cit., pp. 250–3.

M. Dastignac, a *receveur* of the last, secured this object, then it hardly mattered to the employer what were the profits of the agent, more especially if the actual owner was absentee.

Again, the *receveurs* of the *taille* and other taxes were given a fixed sum of three to five *deniers* for every *livre* collected.[1] The ultimate profit was attractive as indeed it needed to be, for the *receveurs* of the *taille* and the *vingtième* had to advance the tax estimate before they collected it. It was more common to collect taxes on a part-time basis, the profits forming a part, but not the whole, of the collector's income. In most cases, tax collection was seasonal work limited to the months immediately after the harvest and rarely employing those engaged in their collection for the whole of the year. Indeed, the most important conclusion to be drawn from an investigation of the sources of income of the *bourgeoisie* of Bayeux is that whether rich or poor, professional or commercial, any individual's income was likely to be drawn from a number of sources rather than from a single one.

It is always possible to pick out the handful of men who would make money under any circumstances, largely by a shrewd appreciation of the circumstances under which they were living. The career of Robert Le Parfait is a case in point. He inherited in the 1740s a small undistinguished inn, hardly likely to attract travellers of any distinction when the Lion d'Or, and later the newly built Luxembourg, were to hand. But the distinguished inns, Le Parfait learned, were not necessarily the best source of profit. His inn was situated on the main road and a careful investment in a couple of nearby meadows brought in the cattle drovers on their long haul between Cherbourg and Paris. The cattle grazed at the most for two days, but the cow dung brought a high price from small subsistence farmers using their land for arable farming and needing manure. So encouraging were the results of the trade that by 1788 Le Parfait had acquired a large part of the sewage rights of the town[2] and did perhaps the best business in manure supplies in the whole area. Apart from individual enterprises of this nature, however, the amount of new wealth being created in Bayeux at the end of the eighteenth century was slight and confined to a small proportion of the population. The rest lived either by exploiting someone else or were dependent on income from property. The town was in fact parasitic upon the countryside and

---

[1] Marion, *Dictionnaire* . . ., p. 471.   [2] Duterque, op. cit., p. 177.

it is impossible to describe the town without continual reference to the surrounding rural area. The relationship between town and country was bad. It was a relationship poisoned by the chicanery of the legal system, by tax-collectors and middle-men, by *bourgeois* landowners who used the land the poor peasant considered his. Echoes of these sentiments are found in the *cahier* of the *bailliage*. The church, which tried to resist the change to pasture farming because of the ensuing loss of tithe, was able to claim that it was doing so in the interest of the small peasant tenant farmer who was elsewhere losing his livelihood to capitalist exploiters of both town and country.[1]

The country had grounds for complaint, but there was another side to the coin. How otherwise was the *bourgeois* of Bayeux to make a living under the conditions prevailing in the town in the eighteenth century? Such industry as the town had scarcely encouraged investment and for many professional men the conditions under which they practised brought endless frustrations. They might well argue that they had no real means of livelihood if they did not exploit some privilege, some abuse. The administrative changes of the fifty years before 1789 struck a severe blow at many of the *avocats* and officials who hoped to make something from their work. The abrupt termination of the creation of offices, together with the abolition of some courts and the reorganization of others, jeopardized the aspirations of many who had hoped for a career in them. Increasingly they were forced to regard their careers as little more than a nominal occupation which often bore no relation to the actual source of income. This was the section of the population most constant in its criticism of the administrative *status quo*, which concentrated all power in the hands of the *intendant* and his overworked *subdélégué*. Equally the knot of bailiffs, notaries, *procureurs*, *contrôleurs des actes*, and minor tax officials, who had all bought their position and expected a return from their investment, might ask with some justification what else lay open to them but the ignominious profits of the anomalies of the judicial system? They can hardly have been unaware of their unpopularity. Criticisms came both from above and below. The higher officials of the *bailliage* and *élection* courts were conscious of the evils which had crept into the administration of justice and readily criticized those concerned with its execution.

[1] A.N. G⁸ 623.

Complaints were reiterated throughout the *cahiers* of the gilds.[1]
The first men to be attacked in Bayeux itself in 1789 were neither
noble nor ecclesiastic, judge nor landowner but the officials of the
aides who made their money from the seizure of illicit alcohol.[2]
It was indeed impossible to live within the framework of a
stagnant economy without being parasitic on someone else—
those who did this the most successfully were those, in Bayeux,
who made money.

[1] A.M.B. AA. *Cahiers des corporations.*
[2] Pezet, op. cit., p. 132.

V

THE POOR

A N examination of the sources of income of the *bourgeoisie* of
Bayeux reveals much of their complexity. The bulk of the
bourgeoisie of the town drew their income from more than
one source and were often dependent on revenues other than
those derived from their occupation. The economy of the artisan
family was no simpler. Over half the total working population of
the town, including the manual labourers, the textile and building
trades, some shopkeepers, tailors, shoemakers, soapmakers,
barbers, haberdashers, police, a few surgeons, public servants,
and school teachers, earned between 10 and 15 *sols* per day and
were those rated at the lowest level of the *capitation* assessment
(2 *livres* 2 *sols*). The purchasing power of 10 *sols* was far from
great. Converted into bread it represented by the end of the old
régime, during a year of moderate harvest, between five and six
pounds. The average daily bread consumption of a family of five,
three of them young children, has been estimated at seven pounds.[1]
Moreover, at the very maximum, with Sundays and obligatory
holidays taken into account, the worker could only be guaranteed
290 working days per year, while he and his family ate every day.

The minimum upon which the average family could survive is
still an object of speculation and probably varied greatly from
one part of France to another. Young, for example, found living
in Brittany cheap in comparison with Normandy where everything was 'extravagantly dear'.[2] Camille Bloch found that the
comité de mendicité of 1790 estimated at 435 *livres* the annual income
necessary for the average family of five. But he also found information on the town of Versailles which showed that with
such a sum a family thus composed could only with difficulty
survive.[3] The Bayeux poorhouse estimated the cost of keeping an

[1] Labrousse's estimate has been used as the basis of all subsequent French statistical studies: e.g. Lefebvre, *Études Orléanaises . . .*, vol. i, pp. 217–18.

[2] A. Young, *Travels in France* (Cambridge, 1950), p. 108.

[3] C. Bloch, *L'Assistance et l'état en France à la veille de la Révolution* (Paris, 1908),
pp. 4–5.

internee to amount to some 150 *livres* per year.[1] This sum was inclusive only of food and clothing. Moreover, bread was obtained at a reduced rate. Heating and housing costs were calculated separately. The humblest shelter of one room cost between 10 and 15 *livres* annually.[2] Working on a very rough estimate if heating and minor costs are added to the hospital's estimate and the average rent, then 200 *livres* would seem to be the minimum on which one man might exist, that is between 10 and 11 *sols* per day. If his wife cost a further 100 *livres* yearly, this must be earned in addition for her. The hospital estimated the upkeep of a child as approximately 3 to 4 *sols* per day[3] and a time would come when the child's wants would be greater, his appetite larger, and his growing body would strain still further the family income. A family of three for basic subsistence probably needed about 20 *sols* per day. Yet the rate of day labourers, carpenters, roof-builders, joiners, and textile-workers fell below 14 *sols* per day.[4] Even when fully employed they did not earn sufficient to guarantee themselves a tolerable personal existence, and this without a wife to add to the problem. Whatever a woman did, be it make lace, spin cotton, take in washing, or make clothes, it was impossible for her to earn in Bayeux more than 6 *sols* a day,[5] which was only sufficient for her own basic needs. Without children, hardship only became really acute in times of bad harvest with the rising costs and unemployment this might well entail. But this is to suppose a situation unlikely to continue. The arrival of children could be an unqualified disaster which could strain a family budget to the full. Nor was there any way out of the situation. The pressure on the number of jobs meant that wages could be kept low and the rising cost of foodstuffs threw an increased burden upon the family income.

   Within the poorer sections of the population there was an acute anxiety to find a further source of income, perhaps by

[1] A.D.C. H. Suppl. 562. B2. *Hôpitaux de Bayeux.*

[2] A.D.C. C5310. *Vingtième de la ville de Bayeux.*

[3] A.D.C. H. Suppl. 562. B2. *Hôpitaux de Bayeux.*

[4] 10 *sols* was the daily wage of a mason and day labourer, 1741–2. A.D.C. H. Suppl. 832. E127. *Hôpital Général de Bayeux.* 14 *sols* was the daily wage of a roof-builder and carpenter, 10 *sols* the daily rate of a joiner, 1771–89. A.D.C. H. Suppl. 898. E193. *Hôpital Général de Bayeux.*

[5] This was a low rate in comparison with the female textile-workers of Rouen who earned up to 15 *sols* a day (Bouloiseau, op. cit., p. xl); and those of Orléans who earned 14 *sols* (Lefebvre, op. cit., p. 60).

renting a strip of land in the town or in the parishes of the town periphery. The nearest parish of St. Vigor was divided into allotments, each perhaps yielding an annual revenue of no more than 10 *livres*, owned or rented by some of the poorest inhabitants of Bayeux. However small, such a patch of land might well be the most constant source of income of the poor artisan. Another chance was to find an extra small job. Amongst the poorer income groups a real proliferation of activities is visible which allowed the man who practised them to make ends meet. The *croquetiers* (egg and butter sellers) of Bayeux were poor men, but two managed to combine the occupation with the manufacture of pottery and candles. Some were part-time gardeners. Odd jobs of this nature could often be found on the vegetable patches of the more substantial property-owners of the town. In a small town where the duties of public employees such as the postman, the fireman, and the town crier were not over demanding, these occupations were invariably coupled with something else, be it shoemaking, candlemaking, soapmaking, or gardening. The church gave a further outlet: someone was needed to ring the bells and clean the churches. These pursuits sound little in themselves but an extra 50 *livres* a year from one of these sources would keep a baby. The school-teachers of Bayeux obviously made very little from their occupation. Two did a little wool carding, another mended shoes. Even with income from these sources they still hovered dangerously on the fringes of destitution.

Of paramount importance to the town was the lace industry because this made a large percentage of the female population relatively independent. Even if the women and girls earned enough only to support themselves this relieved the strain on the main bread-winner. The wife of the artisan was obliged by economic necessity to work[1] as well as the unmarried, but for the unmarried domestic service was a possible alternative, whereas for the married with children this was less practicable. The lace industry was essentially domestic. The baby could lie in the cradle and the children play on the floor while the mother attended to her bobbins. She was paid by the piece and doubtless harshly exploited, for the lace merchants showed a fat profit while the

---

[1] The wives of professional men rarely had employment, however poor their husbands, but otherwise wives of men with a tax rating of under 10 *livres* usually had employment. A.M.B. *États de la population, an IV*.

lacemakers rarely exceeded a daily 6 *sols*. The young girls of the town were taught the craft by the Sisters of Providence, who ran a large lace school designed to help the young of the town to become self supporting and they would train anyone over ten years of age. The girls were paid partly in kind. They were fed and only received payment after they had reached proficiency, but the nuns were popular employers. They were patient with beginners and did not deny instruction to any poor girl who presented herself.

The seamstresses, laundresses, and servants of the town were no better paid than the lacemakers. They worked long hours for a pittance which would only maintain them as long as they were childless or did not have to maintain an aged relative. Many of the women convicted of prostitution and sent to the criminal *dépôt de mendicité* in Caen claimed that they had turned to this expedient because otherwise they had no means of raising extra money and that even though they were in full employment, their wages were insufficient.

The artisan of the town of Bayeux and the unskilled workman shared a common poverty. Their economy was essentially day to day. The wages of the manual worker and his wife were more than fully spent on the purchase of bread and butter, cider and a few vegetables, meagre shelter, and poor clothing. The wills of the townsfolk reveal the scanty nature of their material possessions. A bed, a table, a straw mattress, three or four blankets, a few coarse cooking pots and pans, a wooden crucifix, the whole not valued at more than 40 *livres*, were the extent of their wordly wealth. Families were packed not only into one room but into one bed, and when prices became high, or disaster struck, these scanty belongings were the only thing the artisan had to sell. Any artisan who married and started to raise a family was exposing himself to financial disaster even if he was in full-time employment.

The line between poverty and utter destitution was of no more than a hair's breadth. It only needed a protracted illness which cut off the wages of the bread-earner, a food crisis or a second or third baby to push a family over the brink, and beyond that point recovery was not easy. A sickness in the family, particularly of one of the parents, was an unqualified disaster. Medical attention, even when it could be procured, was not cheap. A bleeding cost 5 *sols* and this was in no way tantamount to a cure. When the main bread-winner ceased to earn or the mother became enfeebled, then the family had no other recourse than to seek charity. Any epidemic left its trail of wrecked households forced to search for some means of existence. Even a small outbreak like the one of miliary fever in the 1760s was still mentioned ten years later as the origin of the poverty of some families.[1]

The disaster no one could foretell was the failure of the harvest, when prices immediately rocketed. Lower Normandy perhaps suffered less at the extremities of the century than elsewhere in France, but the early 1740s, 1769–70, 1784, and 1788–9 were crisis years which hit especially hard the wage-earners of the town and country.[2] Priests of the diocese were quick to describe the pathetic condition of those of their parishioners who found themselves without the means to buy bread, forced to sell the clothes on their backs and their miserable sticks of furniture, and, in the case of the rural dwellers, to dispatch themselves to seek work in other parishes or the nearest town, abandoning wife and children.[3]

These were more exceptional circumstances than the arrival of a second or third child which the family could not afford to support. The birth of a new baby when small children too young to work were already straining the family budget was the most common cause of the utter destitution of a household. Few went as directly to the root of the problem as the *curé* d'Athis in a letter to the bishop of Bayeux:

Les journaliers, les manœuvres, les compagnons de métier et tous ceux dont la profession ne fournit pas beaucoup plus que le vivre et le vêtement, sont ceux qui produisent les mendiants. Étant garçons, ils travaillent, et lorsque par leur travail ils se sont procuré un bon vêtement et de quoi faire les frais d'une noce, ils se marient, ils nourrissent un premier enfant, ils ont beaucoup de peine à en nourrir deux, s'il en survient un troisième, leur travail n'est plus suffisant à la nourriture, à la dépense.[4]

When this happened, he went on to say, they ceased work and the family sought alms for its livelihood, a situation which was common throughout France.

The problem of the poor and the destitute forced itself upon the

[1] A.D.C. C242.
[2] A.D.C. C2731–8, C2740, C2742–6. *Grains.*
[3] A.D.C. H. Suppl. 1308.
[4] Ibid. Letter of 2 December 1774.

attention of observers of French society in the eighteenth century by its overwhelming proportions. Of the 10,000 inhabitants of Bayeux, a third, the poorer artisan class, had barely enough to live on and a sixth, entirely lacking in sufficient means, was dependent upon outside help. In Paris a tenth of the total population was in a state of destitution: in Vendôme 1,200 out of 6,500 inhabitants, some fifth of the whole, were in a similar condition.[1] Bertrand de Molleville estimated that the beggars of Brittany formed a quarter of the total population of the province.[2] Arthur Young bears witness to their pathetic condition as well as to the poverty of the Limousin and the Dordogne.[3] In Orléans the textile-workers turned out to beg on Sundays and holidays and joined the regular beggars in seeking alms.[4] The country districts if anything were worse off than the towns. The replies to the inquest of the archbishop of Rouen in 1774 on the state of the rural parishes revealed, to cite merely a few, that two-thirds of the inhabitants of the village of Martagny had no other resources than what charity afforded them. Twelve of the thirty households in the parish of Neufchâtel were kept going by alms. Over half of those of St. Austrebert lived in the greatest misery. La Ferté estimated 153 out of 620 inhabitants to be totally destitute.[5] Throughout the diocese there were complaints of begging and of vagabondage. The *généralité* of Caen complained that beggars thronged its highways, banding together and ranging over a whole province, terrorizing travellers and isolated farmsteads regardless of police and the militia.[6]

The beggars were the product of poverty: of a recognition that however hard one worked one could do nothing other than drag out a wretched existence. They were drawn in large part from the artisan and labouring class. Bayeux had 3,000 inhabitants hovering on the brink of destitution and 1,800 who had crossed that boundary.[7] Many of the men and women in the first category were in full-time employment. Others were occasional labourers who tried to hire themselves out at harvest time and spent the winter months hoping for navvying jobs in the town. Notwithstanding,

---

[1] Bloch, op. cit., p. 6.
[2] Marion, *Dictionnaire* . . ., p. 371.
[3] Young, op. cit., p. 24.
[4] Lefebvre, op. cit., p. 62.
[5] Bloch, op. cit., p. 7.
[6] F. Mourlot, 'La Question de la mendicité en Normandie à la fin de l'ancien régime' (1902), p. 4.
[7] A.D.C. C628, C955.

they and more particularly their families might at any time find themselves helpless unless they could secure some sort of supplement to their wages.

There was a distinction between the professional beggar and the *indigent*, but it was one which was not always clear to contemporaries and especially to the central government, which gave little official indication that it appreciated any difference at all until the 1770s. In this lack of comprehension the central government lagged far behind the men who headed the administration of the *généralité* and even further behind those who were on the spot.

Reduced to the simplest terms, the beggar, the *mendiant de profession*, owed his entire income to what he could get from alms and had no other resources. The *indigent* was he who earned something by the work of his hands but not sufficient to live on and was forced to supplement it by seeking charity.[1] But, and here the confusion inherent in the situation began, the male *indigent* more often than not had a wife and children who could not find work to support themselves and so turned to begging. This situation was general in northern and north-western France and in the Auvergne, a *subdélégué* commented that babies scarcely knew how to walk when they received their first lessons in how to beg so as not to be a burden to their family.[2] Furthermore, in a society where the number of women far exceeded that of men—in 1774, 58 per cent. of the total population of Bayeux was female and only 42 per cent. male[3]—inevitably many old women found themselves uncared for and without means and were forced to turn to the one way of obtaining a livelihood that lay open to them when they were too old to work.

Even among the *mendiants de profession* differences manifested themselves. There were those who would not work and those who could not work. The latter category included the blind, the crippled, and the mentally defective, who were far more prevalent in the eighteenth century than is commonly realized. Many were crippled from birth. The art of the midwife may have been improving but it was far from perfected and in rural areas she had

---

[1] There was a further category of *indigent*—the *pauvres honteux*. This term qualified families in possession of a little property which prevented their asking for assistance but whose plight merited consideration. In official lists, while they are always counted, they remain anonymous and few details are given. See Appendix IV.

[2] Marion, *Dictionnaire* . . ., p. 371.

[3] See Appendix I.

often received all the instruction she had ever had from the parish
priest. A contemporary remarked:

L'on voit des hommes estropiés, infirmes, impotents dès leur nais-
sance; d'autres dont les organes et les proportions de la tête ont été
dérangés et viciés et cela par l'impéritie de la sage femme qui a tiraillé
ou pressé trop fortement les os encore membraneux et mal assurés
dans leurs articulations; d'où il résulte qu'un grand nombre d'enfants
périssent ou restent contrefaits ou imbéciles tout le temps de leur vie.[1]

The category of *mendiants de profession* included also children
abandoned by their parents, women whose husbands had tired of
the constant poverty a family entailed and who had fled their
marital commitments, and the genuine vagabond and thief.

The urban beggar did not usually become a vagrant. The
unemployed or under-employed agricultural workers, lacking
sufficient income, were far more often thrown back upon the
expedient of begging upon the roads. They banded together and
by strength of numbers could often extort from travellers what
charity might never have given them. They became the terror of
isolated farmsteads and small villages. In Normandy under a
forceful leader, bands of vagabonds might pillage an entire
province, fearless of police or the militia. In the towns the
destitute were brought more effectively to the attention of the
municipality. A large number of unemployed and starving in a
town of some size could menace the security of the rest of the
population and the maintenance of public order, and urban
authorities were unlikely to forget this. It followed that the urban
dweller's problems, as long as he was a resident in the town, were
far more likely to get attention. Moreover, when the central
government did send out direct relief, it tended to be the monopoly
of the urban *indigents* because they were a menace to the town,
centre of the *élection*, which was the unit of distribution. It was
therefore to the advantage of the urban poor to remain in the
town.

In 1785 the parish lists of the *indigents* in the town which were
presented to the *bureau de charité* name some 1,270 individuals.[2]
Of these only about 17–18 per cent. were sick or aged, 25–26
per cent. were women, and 45–46 per cent. young children. These

---

[1] *Encyclopédie méthodique de la jurisprudence*, lx, word '*accouchement*' cited by Bloch,
op. cit., p. 248.
[2] A.D.C. C955. See Appendix IV.

numbers were exclusive of the 200 old, infirm, or imbecile catered for by the *hôpital général*, of the criminal vagabonds and prostitutes who had been sent to the house of correction in Caen, of children abandoned since birth, and of any non-resident beggars who had come to the town. These *indigents* were those who besieged the doors of the churches and hung about the market-place in the hope of relief. The men were mostly day labourers, shoemakers, and out-of-work textile-workers. Some of the women were, or had been, lacemakers. By far the greatest proportion were children. In official lists and references they are described indiscriminately as *indigents* or *mendiants* because if in theory an important differentiation was possible, in practice the difference was slight.

The provisions for dealing with poverty in eighteenth-century France had changed little since the Middle Ages. Then relief of the poor had been the business, firstly of the lord of the manor and later, throughout Christendom, of the church. Ecclesiastical revenues were, according to canon law, divided into two parts, *necessitas* and *superfluas*. The first was for the upkeep of the clerics, the second for the poor. This was a natural obligation incumbent upon the church. In England the system began to disintegrate in the late fourteenth century. The dissolution of the monasteries and the sale of church lands occasioned its complete breakdown; and responsibility for the maintenance of the poor shifted from the church to the parish, which was forced to make provision for its own paupers by act of parliament. In France the same process had not taken place. Sections of the church had maintained its medieval wealth and, it was hoped, its medieval obligations. Little or nothing had been done to create alternative methods of relief for the poor and what little had been done had touched only a small section of the paupers. It had been confined to the great urban centres like Paris, where spasmodic efforts had been made in the sixteenth and seventeenth centuries to create work for the poor. But these had no degree of continuity.

Ecclesiastical charity was of three kinds. Firstly, there existed traditional bequests out of the revenues of any bishopric, chapter, or religious house for the sustenance of the poor. Most of these dated back to the Middle Ages and varied greatly in extent. Usually they consisted of special donations and bread distributions during Lent, the ceremonial washing of the feet of twelve beggars and the gift to them of pieces of silver on Palm Sunday or Maundy Thursday, and were acts intended as much for the good of the souls of the religious as for the benefit of the beggars. Some were of a more extensive nature: the chapter of Bayeux was obliged to distribute to the poor of the town 400 pounds of bread per week and even the bishop spent in a normal year about 3,000 *livres* on helping the urban poor. Secondly, it had been the effort of the Counter Reformation in France to try to help those too weak to look after themselves by the creation of new religious orders designed to fill a useful role in society, and of these the most influential were the Sisters of Charity of St. Vincent de Paul. Lastly, in the late seventeenth and eighteenth centuries the church in Bayeux had attempted several experiments to create new industries, and of these the most successful was the lace *manufacture*, initially sponsored by the chapter and run by the Sisters of Providence.

The Sisters of Charity had first come to Bayeux in the 1650s at the invitation of the bishop, who offered them a house in exchange for charitable services performed by the nuns to the townspeople. They were to help to care for the sick, aid in the distribution of relief during years of hardship, and organize the wealthier women of the town into making contributions to supply soup to families where the main bread-winner was disabled. The house constituted the whole of the initial endowment, and furthermore the nuns were immediately charged with the rearing of eight young girls whom they were to provide, when they left the shelter of the convent, with 150 *livres*, raised out of the dowries of those entering the order. In 1653 the entire revenue of the order at Bayeux was a mere 400 *livres*,[1] but this grew rapidly, for the Charity of Bayeux had the reputation of sincerely trying to alleviate the suffering of the poor. The Sisters were not passive onlookers of the social scene waiting for alms with which to succour the needy. Rather did they, from the beginning, set out to gather together by their own initiative the necessary funds. Just how successful they proved to be was illustrated when, in the mid eighteenth century, their efforts to raise money for the expansion of their house led them to bankruptcy. An inquest into the situation conducted by the *subdélégué*[2] revealed that in order to employ the poor, the Sisters of Charity had, in fifty years,

[1] A.D.C. C251.   [2] Ibid.

established in their house the manufacture of soap, cloth, and lace, to an extent far greater than that of any manufacturer in the town, and also carried on a wide commerce in wine and coffee with which they supplied almost the whole town. But for too much borrowing to build a new chapel, there was no reason why the flourishing business of the Sisters should not have continued; but as it was, in 1776 the Sisters of Charity had creditors demanding payment and every merchant in the town hopeful that their trade would be stopped.

But, the *intendant* was forced to admit, the profits from the trade had been used to keep forty young girls of poor parentage between the ages of ten and seventeen. Moreover, forty-five poor people worked for the house in the making of lace. In addition the Sisters made up parcels of clothing every year for distribution to poor families. Rather than close the religious house and render these forty-five people redundant and forty more homeless, the *intendant* suggested that the Sisters sell their land, re-establish themselves in public esteem, and pay their debts. By the end of the old régime the Sisters of Charity were just managing to balance expenditure and receipts.

More important than the original house, however, was the *hôpital général*, of which the Sisters of Charity assumed direction in the late seventeenth century. This institution had been built with money raised by the bishop in the 1680s to accommodate about 170 beggars, but allowed admission only to those who were disabled, blind, crippled, mentally sick but not violent, and the old and orphaned. Of the 170 in 1724, fifty were disabled, fifty-seven old, and the rest children. Its revenues were based on a few meagre rents and dues which seventeenth- and eighteenth-century philanthropists had seen fit to bestow. Even in normal years the expenditure was very slightly in excess of receipts and the economy of the institution was very delicately balanced and totally unfitted to deal with the high price-rise. The nuns cut costs to a minimum, were grossly overworked, and would not enlist more help because of the increased expenditure this would entail. Each nun needed a yearly sum of 140 *livres* for her upkeep and the money could not easily be found. Nor could they exceed a fixed number of beggars, and had to refuse admission to the rest.[1]

[1] In 1738 the chapter complained of the number needing admission and the

The *hôpital général* of Bayeux, the *inspecteur général des hôpitaux*
said in 1784, compared very favourably with most institutions of
its type.[1] The idea behind the foundation of such an institution
here, as elsewhere in France, was essentially to rescue those
otherwise condemned to a life of vagrancy by interning them in
an institution where they must substitute for a life of idling one
given over to devotions and work and in return receive regular
meals and fresh linen. The concept was indeed charitable but
charitable in a seventeenth-century context. The day began at
five in summer and six in winter. The internees rose and made their
beds and then embarked on an eleven-hour working day interrupted only by morning prayers and benediction. The work was
usually the spinning of cotton and most of the workers were the
orphan children and the aged. Unnecessary talking was forbidden.
The workers might if they so chose murmur prayers as they
worked but nothing more. Meals took place to the accompaniment
of the reading of holy scripture. The pauper's rations consisted of
one and a half pounds of bread and a portion of vegetables and
ration of cider per day.[2] Sunday was the only day that broke the
pattern of the week. There was no work and after a morning
spent in devotions, the afternoon was free. Confession and
communion were obligatory every month. Swearing was forbidden and the offender punished by a diminution of rations.
Occasionally the paupers were hired out for funerals, where the
prayers of the poor following the coffin were held to be particularly
efficacious for the repose of the soul of the deceased. At midday
the paupers' bell could be heard to remind the townspeople that
some of the internees of the *hôpital* would call at their houses to
collect the leavings from their meals. Otherwise the paupers were
forbidden to leave the precincts. The paupers in effect were made
to live the lives of the religious and the nuns enforced all rules.
They feared, and not without cause, that any deviation from the
traditional monastic discipline might mean trouble for them.
The nuns were few in number and deemed discipline of this
nature the best way of keeping control, but it is small wonder that
several rebelled. The old man who broke out and came back
drunk was no exception. The nuns were kinder to the children,

Sisters agreed to take anyone for whose upkeep the chapter would pay, but nothing
was done. A.D.C. H. Suppl. 34, 11. E10.

[1] A.D.C. C630. *Enquête sur les hôpitaux.*   [2] Ibid.

but even so they were subjected to the same discipline until they left the *hôpital* some time before their eighteenth year. The *hôpital général* represented an attempt to deal with the problem of poverty which progressive thinkers by the mid eighteenth century condemned as out of date; but the main complaint in Bayeux was that the *hôpital général* only catered for a handful of the beggars of the town. Competition to gain admission to the house was severe, and the nuns were, perhaps inevitably, often accused of favouritism in respect of those they chose to admit.[1]

The *hôpital général* was not the only institution of seventeenth-century endowment in Bayeux intended to help the poor. On the ruins of the medieval leper houses and hostels to receive those stricken with plague had been organized *hôtels Dieu*, hospitals designed for the impoverished sick and the foundling children of the area. The *hôtel Dieu* of Bayeux had been given a little of the land belonging to a former *léproserie* but otherwise it was wholly dependent on private endowments. Its revenues were inadequate and much less than those of the *hôpital général*, while its expenditure by the mid eighteenth century was much higher.[2] The *hôpital général* was able to refuse admission to paupers, but the *hôtel Dieu* could not so easily refuse entry to the sick who were without shelter or the babies who were deposited on its doorstep. Indeed, the main problem confronting the *hôtel Dieu* in the eighteenth century was how to deal with the steadily mounting numbers of orphan children abandoned by families who could not in a time of rising costs afford to feed an extra mouth, and the expenditure the foundlings entailed was to jeopardize the very continuance of the institution.

From 1760 to 1780 the average number of newly born children deposited every year on the steps of the *hôtel Dieu* was about fifty.[3] This figure does not sound large until the size of the town is considered. In Paris, a city of 600,000 inhabitants, 6,000 babies every year were placed from birth into the arms of charity.[4] These orphaned children had to be looked after until they reached an age when they could look after themselves. It was estimated that a boy could do this at fourteen and a girl at sixteen.[5]

[1] A.D.C. H. Suppl. 1099. 1774.
[2] Its revenues totalled less than 6,000 *livres*: those of the *hôpital général* were 8,110 *livres*. A.D.C. C630.
[3] A.D.C. H. Suppl. 561. B1.   [4] Bloch, op. cit., p. 110.
[5] A.D.C. C800.

In Bayeux the traditional method of dealing with abandoned infants since the time of the foundation of the *hôtel Dieu* in the mid seventeenth century had been to take the children into this establishment where they were cared for by the Sisters of Providence, who then arranged for them to be sent, as quickly as possible, to a foster home. The *hôtel Dieu* was intended primarily for the sick and the children were only an incidental charge upon its revenues. It paid for their upkeep until they reached the age of seven. At this age they passed into the care and charge of the *hôpital général*, which had to supply them with work to help towards their upkeep.[1] The revenues of the two institutions were completely separate and the *hôpital général*, while it lodged the orphan children, did not defray the entire cost of their upkeep, and the rest had to be met by the *hôtel Dieu*.

By the end of the old régime a child cost 100 *livres* a year to keep in a foster home.[2] Thus any foundling baby with the strength and the will to live the full seven years had by its seventh birthday already cost the *hôtel Dieu* 700 *livres*.

The numbers of children can only spasmodically be found. Deaths were frequent. What is evident, however, is the increased burden upon the revenues of the *hôtel Dieu* occasioned by the foundling children. In 1672–3 three years' expenditure on the foundlings was estimated at 320 *livres*;[3] in 1752–3 a year's expenditure was 1,312 *livres* 14 *sols*;[4] in 1769–70 a year's expenditure was 1,933 *livres* 19 *sols*;[5] in 1780 it was 5,181 *livres* 19 *sols*.[6] The reasons for the increase of the 1780s are partly the rise in the price of bread which caused the foster mothers to demand more for the upkeep of the children, and partly the change in the policy of dealing with the young babies.

The increasing numbers and the rising cost of keeping the orphan children had tended to be hidden in the 1760s and 1770s by a policy of sending the provincial orphans to the large *hôpital général* in Paris, whence they were sent out for care to foster parents in the surrounding districts. The foster parents received payment ranging between 30 and 40 *livres* annually. The

[1] A.D.C. H. Suppl. 561. B1. *Dépenses pour les enfants trouvés, 1781.*
[2] Ibid. 1090. G8.
[3] Ibid. 711. E6. *Dépenses pour les enfants trouvés, 1672–1675.*
[4] Ibid. 852. E147. *Dépenses pour les enfants trouvés, 1752–1753.*
[5] Ibid. 889. E184. *Dépenses pour les enfants trouvés, 1769–1770.*
[6] Ibid. 561. B1. *Dépenses pour les enfants trouvés, 1781.*

conditions of keeping a child were simple: boys had to be taught a craft, if taken in by a town-dweller, or to work on the land, if in the country. As a further inducement the foster parents' own children were exempted from the militia.[1]

Any opportunity for shifting the burden of these helpless children on to others was eagerly accepted by the provincial foundling homes. They dispatched their surplus babies into the capital in order to keep their own establishments out of debt. Infants from as far away as Brittany, Normandy, Alsace, and Lorraine, were sent into Paris under the worst possible conditions. It was the usual practice to gather as many of the babies as possible together and pile them either into open carts or in baskets strapped to the back of a man on horseback.[2] The nuns at the *hôpital* in Paris alleged that the carters only stopped to eat themselves and to give the children a drink, which was sometimes wine, not milk, so it is hardly surprising that many died *en route*.[2] Only the exception from Lorraine arrived alive.[2] Three-quarters of those surviving the journey died a day or two after arrival. Moreover, when they arrived, suitable wet-nurses could rarely be found. Often they did not give the children the food their age demanded. There were not enough inspectors to see that they carried out their job adequately, and so the task was added to the duties of the already grossly overworked parish priest and the Sisters of Charity.[2]

Added to this, disease in a large central orphanage of this nature spread rapidly. The problem of syphilis assumed over-whelming proportions. The children contaminated each other and then their wet-nurse, who in turn passed it on to her husband and any children she subsequently bore or fed.[3] There was no provision for washing the linen of diseased children separately. Regulations stipulating that midwives must report the discovery of the disease were difficult to carry out, for the symptoms are not always obvious at the moment of birth and in any case many midwives were too ignorant to recognize them. The association of disease with the children of the Paris foundling home did, however, come to serve as a deterrent to many who might otherwise have taken in a child, and many parish priests tried to dissuade their parishioners from accepting a child on these grounds.

[1] Bloch, op. cit., p. 113.   [2] Ibid., p. 110.
[3] Archives des Hôpitaux de Paris. *Inventaire* III B 24.

However, the provinces were thankful to have an outlet in Paris for children their foundling hospitals could not afford to keep, and the increased numbers of children abandoned because of the poverty of their parents meant a rapid increase in the numbers arriving at the *hôpital* in Paris. In 1680 there had been 890 children abandoned to the care of the Sisters of Charity: by 1740 there were 5,032, by 1767, 6,918, and by 1772, 10,634.[1] The hospital was entirely without the means for making adequate provision for such a quantity of children. After many attempts, it succeeded in calling the attention of the government to the problem. An *arrêt du roi* of 10 January 1779 revealed that 90 per cent. of the children sent to Paris perished before the age of three months and decreed that the practice of sending children to Paris must stop. It promised that a royal subsidy would be given to the provincial foundling hospitals to enable them to keep the children normally sent to Paris.[2]

Had the help been received, all might have been well. Instead it was no more than an empty promise. The *hôtel Dieu* at Bayeux, in 1781, claimed that the children entailed an expenditure of 5,181 *livres* 19 *sols* while the entire revenue of the house was only 6,000 *livres* and from this provision had to be made for the sick.[3] So acute was the financial situation that the Sisters of Providence preferred to try to continue the policy of sending the children to Paris in an attempt to keep their house running. For this Bayeux received a personal rebuke from Necker.[4]

The plight of those who did not undertake the journey to Paris was only slightly more enviable than that of those who did. Detailed figures on the period 1779–85 show that during these six years, 320 children were abandoned to the care of the *hôtel Dieu*, which also had 24 surviving from the preceding years. Of these, 61 continued in the care of the *hôtel Dieu*, 5 were adopted by their foster parents, 16 were given back to their mothers, 26 passed on to the *hôpital général*, and 236 died.[5] A mere third had survived the hazards of a babyhood dependent upon the foundling hospital of Bayeux.

[1] A.D.C. C800.
[2] Isambert, *Recueil des anciennes lois françaises*, vol. xxvi, pp. 7–9. *Arrêt du conseil concernant les enfants trouvés, 10 janvier 1779.*
[3] A.D.C. H. Suppl. 561. B1.
[4] A.D.C. C800. Necker to the *intendant* at Caen. 26 January 1780.
[5] A.D.C. H. Suppl. 1089. G7.

The orphans, who had once been an inconsiderable part of the hospital's expenditure, had thus become, in the course of the century, the largest single drain upon its funds. It followed that because of their needs the sick suffered. The inspection of 1784 revealed that the poverty of the hospital was such that not all the sick could have meat.[1] But more especially it meant that only a little could be spent upon drugs and medicaments. The doctor did not attend regularly, although the surgeon did. Since their payment was slight the hospital could not complain if they turned to more lucrative work.[2]

A lawsuit was to arise out of the poverty of the *hôtel Dieu*. The leading surgeons of Bayeux were anxious to form a surgical school and pressed their right to superintend prescriptions made up and administered by the nursing sisters. The nuns, however, declared that the surgical students were disrespectful in their treatment of dead bodies and, backed by the doctors of the town, tried to get the leading surgeon dismissed from his position at the hospital. Le Tual, the surgeon, responded by pointing out the frequent absence of the doctor from his duties at the hospital and took the matter to court. The Mother Superior revealed the truth in a letter to the *intendant*.[3] The doctor and a surgeon were more than the hospital could afford, the more especially because of the quantity of drugs the latter demanded. The surgeons won their case but the menace of poverty to medical progress was not removed. The nuns regarded the surgeons as intruders whose expensive demands for drugs, however effective these were, only placed a further strain upon an economic situation already desperate and for which they had no remedy. This situation was not peculiar to Bayeux; throughout the hospitals of France the nuns and surgeons were in conflict.[4] But whoever won, the sick poor could not expect much effective treatment for their condition. Nevertheless, the majority of the sick and aged poor of the town probably died in the hospital. They were kept clean, sheltered, and relatively comfortable while awaiting death.

The sick, the aged, and the orphaned were only a small proportion of the beggars of the town. For the rest of the poor who crowded the cathedral, the churches, and market-place of Bayeux,

[1] A.D.C. C630.   [2] Ibid.
[3] A.D.C. C629. Letter of 5 October 1779.
[4] Bloch, op. cit., p. 74.

crying for money and bread, relief was wholly dependent on private alms. There was no obligation upon the community as a whole to give. Neither the town nor the parish imposed any tax, and apart from a slight subsidy from the royal government in times of extreme hardship, the central government at the beginning of the eighteenth century did not regard the bulk of the poor as its concern, and hence did not formulate any provisions at all for local relief.

The attitude of the government towards the destitute no more than echoed current thought on the subject. Whilst recognizing the precarious position of the artisan who possessed nothing more than what he made from the work of his hands, the economists and philosophers of the seventeenth and eighteenth centuries were harsh in their attitude towards beggars. Unless aged or maimed, the beggar was generally regarded as lazy, vegetating on public alms or even as extorting charity under false pretences. The practice of almsgiving, it was said, had debilitating effects upon the character, and made living on the community for some an ingrained habit. 'Un homme n'est pas pauvre', said Montesquieu, 'parce qu'il n'a rien, mais parce qu'il ne travaille pas.'[1]

Until the 1770s the French government turned its attention to only two sorts of beggars, the old and the sick, who were deserving of charity, and the lazy who were the scourge of society. The first should go to the hospitals designed for them, the second should be punished. All legislation was directed towards this end.[2]

The poverty of the poor hospitals was recognized and attempts were made to increase their revenues. A measure of 1721 accorded them dues on alcoholic drinks entering the town.[3] Periodically they were allowed to hold lotteries. The edict of 1724 is representative of royal policy early in the century. Extra financial help was promised to the impoverished sick, the galleys to any beggars

---

[1] Cited by Bloch, op. cit., p. 153.

[2] Edicts for the suppression of begging were published in 1724, 1741, 1752, 1764, 1767. Isambert, op. cit., vol. xxi, pp. 271–3; vol. xxii, pp. 143, 146, 404. A.D.C. A37, A39. Edicts.

[3] These were known as the *droits des pauvres*. At Bayeux the revenue was divided and two-thirds went to the *hôpital général* for the old and infirm and a third to the *hôtel Dieu* for the sick. The total average yearly income from this source was about 3,000 *livres*, falling towards the end of the old régime to about 2,500 *livres*. Michel, op. cit., vol. iii, p. 321.

found banding together to extort alms by force, whilst internment was threatened to anyone actually caught in the act of begging.[1] The edict was circulated to the municipalities to whom it was left to prove its utter ineffectiveness. It would demand, the town of Bayeux pointed out to the *intendant*, the arrest of 1,800 people, an act it was impossible to carry out. Perhaps in deference to the royal edict, the municipality explained that the town prison was small and could not accommodate the town's many beggars but that they had, on receipt of the edict, taken into custody a handful of 'femmes de mauvaise vie, mais non mendiantes'.[2]

Edicts of this nature were impossible to implement: no one could embark upon the arrest of a quarter of the population of the town. The *intendant* wrote to the *contrôleur général* in 1749 urging him to establish categories of beggars in order to single out those who were only accidental beggars through illness or lack of work.[3] Nothing came of the letter.

Between 1724 and 1764 the central government was largely silent and help for the poor was left to local effort or to the *intendant*, who had in his power a twofold method of relief. He could grant tax alleviation, but this was a rather negative help since the urban destitute were not in that condition through being overburdened with taxes—they were not taxed at all. Tax alleviation was of most help to the artisan or shopkeeper who on paper appeared to have enough to manage but whose family was so large that it rapidly absorbed all he possessed.[4] From 1740 onwards, the *intendant* at Caen began sporadically, in times of extreme hardship, to use the funds of the *corvée*, which was converted into a money payment at this time in Normandy, in order to employ the poor on the roads. This was only done in times of dire distress and it tended to be used more for the relief of rural than urban areas, because those living in the country, unless they had a bountiful *seigneur*, had no other source of supply.

The ineffectiveness of royal policy inevitably led in Bayeux to a turning towards the church as the one organization from which

---

[1] Isambert, op. cit., vol. xxi, pp. 271–3.
[2] A.D.C. C626. *Hôpitaux de Bayeux, 1728.*
[3] A.D.C. C602.
[4] For example, Julien Le Moigne, a fishmonger of Bayeux, had an income of a little under 500 *livres* and was usually rated at 3 *livres* 11 *sols* on the *capitation* list. His family, however, was sufficiently large to ensure that he always escaped with the lightest payment. A.D.C. C944. *Secours aux familles nombreuses, 1777–1789.*

consistent relief might be obtained and from which it might be demanded on the grounds that the church had a positive obligation to succour the poor. There were several ecclesiastics in the town upon whom pressure could be exerted. If the bishop could not always be reached the canons could. Reliance on the church and private subsidy meant that in the town a divorce might easily have grown up between current economic thought, which pronounced almsgiving dangerous since it led to sloth and proclaimed that a man should be made to work for whatever he was given, and the traditional principles upon which ecclesiastical charity was based. But the church, which had to a certain extent abandoned its adherence to the blessedness of poverty when poverty implied sloth, chose to talk in modern terms, tried the subsidization of industry and the creation of new ones, and only when these experiments failed reverted to unveiled direct subsidy.

In 1750, when the best the government could do was to order the beggars to return to their own province without suggesting methods to enforce this, members of the cathedral chapter of Bayeux, headed by the Abbé Hugon, drew up a project of relief clearly differentiating between different types of needy. They intended, they said, first to help those whose age or infirmities prevented them from providing for themselves; secondly, to supplement the income of those whose wages were only partially sufficient for their support; thirdly, to make work obligatory for all those who were able bodied; and lastly, and most important, to save the children of poor families from want by giving them work suited to their years.[1] For the first group, the sick and the old, the hospital poor house was the answer; for the second, those whose income was too slight to support themselves and a family, a subsidy; for the third, the lazy, punishment; and for the last, the children, some sort of work which would make them self supporting and give them the habit of working.

The initial stage consisted of the setting up of a *bureau de charité* composed of seven important ecclesiastics, including the bishop, two nobles, five officials of the law-courts, and the *subdélégué*, all of whom were nobles. They were concerned with seeing that the parish priests drew up a document describing the state of the poor within their parishes and stipulating who needed

---

[1] Béziers, op. cit., vol. i, pp. 208–12.

alms. From this, the *bureau* embarked upon the opening of a cotton-spinning school to employ the children. Moreover, it tried, as far as in it lay, to institutionalize almsgiving. Instead of scattering money gratuitously upon perhaps unworthy cases, the *bureau* urged that those who wished to give money should pay it into a central fund. From this, the parish priest would distribute it to cases according to their individual needs as stated by the priest and ratified by the *bureau de charité*.[1]

A year later the results were impressive. The churches were no longer besieged by hordes of beggars and if the children's work brought in little at least they were occupied and their meals provided. The *bureau* suggested that discarded furniture should be placed in a central depot and used to help struggling households.[2] There could be no doubt of the success of the whole enterprise. It gained for Bayeux widespread praise and later served as a model for Turgot in his recommendations for dealing with the poor.[3]

Of the alms which were collected the bishop contributed about a sixth annually. The chapter's donation was about the same; as was that of the nobility. The rest came from individual bequests, many of them given by ecclesiastics, from the magistrature, and from parish collections.[4] The lay members of the *bureau de charité* were anxious to make the church pay as much as possible.

The sort of charity the indigent of the town sought was not so much a sum of money as bread distributions or free meals for their children. If the *bureau de charité* made bread distributions on Mondays and Thursday then the family income could be stretched a little bit further. The plans of the chapter fitted exactly the needs of the poor of the town.

They did not, however, take into account the rural poor, and hence they did nothing for those vagrants from the rural parishes who came into the town. The rural parishes claimed in vain that anything between a third and two-thirds of their parishioners were *indigents* and that they could not help them in any substantial way, and the most perceptive of the parish priests were at length to point out that the root of the problem of vagrancy lay in the countryside.[5] For the rural poor nothing was done. The church

---

[1] Ibid., p. 271.   [2] Ibid., p. 211.   [3] Bloch, op. cit., p. 194.
[4] B.C. MS. 185. *Registre concernant la recette du bureau de charité, 1763–1789.*
[5] A.D.C. H. Suppl. 1308. 11. G5.

in the town could afford to be modern and decry indiscriminate almsgiving and make the pauper work for his living, but what was to happen to the rural poor? What else could the parish priest in the outlying country districts do, when he had no hope of outside help, except urge his parishioners to share their bread with their poorer neighbours and stress the reward in heaven for those who succoured the poor? The difficulty was always that there were so many in this position and that almsgiving could not be made obligatory. The townspeople were deeply resentful of the beggar from outside. They were prepared to share their bread with their own townsfolk but not with strangers. Unless he was prepared to use force, the vagrant could expect little in the way of help.

Government policy was worse than useless. After the Seven Years War the state once more turned its attention in the traditional pattern to the beggars. In 1764 de l'Averdy published an edict ordering that the edict of 1724 be reinforced.[1] The measure had no greater success in 1764 than in 1724. In 1767 another edict declared that anyone recognized as a beggar who was not sick or old must be interned in a *maison de force* which would be erected in the *généralité*.[2]

The *maison de force* and house of correction of the *généralité* of Caen at Beaulieu was under the directorship of a *lieutenant* of the *maréchaussée*, who was endowed with the title of *subdélégué* of the *intendant*. Its finances were regulated by a special official attached to the *bureau* of the *intendance* and it was supported out of the taxes of the *généralité*.[3] It was meant to be an unpleasant place to stay in. In 1777, of the 240 internees, 40 were prostitutes, 35 insane, 22 children (usually of imprisoned women), 6 were put there at the request of relatives for stealing, and 2 were old and blind. The remaining 135 were vagrants and thieves.[4] In 1784, of the 267 in the *dépôt*, 175 worked at cotton spinning, 5 as nurses, and of the rest, at least 50 per cent. were too sick to do anything.[5] It was an institution combining together in a common misery a motley assembly of prostitutes, thieves, and young children. Fontette, the *intendant*, justified the institution to the bishop, who had received ill reports, by saying that his lordship

[1] Isambert, op. cit., vol. xxii, p. 404.   [2] A.D.C. C595.
[3] A.D.C. C611. *Dépôt de Beaulieu*.   [4] A.D.C. C678. *Dépôt de Beaulieu*.
[5] A.D.C. C681. *Dépôt de Beaulieu*.

should not expect the institution to resemble an *hôtel Dieu* in cleanliness. Most of its inmates arrived covered in lice. Many were either syphilitics or covered in sores due simply to their own filth.[1] If added to this is the fact that these institutions were supplied with food and raw materials by a company which had a virtual monopoly throughout most of France, then the other features of the establishment are self explanatory. To save money, soap was never sent. All the washing was done in water alone and the children's wet napkins were just dried and put back. The daily diet consisted of one and a half pounds of bread and a ration of rice or lentils.[2]

Obviously such an institution accommodated only the worst type of vagrant. Elsewhere *dépôts* were to be set up which interned others taken in the act of begging. The treatment accorded them was to be rough and the *dépôt* had to decide whether the beggars should be sent off to a house of correction, a hospital poor house, or released with the threat of harsher treatment if caught begging again.

Such a policy did not strike at the root of the problem. Fontette wrote to l'Averdy pleading for a distinction to be made between the professional beggar and the merely poor.[3] This time he received a reply from l'Averdy who stated in the vaguest terms that the edict was only ever intended to be directed against the first, that the poor must be helped at home and that this was a natural obligation incumbent upon the wealthier sections of the community. He went on to urge that: 'Les archévêques et évêques travailleront à établir des bureaux d'aumônes pour prévenir une imposition. Si elle est établie, elle sera d'autant moins à charge qu'elle sera payée par les nobles, les ecclésiastiques et privilégiés.'[4] The bulk of the beggars were not treated as a problem of the state, which assumed responsibility only for the criminal beggar. The rest were the concern of charity, which, it was hoped, the church would organize. The idea was put forward, however, not as a command in an edict, but in a letter as a tentative suggestion.

Charity and private philanthropy were not lacking in the 1760s in Bayeux. In the late fifties the cathedral canons were worried at the marked diminution in almsgiving. They declared that their

[1] A.D.C. H. Suppl. 1308. 11. G5.
[2] Mourlot, 'La Question de la mendicité en Normandie . . .', p. 9.
[3] A.D.C. C604.   [4] Ibid.

experiments had been so successful that begging in the streets
had stopped, and since the public saw so few poor they no longer
felt the necessity to give alms to the *bureau de charité* and ended up
by not giving any at all. Two canons spent between them in the
1750s 50,000 *livres* on the extension of lace schools and the
cotton-spinning school.[1] This sum was more than the entire annual
subsidy accorded to the whole *généralité* of Caen for the relief of
the poor during the administration of Turgot in the seventies.
The lace schools were an unqualified success and the enterprise
encouraged the *bureau* to undertake the ambitious project of the
industrialization of Bayeux. The enterprise was motivated by
the current belief that only the creation of industry could be the
ultimate solution to the poverty of the town. The founding of a
school to teach cotton-spinning to the children of impoverished
families, using some of the money collected by the *bureau de
charité* and a gift from the Abbé Hugon, was only intended as the
beginning of a larger project. Tragedy struck before the idea
advanced any further. The children employed produced work of
inferior quality and the little money which was paid to them to
encourage them to work caused an expenditure the *bureau* could
not afford. The philanthropic Abbé Hugon contributed 10,000
livres out of his own money to keep the enterprise going and was
so hopeful of ultimate success that he was in process of building a
school to train woollen workers when he died. His place was
taken by another canon of the cathedral, of noble origins, de
Loucelles, who applied himself to the project with equal enthusiasm. Indeed, such was his anxiety to succeed that he travelled
throughout Normandy learning about the manufacture of cloth
so that he would know what faults to look for. Fear of being
tricked by unscrupulous middle-men led him to undertake
personally all purchase of raw material. This led him to fairs,
markets, farms, and to rub shoulders with merchants and
manufacturers.[2]

The thought of such a man, obviously motivated by genuine
philanthropy, is impressive until one remembers the commercial
battle with England for the markets of the world, and that
Bayeux already produced far more cloth than it could sell. Failure
to find a market for the material it produced because of the poor

[1] A.D.C. C630. *Établissement des manufactures des pauvres.*
[2] Ibid.

quality of the work prompted the struggling *manufacture des pauvres* to cut down on the number of children it employed. With adult labour and a preferential tariff in respect of the *octroi* it managed to sell the cloth it produced at the Foire de Guibray. Here it met the opposition of local manufacturers, who already had trouble in selling their goods, and in 1768, four years after its inauguration, the *manufacture des pauvres* ran into trouble with the *hôtel de ville*.[1]

In 1764, at the end of the Seven Years War, the royal government had promised to help the hospital poor-houses by according them a part of the *don gratuit*. The municipal council of 1764 declared that the gift should be divided into three parts, one to go to the hospital poor-house, another to the *hôtel Dieu* for the sick, and the third part to the municipal council which was acutely in need of funds. Out of the two-thirds due to both hospitals, it was decided, a half should go to the new *manufacture*, for the town had no greater problem than the upkeep of the poor.[2]

By 1768, however, the municipal government had changed and Bayeux had its first non-venal municipal council. The latter, in need of funds, refused to be committed by the promises of its predecessors, who, they said, had not submitted the question of the allocation of the subsidy to 'le général de la ville'.[3] It therefore tried to hold back the gift from the *don gratuit* from the hospitals as well as from the new woollen *manufacture*. The matter was hotly contested because in 1767 the hospital poor-house had lost a fifth of its revenues by the suppression of dues on the measuring of corn in the market of Bayeux,[4] and needed the money the council was holding back.

The municipal council enraged the administrators of the *bureau de charité* still further by demanding the keys and inspecting the work of the *manufacture*, all without consulting the *bureau* in any way—a *bureau*, moreover, which was of a pronouncedly more aristocratic nature than the municipal council. The council

---

[1] Ibid.

[2] A.M.B. BB III. *Registre des délibérations municipales*. August 1764.

[3] 'Le général de la ville': the administrators of the *bureau de charité* declared that they were not sure what this meant but that presumably it referred to the old *assemblée générale des habitants*. Such a body no longer met and in any case in 1776 had been officially replaced by an assembly of notables. The municipal council was obviously trying to gain time because they needed the money from the *don gratuit* to meet the expenses of the town. A.D.C. C630.

[4] A.D.C. H. Suppl. 109.

retaliated with the cogent argument that when the subsidy had
initially been promised the purpose of the *manufacture* had been the
employment of children. This had not been accomplished. The
children had been dismissed as soon as it was realized that their
work would not sell.

Whether the *manufacture* ever received the money from the
don gratuit is not known. What is evident is that by the early 1770s
the *manufacture* was no longer in existence. Unable to perfect its
goods, it lapsed. The failure of small-scale industry in areas unsuited for textile production was as patent in France as in England,
where the idea was also finally abandoned.

The 1770s, however, if they saw the failure of one experiment,
were not without hope for the poor of the town. The administration of Turgot inaugurated a new era in the general attitude of the
central government towards the poor. Turgot, as an *intendant* of
one of the poorest regions of France, had viewed the situation at
first hand. Believing that the only remedy for poverty and begging
was work, he proposed the freeing from prison of all except the
criminal vagabonds and the closing of the subsidiary *dépôts de
mendicité*, leaving open only the house of correction for vagabonds
and thieves. For all those beggars who were not physically handi-
capped, work which assured them of enough to eat and a little
over was a prime necessity. The first duty of public assistance was
the organization of work rather than a system of almsgiving,
which was justifiable only in the case of the sick and the crippled.
Those without work should be supplied with it by *ateliers de
charité* which were to be financed out of the *taille extraordinaire*
and in some cases out of the *corvée*.

Whilst the idea of employing the poor out of these funds was
an old one, the universalization of its application, as well as the
admission that work might not exist for the poor and where it
did not it must be created, was new. Moreover, Turgot urged, it
was indispensable to admit to the *ateliers de charité* men and women,
the aged and children. The work these *ateliers* could execute must
inevitably be conditioned by the very diverse nature of the work-
people.[1] The limitations of what could be undertaken were
recognized even from the outset. Turgot stated in an official
pamphlet:

[1] A.D.C. C3416. *Instruction pour l'établissement et la régie des ateliers de charité,
1775.*

On sent bien qu'il n'y a guère que les remuements et le transport de terres, de cailloux et de graviers qui puissent être l'objet des ateliers de charité parce que ce sont les seuls travaux qui puissent être exécutés par toutes sortes de personnes. Ainsi dans les parties de chemin qu'on entreprend s'il se rencontre des travaux plus difficiles, et qui exigent des bras plus exercés, il sera nécessaire de charger des entrepreneurs de leur exécution et de payer ces entrepreneurs sur d'autres fonds que ceux destinés aux ateliers de charité.[1]

The direction of the work would be entrusted to the *ponts et chaussées*, which was to appoint a *conducteur* for each *atelier*. Distribution of work and wages was to be left to the management of the *subdélégué*. The parish priest had the task of drawing up a list of those needing employment and estimating their capacities. He was, moreover, to split them up into brigades of ten or twelve and, if possible, keep members of a family together. Specific tasks were to be allotted to each brigade, which was to be paid only when the work was completed and not by the day. A regulation such as the following illustrates the thoroughness of the plan: since the brigades were composed of men, women, and children, whose working capacity obviously varied, the children were merely given food, whilst the men and women needed also a supplement in money because, very often, they had younger children to feed.[2]

Turgot's plan showed that the poor of France had at last been recognized in government circles, not as criminals, but as people in need, and a project, inadequate though it proved to be, had been put forward to solve their problem. They were, moreover, effectively categorized and seen not only as men, but also as women and children, each needing separate and different treatment.

The *ateliers* were financed by a part of the *corvée en argent* and the sum the king granted yearly out of the *taille* for the help of the poor.[3] They were, however, still dependent largely upon private contributions. The type of work undertaken was planned with a view to obtaining financial help from the great landowners and hence was designed to be beneficial to them.[4] Private contributions covered anything up to about a third of the total cost.[5]

---

[1] Ibid., Article 1. [2] Ibid., Article 3*c*.
[3] This was usually 45,000 to 50,000 *livres* for the *généralité* of Caen. A.D.C. C3417.
[4] Ibid. Letter from Necker to the *intendant* at Caen, 7 May 1778.
[5] Mourlot, 'La mendicité en Normandie . . .', p. 19.

Thus the bishop of Bayeux contributed about a sixth of the cost of the building of the road from Bayeux to Sommervieu where his palace lay.[1] For this reason the grant of individual contributions was apt to decide where a road should be built rather than considerations of general utility.[2] The general application of this principle was ultimately to lead to complaints in the *cahiers* that the *corvée* was used only to build roads for nobles and *seigneurs* rather than for the benefit of those who paid the actual tax.

The *intendant* was the pivotal figure in the whole procedure and he had a certain amount of licence in the type of work undertaken.[3] The *contrôleur général*, for example, was not convinced of the value of building a sloping approach to the cathedral of Avranches. Fontette pressed his point, saying that not only did it need doing but that its construction would help to alleviate the poverty of Avranches, which was unparalleled throughout the *généralité*.[4]

By the early 1770s, Bayeux, St. Lô, Avranches, Cherbourg, Granville, all had *ateliers de charité*. The moment was opportune for Bayeux, since the *parlement* of Rouen had just been exiled and the king had authorized the setting up of a *conseil supérieur* in its place at Bayeux. The *intendant* proposed the demolition of the ancient *château* and the levelling of the site for the building of the new *palais de justice*.[5] The work was continued until 1774 and then abruptly suspended when it became obvious that the *parlement* would be recalled.

The difficulties inherent in the running of *ateliers* soon became apparent. Fontette in a letter to Turgot complained that money was the main difficulty.[6] The *seigneurs* and those who were willing to subscribe to work done by the poor preferred to pay afterwards, but in the meanwhile, money had to be found for the wages of the work-people. Moreover, Fontette claimed, subscribers seemed to fear lest their donations should be changed into an obligatory tax and were withdrawing their previous promises. This lack of funds meant that the *ateliers* were unable to pay the

---

[1] A.D.C. C3421.
[2] M. Noel, *directeur des mines de Littry*, said that the road between Bayeux and Littry, a necessary communication, was too hazardous to use in winter, but since he only offered 400 *livres* towards its repair the project was postponed till he should offer more. None the less, the importance of the communication was generally accepted. A.D.C. C7655. *Registre des délibérations de la commission intermédiaire de Bayeux, 1787.*
[3] A.D.C. C3421.
[4] A.D.C. C3471.
[5] Ibid.
[6] Ibid. Letter of May 1775.

wages of those who turned up to work and once more the pauper found himself obliged to beg. So unsatisfactory did the system prove that Clugny, Turgot's successor, decided that they were no real substitute for the old punitive *dépôts de mendicité*, which he reopened. Still, the *ateliers* represented the one positive effort to employ the poor made by the governments of the old régime, and even after the fall of Turgot from office the effort they represented was not entirely abandoned. Indeed, after the mid 1770s Bayeux had recourse almost every winter to the expedient of opening some sort of public workshop for the employment of the poor during the most difficult season of the year to find work. The greatest problem which confronted the town administration, apart from the serious lack of funds, was how to employ the poor in a way that did not demand overmuch skill and took into account the fact that many of them were women and children. Such work was difficult to find especially if the ground was frozen hard or waterlogged. On 3 July 1785 the municipal council wrote to the *contrôleur général* to inform him of the high proportion of destitute within the town and to state that they feared a rapid deterioration of the situation. They declared:

Les temps de calamité qui se font sentir depuis longtemps dans cette ville et qui s'annoncent devoir être plus rigoureux l'hiver prochain fait tout appréhender pour la classe des misérables journaliers et autres malheureux artisanats qui sont, dès à présent, restés la plupart sans occupation et exposés à manquer bien d'avantage après la moisson. En effet, la récolte de cette année sera très peu abondante et par conséquent n'occupera . . . que très peu de bras et pendant un très court espace de temps . . . d'où il résultera que le plus grand nombre de pauvres ouvriers qui trouvaient leur subsistance et celle de leur famille dans les travaux, soit de la campagne, soit de la ville, vont être exposés à succomber sous le poids de l'indigence et de la misère.[1]

Following this cogent preface the members of the council made two suggestions for the employment of about eighty workers, a mere fraction of the destitute, which they hoped would secure approval and a government subsidy. First, they put foward the idea of levelling and paving the market-place, which was often waterlogged; secondly, the demolition of the Tour Louise, part of the ancient fortifications of the town. The *contrôleur général* replied briefly that the municipal officials had not given sufficient thought

[1] A.D.C. C3421.

to the work they wished to be undertaken. Paving was skilled work. The demolition of the tower was a sounder idea and the minister asked for an idea of the cost.[1] Eight months later the central government had taken the matter no further and the municipal council wrote to the *intendant* for relief in a pathetic note:

> Le froid rigoureux que nous éprouvons ici depuis quinze jours, la terre endurcie et couverte de neige dans tous nos alentours ôtent entièrement aux malheureux journaliers tous les moyens de travailler pour subvenir à leurs besoins. Nous vous avons présenté l'année dernière la liste de ces indigents qui forment presque un septième de la population de cette ville, sans y comprendre la classe de citoyens au dessous du médiocre qui pour la plupart sans, ou avec peu de fortune, ne végètent que par leur faible travail et que le prix excessif des denrées ordinaires et surtout les moindres comestibles, réduit insensiblement à celle des nécessiteux.[2]

This reminder was sufficient for the *intendant* to grant the town 1,500 *livres* to alleviate as best it could over 1,200 suffering people.

The council decided to open an *atelier de charité* and raise what funds it could from the government and its own *bureau de charité*. The major problem was still regular payment of those who came to work. Government funds were particularly unreliable. The *corvée* had to be paid first into the office of the *intendant* and from thence into the hands of the *entrepreneur*, who paid the wages of the workers. The *intendant*'s office was always inundated with business and any suggestion that the tax should be paid directly into the hands of the *entrepreneur* was utterly unacceptable to the *Assemblée Provinciale* of 1788 for the *entrepreneurs* formed a class notorious for prosperity based on private profit and the malversation of public funds. Delay in payment to the workers meant that they and their families must go without food for they had no other resources than their wage from the *atelier*. The *subdélégué* at Bayeux and the *conducteur* of the town *atelier* claimed in 1789 that so desperate was the situation that some of the workers in the *ateliers de charité* had had nothing at all in their stomachs for several days but blood from the slaughter-house with which they had sought to appease their hunger.[3]

---

[1] A.D.C. C3421.   [2] Ibid. Letter of 7 March 1786.

[3] A.D.C. C3088. Letter from Maillard to Lefebvre, *ingénieur en chef*, Bayeux, 2 May 1789.

For this, the blame did not rest entirely with the *entrepreneur*. There was a general reluctance amongst both town and country people to pay the *corvée en argent*, and the townspeople especially put up a stubborn resistance since they had not fallen liable to the tax before it was commuted into a money payment.[1] The *corvée* estimates throughout the *généralité* were rarely realized. In 1789 promissory notes were drawn up and given to the *entrepreneurs* of the preceding year. But by this time few were ready to advance money for the creation of *ateliers*.[2] Indeed at the *atelier* of Goville near Bayeux unpleasant scenes occurred during the summer of 1789, inspired not by workmen who had not received payment but by *entrepreneurs* to whom the administration was greatly in debt.[3] By the end of the old régime the bankruptcy of the scheme was apparent enough, but both the central and local government hesitated to abandon it. They could envisage no other solution to the problem of unemployment and under-employment.

During the crisis of the late 1780s the church continued and indeed increased its almsgiving. Emergency measures such as the organization of a daily soup kitchen by the Sisters of Charity at the bishop's expense were adopted in the autumn of 1788. The *bureau de charité* throughout 1785, 1786, and again in 1789 paid out more than it received.[4] Rapidly rising costs were not productive of philanthropy, but the bureau succeeded in 1788 and 1789 in increasing its revenues by half.

The measures did not solve the problem. The poor artisan and the utterly destitute together constituted the greatest social problem of eighteenth-century France. An analysis of the poorer population of Bayeux reveals a situation bleak by any standards. On the other hand, somehow the townspeople managed to survive. Their economy was precarious: their existence day to day. It depended on finding an odd job to earn a few extra *sols* or perhaps joining the *atelier de charité* during the winter months, or doing a little gardening in summer. It might mean taking in washing as well as making lace all day, and turning the children out to ask for bread, which if it was too old to eat could be sold to the horse-dealers for a few pence when enough had been

[1] A.D.C. C8262. *Mémoire sur la corvée adressé par le bureau intermédiaire de Bayeux à la commission intermédiaire de l'assemblée provinciale de Caen.* 23 September 1788.
[2] Ibid.
[3] A.D.C. C7657. Letter of 27 November 1789.
[4] B.C. MS. 185. *Registre concernant la recette du bureau de charité.*

collected. Perhaps a little help would come from a bread distribution by the chapter and the *bureau de charité* and from a parcel of clothes made up by the Sisters of Charity. The really sick and dying could spend their last days in the *hôtel Dieu*: an extra child might with good fortune be taken into the small choir school run by the chapter or be accepted by the Sisters of Charity if a girl. An unwanted baby could perhaps be left to the Sisters of Providence. In this way the poorer population of the town managed a miserable existence. Their greatest buffer in Bayeux was the church and the *bureau de charité* which, inadequate though they were, survived when more ambitious experiments failed.

VI

MUNICIPAL ADMINISTRATION

THE business of running a town under the old régime was far from straightforward. Participation in municipal government was a high social honour accompanied, in fifteen towns at least, by the immediate conference of personal nobility; but to be set against this was the constant struggle, if one held office, involved in defending the town against the policy of the royal government which regarded municipal office mainly as yet another source of revenue. The picture doubtless differed from province to province and town to town, but the parallels and contrasts between the administration of Bayeux and the neighbouring town of Caen are illustrative of the complicated scenes which were being enacted throughout France. Moreover, they are indicative of a narrow-sighted royal policy which at times stultified—indeed wrecked—the effective functioning of municipal administration, to the general detriment of the welfare of the town.

Before 1788 local government in France was threefold. It was divided among the *intendant*, the most important figure in provincial administration, with his personnel, the law-courts, and thirdly, the municipal councils. By the end of the period, each had strictly defined spheres of activity. In Bayeux the *subdélégué* was the agent of information for the *intendant* on all matters concerned with the administration of society. He was the main link of the community with the government and he was at hand to see to the implementation of the orders of the *intendant*. He had control over the allocation of certain taxes. The law-courts each had their separate responsibilities and the *bailliage* usually judged in the first instance all those cases for which no other specialized court existed. The municipal government was concerned with purely municipal affairs, of which the most important was the management of the town's finances. This included its income from *octroi* and municipal property, and expenditure either on debts to the central government such as payment of the *abonnement* for the *taille*, on the repair of buildings owned by the town and the upkeep of roads within the municipal boundaries, or on the quartering of the militia. The division of the *capitation des arts et métiers* was also the concern of the municipal government.

All these bodies, however, had a common function, to see that the community was justly administered and ran smoothly. Up to the early eighteenth century, this basic common denominator had fused the separate spheres together. In Caen, during the medieval period, the *bailli* and subsequently the *lieutenant général du bailliage* considered himself *maire né* of the town.[1] This pattern was repeated throughout the *généralité* in towns where *bailliage* courts existed. Bayeux, on the other hand, had an almost unique form of government which was a relic of the early Middle Ages. The *vicomtes* of Merovingian France had had positions of scarcely rivalled importance in provinces such as Normandy which were but loosely knit to the crown. Their functions were to hear law-suits, regulate the police, see that roads were repaired, punish the wrong-doer, and receive the revenues of the ducal demesne.[2] This last consideration rendered the position highly lucrative. Bayeux, as capital of the Bessin, had been centre of a *vicomté* and the *vicomte* carried out duties which elsewhere, in towns which were then less important, were given to a *maire*. The system gradually crystallized during the late Middle Ages into a *vicomté* court which assumed the functions of the former *vicomte* whilst his style and revenues passed to the bishop. But the title *vicomte-maire* was used to qualify the man who exercised the positions of first judge of the *vicomté* court and *maire* of the town.[3] They were always, until 1749, exercised conjointly. Added to this, the intermingling of branches of local administration was further accentuated in Bayeux during the period 1725–49 when the *vicomte-maires* were also *subdélégués* of the *élection*.

In theory, in Bayeux, the position of *maire* was elective at the beginning of the eighteenth century. The elected *maire* automatically became *vicomte*, the chief judge of the *vicomté* court. The *subdélégué* was, in theory, chosen by the *intendant*.[4] The burden of the post of *subdélégué* was such that any man who was not diligent

[1] J. Yver, 'Les Offices municipaux à Caen au XVIIIᵉ siècle', *Mémoires de l'Académie des Sciences, Arts et Belles Lettres de Caen*, vi (1931), p. 5.
[2] C. E. Lambert, *Les Vicomtes de Bayeux* (Bayeux, 1879), p. 11.
[3] Ibid., p. 15.
[4] Marion, *Dictionnaire . . .*, pp. 519–20.

in his duties would never be granted the position, since he was an agent upon whom the *intendant* was forced to place great reliance.

The division of the municipal government into a *corps de ville* of *maire* and *échevins* and the *assemblée générale des habitants*, who elected two notables per parish, who then elected the *échevins*, no longer had any real meaning in Bayeux by the eighteenth century. As early as 1658 it is recorded that of the 822 male inhabitants of the town who were eligible to meet to elect new officials only 97 in fact gathered.[1] The situation grew worse, not better, and the *assemblée générale des habitants* became a mere formality never seriously changing the character of the *corps de ville*. The *maire* and *échevins* until the mid eighteenth century were never other than the leading magistrates. Municipal councils were, in fact, rarefied meetings of the *bailliage* and *vicomté* courts, freed from their minor personnel. The *maire*, his deputy, and four *échevins* were practically self-perpetuated in office and received only a token payment for duties demanding both time and energy. A *procureur syndic* was the executive agent of the *corps de ville*, responsible for seeing that its decisions were put into effect. Usually an official of one of the courts filled this position. A *receveur* was responsible for the town's treasury. Like the *receveurs* of the royal taxes he had often to dive into his own pocket before the town's revenues were fully collected, in order to deal with expenses. Theoretically, he was paid a number of *sols* per *livre* of the receipts. Sometimes he worked at a loss. Not infrequently an experienced collector of seigneurial dues held the position at Bayeux.

In the early part of the century this small town council had considerable scope for private initiative and had the means whereby to implement its decisions. During the periodic grain shortages of the eighteenth century the town had to depend on the efforts of its administrators almost alone to stave off the worst effects of the crisis. In 1709, 1724, and again in 1739, when neither Paris nor the *intendant* in Caen could offer any help, the council sent envoys directly to England to buy grain out of municipal funds and a loan raised largely amongst themselves and by which they were in effect subsidizing the town.[2] They had a tradition of public service and expected hard work especially in times of crisis.

[1] A.D.C. C1075. *Offices Municipaux, Bayeux.*
[2] E. Anquétil, 'La Municipalité de Bayeux et les disettes, 1709–1739', *Mémoires de la Société des Sciences, Arts et Belles Lettres de Bayeux*, vol. x, p. 154.

The destruction of this closely knit network of high magistrates and urban nobles, working together in all spheres of the local administration, as well as the decline in the effective power of the municipal council in acting for the welfare of the community, was brought about in the *généralité* of Caen by the introduction of venality in the municipal offices. The partial divorce between the different sections of municipal administration was not effected easily, nor overnight. Protracted struggles occurred in some towns between *bailliage* officials and municipal councils over questions which would never have arisen when the high personnel of the former were, by a custom which had the force of law, also members of the latter. Minor quarrels were frequently enacted over questions of precedence in public ceremonies. In some cases they had to be settled by instructions from the central government.

In spite of the constant creation of offices during the seventeenth century, the effective power of the medieval *bailliage* was, by the beginning of the eighteenth century, clearly on the wane. None the less, the *bailliages* retained a psychological hold over the population and an alliance with municipal government, if not with the members of the municipal council, which proved difficult to destroy. Even by the end of the *ancien régime* the situation was far from clear. In towns where the municipal council had no *procureur syndic* to attend to the execution of municipal decisions and business affairs, the *procureur du roi* of the *bailliage* performed this function. In the food crisis of 1784 the people of Bayeux appealed for help not to the municipal council, nor to the *subdélégué*, but to the *procureur du roi* of the *bailliage* as the traditional protector of their interests.[1] Furthermore, the *procureur du roi* at Bayeux was at this time the son of the *subdélégué* and had the old forms of administration continued would, in all probability, have succeeded his father as *subdélégué* as the father had succeeded his uncle before him.

Municipal government in France throughout the eighteenth century was subjected to two pressures, both emanating from the central government but working at cross-purposes. The first came from the *contrôleur général des finances*, interested in extracting the maximum he could from the town for the benefit of the royal treasury, and the second from royal officials like the *secrétaire*

[1] A.D.C. C2643. *Grains, Bayeux*. 8 July 1784.

d'état chargé de la province, who wanted the smoothest and most efficient administration for the town.

The venality of municipal offices was inaugurated by Louis XIV in 1692. His intention, he said, was above all to substitute for the elected *maires* more impartial ones who would have bought their offices and hence would be independent of the electorate; secondly, to replace temporary *maires,* who had only a term of office, by perpetual ones who would be irremovable and so would ultimately have more experience.[1] After this first creation, in 1702 he ordered the sale of the office of deputy *maire* and in 1704 those of *échevins perpétuels.*[2]

Bayeux and the neighbouring town of Caen ignored the letter but grasped the motivating spirit of the royal edicts, paid the requisite amount to the royal treasury and continued to choose their own officials, from whom they demanded a sum on entry into office. Hence, at Bayeux, the edict occasioned no breach between the old officials and the new. The sums demanded were not large. For the position of first *échevin* Bayeux was asked to pay 400 *livres,* for the third only 300 *livres.*[3]

These sums appear small in comparison with the demands of 1722, when municipal offices were once more put up for sale. From the towns of the *généralité* of Caen astronomical sums were requested: Bayeux was asked to pay 125,300 *livres,*[4] an assessment which appears to have been made upon the prestige of the town

---

[1] Isambert, op. cit., vol. xx, pp. 158–64, *Édit portant création des maires et assesseurs en chaque ville et communauté du royaume, à l'exception de Paris et Lyon, le 27 août 1692.*

[2] Ibid., pp. 441–2. *Édit portant création des offices d'échevins, consuls, capitouls, jurats et autres officiers municipaux et de concierges et gardes meubles des hôtels de villes et maisons communes. Janvier 1704.*

[3] A.D.C. C1076. *Administration des villes.*

[4] A.D.C. C1050. *Administration des villes.* The towns of the *généralité* of Caen were asked to pay:

Town	Total sum livres	Town	Total sum livres
Avranches	38,200	Montebourg	27,100
Barentan	23,500	Mortain	39,000
Bayeux	125,300	Periers	26,200
Caen	349,000	St. James	28,900
Carentan	51,200	St. Lô	109,300
Cherbourg	38,200	St. Sauveur le Vicomte	28,700
Condé sur Noireau	29,300	Tinchebray	28,900
Coutances	79,400	Valognes	59,600
Granville	21,800	Villedieu	28,700
Isigny	25,500	Vire	83,800

and its administrative importance rather than on any considerations of size, for Bayeux, Granville, and Vire had roughly the same number of inhabitants, yet Granville paid four times less than Vire and seven times less than Bayeux. St. Lô, on the other hand, paid almost as much as Bayeux and was only half as large. The cathedral city doubtless suffered from its former importance as an administrative centre and the lustre surrounding its name. There was, Fontette remarked, always a deceptive apparent opulence associated with the town of Bayeux which bore little relation to reality.[1] None the less, the towns of the *généralité* of Caen appear to have paid what was demanded of them and to have reverted to their former methods of choosing municipal officials. The Sieur Dumartel in 1730 still styled himself *vicomte-maire* and *subdélégué* of Bayeux:[2] the *lieutenant général du bailliage de Caen* still considered himself *maire né* of that town.

Difficulties began in 1733 when, after an interim of only eleven years, offices were once more confiscated and put up for sale. A general reluctance to buy characterized the towns of the *généralité*, and the towns continued to maintain the holders in office. This almost unanimous reluctance to buy substantiated the fear in the mind of the Paris government that the old principle of law-court officials who considered themselves *de iure* mayors of the town menaced the effective implementation of royal policy, because it prevented the sale of office to the highest bidder. There probably existed men anxious to buy who would not contravene a deep-rooted practice by purchase of an office which it was claimed by right belonged to another. By 1734 no step towards purchase of the offices had been taken and the *contrôleur général*, Orry, wrote to the *intendant* in Caen:

Monsieur,

Je vous envoie deux exemplaires d'un arrêt portant qu'il sera instamment commis aux fonctions des offices municipaux auxquels il n'a pas encore été pourvu. Les motifs de ces arrêts vous feront connaître la nécessité qu'il y a de commettre à ces offices et de faire choix de gens capables de les remplir. Vous n'ignorez pas que la plupart des officiers des présidiaux et des bailliages se prétendent maires nés; que plusieurs juges des seigneurs s'arrogent le droit de maire et se font commettre à ces places par autorité ou autrement et que

[1] A.D.C. C1051. Letter from Fontette to Terray, 16 June 1772.
[2] A.D.C. C2861.

ces prétensions des uns et autres éloignent ceux qui auraient dessein d'acquérir ces offices.[1]

Orry began by implying that the *maires nés* might be incapable. The second part of the letter shows, however, that his real fear was that they might not pay. It was tantamount to an order that any man pretending to be *maire* by virtue of holding a particular office must be disillusioned in his beliefs. In actual fact, so long as the money was forthcoming, the central government did not care who exercised the position. Bayeux preserved its traditional pattern by agreeing to purchase the offices by payment of a yearly sum into the royal treasury until the debt was liquidated. The *maire* of Bayeux from 1740 to 1749 continued to be François Genas, Sieur Duhomme, *conseiller du roi, vicomte-maire de Bayeux et commissaire subdélégué pour l'élection dudit lieu.*

At Caen a more confused situation ensued. The magistrates who considered municipal office their prerogative refused to pay. The town for ten years resisted the central government, which in 1737 had reluctantly admitted that the former *maire* (the *lieutenant général du bailliage*) should continue in office until new elections were held.[2] In 1747 the king declared that all officials who had not yet done so must pay for their offices. The town eventually proceeded to gather together the required sum.

The purchase of offices ordered in 1733 appears to have met with opposition throughout France and the old custom of magistrates who considered themselves *maires nés* died hard. Where the towns could only pay for the offices by selling them to a bidder, the ousted magistrates retaliated by open opposition. In 1774 an edict was circulated which expressly forbade

tous baillis, sénéchaux et leurs lieutenants, prévôts, vicomtes, juges-consuls, syndics et à tous autres, de prendre la qualité de maire . . . ni de troubler les maires et autres officiers municipaux, et excluant des assemblées des hôtels de ville tous les particuliers qui, de leur autorité privée ou des magistrats desdites villes, s'y sont procurés l'entrée sous les titres de conseillers de ville, pairs, anciens échevins et autres titres.[3]

The abolition of the *vicomté* and *prévôté* courts in 1749 marked the end of the dual office of *vicomte-maire* at Bayeux, but the same man continued for a few years to be both *maire* and *subdélégué*.

[1] A.D.C. C1051.   [2] Yver, op. cit., p. 9.   [3] A.D.C. C1051.

The law-court officials could by the 1750s make no claims that the positions in the municipal council were theirs *de iure*. This did not mean, at least for the present, in Bayeux and Caen, that municipal government ceased to be the *de facto* monopoly of the courts. Béziers recorded that on 10 November 1760 a Sieur Nicholas Eurry, *conseiller au bailliage* and first *échevin* of the town, was elected *maire* in the place of the Sieur Crepel, *avocat du roi au bailliage*, whose ill health prevented continuance in office. Crepel had succeeded the Sieur Le Parsonnier des Rougesterres, who was simultaneously *procureur du roi au bailliage* and who, before he died, had been *maire* for twelve years. Des Rougesterres had assumed office when Genas resigned.[1] The latter continued his arduous position of *subdélégué*, which by this time was too burdensome to be exercised in conjunction with any other.

To pay for the offices created in 1733, Bayeux and the other towns of the *généralité* of Caen had been forced to borrow and were left with a debt whose repayment was a dead weight upon municipal revenues. Moreover, the years of repayment coincided with a further drain on municipal income resulting from the Seven Years War. Bayeux lay very near the coast and the continued bombardment of the Channel ports by English vessels engendered in the late fifties a genuine invasion scare. As a result, the town was constantly expected to garrison two regiments, and the lack of accommodation was such that new barracks had to be built.[2] War costs also meant that the central government needed more money and it chose as one method of raising it to continue the payment levied on offices in 1733, which Bayeux had in fact completed by about 1752. Largely because of this demand, the municipal government of Bayeux was confronted with a permanent situation wherein yearly expenditure exceeded receipts to the extent of some 5,000 *livres*.[3] The debts began to accumulate and a bemused municipal council did not know which way to turn.

Throughout France, municipal finance was based upon two sources, upon landed property and the *octrois* or *aides de ville*. These consisted of dues levied on goods entering the town according to a tariff established only after royal sanction. In Bayeux the tariff had been fully worked out in 1704 when the town purchased

[1] Béziers, op. cit., vol. i, p. 137.   [2] A.D.C. C1433. *Octrois*. Bayeux.
[3] Ibid.

abonnement from the *taille*.[1] It was granted that this yearly indemnity should be raised from taxes on consumer goods entering the town for the use of the unprivileged orders. The municipal council had no power to alter or add to the tariff in any way.

So desperate did the municipal council of Bayeux become for funds that it turned to reinterpreting the tariff by a merciless exploitation of any minor loophole. It found its best solution in an interpretation of the phrase relating to the tax on raw wool which ran: 'chaque cent pesant de laine avec le suin payera en entrant 15 sols.'[2] The letter of the tariff left unclear whether the tax should be *au cent de livres pesant* or *au cent de toisons*. Obviously if the previous tax which was on every hundred fleeces were changed to be on every hundred pounds of raw wool a substantial gain might be expected. Hence the section of the population that first felt the impact of the shortage of municipal funds was the manufacturers, the carders of wool, and stocking-makers whose plight was already causing concern and who were already facing unemployment.

The period of the Seven Years War appears to have created general havoc in municipal government throughout France. The bankruptcy of towns was quite general and it became obvious by 1764 that something would have to be done to remedy the situation. In August 1764 the central government brought out the first major edict concerning municipal government in the course of the century which was not merely intended to be of benefit to the royal treasury.[3] The solution to the financial chaos was, however, not approached in any systematic way. It was stated that:

En cas de l'insuffisance des deniers patrimoniaux, pour fournir aux charges desdites villes et bourgs, obligeât lesdits officiers municipaux de recourir à notre autorité, pour y suppléer par l'augmentation, la prorogation ou l'établissement de quelque octroi, ils demanderont audit commissaire départi, permission de convoquer une assemblée des notables habitants à l'effet d'être délibéré sur ladite demande, et ladite délibération contiendra la situation des affaires de ladite ville, et les motifs de la demande.[4]

[1] A.D.C. C1432. *Octrois*. Bayeux.
[2] A.D.C. C1433.
[3] Isambert, op. cit., vol. xxii, pp. 405–23. *Édit contenant règlement pour l'administration des villes et principaux bourgs du royaume*. August 1764.
[4] Ibid., p. 411, art. 24.

The payment on the offices of 1733, however, continued for the town of Bayeux and others of the *généralité* of Caen.

De l'Averdy's edict of 1765 followed the edict of 1764 and was intended to restore some order to the situation. It established freedom in municipal elections by the suppression of the practice of the sale of offices.[1] It was followed in July 1766 by another edict with complete details of municipal organization for Normandy. Municipal administration was from henceforth to be conferred upon councils varying in size according to the importance of the locality. The ultimate choice of *maire* was given to the king, but he was to choose from a list of three names submitted by the town. The town had the right of nominating its *échevins*. Together *maire* and *échevins* formed the *corps de ville*. A special body of *notables* formed the *conseil général de la ville* and were to be composed of forty or ten or six members according to the size of the town. Precise ruling defined the election processes, two stages for the *notables*, three for the *échevins*, and gave the duration of their functions and methods of convocation. The *notables* should be elected by an assembly composed of a deputy from each of the following—the cathedral chapter, the clergy, the nobles, the *bailliage*, each of the other jurisdictions, and one from each gild or *collège*. A year later an interesting amendment was made to this ruling. The artisans, in 1765, had been given far wider powers than ever before: in 1766 these powers were cut by decreeing that only those artisan gilds of eighteen or more members might elect a deputy. The *déclaration* ran:

Nous avons remarqué que les corps et communautés des artisans, en s'assemblant séparément et nommant . . . chacun un député, donnaient une si grande quantité de députés dans toutes les villes, que leur nombre se trouvait, dans plusieurs endroits, excéder celui des députés des compagnies et autres classes des habitants, et leur assurait conséquemment la prépondérance dans les élections; qu'il en pouvait résulter un inconvénient, en ce que le concert entre ces députés des artisans, et même quelquefois les brigues et cabales entre eux, pouvaient anéantir le choix le plus éclairé, et donner, contre notre gré, à l'administration, des officiers municipaux mal choisis, même souvent incapables. . . .[2]

[1] Isambert, op. cit., vol. xxii, pp. 434–47. *Édit portant règlement pour celui du mois d'août 1764, dans les villes et bourgs du royaume.*
[2] Ibid., p. 455. *Déclaration interprétative de l'édit de mai 1765 pour l'administration des biens des villes.*

This amendment was not entirely a gratuitous piece of prejudice against the artisan vote. On the contrary, the year's delay between the initial edict and the amendment illustrated some of the difficulties likely to arise from the reform. Bayeux was anxious to be rid of officials whose financial malversations and unfortunate term of office had not gained them general support. On the other hand, the actual means for proceeding to election and details on the number of *échevins* and *notables* for each town were not forthcoming until the second half of 1766. In the meanwhile the magistracy asserted its ancient prerogatives, the carders of wool attempted to take the *adjudicataire du tarif* to court, and town government seems to have broken down for a few months. Faced with chaos, the *subdélégué* sent a list of suitable officials to the *intendant*, who forwarded them to the central government. The king then ordered the installation of these officials for a year until the new regulations were finally worked out.[1]

The elections which took place in 1766 did not produce a *corps de ville* much different in composition from its predecessors. The *maire* was a noble and official of the *bailliage*, three of the *échevins* were officials of the courts, the fourth was a doctor, the *receveur* of the town was a collector of dues for the Marquis de Balleroy and a surgeon was *adjudicataire du tarif*.[2] Nor did this body succeed where its predecessor had failed—in finding a solution to the town's financial problems. This council was called upon to answer for what its predecessors had done in interpreting the tariff. Indeed, they themselves were forced to continue the practice because of their own poverty. By holding back the share of the *don gratuit* destined for the hospitals and alleviation of the poor, they ran into direct conflict with the *bureau de charité*. The unpopularity of this municipal council was due again to its financial difficulties. Nothing fundamental was done to augment the inadequate town funds. The only minor concession was a small sum from the *don gratuit*. The difficulties of these years, however, were to seem small compared with those that appeared when the situation grew really out of hand in the 1770s.

Terray's demand, in 1771, that the towns should once more purchase their municipal offices must be viewed against this background of financial deadlock. No one seemed to know whence money might be obtained. Certainly in Caen and Bayeux no new

---

[1] A.D.C. C1051.   [2] A.D.C. C1079.

acquirers volunteered the sums which were demanded. More-over, a letter of 1786 reveals that not only was the town asked to buy the offices but it was expected to continue the payments on the offices of 1733 which had in effect been paid off by the early 1750s.

The municipal council of 1786 wrote to the *intendant* explaining their dilemma:

cet octroi est celui qui prend son principe dans la création des offices municipaux qui fut faite au mois de novembre 1733. Ceux de ces offices qui ne furent point levés ayant été réunis aux corps des villes et communautés, la ville de Bayeux fut une de celles qui subit cette réunion dont le prix fut, à son égard, fixé à 30.000 livres. Ne pouvant point acquitter cette somme, elle éprouva le sort des autres villes de la généralité qui se trouvaient dans le même cas et qui furent toutes taxées à des droits de sols pour livres imposés sur le tarif de leurs octrois. . . . Tandis que la plupart (des villes) ne payent que 2 ou 4 sols pour livre . . . Bayeux et Condé sur Noireau furent les deux seuls imposés à 8 sols. Cette imposition ne devait d'abord durer que neuf ans, cependant après une première prorogation qui eut lieu en 1755 la perception en fut encore prorogée jusqu'au dernier décembre 1767. Depuis encore . . . la perception en fut prorogée jusqu'au dernier décembre 1777. . . . Ces droits ont produit aujourd'hui plus de 450.000 livres.[1]

Rouen, a city of 80,000 inhabitants, refused in 1771 to pay for Terray's new creation on the grounds that over the years 1722–71 it had paid two and a half million *livres* for municipal offices.[2] It is even more remarkable that Bayeux, whose population ranged between 8,000 and 10,000 over the period 1722–81, had paid over half a million *livres*.

The twenty-one towns of the *généralité* of Caen which Terray instructed to proceed to buy their municipal offices were warned by the minister that if they neglected to do so, a company was waiting which was anxious to buy them up in bulk. Prices were lower in 1771. Whereas in 1722 Caen had paid 349,000 *livres*, now the demand was for 118,000 *livres*. Bayeux in 1772 had been mulcted to the extent of 125,300 *livres*, now only 24,000 *livres* was asked.[3]

[1] A.D.C. C1433.
[2] E. le Parquier, 'Un Essai d'organisation municipale au XVIIIe siècle; le règlement pour la ville de Rouen du 15 juin 1767', *Nouvelle Revue historique de droit français et étranger* (1922), p. 733.
[3] A.D.C. C1433.

The preamble to the edict of 1771 was cloaked in the hypocritical terms that French governments used when they needed money. It was pointed out that the edicts of 1764 and 1765 had produced nothing but disruption in the towns, and, returning to Louis XIV's pretexts, it was declared that only venal officials independent of an electorate could be impartial administrators, and ones who would ultimately have experience because irremovable.[1] At the same time as the circulation of this edict and the note threatening the buying up of unredeemed offices by an outside company, the *intendant* received another letter from the *secrétaire d'état chargé de la province*, Bertin. The latter, intent upon keeping the existing administration working until the regulations for the sale of offices had been settled, declared that the present administrative assemblies should continue to function until that event.[2]

The *intendant*, the energetic Fontette, replied to the *contrôleur général* that the officials actually in place had no wish to continue to exercise their functions and that no one in the towns wished to buy these offices or assume control in towns facing bankruptcy. He wrote to Bertin in early May that instead of expecting to sell the town offices, the government should take some steps to help the towns out of the severe financial difficulties in which they were currently placed.[3]

He was equally firm with Terray and told the *contrôleur général* frankly that the project for the sale of offices had met with very little attention in his *généralité*; that all the towns were in debt and that far from seeming an attractive proposition, to hold municipal office appeared a financial liability of interest to no one.[4] Terray's only rejoinder was that surely the towns would prefer to buy the offices rather than have an outsider purchase them.[5]

The attitude of the towns of the *généralité* towards Terray's new demands was, Fontette stated, largely affected by the attitude of Caen, its largest and most important town. The refusal of Caen to pay determined Terray to put his threats into effect and he hoped, by forcing the hand of the municipal council of Caen, to persuade the rest of the towns to pay.

In October 1772 a certain Sieur Léon presented to the *hôtel de*

[1] Isambert, op. cit., vol. xxii, pp. 539–40.
[2] A.D.C. C1051. Letter of 9 June 1772.
[3] Ibid. Letter of 1 May 1772.
[4] Ibid. Letter of 16 June 1772.
[5] Ibid. Letter of 7 June 1774.

ville in Caen letters providing him with the two venal offices of *receveur* and *contrôleur des deniers de la ville*. Theoretically, the position of *contrôleur* had been created to serve as a check on the financial manipulations of the *receveur*, but the royal government was not concerned with such trivialities provided the offices were sold. Léon was an outsider. He proved that he had no desire to reside in Caen, he merely wished to receive the taxes collected by an agent of his and appropriate them for his own ends. In fact, Fontette claimed, the municipal council had not seen him at one of its meetings since he had assumed office. They sent him municipal bills but he took no notice since he was only concerned with assuming the town's income, not in coping with its expenditure. In such a situation, Fontette stated in a letter to Paris, the town would not pay for the other offices created for the sole purpose of raising money for the state and which might well be put up for sale again within a few years.[1]

By 1774, unable to gather funds for the day to day running of the town, the municipal council took matters into their own hands and tendered their resignations to Bertin. Fontette added a letter justifying their action.[2]

Terray did not conceal his anger. On 16 July 1774 he wrote to Fontette expressing his displeasure and conveying to the *intendant* and the municipal officials that he did not expect administrators to act in this way. At the same time, he was forced to take notice and promised a partial repayment of some of the money appropriated by Léon. Turgot found the ultimate solution; shortly after he became *contrôleur général* he reduced the 118,000 *livres* demanded by Terray to some 20,000. The town paid and was once more freed from debt.

The appearance of the Sieur Léon in Caen decided the town of Bayeux that the evils inherent in non-payment might very well be worse than payment. The town's financial state was critical and the municipal council managed to convince the government of their poverty and to reduce the 24,000 *livres* demanded to 6,000 *livres*. In August 1773 a *lettre patente* was sent from the king to the effect that His Majesty was satisfied that the town had seen fit to suppress the offices created in 1765 and that it might now proceed to new elections of its *maire* and *échevins* 'in the manner that it judged

[1] Yver, op. cit., pp. 20–21.
[2] Ibid., p. 24.

best'.[1] In this phrase lay the origin of the town's difficulties. Nowhere, in fact, was it laid down how the town should proceed to the election of its new officials. Louis, by the very framing of the edict of 1771, had been forced to pour scorn on those of 1764 and 1765. In so doing he had rendered questionable the whole electoral procedure created by these edicts without specifically putting anything in their place.

The town paid the 6,000 *livres* and temporarily continued its old officials in office until elections might be held. But what form these elections should take occasioned universal controversy. The old officials continued in office and when vacancies occurred no steps could be taken to fill them without complete disruption.

Esmangart in 1776 appealed to Bertin for some solution to the problem. He claimed that municipal government at Bayeux had been brought to a standstill because whenever the question of the election of a new official arose half of the community demanded that the new elections should take place according to the principles laid down in 1766, when new officials were elected by deputies from the gilds and communities, and half claimed that this method of election had been nullified by the edict of 1771 and that when a member of the council retired the officials left should choose his replacement.[2]

Esmangart was not exaggerating. It is difficult during the years 1772–6 to find out what business was transacted by the municipal council, which on occasion consisted of no more than one or two men. Bertin, the *secrétaire d'état chargé de la province*, responded to Esmangart's plea for help by sending the copy of a provisional ruling he had already had to send to the towns of Champagne. He suggested that the *intendant* should make the modifications the locality seemed to demand in consultation with the principal inhabitants of the town. Failing the success of this, the king must use his authority to nominate the municipal officials.[3]

On 28 April 1777 a *lettre de cachet*[4] ordered that municipal government at Bayeux should consist of a *maire*, four *échevins*, a *procureur syndic*, a *secrétaire greffier*, and twelve *notables*. The last should be

[1] *Mémoire présenté au roi par les citoyens de la ville de Bayeux* (Bayeux, 1789), p. 15.
[2] A.D.C. C256. Letter from Esmangart to Bertin, 13 December 1776.
[3] Ibid. Letter from Bertin to Esmangart, 23 December 1776.
[4] *Mémoire présenté au roi par les citoyens . . . de Bayeux*, p. 11.

chosen from the same corps as stipulated by the edict of 1766. *Échevins* must have been either former *notables* or former *échevins*. Tenure of office was to be six years but this could be prolonged because experience in government was of value. The king in the meanwhile, to prevent any further controversies, arbitrarily nominated the new officials from a list presented by the *intendant*.

Hence the town of Bayeux, although by 1776 the only town, with Carentan, of the *généralité* of Caen which had in any way paid for the offices declared venal in 1771, now found that it must surrender all freedom to choose the men who should fill them.

The edict of 1771 caused difficulties throughout France. In Rouen a group of wealthy merchants willing to buy offices ousted the magistrates and nobles elected in 1766 who refused to pay.[1] In Lisieux a number of woollen merchants seized control. The upheaval occasioned by Terray's edict in fact created so much anxiety for the central government during the period 1771–6 that succeeding ministers seem to have opted for peace at any price. Indeed, they probably feared change too much. The *lettre de cachet* which settled the government of Bayeux in 1777 expressly emphasized that those given office could remain there without re-election.[2] The men placed on the municipal council in 1776 left office only when outside pressure of work occasioned resignation. Then the other members of the council co-opted one of their friends into the vacant office. The council remained the prerogative of the moderately wealthy urban *noblesse* and the personnel of the courts. Commercial interests were ignored. The three *notables artisans* were never changed and in actual fact though technically qualifying for artisan status they were wealthy manufacturers.

This self-perpetuated body occasioned keen resentment even from its colleagues in the law-courts and from the merchants. In 1789 a memorandum was presented to the king appealing for the revocation of the *lettre de cachet*.[3] It also created many problems for those actually in office. In 1788 when opposition to the payment of the *corvée* tax caused a general revolt at Bayeux the *maire* claimed that it was, to his certain knowledge, stirred up by the personnel of the preceding administration.[4]

[1] Le Parquier, op. cit., p. 733.
[2] *Mémoire présenté au roi par les citoyens . . . de Bayeux*, p. 6.
[3] Ibid.
[4] A.D.C. C8262.

By the end of the *ancien régime* local government had undergone a marked change and not one of the component elements
was left with even an approximation of its original power. The
multiplication of court personnel and the continuation of ob-
solete courts had brought profit to the central government only
at the cost of preventing the effective working of the judicial
system. The enforced purchase of municipal offices for the purposes of the royal treasury was at the price of disrupting town
government, jeopardizing town funds, and destroying the power
of the municipal bodies to act for the good of the community.
The independent body of 1729 which had been sent from Bayeux
to England in search of grain was hard pressed in 1786 to raise
1,000 *livres* to help in employing its poor.[1] More than this,
the successive changes in municipal government had made each
new municipal council in turn a source of discord. The presence of
men who were not officials of the courts in municipal office was a
constant reminder to the judges of the *bailliage* of their declining
power. In public ceremonies at the cathedral they attempted to
assert their precedence over the *corps de ville*.[2] In Rouen, after 1771,
the law-court officials were in conflict with the merchants who
had purchased municipal office.[3] The same happened at Lisieux.
At Bayeux a knot of law-court officials retained and jealously
preserved control, hedged in by financial chaos and opposition
from preceding administrations.

The increasing impotence of the municipal councils and of the
bailliage courts made the *subdélégué* an even more important agent
and gave him a power which Colbert, who mistrusted *subdélégués*
because they were local and therefore partial men, would have
deemed unwise. Strangely enough, and it is an interesting comment
on the power of the *subdélégué*, the position was never rendered
venal after 1712.[4] At some stages in the century he was the sole
effective administrative agent in Bayeux and the sole means by
which the orders of the central government were conveyed
to the town. One man, however, could not do everything.
At the end of the old régime the need to undertake a thorough
reform of the French administrative system, to redistribute

[1] A.D.C. C3421. Letter from the municipal council of Bayeux to the *intendant* in
Paris, 7 March 1786.
[2] Laffetay, op. cit., pp. 72–73.
[3] Bouloiseau, op. cit., vol. i, pp. lxxiv–lxxv.
[4] Marion, *Dictionnaire . . .*, pp. 519–20.

work, to define duties, and to make adequate provision for municipal finance was recognized to be of paramount importance, and both the town *cahier* and that of the *bailliage* urged it upon the government.[1]

---

[1] E. Anquétil, *Cahier du Tiers État de la ville de Bayeux* (Bayeux, 1886).

VII

THE ELECTIONS OF 1789

THE elections held in 1789 for the deputies to go to the Estates General were to reveal the extent to which society at Bayeux was divided. A clergy rent by internal conflict between the rich who were powerful and often virtually parasitic and the poor who were powerless and often grossly overworked; a *noblesse* with ancient and wealthy elements, others of moderate means occupied in much the same functions as the officials of the courts and the professional sections of the *bourgeoisie*, together with a fraction who were almost destitute: these were temporarily bundled together for electoral purposes under the respective headings of clergy and *noblesse*. The third estate was composed of elements no less disparate. It comprehended alike the official class with its dwindling power, the few wealthy merchants, shopkeepers varying in prosperity, a large artisan section which was for the most part poor, and the rural vote—itself divided by economic interests and severed from the town which exploited it. It was from the outset apparent that within these traditional sections momentarily grouped together lay elements with irreconcilable differences, and their conflicting attitudes were to be instrumental in the destruction of the old social order.

Bayeux was the centre of a secondary *bailliage* annexed to the *grand bailliage* of Caen and as such was the scene only of the preliminary elections of the third estate. The gilds and professional *collèges* first met to choose representatives to go to a town assembly at which they and the *corps de ville* elected delegates for the *bailliage* assembly. At this meeting, also held in the town, under the presidency of the *bailliage* officials, the town and parish representatives decided which of their number to send to Caen to meet in concert with the representatives of the *grand bailliage* of Caen and the secondary ones of Falaise, Thorigny, and Vire and make the final choice of whom to send to Paris. The clergy went directly to the assembly of their order in Caen, as did the *noblesse*.

The elections for the town and parish representatives, and ultimately for those of the *bailliage*, were so arranged that they played directly and clearly into the hands of the official groups. These succeeded in securing a representation out of any proportion to their numbers or their wealth and this, in the *généralité* of Caen, assured their ultimate victory in the final elections for the Estates General. The clue to their success lies largely in the rules governing electoral procedure laid down in the *déclaration* of 24 January 1789 : these accorded the gilds only one representative for every hundred members or less at the town assembly, whilst they allowed every professional *collège, corporation d'arts libéraux*, or other professional body, twice that number. The government obviously intended to give all possible scope and weight to the vote of the official groups and professional classes—perhaps out of fear that if the impoverished artisan class were to monopolize by weight of numbers the urban elections representatives hostile to the government might be elected. Whatever the reason, the power of the artisan vote was severely limited and the victory of the men of the courts at Bayeux made easy by the rubric. Courts like the *élection, grenier à sel*, and *eaux et forêts* at Bayeux, although officially re-established, had never been reopened after their abolition in 1788; nevertheless they were fully authorized to elect two representatives each, to send to the town assembly, and were duly instructed to do so by the *lieutenant général du bailliage*, M. Jean Antoine Eudes, Sieur de la Jumellière, when he ordered the gilds and professional *collèges* to proceed to the election of their deputies on 17 February.

Ten days later, the results of these primary elections had all been gathered in and preparations could be made for the calling of the town assembly. They were as follows :[1]

	No. of electors	No. of representatives
Officials of the *amirauté*	3	2
Officials of the *élection*	4	2
Officials of the *grenier à sel*	2	2
Avocats au bailliage	35	2
Procureurs du bailliage	9	2
Procureurs en élection	4	2
	57	12

[1] 'Études sur la Révolution à Bayeux', *Mémoires de la Société des Sciences, Arts et Belles Lettres de Bayeux*, xx (1945), pp. 38 ff.

COLLÈGES

Doctors	4	2
Surgeons	12	2
Bourgeois non corporés[1]	23	2
Drapers	30	2
Grocers	23	2
Printers	3	2
Painters	12	2
Clockmakers	8	2
	115	16

GILDS

Barbers and wigmakers	27	1
Tanners	17	1
Carpet-makers	3	1
Bakers	46	1
Glass-makers	8	1
Saddlers	7	1
Hotel and restaurant-keepers	16	1
Hatters	16	1
Carpenters	14	1
Egg and butter vendors	8	1
Plumbers	12	1
Café owners	7	1
Joiners	41	1
Weavers	50	1
Stocking-makers	22	1
Tailors	25	1
Dressmakers (male)	14	1
Cutlers	3	1
Potters	6	1
Butchers	16	1
Locksmiths	8	1
Carders of wool	25	1
Masons	17	1
Tinsmiths	3	1
Roof-builders	10	1
Fruiterers	4	1
Trouser-makers	4	1
	429	27

The deputies elected by the gilds and *collèges* then proceeded to the town assembly, which was composed of themselves and the *corps de ville* and presided over by the mayor. The fact that the venal municipal council was given so much power at the municipal

[1] The *bourgeois non corporés* were retired court officials, professional men, collectors of seigneurial dues, and in a few cases those who lived on their *rentes*. A.M.B. AA. *État des Corporations*.

elections aroused much criticism in the town; and some twenty *avocats* and officials went so far as to address an urgent petition to the king, urging him to revoke the *lettre de cachet* of 1771 which arbitrarily conferred office upon the existing members of the municipal council, on the grounds that unless this was done the town could not regard itself as being truly represented at the Estates General since those in control of the elections were not of its choosing.[1] The petition went unheeded and the suggestion that new municipal elections should take place was hardly practical at this late date. Two members of the *corps de ville* were in fact amongst the six men elected to represent the third estate of the town at the forthcoming *bailliage* assembly: the mayor, de la Londe, and the *procureur syndic*, Delauney, who was also an *avocat au bailliage*. The others were Tanqueray, an *avocat* of some note in the town, Delleville, *lieutenant général de l'amirauté*, Le Fort, *bourgeois vivant de son bien*, and Le Boucher, *doyen des apothicaires* who, though theoretically a representative of the gilds, was a former *échevin* and exploiter of the *seigneuries* of Surrain and St. Laurent sur Mer.[2] The artisan had completely failed to obtain any representation at the *bailliage* assembly and the same held true in the other nearby towns of the *généralités* of Caen and Coutances.

Within a week the town representatives had joined those of the rural parishes at the *bailliage* assembly. The elections held in the country parishes had afforded another chance to the officials of the *bailliage* court and the *avocats* to secure election as representatives at the *bailliage* assembly, for the declaration of 24 January stipulated that parish assemblies were to be held under the presidency of the seigneurial judge or *bailli* aided by the parish *syndic*—positions often held by *avocats au bailliage*. These, even if not resident in the parish, might be elected as parish representatives. Deeming their chances of election better in the parishes than the town, the officials of the *bailliage* court of Bayeux did not assemble as a body to elect representatives to the town assembly. Nor did twenty-eight of the sixty-three *avocats* inscribed on the court register of Bayeux. Instead, they went to the parish elections where their victory was from the outset assured because, like the *corps de ville* in the towns, they directed electoral procedure and were the outstanding figures at the village assemblies.

[1] *Mémoire présenté au roi par les citoyens . . . de Bayeux*, p. 8.
[2] Anquétil, *Cahier du Tiers État de Bayeux*, p. 55.

Sixteen of these twenty-eight *avocats* were chosen to go to the *bailliage* assembly, which was presided over by the *lieutenant général* of the *bailliage* and the *procureur du roi* of the same court. The numerical strength of the *avocats* and officials of the courts was such that at least sixteen of the eighty-one representatives sent to the final assembly at Caen were *avocats* or high officials of the *bailliage* of Bayeux.[1] They were by far the largest cohesive interest represented at the gathering—a cluster of men who knew each other far better than the isolated, large landowners chosen by the other rural parishes.

One Bayeusain, Delauney, was chosen at the assembly held in Caen to go to Paris; the other five delegates included three officials of the courts, one *négociant*, and a *cultivateur*.[2] The men of the courts had, at Bayeux, won the first battle for power virtually uncontested.

As in the case of the third estate, so in that of the clergy a group succeeded in assuming control. The electoral regulations of 24 January 1789 stipulated that chapters of secular clergy might only send one representative for every ten members to the *bailliage* assembly, whilst it authorized the presence of every ecclesiastic holding a benefice with cure of souls and furthermore allowed unbeneficed clergy to assemble under the directions of the *curé* of the parish in which they were domiciled and elect one deputy for every twenty or less men present. The first provision struck directly at the power of the cathedral chapter of Bayeux, for it meant that the forty-nine canons could only send some five delegates to the *bailliage* assembly. They realized immediately how little voice this would give them at the meeting of the clergy of the *bailliage* to be held in Caen on 16 March and wrote in haste to Paris:

D'après le règlement il est possible que nul évêque ne soit député aux États Généraux. Il est à craindre que le nombre prodigieux de jeunes ecclésiastiques sans bénéfices, appelés aux assemblées électorales, ne puisse guère accroître la masse des lumières de l'assemblée particulière de l'ordre du clergé et qu'il n'ajoute infiniment à l'embarras de ses délibérations. Leur nombre est tel, surtout en Normandie, que par cet avantage seul, ils pourraient concentrer en eux-mêmes la députation

[1] Hippeau, *Le Gouvernement de Normandie . . .*, vol. iv, p. 251.
[2] A. Brette, *Les Constituants* (Paris, 1897), p. 98.

de l'ordre du clergé aux États Généraux. Du moins, ils influeront très puissamment, s'ils le veulent, sur le choix des députés.[1]

The bishop of Bayeux was no less disquieted. He proclaimed his belief that there existed 'deux ordres distincts dans le clergé, l'un qui gouvernait, et l'autre qui était gouverné' and he considered the regulation of 24 January to be grossly *inconstitutionnel* in that it permitted 'aux vicaires et curés aigris de humilier leur évêque'.[2] Both bishop and chapter had grounds for concern. The individual *cahiers* drawn up by the priests of the parishes of Bayeux remain as witness to their bitter hostility to the higher clergy and their anxiety for change. Moreover, there is every indication that before the *bailliage* assembly of 16 March, the parish priests of the diocese of Bayeux had already determined upon the course they intended to take. This consisted mainly in the exclusion of the higher clergy from the deputation which would be sent to Paris. As early as 6 March, ten days before the opening assembly, the Abbé Soulavie, *curé* de Septvents and one of the main agitators of the lower clergy, wrote to Necker: 'L'ordre du clergé ne veut que des curés pour députés et leur choix paraît déterminé.'[3] Again four days after the opening session he wrote: 'L'assemblée élira trois curés pour Paris; et depuis plusieurs mois le parti qui était pris avait nommé trois à quatre sujets qui réunissent les voix.'[4]

News of this intended seizure of power undoubtedly reached the bishop of Bayeux, for on 14 March Le Tual, *curé* of St.Vigor le Grand, wrote a complaining letter to Necker in which he said that the bishop had forbidden him to leave his parish for elections since he had no substitute to attend to his spiritual duties in his absence. Le Tual had no doubt of the bishop's motives: 'Le but de la conduite de Monseigneur est d'empêcher que ce ne soit trois curés d'être députés aux États de Versailles, et d'y en faire parvenir selon son vœu.'[5] He went on to state that he had, notwithstanding the bishop's injunctions, every intention of going to Caen and he urged others to do the same in open opposition to their superior.

The victory of the lower clergy was apparent from the very

[1] A.N. B. 27. 1. Cited by F. Mourlot, *La Fin de l'ancien régime et les débuts de la Révolution dans la généralité de Caen* (1911), p. 187.

[2] Ibid., p. 188.

[3] A. Brette, 'Les Élections du clergé de Caen en 1789. Bulletins de l'Abbé Soulavie, curé de Septvents', *La Révolution Française* (1894), p. 162.

[4] Ibid., p. 166.

[5] Mourlot, *La Fin de l'ancien régime* . . . .p. 191.

opening of the assembly, but it was equally plain that the canons would not allow them to triumph so openly without registering some protest. On 22 March 1789, six days after the opening of the meeting, Soulavie wrote to Necker:

... les députés du chapitre ont décidé que la formation de l'assemblée du clergé était illégitime et se sont retirés ... l'évêque y a adhéré et a quitté l'assemblée sur le champ. Un vieillard moribond s'est saisi du fauteuil et s'est nommé président, on l'a reconnu: suite des élections des rédacteurs. . . .[1]

The next day he wrote another letter to Necker with yet more details:

Les moines, les chapitres, les abbés ayant adhérés aux oppositions du chapitre, ce chapitre a enfin montré ses pouvoirs et capitulairement assemblé ... avait déclaré ... que l'assemblée ... était illégale, non constitutionnelle.[2]

In a mere week, the important ecclesiastics had withdrawn from the assembly, declaring plainly that they considered the whole gathering illegal and that they were in full accord with the actions of the chapter of Bayeux. Their conduct precipitated an outburst of antipathy towards the higher clergy from the townsfolk. Soulavie faithfully described the situation to Necker: 'Les cinq lettres de pouvoir du chapitre sont un tissu de mauvaise foi, d'ignorance, de sottises contre les ministres et le roi, toute la ville en est indignée.'[3] Soulavie's account of the events at the assembly during the next few days indicated the confusion caused by the withdrawal of the bishop and the almost unexpected ease of the victory of the lower clergy. He was rapidly disillusioned by the conduct of the meeting and reported despairingly to Necker:

L'Asemblée est des plus orageuses. Six à sept ecclésiastiques pour quatre ou cinq hommes de génie et intriguants avec des voix assurées, promises fermes, avec un évêque tiré de son chapitre et une commission pour dresser les cahiers que j'avais d'abord à moi en pluralité et qui se divise ne me laissant que deux honnêtes gens seuls qui me restent pour soutenir mes quatre fondements; grand Dieu, quel ouvrage avez-vous entrepris, incomparable Necker, et comment pouvez-vous soutenir cet édifice? Ce me semble impossible à réparer, les bases étant aussi pourries.[4]

More than this is not known. Apparently the priests, united in

---

[1] Brette, 'Les Élections du clergé . . .', op. cit., p. 166.   [2] Ibid.
[3] Ibid., p. 168.   [4] Ibid.

their anxiety for reform and improvement of their circumstances, were divided as to the method by which this should be achieved. Some perhaps felt themselves more deeply bound in deference to the authority of the bishop than others and watched the trend of events with troubled eyes. Certainly of all those elections held in the area those for the clergy were the most bitter and the most decisive.

The electoral process of the *noblesse* was subject to the simplest procedure of all. The *noblesse* of the *bailliage* of Caen and its four secondary ones were summoned by personal letter to the elections in Caen. The poorest town nobles of Bayeux did not trouble to take the journey and although widows were allowed to send someone to represent them, those of Bayeux did not take advantage of this. Moreover, the silence of the urban *noblesse* of moderate as opposed to great wealth is striking. Many did not attend but opted to try their chances elsewhere or as they were obliged by the ruling of 24 January. The judges of the *bailliage* of Bayeux, for example, although noble, preferred to try their fortune as presidents of the rural assemblies of the third estate.[1] De la Jumellière, as *lieutenant général du bailliage*, though noble, did not appear at the noble assembly, but had to preside over that of the third estate of the *bailliage secondaire* of Bayeux. So had Genas, the noble *procureur du roi*, though his father, the *subdélégué*, perhaps estimating his chances at an assembly of the third estate as indeed slender, was present at the assembly of the *noblesse*. Again, de la Londe, noble and *maire* of Bayeux, presided over the town assembly and did not appear at that of the nobles. Indeed, in the main, the petty *noblesse de cloche* affiliated themselves not with their own order, but with their colleagues of the courts.

Their absence from the assembly of nobles prevented their serving as an intermediary body between the nobles of great wealth and distinction and the poor parish *seigneurs* who found themselves differing on one essential principle, whether the *noblesse* should renounce its pecuniary privileges. On 6 March, ten days before the assembly opened, Soulavie wrote to Necker: 'La noblesse même, malgré quelques factieux, va, dans l'assem-blée du bailliage, prononcer sa renonciation solennelle à tout privilège pécuniaire.'[2] The 'quelques factieux' of Soulavie's letter

---

[1] Hippeau, *Le Gouvernement de Normandie* . . ., vol. iv, p. 251.
[2] Brette, 'Les Élections du clergé . . .', op. cit., p. 164.

were more numerous and more adamant in their opposition to any renunciation of their privileges than the *abbé* suggests. The question had been hotly debated from October 1788 to the opening of the assembly in March. Indication of this appeared in correspondence between one noble and another and the Comte d'Osseville went so far as to circulate a pamphlet to the local *noblesse* stressing the desirability of sacrifice on the part of the nobles if they were to forestall opposition from the third estate. But nothing d'Osseville could say could persuade the poorer *noblesse* of the rural parishes of the necessity for such a step. The latter insisted that their status demanded special privileges to mark them off from the rest of the population and held that their exemption from the *taille* was the best expression of this. For them tax exemption was a jealously guarded privilege and indeed, in some cases, seemed a necessity, but they did not advance their argument in such open terms. Instead they gave their support to a plea written by the Sieur de Touchet and widely circulated:

Quoique tous les hommes soient de même condition dans les principes de la nature, il doit y avoir néanmoins parmi eux certains avantages particuliers qui servent à les distinguer dans la société civile. Cette demande n'est point dictée par la passion, ni par esprit de parti, mais par une élévation d'âme, une pureté de mœurs, une délicatesse de sentiments qui forment l'essence de la vraie noblesse.[1]

A few days before the opening of the assembly, the Duc de Coigny, who had the task of presiding, wrote to the Duc d'Harcourt that it was clearly visible that the *noblesse* were bitterly divided.[2] The assembly's debates were to justify his worst fears.

The poorer nobles needed persuasion and careful handling if the wealthy liberal nobles who were prepared to surrender the most criticized of the prerogatives of their order were to achieve their purpose. Only after protracted debate and days of deadlock did a speech from the Baron de Wimpffen, recently returned from the battlefields of America, serve to lend some cohesion to a disturbed assembly. It was a speech designed primarily to coax the poorer nobles to renounce their pecuniary privileges by promising new careers which they might follow, without fear of *dérogeance*,

[1] *Discours adressé à la noblesse du bailliage de Caen par M. de Touchet, 16 mars 1789.* Cited by Mourlot, *La fin de l'ancien régime . . .*, p. 193.
[2] *Archives du Château d'Harcourt. Liasse 339.* Cited by Mourlot, op. cit., p. 196.

and indicating new sources of economic benefit which might be exploited without loss of status.

Le maintien du gouvernement exige l'existence d'un ordre intermédiaire entre le peuple et le souverain: et la nature des choses exige que cette démarcation soit sensible; mais pour qu'elle le soit, l'ordre qui la constitue doit être un objet de respect et d'émulation . . . Si nous supposons qu'un décret national ouvre de nouvelles carrières à la noblesse . . . nous trouvons qu'il ne résulterait qu'une plus grande confusion dans les ordres tant que rien ne distinguerait le gentilhomme du plébéien et que très peu de gentilshommes profiteraient de cette invitation par cela seul qu'ils craindraient d'être inconnus dans les professions.[1]

De Wimpffen suggested, to obviate this result, the inauguration of the custom of each noble's wearing a small, gold medal to mark him out from the rest of the population. The speech continued at great length to accentuate the benefits which would result from such a practice. Any doctor or retail trader with such a badge of distinction would immediately be recognized, not as a doctor or as a retail trader, but as a noble. He would immediately, however low his profession, be singled out from the rest of the population.

Slight as the speech would seem to have been, it succeeded in appealing to the lesser nobles, who were above all intent upon the preservation of their existing privileges and feared confusion with the third estate. Guaranteed in this way by de Wimpffen that the group of nobles anxious to surrender some of the privileges of the *noblesse* were firmly intent upon retaining and indeed enhancing the dignity of their order, the poorer nobles withdrew their opposition. Perhaps for the petty *noblesse* absence from the tax rolls was all that remained to them as a reminder of past social distinction. Certainly after de Wimpffen's reassurances the meeting immediately assumed a quieter tone and the elections proceeded apace. The choice of de Wimpffen, the Duc de Coigny, *grand bailli* of Caen, and the Comte Louis de Vassy, who were elected as delegates, represented the triumph of the wealthy provincial nobility with more liberal ideas,[2] but it was only the narrowest victory.

---

[1] Hippeau, *Le Gouvernement de Normandie* . . ., vol. iv, pp. 231–5.

[2] De Wimpffen's fame was already widespread. De Vassy belonged to one of the oldest families of the area. The Duc de Coigny was *pair de France, chevalier des ordres*

The assemblies of 1789 met for more than purely electoral purposes. Each of the assemblies legally constituted as electoral bodies had the right to draw up *cahiers de doléances*. In addition, priests and ecclesiastics appearing in person at the assembly of the clergy might present their own individual *cahiers*. Since each of the electoral assemblies at Bayeux was directed or monopolized by a particular group, most of the *cahiers* present a case for one or another interest. They provide some interesting comments on the society of the town under the old régime for they reflect the differences, patent self-interest, petty snobberies, or rank hostility which motivated many elements in the population of this small country town. Obviously all of them were concerned with the burning issues of the day : they demanded constitutional reforms such as the regular calling of the Estates General; they called for the taxation of every individual according to his means and not according to his order, and even the *noblesse* were finally prepared to sacrifice their privileged position to this end. All the *cahiers* condemned existing methods of indirect taxation and the evils involved in its collection. Apart from the recognition of general principles of administrative and constitutional reforms, however, the *cahiers* of the town, the clergy, and the *noblesse* are chiefly characterized by articles concerned with the special problems of their compilers and indicate the sort of changes they hoped the Estates General would make. The gild *cahiers* are disappointing for they are brief and do not go beyond the commonplace administrative and constitutional reforms, except for a general condemnation of the free-trade treaty made with England in 1786, which they claimed was the ruin of the town manufacturers. This grievance did not appear in the town *cahier*, for the lawyers and officials responsible for its compilation[1] were fully preoccupied with lengthy projects for the reorganization of the judicial system, careful plans for granting full compensation for any abolition of seigneurial rights or privileges, or of superfluous offices, and with a bitter onslaught upon the wealth of the church.

In the lengthy chapter on the reform of justice, the compilers of

du roi, lieutenant général de ses armées, chef de division des troupes de la province de Normandie, gouverneur de la ville et du château de Caen. Brette, *Les Constituants* . . ., pp. 97–8.

[1] Jean Tanqueray, *avocat au bailliage*, was the main compiler of the town *cahier* and responsible for framing the clauses. He was aided by a further fourteen men, nine of whom were officials of the courts, four wholesale merchants, and the rest of whom lived on income from property. Anquétil, *Cahier du Tiers État de Bayeux*, p. 19.

the *cahier* of Bayeux envisaged a new system whereby tribunals of
first instance would be set up, with secondary courts of appeal.
To this end they were prepared to sacrifice seigneurial jurisdictions, but with the following reservations:

Que pour améliorer l'administration de la justice qu'il vaut mieux
trouver bonne à quelque distance que d'avoir mauvaise et imparfaite
sur les lieux, toutes les hautes justices, tant seigneuriales que domaniales,
d'ancienne ou nouvelle création, ressortissantes médiatement ou
immédiatement aux cours de parlement, soient supprimées, sans
préjudice du droit des seigneurs haut-justiciers relativement à la
quotité des arrérages exigibles de leurs rentes et cens, et leur compétence
et ressort remis au bailliage ou sièges royaux dont ils ont été détachés.[1]

It was proposed to detach the *bailliage* courts, which were to be
tribunals of first instance, from *présidial* courts in those places
where the central government, in an attempt to reduce the delays
of the judicial system, had amalgamated the two courts. The
bailliage court would thus be buttressed on two sides, from below
by the abolition of the seigneurial jurisdictions and from above by
the separation of its powers from the *présidial* courts. *Parlement*
was to be preserved, but the chief magistrates of the court were
no longer to be able to buy their positions; they were to be chosen
from those who had proved themselves most proficient in their
duties in the courts. Full compensation was proposed to those
who owned offices in the seigneurial courts—the means by which
the *avocats*, bailiffs, and notaries of the town had increased their
income from the law and whose loss would be felt.

The church was singled out for the bitterest criticism of all.
Annates, the right of *déport*, plurality of benefices, the poverty of
parish priests, extraneous religious houses, the possession by
wealthy ecclesiastics of secular titles, over-rich prelates, ecclesiastical jurisdiction, the tithe, were each separately treated and the
demand made for the abolition of each separate abuse. The third
estate of Bayeux expressed the wish for a church without land or
privileges, whose only officials would be those fully engaged in
diocesan or parochial administration.

The *cahier* of the third estate of the town of Bayeux contained
nothing which, if carried out, would not be to the advantage of
this group of lawyers, officials, and professional men concerned in
its compilation, anxious above all for administrative reform which

[1] Anquétil, *Cahier du Tiers État de Bayeux*, pp. 38–39.

would enhance their own power and increase business in their dwindling courts.

The individual *cahiers* drawn up by the priests of the parishes of Bayeux remain as evidence of the hostility felt by the poorer clergy to their rich and powerful superiors. The priests of St. Sauveur, St. Martin, St. Malo, St. Jean, and St. Exupère together requested:

> Qu'il n'y ait plus en France de religieux, chanoines réguliers ou séculiers, abbés ou prieurs et tous autres ecclésiastiques, excepté MM. les archévêques ou évêques, qui puissent se dire seigneurs, marquis, comtes et barons; mais que toutes les seigneuries attachées aux terres de leurs bénéfices soient vendues, et le prix employé à acquitter les dettes du clergé, et que toutes les nominations aux cures dépendantes des susdits bénéficiers soient dévolues aux ordinaires.
>
> Qu'il n'y ait plus en France que deux ordres religieux: l'un se dévouera à l'éducation de la jeunesse et l'autre embrassera la réforme de la Trappe . . . et qu'on diminue la longueur des offices, et qu'on y substitue le travail des mains, et que la clôture la plus exacte soit observée.[1]

They protested against the mere pittances which constituted their income and their need to collect the *casuel*. They deprecated the practice of *déport*. They urged the desirability of a pension scheme for retired ecclesiastics and above all, stressed their need for a decent personal income of something between 1,200 to 2,000 *livres* per year, an assertion which was echoed in the composite *cahier* of the clergy of the *grand bailliage*. They did not, however, envisage any payment of ecclesiastics which was not dependent on the tithe and demanded, on this issue, that the royal declaration of 1786 be put into effect and the *arrêt* of the *parlement* of Rouen nullified. If the clergy of the diocese of Bayeux had had their way, the income of the Gallican church would have been distributed more evenly amongst all churchmen: they did not envisage any surrender or sacrifice of the wealth of the church. The poor clergy, no less than the rich, were anxious to preserve the constitutional privileges of the church in deliberating at the Estates General as a separate order. Their grievances, expressed in the *cahier*, are in fact those of the poor members against the rich of the same body, and the criticism and reforms involved are of a purely economic nature.

[1] Hippeau, *Le Gouvernement de Normandie* . . ., vol. iv, pp. 178–80.

Similarly, the *cahier* of the *noblesse* is a partial commentary upon the divided nature of the noble order of the area. The problem, from the very start of the assembly, was how to bind together men who, ostensibly, had very little in common beyond a few pecuniary and honorific privileges, the more especially when a section of those present at the assembly were prepared to sacrifice the first of these. In its search for a common bond among men whose wealth and interests were so widely different, the *cahier* of the *noblesse* of Bayeux became remarkable for a series of clauses bent upon opening occupations and opportunities to the *noblesse* whilst preserving it as a closed caste.

> Article 4. Les États Généraux détermineront, par un décret national, les professions et arts libéraux auxquels la noblesse pourra se livrer sans dérogeance.
>
> 5. Les députés solliciteront des bontés du Roi la suppression de toutes les charges qui donnent la noblesse, afin qu'elle ne soit à l'avenir, que le prix du mérite et des vertus.
>
> 14. La jeune noblesse prolongera son éducation jusqu'à dix-huit ans et n'aura accès dans le militaire qu'à cet âge; mais alors la croix de St. Louis serait, sous le bon plaisir de Sa Majesté, le prix de vingt années de service.
>
> 18. Il est encore expressément recommandé à nos députés de solliciter des bontés de Sa Majesté une marque distinctive pour la noblesse.[1]
>
> 22. Il sera également formé des chapitres nobles, des écoles militaires et autres pour les enfants de la noblesse la moins fortunée.

The *cahier* went on to suggest that all hereditary offices of any importance should be abolished and from henceforward these offices should be awarded to the *noblesse* alone, on merit. The whole document was so constructed as to weld together the noble order into an indivisible whole and to try to illustrate that noble status was sufficient to join rich and poor in spite of the utter lack of homogeneity illustrated in the assembly. Agreement on its clauses was only reached with much difficulty.

The elections for deputies to go to the Estates General, and the ensuing drawing up of the *cahiers*, were the first round in a battle for power which began in early 1789. They illustrated on a large scale many of the cracks in the social pattern. The results of the issue were clear cut and there could be no doubt, in the Normandy

---

[1] *Cahier de la noblesse du grand bailliage de Caen et ses quatre bailliages secondaires* . . . *Archives Parlementaires* . . ., vol. ii, pp. 490–1.

Bessin, who were the victors—a poor clergy, anxious to redress inequalities but preserve the power of their order; a *noblesse* ready for some reform but intent upon the preservation of the privileges of their caste in matters of government; and the professional groups of the *bourgeoisie*, the lawyers and officials of the courts or municipal councils, whose administrative power and scope for activity had gradually narrowed during the eighteenth century and who were anxious to assert themselves. The artisan, the merchant groups, the small tradesmen, the dweller in the rural parishes, had each played a minor role and had been forced to retire. So had the bishop and chapter, who had disassociated themselves from the assembly of their order, and the little *seigneur* of the isolated communes, who was unwilling to sacrifice any of the privileges of his caste.

In April the deputies left Normandy with a set of *cahiers* which included the grievances, hopes, and aspirations of the interests which had won the elections. By 4 May 1789 they were in Versailles for the opening of the Estates General.

PART TWO

Bayeux during the Revolution

I

ADMINISTRATIVE REORGANIZATION
1789–1790

THE summer of 1789 was perhaps the hardest Bayeux had experienced since the early 1740s or 1770–1. Its severity was felt the more because only four years previously the town had undergone a severe shortage and because the crisis took place against a background of political ferment. The pattern of shortage was a familiar one. The price of bread in the market began to mount rapidly after September 1788. By July 1789 it had reached peaks unprecedented since the crisis of 1770. The obvious scantiness of the harvest led anyone who had grain to hold on to it. The producers in the country refused to surrender to the town what they feared they might need for their own consumption. At best they could only be persuaded to sell at the highest prices. The consequences were not unfamiliar. Shortage always hit the small manufacturers and shopkeepers, especially if the crisis was in any way prolonged. In these conditions, to the perpetually indigent were added many of the day-labourers of the town and country and the artisans who in normal times could just manage to subsist. It was estimated in the early summer of 1789 that some 2,000 of the inhabitants of Bayeux were in need of some sort of relief— a fifth of the entire population. No precise figures exist on the numbers of beggars and needy in the rural parishes, but again the traditional pattern manifested itself. The same number of hands had not been needed to reap the harvest of 1788. Winter employment diminished because no one took on extra men during a time of hardship. When clothing and furniture had been sold to realize what little they would in a time of stress, and no other source of income was forthcoming, the only recourse was for the unemployed to take to the roads and to disperse themselves in other parishes in search of work, and when that did not materialize to beg. The doors of the cathedral of Bayeux were besieged by the indigent seeking alms.

The spring and summer of 1789 were marked in Bayeux and the

surrounding villages by manifestations of public discontent only too familiar to administrators of the old régime. The townspeople attributed their hardship not to the forces of nature, but to the municipal and government officials, whom they singled out as agents of a corn monopoly aimed at keeping prices high. A hungry crowd sought out the *procureur du roi* of the *bailliage*, Genas Duhomme, demanding that he take action. In early July carts passing through the town carrying grain at the dead of night, the only time they dared travel because of the hazard of pillaging, were held up by an angry mob, who claimed that they had discovered those responsible for sending grain away from the area so that they could keep up the price and starve the inhabitants of the city. The *commissaire de police* was forced to distribute the grain from one of the carts in order to restore order and the only loss of life was that of the horse leading the first cart. The whole populace, Genas complained, was thoroughly persuaded that there was no real shortage and nothing could convince them to the contrary.[1] The police registers give indications that similar outbursts against deprivation were taking place in the neighbouring villages too. Supplies on the way to the town were pillaged: local officials were surrounded by groups of hungry women demanding food for their children at what they considered a fair price and every market was a scene of potential disorder.

Matters were made worse by the virtual vacuum of power occasioned by the breakdown of provincial and local government which followed the calling of the Estates General. In 1709 and 1725 the municipal government had taken the initiative and had dispatched representatives to buy corn in Le Havre or Great Britain from municipal funds. More commonly, the council had attempted to fix prices and the *intendant* at Caen had done what he could to alleviate the situation. But in the summer of 1789 even these slight aids were lacking. The estimates of the *Assemblée Provinciale* failed to materialize and the very continuance of this body seemed unlikely. The *intendant* in Caen had lost control of the finances of the *généralité* and was relatively impotent. Indeed, in Caen he was regarded as the most important agent of the corn monopoly.[2] The municipal council had no means at their disposal to help in any way.

---

[1] A.D.C. C2643.   [2] Mourlot, *La Fin de l'ancien régime* . . ., p. 175.

The crisis reached a climax in early July. Even during a normal year in the north of France the months between April and September tended to be the most difficult, because the old stocks of corn were approaching exhaustion and the new crop had not yet reached fruition. For any proprietor in time of shortage these months were especially anxious because the hungry people of the countryside, if sufficiently hard pressed, might attempt to cut down the crops before they ripened. Already in June there were isolated instances of this in the villages around Bayeux. For everybody these were the months of highest costs. By July the cost of bread exceeded the sum of 5 *sols* a pound in the *élection* of Bayeux. In the nearby Pays de Caux, it stood at six.[1] The sporadic bread riots which had begun in the villages now became more frequent. They were directed not only against the convoys, and against government officials, but also against the privileged, against the owners of seigneurial rights, and anyone who had taken a cut of the harvest or was suspected of having grain.

It was against this background that Bayeux received news of the political changes at Versailles and, on 17 July, of the fall of the Bastille. The town showed no immediate reaction but the countryside was far from quiet. As shortage grew worse the fears of the proprietors that the next harvest might be prematurely cut down were enhanced. The net result was an atmosphere as tense in the Bessin as elsewhere. Fear bred panic. News from Paris was always late and the political deadlock of June and early July had given rise to all sorts of suspicions. Rumours were disproportionately exaggerated and distorted beyond recognition and prominent amongst these rumours was that of the *complot aristocratique*, the design of the wealthy *noblesse* to wreak vengeance on the third estate for forming the National Assembly and to impede the granting of freedom from seigneurial obligations to the peasantry. The Norman Bocage was one of the areas where *la Grande Peur* was most acutely felt but enclaves in the Bessin did not escape. By 24 July rumours had circulated that the town of Bayeux was completely encircled by brigands and that others were gathering for attack on the villages bordering the forest of Cérisy,[2] always the haunt of robbers and vagabonds. The villages surrounding the town were shaken with fear. The peasants took counter-measures against brigands, who did not exist, and against those unfortunate

[1] A.D.C. C2643.   [2] G. Lefebvre, *La Grande Peur de 1789*, p. 206.

nobles whom they suspected of being the brigands' paymasters.
The town registers record incident after incident in the last days
of July. At Vidouville the *seigneur* was forced to burn the papers
relating to his seigneurial rights; his *château* was devastated and he
fled. The Marquis de St. Vast was chased from his *château* by
peasants armed with pitchforks. The Marquis de Hottot and
the Sieur d'Ecrammeville sought refuge in Bayeux against the
hostility of their tenants.[1] The Duc de Coigny, who represented
the *noblesse* of the *grand bailliage* of Caen, was seized at Ver sur Mer
by mistrustful peasants who declared that the *duc* was attempting to
flee the country to avoid the consequences of his actions. Philippe
Delleville, *lieutenant* of the *amirauté* of Bayeux, rushed to Coigny's
defence and declared his innocence to an unconvinced crowd.
His only reward was imprisonment by the people of Ver as an
accomplice. No one would believe that the *duc* was merely
returning to Paris by sea with the full authorization of the
amirauté. A deputation was speedily organized by the municipal
council of Bayeux to go to the defence of a man with whom it was
closely associated, and succeeded after much argument in securing
his release.[2]

The town authorities were in the main powerless against these
peasant riots and watched them with dismay. Requests from
seigneurs in neighbouring parishes to send troops to their aid
received the uneasy reply that they could do nothing which might
provoke civil war, but sections of the town population and
indeed the council itself were not unsympathetic to the plight of
the *seigneurs*. They had, after all, everything to lose and nothing
to gain from the activities of the peasants. Their dilemma was
the same as that of the National Assembly. The *bourgeoisie* of the
Assembly had secured what it wanted in the abolition of the
juridical rights of the other two orders, but the peasantry now
forced them a step further into the formal abolition of seigneurial
dues and rents on the celebrated night of 4 August. Perhaps many
of those who sat in the Assembly were owners of the very rights
which were at stake, but the step was necessitated by the urgent
need to restore order in the countryside.

Complete peace in the country districts around Bayeux was not
secured by the promises of 4 August. The formation of the

[1] A.M.B. *Registres des délibérations du corps municipal*. July 1789.
[2] Pezet, *Bayeux à la fin de l'ancien régime*, p. 128.

National Guard was indicative of an alliance in defence of property rights which grew up during the summer months between the property-owners living in the town, the owners of seigneurial rents, and the *noblesse*, who were in the same position. The Baron de Wimpffen was chosen as its honorary head and its acting head was Le Roy, another noble and former royal pensionary. The Guard of Bayeux was of an essentially aristocratic nature. Its purpose was to keep order, but the peasantry of the surrounding villages were doubtful of what the Guard of Bayeux understood by order. The peasant riots had been against aristocrats and vagabonds. As far as they were concerned, these were the real enemies. But the composition of the Guard of Bayeux seemed to indicate that it was a body much more likely to sympathize with the *seigneur*. In order to defend themselves, and because they were distrustful of the intentions of the town Guard, the peasantry of the *bailliage* combined to form their own, one which would recognize and protect their interests.[1]

An inflammable situation continued well into the autumn. Work on the harvest absorbed some, but the new crops did not bring full alleviation and a diminution of prices overnight. The town had been quiet during the peasant disturbances of July, but September brought the artisan into line with the peasant in a refusal to pay taxes of any kind and in particular those imposed on food and drink. During early December the *directeur des aides* was chased from the town and stoned.[2] Badly hurt, he escaped death only by the intervention of Le Roy and a senior officer of the National Guard, who bargained for his life with the crowd and promised that he would never again return to the town. Several employees of the *aides* were attacked. Many of these were quite humble officials, but they were well advised to shake the dust of the town from their feet. The *droit de trop bu* disappeared overnight.[3]

In the face of difficulties of this kind, the old municipal council abandoned office. It had no funds at its disposal and the direction of a town with some two thousand destitute, surrounded by a countryside at least partially in revolt, was a task it was willing enough to renounce. After August 1789 the councillors refused to accept any responsibility and the town was left without direction.

[1] G. Lefebvre, *La Grande Peur de 1789*, p. 109.
[2] A.M.B. *Registres des délibérations du corps municipal*. December 1789.
[3] Ibid., December 1789–January 1790.

This situation was far from being confined to Bayeux. The breakdown of local government was general and indeed the National Assembly was anxious to provide some stop-gap until new legislation on local and provincial government had been prepared. During late August towns were ordered to set up *comités nationaux* of responsible citizens in order that central contact with them should not break down completely. But all the old officials refused. No one wanted the responsibility of running the town without funds. In face of general recalcitrance, one man came forward to assume direction. It was the bishop. As always in time of crisis, Bayeux turned to the church. During August the bishop supplied some 6,000 *livres* for the distribution of bread to the poor, whilst the chapter paid for a soup kitchen run by the Sisters of Charity. There was little pretence at real government. The aim was merely to preserve some sort of order until the harvest brought alleviation and a new provision for local government was made by the National Assembly. But rarely had Bayeux leant more heavily on its cathedral than it did during the last months of 1789, a time, ironically enough, when the confiscation of church lands was already under discussion in Paris.

The *comités nationaux* were essentially makeshift and provision for a more permanent form of provincial and local government was the immediate concern of an Assembly anxious to establish order and above all to render France taxable and bring an end to the economic deadlock. But plans for a uniform administrative system which was to sweep away the anomalies of the old, demolishing *pays d'états* and *pays d'élections*, *intendant* and provincial estates, old municipal governments and parish *syndics*, could not be elaborated overnight. If the form of municipal government was decided upon in early December and could be speedily implemented, the rest of the scheme to divide the provinces of France into departments, each with its separate governing authority responsible to Paris, and the departments into districts responsible to the departmental authority, was far more difficult to complete. There were lengthy debates upon departmental boundaries, upon the choice of departmental centres, the number of districts and their *chef-lieu*, even in some cases the name of the department. The details of the work were entrusted to the deputies of the province in question and these were constantly subject to pressure, both from towns anxious to conserve an administrative importance they had previously enjoyed and more so from an Assembly which wanted to get its taxes in and could not do so until the mechanism for their distribution and collection was complete. In spite of the exhortations of the Assembly to finish the work, it was March 1790 before Bayeux had emerged as *chef-lieu* of the district of Bayeux in the department of the Calvados, whose centre was in Caen; and it was August of that year before district and departmental elections were completed.[1]

Provision for new municipal elections was accomplished by the law of 14 December 1789. The creation of these new bodies involved less problems than any other, since the unit of election was unchanged. The difference was in the nature of the electorate. The male population was roughly divided into active and passive citizens, of whom the former—those over twenty-five paying a tax equal to the wages of three days' work—alone possessed the right to vote. This qualification was calculated in Bayeux, as in most places, at not less than 20 *sols* per day.[2] To be eligible for municipal office, in addition, it was necessary to pay a tax equal to the wages of ten days' work calculated on the same basis. On these assumptions, 629 at Bayeux were qualified as active citizens and 352 as eligible for election. The new councils were to consist of a mayor and three to twenty municipal officials, depending on the size of the town. Bayeux could expect six.[3] The electorate was wider than ever before, though it excluded the poorest of the artisan class, and only the relatively affluent, those paying 10 *livres* of *capitation* and above, could hope for office. There was no difficulty in assessing the urban population for electoral purposes because the *capitation* rolls were in the hands of the municipalities.

The results of the elections held in Bayeux in January 1790 are best explained by reference to the events of the last months of 1789. Those who in January of that year had been anxious to gain power in municipal government and who had pressed for the

[1] Full details on the difficulties incurred in the formation of the department of the Calvados are given in Le Brethon, 'La formation du Calvados', *Nouvelle Revue historique du droit français et étranger*, 1893, pp. 746–73, and 1894, pp. 96–124, 236–77, 372–402.

[2] J. Godechot, *Les Institutions de la France sous la Révolution et l'Empire* (Paris, 1951), p. 99.

[3] 'Études sur la Révolution à Bayeux', *Mémoires de la Société des Sciences, Arts et Belles Lettres de Bayeux* (1945), p. 57.

revocation of the *lettre de cachet* which had bestowed power upon the then existing officials, far from showing enthusiasm or at least an active interest in gaining control of the town, now showed instead a positive recalcitrance. The harvest of 1789, although a good one, was slow in bringing relief: prices remained high well into January and with high prices continued the customary unrest. The attacks on town officials in the summer of 1789 and in particular on those concerned with the collection of local taxes had not been forgotten. Few came forward or were willing to accept nomination for office. Only a half of the town's electorate turned out to vote for the new mayor. Their choice, by an overwhelming majority, was the bishop. To the townspeople the bishop stood for order and authority; he would not abdicate in face of a crisis, food shortage, or civil disorder. De Cheylus was run second by the former mayor, who owed his position to the arbitrary nomination of a *lettre de cachet* and who had been the subject of complaint on the eve of the elections for the Estates General. Nobles and lawyers with experience of aldermanship were the only others even considered. De Cheylus, by accepting immediately, saved the town from having to go further down the list, with the likelihood of refusal from the other nominees. The real problem came with the election of the six municipal officials. Only 294 turned out to vote. Of the first six chosen, only two, Gardin de Néry, *avocat*, and De la Londe, noble and *lieutenant au bailliage*, were willing to accept office; the others refused. The next four on the list were then offered the positions but of these, only one, Septier, *avocat*, accepted. Three more were called, of whom one, Tavigny Duclos, *avocat*, with some seventy-seven votes, accepted. Two more had to be found. The situation was growing delicate. Obviously, the further one went down the list, the less the number of votes the candidate possessed. The question was bound to arise whether men with such a small number of votes could possess public confidence. Of the next five, only one, Hallot, a *procureur* of the *bailliage*, accepted and he had only forty-eight votes. Twelve more were approached, of whom the last, a minor noble who accepted, had under twenty votes.[1] At least four of the six had previous experience of municipal office. None of them accepted government of the town without much hesitation and most of them gave as their reason for hesitation the lack of funds. The

---

[1] 'Études sur la Révolution à Bayeux', op. cit., p. 57.

government had not assured the towns of any other immediate source of supply than the old *aides* and *octrois*, which simply could not be collected in the conditions prevailing in Bayeux in 1790. In any case, these had been insufficient for the day-to-day running of the town. The urban officials refused outright to reimpose them, stating their case cogently to de Wimpffen in Paris:

Le rétablissement des commis est impraticable. L'opinion publique est trop contre eux. Leur retour serait la cause de la guerre civile. Ils seraient massacrés. Nous préférerions abandonner nos fonctions à l'horrible nécessité de mettre notre ville à feu et à sang.[1]

What existed by February 1790 in the way of urban government in Bayeux was a powerless little aristocratic body, totally without funds at its disposal and pathetically anxious for the speedy construction of the rest of the mechanism of local government. The officials of the town had accepted office reluctantly, perhaps largely out of a sense of public duty, and their first months in office were marked only by their efforts to prevent civil disorder and to defer action until the district and departmental authorities had been elected.

The conditions in which the elections for the departmental and district administrations took place were far more optimistic than those in which the urban elections had been completed. During the early months of 1790 food supplies reached the town more easily, prices were stabilized and the crisis of the preceding months passed. Prospects looked decidedly brighter for whoever assumed control. Positions in the district and department were far more attractive to those with political ambitions than the government of the town. Electoral procedure and results were followed with keener attention and aroused much criticism. The departmental administration was to be composed of a *conseil général* of thirty-six members, elected for two years and renewable by a half each year. The district body was comprised of a *conseil général* of twelve, subject to the same conditions. Once elected, these *conseils* would chose within themselves *directoires*. That of the department was to consist of eight members and that of the district of four. The *conseil* of the department was to meet for a month each year, that of the district for two weeks. The *directoires*, on the other hand, of both district and department, would be virtually permanently in

---

[1] A.M.B. *Registre de correspondance*. 25 February 1790.

session. For electoral purposes the districts were split into cantons and primary elections were to be held in the *chef-lieu* of the canton : representatives were to be sent from it to the elections which were then to be held in the *chef-lieu* of the district for the district assembly and to the department centre for those of the department.[1] The rural parishes of the district of Bayeux were very clearly dissatisfied with the electoral arrangements. The singling out of the larger villages and towns as *chefs-lieux de canton* meant, they declared, a clear mingling of very different interests in which the larger towns and villages would outvote the smaller. Angry petitions were drawn up and sent to Paris by the villages of the canton of Bayeux demanding that the peasants be allowed to hold at least primary assemblies distinct from those of the town, in which their interests would be fully represented.[2] Those of the districts of Lisieux and nearby Orbec made the same claims on the grounds that otherwise only the will of the larger villages would prevail. Their petitions were unheeded.[3]

The *conseil général* of the department of the Calvados did in fact represent the interests of the more influential landowners. Fourteen of its members were prosperous *laboureurs*, nine lived on their *rentes*, nine were men of the courts, and there were two doctors and two *négociants*. But, and this was to be of paramount importance in determining the nature of the departmental administration, whilst the agricultural and landowning interests which composed the *conseil général* were prepared to spend a month of the year in dealing with departmental problems, they were not prepared to spend the whole year in such pursuits. The men they chose for the *directoire* are sufficient evidence of their anxiety to opt out of the most active part of the administration. Those elected were three *avocats*, one of them belonging to Bayeux, three officials of the courts, and only two *laboureurs*.[4] The elections held for the district assembly of Bayeux showed the same characteristics. Genas, former *procureur du roi* of the *bailliage*, and son of the *subdélégué*, was elected president. The assembly of twelve did in fact include six *laboureurs*, but only one was elected to the *directoire* of the district and the other three members of it were members of the law-courts, two *avocats*, and a *conseiller au bailliage*. The *procureur syndic* was de la Rue, *avocat*, whilst the secretary of

---

[1] Godechot, op. cit., pp. 98–103.   [2] A.D.C. L3/87.
[3] Ibid.   [4] A.D.C. L599.

the district was Pierre Basley, *procureur* and former secretary to the *subdélégué*.[1]

The government of the district of Bayeux, and indeed of the whole department of the Calvados, passed in the early summer of 1790 into the hands of the lawyers and officials of the old régime. The large landowning and agricultural interests chosen by the cantons were only too willing to surrender the most active role in provincial government to them and occupy themselves the role of a yearly court of appeal to judge the work of the *directoire*. Like the royal officials of the old régime, the members of the *directoires* were paid a token sum rather than a salary. Those of the departmental assembly were paid some 2,000 *livres* and those of the district of Bayeux some 1,200.[2] None of the Bayeusains elected needed to depend on their official salary as their sole income.

The men who formed the new *directoire* of the district of Bayeux were, apart from Genas and Basley, inexperienced in office. The municipal government placed no confidence in their capabilities. When Genas decided to refuse the presidency of the district in favour of the position of a judge of the newly formed tribunal and the position was offered to Moisson de Vaux, a noble and former *conseiller au bailliage*, the town council addressed an anxious letter to the deputy, Delauney, in Paris:

L'honnêteté des membres choisis ne nous empêche pas d'avoir de l'inquiétude. Il va être question de former des bases et l'administration va être confiée à des personnes sans expérience d'autant plus que M. Duhomme ne peut être dans le directoire.[3]

They were even more doubtful about the composition of the departmental assembly. A letter addressed to de Wimpffen on 4 July 1790 ran:

Notre département est formé; rien au monde de si faible; il n'y a pas été appelé un seul homme au fait de la comptabilité, pas un qui ait la moindre connaissance administrative, pas un négociant.[4]

They blamed the composition of these assemblies on the overwhelming preponderance of the rural vote, which had resulted in the choice of men for the *conseil général* who were only too anxious

[1] A.D.C. L. *Registres des délibérations du directoire du district de Bayeux.*
[2] Le Brethon, op. cit. (1894), p. 113.
[3] A.M.B. *Registre de correspondance.* 25 May 1790.
[4] Ibid., 4 July 1790.

to return to their agricultural pursuits and resign power to whoever was left. In particular, the municipal council of Bayeux regretted the failure to choose someone who had worked for the *intendant* and, most especially, the setting aside of the *subdélégués*.

The net result of the elections in Bayeux, and there are ready parallels elsewhere,[1] showed some irreconcilable features indicative of potential difficulties. On the one hand, the elections for the municipal council, because of the time at which they were held, had played directly into the hands of the bishop, the urban *noblesse*, and a few officials of the law-courts: the majority of the members were of as conservative a nature as it would have been possible to envisage and the mayor himself was utterly antipathetic to change. On the other hand, the active administration of district and department had gone by a circuitous path into the hands of those who in this area had been the greatest critics of the old administrative régime. The next few months after August 1790 were to illustrate the difficulties involved, and in particular, the failure of the municipal government of Bayeux to keep pace with the more advanced views of the department and district.

The administrative reorganization of France had been slow to complete. Not until late summer could the new assemblies embark upon the weighty task of assessing the tax liabilities of the new departments. They were dependent on the information in the possession of the old *intendants* for the calculation of tax arrears. But the *intendants* declared, often rightly, that they had surrendered all the information they possessed to the *Assemblées Provinciales* of 1788. It took at least a month to get a letter to Delauney, the last *intendant* of Caen, and to elicit a reply from him. By the end of the year the *directoire* of the Calvados was threatening the last three *intendants* of the *généralités* of Caen and Alençon with legal proceedings if they did not immediately surrender all information they held.[2] The new régime did not mean, the people of France were made to learn in 1790, the evasion of old taxes. Redistribution was under way, but in the meantime, whether just or unjust, the old taxes must be paid: the government needed money. The districts were ordered to appoint their *receveurs* for taxation purposes and were recommended by the departmental authority to choose those who had collected taxes under the old régime, since they would

---

[1] Le Brethon, op. cit. (1894), p. 240.
[2] Ibid., p. 241.

know the best methods. The man chosen at Bayeux was Varin, former *receveur* of the revenues of the cathedral chapter. Not until July 1791 had anything which approached order been introduced into the departmental finances of the Calvados.[1] Before this the state had been forced to look around for alternative ways of ending the financial deadlock. It chose the annexation of ecclesiastical property, a step which, when its wider implications were realized, was to test the relationship between the separate parts of the administration to the full and to have a profound effect upon the life of the town.

[1] In November 1790 arrears were still owing in the department for 1787. Ibid., p. 242.

THE CIVIL CONSTITUTION OF THE CLERGY

THE political, economic, and social changes of July and August 1789 had an immediate repercussion on the church of the old régime. Ecclesiastical landlords were left totally undisturbed during the peasant riots of these months in the area surrounding Bayeux, but the night of 4 August struck at their rights no less than at those of the lay *seigneurs*. The renunciation of privileges shattered the existing economic organization of the church. Many of the clergy, like the bishop of Bayeux, derived much of their income from seigneurial dues, the leasing of seigneurial rights, and the exercise of seigneurial justice. The imminent abolition of the tithes was also implied in the measure, though the issue was postponed for discussion at a future date since no suggestions for an alternative source of income were immediately put forward. In fact, the landowners, small and large, of the diocese of Bayeux ceased to pay the tithe when they ceased to pay other seigneurial taxes. It was, in this area, the most bitterly resented of all the impositions of the old régime. Duhamel de Vailly, the notary who had taken the rights of the bishopric of Bayeux on lease, complained bitterly of his failure to realize what was his due.[1]

Once the future of the National Assembly was assured, some reorganization of church wealth was inevitable. The need to redistribute ecclesiastical revenues within the church hierarchy had long been urged by both the lower clergy and the third estate; but the former were anxious to do so only to secure for themselves a living wage, the latter to deprive the church of its lands and its privileges. During late 1789 the state, on the verge of financial collapse, saw in the annexation of church lands the possible solution to the problem of meeting its immediate needs and in return agreed to pay for the clergy and the maintenance of religious

[1] A.D.C. Q. *Biens de l'Évêché.*

services. It was not, however, prepared to pay indefinitely for the regular clergy. It forbade the taking of religious vows after the end of October and gave existing religious the alternative of leaving their communities and receiving a generous pension or staying, being grouped with religious from elsewhere and receiving less in payment. Charitable establishments were exempt from the decrees.

The monks of Bayeux were in fact the first victims of change since most of the female communities, except the Benedictines and the Ursulines, could claim continuance as charitable institutions. The Cordeliers and the Capucins could not. The alternative to disbanding and collecting the generous government pension of 1,000 *livres* was to wait for instructions to repair to another house, perhaps at a great distance, designated by the government for those who insisted on maintaining a life in community. In such a place, the orders gathered indiscriminately together would be expected to evolve some rule catering for the tastes and habits of all. The prospect must have been as distasteful to the ascetic as to the worldly minded and the monks of Bayeux to a man chose secular life and a state pension.

The female orders responded quite differently to the legislation perhaps largely because it treated them less harshly than it did the male orders. If they decided to stay they were not obliged to leave their house or their community. In addition to this, the transition to secular life involved greater problems, such as returning to families which had contributed a dowry at the time of their entry into the order, expecting to be relieved thereafter of the necessity of providing for their daughters. The loyalty of the women to their vows was exemplary. They exercised also an extraordinary degree of moral pressure over each other, which made some who genuinely wanted to return home decide to stay. Two who tried to leave the house of the Sisters of Providence were ostracized by the rest of the community and denied egress.[1] Nor was the municipal council anxious to be quit of their services. The work they performed as nurses and teachers was sufficient, as yet, to allow them to continue undisturbed.

The measures affecting the religious orders were implemented on the whole without difficulty or regret. It was to be otherwise with the secular clergy. The Civil Constitution of the Clergy,

[1] A.M.B. *Registres des délibérations du corps municipal.* April 1790.

enacted in July 1790, was to plunge France into a tragic conflict—tragic because in essence the decrees embodied the sort of reforms which were needed in the church. They reduced the large numbers of secular clergy by redrawing diocesan boundaries to coincide with those of the department, and amalgamating smaller parishes. Cathedral chapters were suppressed. All church personnel would be state-salaried and elected officials. Bishops would be elected from those who had been priests for at least fifteen years by those who chose the departmental assemblies, and priests from those who had been *vicaires* for five years by those who chose the district officials. The new bishops were to dispatch a letter to the pope indicative of unity of faith, but would receive canonical institution from their own metropolitans. The salaries offered were generous. The minimum a priest would receive was 1,200 *livres*. But lay election and the utter reduction to impotence of Rome had never been envisaged. Moreover, the clergy had in no way been consulted about changes which would shake the church in France to its foundations. In the four months between the promulgation of the decrees and the decision in November that the clergy must take an oath to the new constitution, the church in France surveyed its position. For Bayeux, the religious policy of the Assembly in 1790 was to provide the first real break with the old régime. In the measures promulgated lay the implication of changes which would affect the fundamental character of a town which had for so long been parasitic on the church. An affluent bishop and wealthy chapter, charitable religious houses, had all contributed to the upkeep of a society with few other resources. There is little evidence of any great spiritual awareness amongst the townsfolk. Indeed there was a definite nucleus of anti-clericalism in the judges and lawyers of the courts now entrenched in the district assembly. The town *cahier* had been severely critical of the wealth of the church, and the more prosperous townsfolk were as eager as any to lay their hands on church lands; but that done, they wanted to conserve the material benefits that Bayeux had so long derived from the church. The bishop, however, was a figure commanding the respect of the townsfolk. He had but newly been elected mayor. The attitude of the town towards the new innovations was inevitably ambiguous.

A few of the bishops of the old régime had been sufficiently popular to secure election to the Estates General in 1789. A handful were prepared to accept the proposed changes. A moderate group under the leadership of de Boisgelin, bishop of Aix, hoped that some compromise might be reached by referring the whole question to a national council. Joseph Dominique de Cheylus, bishop of Bayeux, however, belonged to neither of these groups. From the very beginning he had adopted a position of uncompromising opposition to the acts of the National Assembly. Faced, as mayor in 1790, with a choice between his duty to the government and to the church, there was no doubt where de Cheylus's adherence lay. He saw every move of the Assembly as an attack on the church.

The measures nationalizing church property brought the first difficulties. De Cheylus at once attempted to impede government plans by calling the rural deans to Bayeux to instruct them to encourage parish priests not to send in estimates of the value of their benefices. The Abbé Voisvenal, secretary to the bishop, was charged to draw up a circular to this effect for distribution throughout the diocese.[1] The storm of opposition this aroused taught de Cheylus an important lesson. It was apparent that public opinion and the support of the lower clergy could never be won on the property issue. Drop that and something might well be salvaged before the church was changed for ever. Already on the property question the rest of the municipal council was writing to Paris to dissociate itself from the subversive policy the bishop was pursuing.[2] But there was every indication that he might secure support in resisting attempts to change the French clergy into salaried officials of the state. De Wimpffen in Paris was openly hostile to the civil constitution, then only projected, and the municipal council backed him wholeheartedly, going so far as to ask him to speak out in the Assembly against change and the wild projects of the Abbé Sieyès which, they feared, might make the French priesthood like the church of England—without a distinctive clerical garb and perhaps not celibate.[3] De Cheylus therefore now declared himself willing to pay his share of taxes and renounce all financial privileges.[4] But when the dioceses were redefined and Bayeux became the obvious choice for the

---

[1] A.N. DXIX 53 (120).
[2] A.M.B. *Registres des délibérations du corps municipal.* April 1790.
[3] A.M.B. *Registre de correspondance.* 12 May 1790.
[4] A. Dédouit, *Bayeux sous la Révolution, le Consulat et l'Empire* (Bellême, 1892), p. 6.

seat of the bishopric of the Calvados, including that part of the diocese of Lisieux which fell within the department of the Calvados, de Cheylus wrote to de Ferronays, bishop of Lisieux: 'Je ne me regarderai comme évêque de Lisieux, non seulement que lorsque vous y aurez congédié, mais encore lorsque l'église aura prononcé.'[1] All applications from Lisieux for faculties to hear confession and special licences received the same unbending reply.

The local authorities viewed the bishop's activities with alarm. The departmental and district assemblies were both aware of the policy of Paris and anxious to assert their new power. The municipal council, on the other hand, was composed of men older in office and conservative to the core, but they were not prepared to back the bishop. Instead they tried to appease him in the vain hope that they could buy his silence. In late July they purchased the land and palace of Sommervieu and made a gift of it to the bishop so that he might continue to enjoy his hunting in the old familiar surroundings.[2] De Cheylus was in no mood to be won over. On 6 November 1790 he resigned as mayor and from then on, until his departure for Jersey in May 1791, he was the nucleus of opposition to the Civil Constitution of the Clergy in Lower Normandy.

The papacy, anxious not to jeopardize the papal territory in Avignon, hesitated to condemn the ecclesiastical legislation of the Assembly, but the French episcopate could not afford to delay. They drew up a sixty-page brochure, the *Exposition des Principes*, which explained to the clergy of France why a truly Catholic church could not accept the Civil Constitution of the Clergy. De Cheylus and 118 other bishops declared their full adherence to the document and by late November the *exposition* was the platform of the French opposition.[3]

De Cheylus was quick to convey the essential elements of the *exposition* to his diocese. On 20 November he published an instruction to the parish priests proclaiming the illegality of the religious changes proposed by the Assembly. He threatened to suspend immediately any priest who accepted the national decrees. He denied the authority of the state to embark upon diocesan reorganization or the dissolution of the chapters. The instruction

---

[1] A.N. AA 62. 2A. Dossier 1549. Letter of 10 October 1790.
[2] A.M.B. *Registres des délibérations du corps municipal.* 25 July 1790.
[3] A.N. AA 62.

was circulated throughout the diocese together with the injunction that it should be read out to all congregations after high mass.[1] The municipal government, alarmed at the tone of the document, forbade the urban clergy to read it. Five out of thirteen parish priests of the town put the injunctions of the bishop before the orders of the municipal council and read the document.[2]

The priests of Bayeux were thus called upon at an early stage to declare their views on the canonical legitimacy of the decrees issued by the Assembly. Surprisingly, of the five who read the instruction, one later took the oath, while five of the eight who refused to read it were later non-jurors. The incident reflects the state of extreme confusion which must have prevailed in the minds of most of the clergy, but more especially it reveals a not uncommon attitude amongst the members of the lower clergy in France. The idea of an adequate salary was attractive. Moreover, it was mistakenly assumed that the government measures applied only to bishops and chapters and the election of future parish priests. They therefore refused to commit themselves on the issue and left the struggle to the bishop—who commanded very little sympathy—and the government.

The government's next move was to force them into a more positive attitude. In the light of the intensive propaganda campaign against the civil constitution carried out in almost every corner of France by the higher clergy, the Assembly decided upon a decisive counter measure. On 26 November 1790 Voidel, speaking in the name of the *comité ecclésiastique des rapports d'aliénation et de recherches*, reported on the opposition of many of the French clergy to the new constitution and more particularly on the writings of various bishops against the new diocesan framework and the electoral system of appointment. The only thing, he said, which inspired the higher clergy to hinder reform was greed.[3] The following day the Assembly decreed that an oath of loyalty to the constitution was obligatory for all elected churchmen and that no cleric would receive his salary without taking the oath: 'De veiller avec soin sur les fidèles de la paroisse qui lui est confiée, d'être fidèle à la loi et au roi et de maintenir de tout son pouvoir la constitution décrétée par l'Assemblée Nationale et

---

[1] Sévèstre, op. cit., p. 137.   [2] Ibid.
[3] *Procès Verbal de la Constituante et de la Législative, 10eme livraison*, vol. xxxvii. Report 7.

acceptée par le roi.'[1] It was to be the ecclesiastical equivalent of the oath taken by all lay officials on assuming their posts and it emphasized the new state organization of the church.

The clergy of Bayeux would, therefore, in the course of the next two months have to declare themselves openly for or against the civil constitution. On 5 December the municipal council wrote to the chapter to inform the canons that they were to disband immediately. The canons did not resist. They left peacefully, declaring that in the light of recent events they had expected their fate. Only the vicar general made a speech stressing the need for a church united under one head, the pope.[2] No one uttered a protest in their favour save the bishop. The townspeople watched their dissolution with a curiosity verging on indifference.[3] The battle for the support of the lower clergy was left to de Cheylus almost alone. Throughout December and January he undertook an intensive propaganda campaign designed to ensure that the lower clergy did not take the oath. Printed circulars were distributed to each individual parish setting forth the theological impropriety of the civil constitution and the oath. De Cheylus declared that he was prepared to renounce both his privileges and his revenues, which he knew to have been the greatest source of irritation to the lower clergy, but he was not prepared to submit to government decrees which struck at the very foundation of the Catholic church.[4]

The oath was to be taken in late January, after mass, by each *curé* and *vicaire*, in the presence of the officials of the commune and the faithful of the parish.

The week before the oath fell due, the seminary of Bayeux showed its hand and, after months of silence when other ecclesiastical foundations had been waxing eloquent on the theological implications of the oath, came out unreservedly against the policy of the government. The event was significant. The majority of the priests in the town had received their training with the seminary and now their former teachers, who were well versed in theology and canon law, were demonstrating that to take an

---

[1] *Procès Verbal de la Constituante . . ., 10eme livraison,* vol. xxxvii. Report 434.

[2] A.D.C. L. *Fonds du tribunal du district de Caen. Déclaration et profession de foi du chapitre de l'église cathédrale de Bayeux sur la nouvelle constitution du clergé lors de la signification qui lui a été faite du décret portant suppression du chapitre le 12 décembre 1790.*

[3] Ibid.

[4] Sévèstre, op. cit., p. 211.

oath to an unsound civil constitution would be tantamount to error. About four days before the oath-taking ceremony fell due, the superior and four teachers of the seminary drew up a document to which eleven of the priests and curates of the town appended their signatures. It was hastily circulated to many of the parishes of the diocese—though in most cases it failed to arrive in time. The tenor of the document was unmistakable:

> Soumis à la puissance civile comme citoyens, en ce qui concerne nos droits temporels nous sommes disposés à en faire le sacrifice, s'il le faut, pour le plus grand avantage de la patrie; mais nous ne nous écarterons point des règles inviolables de la loi de l'Église et avec la grâce du Seigneur que nous implorons, nous soutiendrons la pureté de ses dogmes; . . . Plutôt mourir et mourir mille fois que d'abjurer notre foi, celle des Exupère, des Regnobert, des Vigor, des Révérent et des Marcoulf, par un serment que notre conscience désavoue.[1]

This was a substantial triumph for the efforts of de Cheylus. Even some of the urban clergy who had compiled personal *cahiers* condemning the wealth and lack of responsibility of the higher clergy now refused the oath. Thirty-two of the forty-two priests in the city were non-jurors.[2] Once the seminary had so plainly condemned the oath a strong *esprit de corps* obviously exercised itself among the clergy of the town. In the closely knit ecclesiastical society of a small town like Bayeux the issue was hotly debated and waverers were won over on the plea of the need to maintain a united front. To be a juror at all in the town one needed strong convictions. Only four parish priests of the town took the oath. Only two took it in January. One of them, Michel Moulland, priest of St. Martin, was a young man of great personal courage and convictions, whose later efforts to restore the church in 1796 are sufficient to mark him out as a man of great faith and personal energy. Of Menand, parish priest of St. Sauveur, less is known, but his curate, Delauney, a young man well known for his advanced left-wing tendencies, was the stronger character and the two took the oath together. Of the two who took the oath in late February, one, Lecuyer, parish priest of the large and poverty-stricken parish of St. Jean, had long led the priests of Bayeux in opposition to the episcopal vicars in the period

[1] Ibid., p. 216.
[2] E. Sévèstre, *Le Personnel de l'Église Constitutionnelle en Normandie* (Paris, 1925), pp. 31–32.

preceding the calling of the Estates General. Yet even Lecuyer
hesitated and went so far as to read the November instruction of
the bishop to his parishioners. His slowness in taking the oath is
in itself indicative of his deliberation on the matter. The parish
priest of La Madeleine had even more scruples. During the
Sunday mass when voices were heard shouting: 'Ne jurez pas.
Ne vous damnez pas!', others yelled, to all accounts the more
loudly: 'Jurez ou ne jurez pas, cela ne nous fait rien du tout!'[1] He
took the oath.

The clergy of the rural area around Bayeux accepted the oath to
the constitution with much more readiness than those of the town,
though many were later to add qualifications which rendered it
virtually meaningless. Fifty-five per cent. of the rural clergy took
the oath without qualification, 28 per cent. with reservations,
and only 17 per cent. refused it outright, compared with the outright refusal of ten of the fourteen *curés* in the town.[2] The striking
difference in attitude between the urban and rural clergy was
perhaps due in part to the failure of the bishop to rally an effective
nucleus of men to serve as his agents in the countryside. De
Cheylus had for long been out of touch with his diocese and
whereas he had been able partially to retrieve this situation in the
town with the aid of the seminary, in the case of the more remote
rural clergy this was not so. He had to depend on the rural deans
for the distribution of letters and pamphlets explaining the finer
points involved in the oath. It was not easy, however, to convey
the letters to the deans themselves because of the hostility of the
local administrative bodies. At Caen the sacristan of the Carme-
lites served as intermediary. The priest of Bretteville sur Odon
received his copy by way of a butcher, Pierre Leherpeur.[3] But
these were isolated examples: the parishes far from the beaten
track remained ignorant of the intellectual arguments involved in
acceptance or rejection of the oath. More than this, however, and
this feature has been revealed time and again in an examination
of the clergy of France in 1790, the rural clergy did not have the
same *esprit de corps* as those of the town. Their closest associations
were not with other ecclesiastics but with their flock, whose
poverty and problems they shared. In the diocese of Bayeux they
were men of the region, anxious to retain their positions, remain

[1] A.D.C. Lv. *Liasse des serments. District de Bayeux.*
[2] Sévèstre, *Les Problèmes religieux . . .*, pp. 189–92.   [3] Ibid.

near their families and friends and completely antipathetic towards the exhortations of the bishop and higher clergy. Their thinking was confined to their own limited experience and their outlook more purely parochial than that of the town.

The high proportion of non-jurors in Bayeux itself was sufficient to occasion the municipal council some alarm. On 25 January 1791 they wrote to de Wimpffen in Paris for guidance on how to win over the urban clergy.[1] They could see no prospect of it themselves. They had heard, however, they said, that the Assembly was considering some modifications in the law. But when this proved a false hope the council had to think reluctantly of implementing the provisions of the law of 27 November.

The law stipulated quite clearly that refusal to pledge obedience to the Civil Constitution of the Clergy was no crime but that non-jurors would be considered to have resigned their benefices and would be replaced by the form of lay election laid down on 12 July 1790. The displaced ecclesiastics were promised an adequate pension. Bayeux would have to replace its bishop, its episcopal vicars, and many of its priests. The city had far too many parishes, but the question of which to suppress could not be decided immediately. The non-juring priest of a suppressed parish might arouse his parishioners to support the old order and the new authorities wanted as little trouble as possible. Moreover, Lent was fast approaching and the Easter confession and the days of obligation provided opportunities for the non-jurors to exert pressure on the faithful. The sooner the elections of both bishop and priests took place, the sooner the local authorities could breathe easily.

On the other hand, in the vain hope that the government would modify its claims and that then the recalcitrant would be won over, the department of the Calvados took longer than the other departments of Normandy in trying to persuade the clergy to take the oath and was the last to call the electoral assembly to choose the new bishop. Many of the electors were reluctant to proceed until every attempt had been made to win over the non-jurors, and replied to the invitation to attend the elections in terms indicative of their feelings. Most expressed the wish that de Cheylus would change his mind before the last minute. Others, like de Vailly, the ex-apostolic notary, replied that they would not

[1] Ibid., p. 138.

allow personal feelings to come before the public good and would obey the mandate to attend the elections.[1]

Throughout February and March de Cheylus had remained in Paris, where he could be in immediate consultation with other leading ecclesiastics. He was in constant contact with his diocese by means of his secretary and two of the former canons. The elections of the new bishop were fixed for 12 March. On the eleventh a new pastoral letter issued by de Cheylus denounced anew the whole ecclesiastical policy of the Constituent Assembly. The members of the electoral assembly were warned: 'Si vous persistez dans le dessein de me donner un successeur... votre choix ne peut faire qu'un intrus . . . je le poursuivrai partout comme un loup ravissant. J'invoquerai l'anathème sur sa tête.'[2] The outburst was fully expected at the electoral assembly. The *procureur syndic* of the department made a lengthy speech in praise of the civil constitution and in denunciation of its critics and 314 out of 395 electors brought Gervais de la Prise, parish priest of St. Pierre at Caen, to the episcopal seat.[3] The municipal council of Bayeux looked on the choice with some alarm. Caen was already agitating for the transfer of the seat of the bishopric from Bayeux to Caen, the centre of the civil administration, and the choice of a Caennais seemed a step in this direction.

The new bishop, however, was hesitant about accepting office. He had grave doubts about the canonical validity of his election. He was a follower of the middle of the road group of the bishop of Aix, who believed that the church in France could be reconciled to the civil constitution if only it were allowed to discuss the matter at a national church council. He hoped somehow to reconcile the juring and non-juring elements in the church and pressed the view that his election by a secular assembly should be followed by the conferring of spiritual jurisdiction by a national church council. He was uneasy in his mind about the changes that had taken place. The department urged him to make a decision. The delay meant that the date for the election of parish priests could not be determined and the implementation of the religious policy of the Constituent Assembly simply could not take place. For a fortnight de la Prise turned over the issue. Finally on 1 April he replied to the departmental *directoire* that if the

---

[1] Sévèstre, *Les Problèmes religieux* . . ., p. 387.
[2] A.N. DXXXIX bis 21.
[3] A.N. F¹ CIII. *Calvados.*

Constituent Assembly refused to hold a national church council, then he could not accept his nomination to the bishopric.[1] The department had no alternative but to order new elections.

The situation was becoming more and more difficult. Three days after the election of de la Prise, the pope, faced with the news of the consecration of the first constitutional bishop, issued the declaration for which the French church had been waiting so long. 'Charity suffereth long, but charity hath suffered long enough . . .', and with that beginning Pius VI proclaimed the elections illegal and the authority of the Assembly in ecclesiastical affairs non-existent.[2] Armed with this weapon the position of the non-jurors was strongly reinforced. Moreover, many who had taken the oath with restrictions now drew back and retracted altogether. The refusal of de la Prise meant that the organization of the constitutional church was even further retarded. Then, on 29 March when no one was expecting him, de Cheylus descended on Bayeux.

The move was nothing short of a *coup de théâtre*. Those chaplains and clerics who had obliged the municipal council by chanting the office in the cathedral, so that the townspeople should not notice the absence of the canons, quickly evacuated the premises.[3] The municipal council had no doubt why he had come. The election of the clergy of the constitutional church was impending. De Cheylus's intention was to prevent, if he could, these elections taking place. At the same time a large group of ordinands were staying in the seminary awaiting the conference of orders by the bishop. De Cheylus made no secret of the fact that he intended this ceremony to take place. Anxiously the municipal councillors wrote to the departmental authority to obtain an order annulling the ordinations and expelling de Cheylus from the bishop's palace. In the meantime they ordered the young clerics to leave the city.[4] On 3 April the order of expulsion came. The bishop took refuge in the house of Madame de Campigny and from there continued his efforts. Non-juring priests were instructed to warn their flocks that attendance at the elections of constitutional priests was a grave sin. One municipal councillor bemoaned the fact that the whole tiresome business had not been completed long before.

[1] A.N. F^{19} 865. 410–11.
[2] A. Latreille, *L'Église catholique et la Révolution française* (Paris, 1946), pp. 90–93.
[3] A.M.B. *Registre de correspondance.* 29 and 30 March 1791.   [4] Ibid.

Lent, he declared, had multiplied their difficulties, for it was the time when the influence of the clergy was the greatest.[1]

Perhaps for this reason the numbers at the second electoral assembly dropped steeply. Only 250 turned up to vote a successor to de la Prise.[2] This time the chances were fairly evenly divided amongst the three candidates: Hébert, a brilliant theologian living in retreat at Maizières, and two complete outsiders—Mulot, a former canon of St. Victor in Paris and well known as an ardent supporter of the civil constitution, and Claude Fauchet, a highly controversial figure very well known in the capital. Fauchet enjoyed a political reputation singling him out from every ecclesiastic of the day, with the possible exception of the bishop of Autun. In the days before the Revolution his outstanding oratorical gifts had made him a popular court and society preacher, but as early as 1776 he had only narrowly escaped being put under an interdict by the bishop of Paris for urging the destruction of the *noblesse* as a social order in the state. He had taken part in the storming of the Bastille, founded the Cercle Social with its organ the *Bouche de fer* to propagate a kind of Christian socialism, and had been one of Mirabeau's private group of advisers and as such was responsible for most of the speeches Mirabeau made on religious matters. He believed he had a mission to renew and reform a nationalized Catholic church. All this he combined with a hasty temper, liability to hysterical outbursts, and rumours of a doubtful private life. His name had been proposed for the see of Paris but his extremist views had gained him powerful enemies and he did not secure election. Even for the see of the Calvados the Amis de la Constitution in Paris and their press actively backed Mulot rather than see the power of Fauchet increased. Only at the third ballot did he obtain the necessary majority of 152 votes out of 250—a narrow enough victory—but he did not hesitate to accept office.[3]

Neither the departmental nor the district assembly was altogether happy about the choice. Fauchet's victory was probably secured by virtue of being the one name known in advance to the electors. The *procureur syndic* of the department, evidently fearing

---

[1] A.M.B. *Registre de correspondance.* 29 and 30 March 1791.

[2] J. Charrier, *Claude Fauchet* (Paris, 1909), vol. i, pp. 229–31.

[3] P. Pisani, *Répertoire biographique de l'épiscopat constitutionnel* (Paris, 1907), pp. 169–72.

the worst, wrote off to Fauchet to urge moderation when he came to the Calvados.[1] Local pamphleteers had rarely had the opportunity for so much scurrilous talk. They exaggerated the picture of Fauchet's private life out of all proportion. 'Mes respects à Madame, est-elle bien rétablie de ses couches?'[2] one ended; while another speaks of the departure of a young woman from Bayeux to Paris 'où on ajoutera une petite branche à celles de l'humanité entière'.[3] Even the moderate constitutional bishop of the Eure could not resist the remark in a letter to his brother: 'L'abbé Fauchet, évêque du Calvados, est donc arrivé, précédé de la réputation d'avoir femme et enfants . . . Je ne sais si sa dame est du voyage, ou plutôt j'imagine qu'elle le laissera s'aspiéger.'[4] Never had an old régime bishop arrived in Bayeux with a more questionable reputation.

The municipality had more on its mind than scandal, however. De Cheylus had promised opposition to the elections and he kept his promise. With guards outside the house where he was staying, and in which he was virtual prisoner, he published, in an ordinance, a long series of questions addressed to Fauchet: 'Qui êtes-vous? D'où venez-vous? Si c'est au nom de l'Église nous sommes prêts à vous céder notre place; mais montrez-nous vos titres; montrez-nous le mandat apostolique qui vous institue; montrez-nous la sentence qui nous dépose.'[5] He cited the pope's condemnation of the elections. The difficulty was increased for the council in that now the bishop had been elected, the elections of the parish clergy for the district had to follow; and they were to be held not at Caen but at Bayeux, where the presence of a bishop ever ready to urge the schismatic nature of the constitutional church was looked upon by the council with some distaste. On 6 May they decided that the only way to silence de Cheylus was to put him under lock and key. But the bishop of Bayeux was a step ahead. Disguised as a merchant he left the house of Madame de Campigny and headed for Cherbourg, where with the help of a parishioner, Chaumontel, captain of the *Vaillant*, he sailed for Jersey.[6]

---

[1] A.D.C. L. *Correspondance du directoire de département.* 25 April 1791.
[2] Bibl. Mun. Caen. *Réserve fonds normand*, B181.   [3] Ibid.
[4] A. Montier, *Correspondance de Robert Lindet pendant la Constituante et la Législative* (Paris, 1899), p. 274.   [5] B.N. Ld 4/7726. 27 April 1791.
[6] Le Mâle, 'Départ de Monseigneur de Cheylus pour l'exil', *Baiocana* (1912), pp. 15–26.

He was not actively pursued by the council; his disappearance had removed a major difficulty. The elections of the new parish clergy were quickly accomplished without any new obstacle. True, only fifty electors turned up out of the entire district electorate and they in large part composed of the administrative officials.[1] The high proportion of jurors in the area meant that there were only sixty-four cures to be filled compared with 122 in the nearby district of Caen. Those chosen were former priests, chaplains, curates, *habitués*, and monks. The jurors were all re-elected to their parishes. The former curate of Carcagny, elected to the parish of St. Loup, was the only man new to the parishes of the town. The others went to an ex-Benedictine, an ex-Cordelier, the ex-prior of the Abbey of Mondaye, a former teacher at the *collège*, and a chaplain from the hospital.[2] The vexed question of parish reorganization was put on one side, to the intense annoyance of the departmental *directoire*, but at least Bayeux could present to the incoming bishop the appearance of a working organization and the skeleton of a constitutional church. It could do no more. The municipal authority of Bayeux had carried out the letter of the law, if without enthusiasm. The bishop, the chapter, the male religious houses, had each in turn been sacrificed as part of the new plan for the state church of France. The non-juring priests obviously commanded, in early 1791, more allegiance from the townspeople, in that they heeded their injunctions about not attending the elections, but there was no demonstration against the appearance of the new priests by the townspeople. The people of Bayeux did not as yet realize the full consequences of the change and most especially what it would do to their pockets. The old bishop, as far as they could see, had merely been replaced by another. They were not interested in the niceties of what one could or could not do within the confines of canon law.

On the other hand, persecution had not united the opposed elements in the *ancien régime* church. To the very end, the different groups within the clergy lacked cohesion. Bishop, disbanded canons, non-juring priests, presented a united front only on the issue of not taking the oath and the principle of not admitting ultimate state control over the church. No non-juring priest had

[1] Sévèstre, *Les Problèmes religieux* . . ., p. 529.
[2] Sévèstre, *La Vie religieuse* . . ., p. 89.

raised his voice to protest against the disbanding of the religious orders or the dissolution of the chapter. Until the last possible moment they had tried to stand apart.

Within days of his departure, de Cheylus's palace was occupied by the municipal council. They decided that Fauchet should be lodged in the far less sumptuous dean's house, which also lay empty. A few months later the former bishop's effects were auctioned. The canons were prominent amongst those bidding for pieces of furniture they had had more chances to survey than others. The townsfolk seized the opportunity to buy a mattress, a cupboard, a cooking pot: those with finer tastes and a little more money, an *objet d'art*: the wealthy *noblesse* paid a good price for the contents of the wine cellars, which realized twice as much as everything else. One man at least thought of the former bishop: an old chaplain attached to the cathedral invested more than he could afford in a bottle of claret to send to de Cheylus to gladden his exile and to show he was not entirely forgotten.[1] Otherwise each in his way in the summer of 1791 accepted the departure of de Cheylus from Bayeux and profited as he was able from the event.

[1] A.D.C. Q. *Biens de l'Évêché.*

III

POLITICS AND RELIGION

MAY 1791–SEPTEMBER 1793

ONE bishop had fallen at Bayeux in the defence of the church to which he was wholly committed: strangely enough, his successor was to undergo a similar fate for what was for him essentially the same cause.

It was ironical that the trend of political events in the old ecclesiastical city under the new régime, as under the old, was to be conditioned so largely by its choice of bishop. Fauchet arrived in Bayeux on 14 May 1791 for the installation ceremony. Such an event had always been accompanied by a spectacle of some magnificence. The municipal council hoped that a splendid demonstration would dispel any mistrust the townspeople might have of the new church. Traditionally, the heads of the two oldest noble families the town could muster had set out to welcome the new bishop to the town, followed by the priests of the town carrying precious ornaments for the ceremonial washing of hands. Obviously the form would have to be changed a little for the bishop of the new church, but the municipal council were determined that the ceremony should not be deficient in splendour. No expense was spared. Representatives from Caen, Lisieux, Pont l'Evêque, Balleroy, Creully, and Isigny were to attend in full force. Police protection of the new bishop was reinforced by the municipality, who feared lest some fanatical supporter of the old church should make an attempt on Fauchet's life, but the day was not marred by such an event. One man was arrested for spitting in Fauchet's direction. The non-juring priests had forbidden the townspeople to attend, but rarely had Bayeux witnessed such a spectacle. All the new administrative bodies and the law-court turned out: a detachment of the dragoons of the regiment of Aunis and the 47th regiment of Lorraine added to the magnificence of the procession and Fauchet himself, extrovert, intense, and with a fine sense of the theatrical, commanded the occasion. The townspeople, as was intended, were thoroughly impressed.

For Fauchet, once the inauguration ceremony was over, Bayeux must have come as something of a shock. Basically conservative, with little apparent political vitality, the town had little to offer in comparison with Caen. The municipal council, half aristocratic, half composed of men of the courts, although it had spent so lavishly in its welcome of Fauchet as bishop, was doubtful about the political leanings of this highly individualist ecclesiastic and even more dubious about his personal conduct. But both bishop and council were anxious to use each other. Fauchet was bent on a political career: the municipal authority wanted the rapid installation of a bishop to restore stability. It desired a figurehead, a symbol of order in the church, and nothing more. Relations between Fauchet and the council were, from the beginning, on the one part openly scornful and on the other profoundly suspicious. For Fauchet Bayeux was a hotbed of 'aristocracy' and 'fanaticism' and its ruling clique were interested in self-preservation rather than progress.[1] He found Caen a much more congenial, a more vital city with more advanced ideas. In the *société populaire* of that city he might secure much more influential support than he could ever hope to receive at Bayeux, the sort of support which would embark him upon a more important political career.

Fauchet had arrived in Bayeux with a clearly defined political philosophy. Aulard has described him as a Christian socialist.[2] For him politics and religion were intricately knit together. The Revolution was a step in the realization of an ideal state devoid of social inequality, where the central authority as embodied in the representatives of the people had full control. Religion was to be the means by which the people of France were directed into the path of progress and reform. Fauchet wanted the officials of his church to understand and work for these ideals.

The juring priests of Bayeux had been hopeful that they would be chosen as episcopal vicars by the new bishop to help in the running of the diocese. As men of the region, with knowledge of the diocese and the reputation of having stood by their oath in defiance of their former bishop, they seemed the obvious choice.

---

[1] A.N. DXXIX 3. Dossier 31.
[2] A. Aulard, *Histoire politique de la Révolution française* (Paris, 1926), p. 50.

Fauchet had other ideas. He intended to confer office on men he knew, men who would owe him allegiance and who would be prepared not only to propagate his views from the pulpit but organize the *sociétés populaires* and any organs of public opinion the district and department might possess. In June 1791 he began, very carefully, to build up such a nucleus from his former colleagues and men of similar left-wing views in church administration and politics. He chose from Paris Louis Marin Bajot, chaplain of the hospital of St. Jacques, and Chaix d'Est Ange, almoner of the hospital of the Salpêtrière, both known to Fauchet from his Cercle Social days. Despreaux and Charbonnel, of Nevers and St. Flour respectively, were also political churchmen of note. Prudent Gasnier, former administrator of the *collège* at Lisieux, and Hébert of Maizières, a rival with Fauchet for the diocese, were the only relatively local men apart from Le Gros of Gray, and they were all celebrated for the outspoken nature of their support of the state church. Bonneville and La Cauve were also former Paris associates of the bishop and a hint of nepotism crept in with Nicolas Donet, Fauchet's nephew, from Dornes, a very young priest who was rapidly promoted by his uncle.[1]

In Chaix d'Est Ange and Gasnier especially Fauchet had the support he sought. Chaix d'Est Ange was rapidly nominated by the bishop to the important parish of St. Étienne at Caen and quickly became Fauchet's spokesman in the *société populaire* there.[2] Gasnier within a few weeks had taken over the rather sleepy *société populaire* of Bayeux and become its president. Fauchet's pastoral visit to his diocese in the late spring of 1791 was nothing short of a political tour. In Caen, in Bayeux, in Lisieux, in Falaise, he spoke in the larger churches and, equally important, addressed the *sociétés populaires*. The club in Bayeux assumed an air of political excitement hitherto unparalleled in the town. It became the centre of all political activity, chiding the municipal council and the district assembly for any recalcitrance in implementing government decrees. In a matter of months it was a rival authority to the municipal council and the centre of Fauchet's power within the town.

This nucleus of support was important. It meant that Fauchet's opinions were assured of a 'forum' and, as long as his men were in

[1] Charrier, op. cit., vol. ii, p. 33.
[2] Sévèstre, *Les Problèmes religieux . . .*, p. 497.

full control, of acceptance. Especially on religious matters, Fauchet's views were far more extreme than anything envisaged by the Assembly in 1791. These views were to be presented to the political societies of the towns of the Calvados and in turn pressure was brought to bear on the departmental and district authorities. The official government attitude towards non-jurors in mid 1791 was one of general tolerance. The proclamation of 18 March 1791 declared that all non-jurors were deprived of their public ministry but that refusal to take the oath was no crime. Non-jurors were disqualified from taking a position in the constitutional church but they were entitled to a pension. The majority in the Assembly were clearly of the opinion that as few as possible should suffer from the changes that they had introduced. On 7 May the non-jurors were promised that they might use the parish church to say mass as long as no disorderly scenes occurred and the priest refrained from anti-revolutionary sermons.[1] The Assembly was far more influenced by the situation in Paris than by what was happening in the provinces. In Paris the large number of churches made toleration feasible: in the provinces it too often meant that the non-juring priest and the juror had to share the same church, the same ornaments, and, even worse, the same congregation. Where the juror was an outsider he often failed to command the support of the faithful of the parish and had the humiliating experience of preaching to an empty church while the masses of the non-juror were well attended. Thus ugly scenes occurred at St. Sulpice, Trevières, and Crépon in the district of Bayeux,[2] where the jurors found they could not command allegiance, and the situation was worse in the district of Caen where the proportion of non-jurors was higher. There was no doubt that wherever Fauchet looked in his diocese the non-jurors were a distinct impediment to the authority of the constitutional church which the bishop was so anxious to enhance.

The new bishop, from the moment of inception, adopted an attitude of open hostility towards the non-jurors: nor could they command the support of the local administrators against him, for during the later months of 1790 the difficulties involved in the

[1] W. Edington, 'An Administrative Study of the Implementation of the Civil Constitution of the Clergy in the Diocese of Lisieux' (an unpublished doctoral thesis of the University of London, 1958), pp. 193–4.
[2] A.D.C. Lv. *Liasse des serments*.

implementation of the financial clauses of the Civil Constitution of the Clergy, and the fundamental impossibility of a prompt and effective payment of one, let alone of two bodies of clergy, was rapidly becoming apparent to district and department. The machinery which organized this payment creaked only very slowly into operation. By the terms of the decree of 6 August 1790, the district authorities were to undertake a full assessment of the value of ecclesiastical property based upon detailed accounts submitted by every priest, whatever his status, of his ecclesiastical revenues. This, together with a list of every cleric in the district and his status, was to be submitted to the government. But this was no easy task. De Cheylus forbade his clergy to supply estimates. At the beginning of December the government was still in the dark on these points. The district administrations were new and only worked slowly. For 1790 the clerics were supposed to enjoy the income they had possessed under the old régime, with a government subsidy if it did not reach the stipulated minimum laid down in the civil constitution. After December 1790 the state declared its intention to assume full control. It promised that the first payments should be made to the clergy for the quarter January to April 1791 in January, together with any supplement needed for 1790. The first real lump sums from the government were thus due at the beginning of 1791, before the complications of the issues between jurors and non-jurors arose.[1]

The district of Bayeux had estimated that for 1790 it owed to the ecclesiastics of the district some 480,000 *livres*. Towards that sum it should have obtained in revenues from ecclesiastical property some 360,000 *livres*. It therefore sought some 120,000 *livres* from Paris. In fact, the projected 360,000 *livres* only realized some 32,000, since those owing rents and dues to the old church refused to pay.[2] A tentative estimate of what was owing to the jurors was made in January 1791, but as yet few had taken the oath, and every day estimates changed. In June 1791, in answer to a complaint by the government that estimates still had not come in, the district outlined some of the difficulties involved in trying to assess clerical incomes in the area especially because those who were in debt to the church took advantage of the confusion.

---

[1] Edington, op. cit., pp. 80–113, examines in great detail the problems involved in the financial arrangements of the Civil Constitution of the Clergy.

[2] A.N. F¹⁹ 1380. 1 January 1791.

Provision had to be made too for many who were not parish priests—men like Michel Grimouville, aged seventy-one, a priest of Bayeux who wrote to the district in April 1791 explaining that he was really too weak to hold any sort of position. He had scraped along for years as one of the chaplains to the Sisters of Charity and a part-time teacher at the *collège*. He was willing to take the oath but was really too worn out to work. Surely he could have a pension of some kind?[1] People like him, who were extremely numerous, had to be fitted into the framework of the provisions. In fact, the position of each ecclesiastic had to be considered individually. In view of the general dearth of clergy, in many districts every incentive was used to encourage the members of religious orders to stand for election as parish priests, and it was usual to grant them the full salary of the living attached to the parish plus half their pension as regulars. The prospect was meant to be financially attractive and several of the regular clergy of Bayeux seized the opportunity. Some, however, wanted to move out, to return to their families, and the district authorities had to make provision for their payment elsewhere; while others wanted to move in and then the district had to wait for information from outside. All this took time and impeded the compilation of accurate estimates. In September 1791 the department of the Calvados sent a letter complaining to the district of Bayeux of its lateness in sending in accurate lists. It asked to be informed immediately of the arrears still owing for 1790 and the sums required for each of the quarters of 1791. The estimates, it said, must be submitted at once because the treasury at Caen was empty and Paris wanted exact information before any more funds were sent.[2] Bayeux was the last district of the department to send in estimates, partly because it had a far higher number of clerics than the others. Caen reminded Bayeux of the hardship lack of funds could occasion the ecclesiastics. In fact, the district did not need to be told. Theoretically, the clerics were supposed to be notified by the district authority when the money came. In practice, whether jurors or non-jurors, they hung around the doors of the district assembly waiting for it to arrive. Those on the spot could then share in whatever there was to be had.[3]

Nor, even when the final estimates were submitted in October, was the government able to show any speed in payment. The full

[1] A.D.C. Lv. *Pensions ecclésiastiques.*   [2] Ibid.   [3] Ibid.

extent of the cost of financing two churches was far greater than had ever been anticipated. Taxation was slow in coming in. The profits from the sale of national property were entering the national treasury at a rate far less speedy than had been anticipated in 1790. By April 1791 the government, trying both to compel the payment of taxes and postpone the day when the second quarter of ecclesiastical pensions would fall due, warned pension and salary holders that they would not be paid the second instalment of their pensions for 1791—should they have been fortunate enough to receive the first—until they had paid their *contribution patriotique*; though, if the department was in agreement, this could be deducted from their pensions at source. By mid 1791 the government was seeking as far as possible to curb its payments.[1]

The difficulties involved in payment of two sets of clergy encouraged the administrative bodies of the Calvados to adopt a much harsher attitude towards the non-jurors, a situation which Fauchet was quick to exploit. In his opinion non-jurors were traitors who ought to be neither tolerated nor paid. The flight to Varennes was used by the bishop to attack the lukewarmness of the departmental and district authorities in carrying out the decrees of the government.[2] The departmental *directoire* was split by this attack into moderates and extremists, with the latter in the majority. Measures were pushed through ordering all non-jurors to leave their former parishes within a week. Clergy who preached against public order were to be immediately imprisoned.[3] These provisions were exactly what Fauchet wanted, but went far beyond anything the government had decreed. De Lessart pointed out the illegality of the proceedings in a letter to the *directoire* on 7 September,[4] but in the meantime the decrees had been implemented. The *société populaire* at Bayeux had ordered a number of its members to drive the non-jurors from the town. The town council, not being prepared to go to these extremes, dispatched the National Guard to defend the clerics.

Neither the municipal nor district authority of Bayeux was prepared to go as far as Fauchet wished in its treatment of the non-jurors—that is, unless profit were to be had. It was precisely for this reason that the district agreed to close, quite illegally, all

[1] *Moniteur.* 2 April 1791.   [2] Charrier, op. cit., vol. ii, pp. 134–40.
[3] Bibl. Mun. Caen. *Réserve fonds normand*, C985.
[4] Ibid. Letter of 7 September 1791.

the male religious houses of the area left open to receive the handful of clerics who had chosen to stay but which, it declared, were centres of disaffection to the new bishop; and in reply to an address from the *société populaire* of the town that the churches attached to religious orders were being used by non-jurors and were drawing large crowds whilst the cathedral was relatively deserted, it promptly put their property on the market.[1] Indeed, Fauchet learnt during his brief stay in the Calvados that the best way to undermine the old church and buttress the new was to stress the uneconomic nature of the attempt to subsidize two distinct churches. On other issues he commanded less support. His attempts to force the administrative bodies of the area into a more extreme position *vis-à-vis* the church always met the hostility of a hard conservative core as yet entrenched in office.

The first clash between Fauchet, backed by his episcopal vicars and the *société populaire*, and the municipal and local authorities was not long in coming. The flight to Varennes in June 1791 found the profoundly conservative municipal council anxious to prevent an anti-monarchical demonstration. They declared that any disturbance would lead to immediate imprisonment. The *société populaire* registered a formal protest at the council's attitude and two of the younger members tore down the sign that indicated the Place Louis XVI. The municipal council, headed by de Littry, a wealthy noble, decided to make an example of the pair. They were imprisoned and a petition from the *société populaire* urging their immediate release was ignored. The municipal government thought it had succeeded in reducing the *société populaire* to its rightful size. The episcopal vicar, Chaix d'Est Ange, however, took the side of the imprisoned men. Fauchet, from Caen, sent a letter to be read by each juring priest after the Saturday (market-day) mass, denouncing the illegality of the municipal council's action in no uncertain terms. Minor clashes occurred in the city between those who had heard Fauchet's missive and the National Guard. Fauchet himself appeared in the cathedral on 28 July and in full pontifical robes denounced the municipality from the pulpit. He threatened the transference of the bishopric to Caen if the authorities of Bayeux did not demonstrate more patriotism and fervour.[2]

[1] A.D.C. L. *Registres des déliberations du directoire du district de Bayeux*. September 1791.   [2] Laffetay, op. cit., p. 268.

The municipal council reached the not surprising conclusion that Fauchet and the club were attempting to undermine their authority and that the time had come to make a stand against the pretensions of the bishop. The council referred the issue to the district tribunal, which ordered Fauchet's arrest for inciting the townspeople against the local authorities, and sent off representatives to Paris to complain of the bishop's conduct. They alleged:

L'Assemblée Nationale a décrété une constitution monarchique, la monarchie lui est odieuse; une constitution représentative et il voudrait que le peuple exerçât lui-même ses pouvoirs. Il prêche la réformation d'un gouvernement qui n'est point établi. Il excite les hommes à l'insurrection. Son orgueil gigantesque ne reconnaît aucune autorité, ni des corps administratifs, ni des tribunaux, ni même celle de l'Assemblée Nationale et du roi. Il emploie un grand étalage de principes, les grands mots de patriotisme, de fraternité religieuse pour égarer le peuple. Il parcourt actuellement les campagnes, il prêche même à Caen ces principes dans les rues.[1]

The *société populaire* of Bayeux addressed a letter to the departmental *directoire* urging the immediate dismissal of the municipal council for its insolent behaviour. The department could not in fact ignore the incident, since it was no small matter to order the bishop's arrest. Moreover, the departmental *directoire* already contained a faction strong in support of Fauchet and extremely sensitive to the opinion of the clubs in Caen. Already the *directoire* had been split on the issue of the punishment of the non-jurors: now the rift became even more marked. Fauchet's chief supporter in the *directoire* was Vardon, called his '*âme damnée*'. Vardon urged that the *directoire* take Fauchet's side in the dispute. Fauchet himself launched a vicious attack on the administrators when they hesitated, saying that they must be hand in glove with the councillors of Bayeux. Vardon and his clique attacked the *procureur syndic* of the department, who was the leader of the moderates, for a financial error which he had long since rectified and forced his resignation, along with that of Maheust, a lawyer of Bayeux who had put forward the case of the municipality, and another supporter, de la Croix.[2] The resignation of the three officials brought the matter to a national level. De Lessart demanded their immediate reinstallation in the interest of peace

---

[1] Pezet, op. cit., p. 182.　　　　　　　　[2] A.N. F^{19} 410.

in the department, and the condemnation of the bishop by the municipality of Bayeux was read out in the Assembly:

Courant de paroisse en paroisse dans les campagnes, faisant des chaires de leurs églises autant de tribunes, autant d'harangues, il étonne, séduit, aveugle, présente l'administration comme remplie de gens corrompus, s'annonce comme un centre de lumière et de vérité, comme l'homme unique qui puisse conserver les vrais intérêts du peuple. . . . La réunion dans sa bouche de la religion et de la politique lui donne la consistance de ces grands novateurs qui ont autrefois renversé des empires.[1]

De Wimpffen followed with a letter complaining that the municipality simply dared not send any representatives to Caen to put forward their case, since Fauchet had the support of as many as five or six thousand in the clubs there and they feared for their lives. De Wimpffen received a sympathetic hearing, for Fauchet had always had many enemies in Paris. Many, even of the constitutional church, considered him an extremist whose views would be destructive of order. On 20 August 1791 Joubert, constitutional bishop of the Charente Inférieure, called for Fauchet's arrest and denounced his conduct as the direct negation of that expected of a man of the church.[2]

Fauchet had ignored the order for his arrest when put forward by the tribunal of Bayeux but he could hardly ignore the issue when it was raised in the Assembly. He was hopeful of election as one of the department's representatives to the Legislative Assembly in the coming September. The municipal council had urged the current Calvados deputies, de Wimpffen and Delauney, to try to prevent this. De Lessart strongly condemned the bishop's activities since his arrival in the Calvados. Pétion objected that the order of the tribunal for the arrest of Fauchet was an extreme step. But no one was prepared to go to the bishop's defence. Even his friends were silent. Fauchet decided it was politic to climb down and apologize to the municipality. The council really wanted nothing more. It was out to prove its strength, assert itself over Fauchet and the *société populaire* and that done was willing to drop the whole issue.[3] The apology was immediately accepted. The only institution to feel in any way dissatisfied was the tribunal which had ordered the arrest, but Genas Duhomme, the judge, was to

[1] A.N. DXXIX 3. Dossier 31.   [2] Charrier, op. cit., vol. i, p. 371.
[3] Laffetay, op. cit., pp. 271–80.

be disappointed. Nothing he could do would bring Fauchet before the tribunal. The municipal council was satisfied with the apology and a vote of the Assembly that Fauchet should limit his activities to ecclesiastical matters and not meddle in politics.[1]

At the departmental level too Fauchet sustained a reversal. In spite of the strength of his supporters in the *directoire*, the three members were reinstated by the Assembly. Moreover, the religious policy advocated by the bishop and translated into decrees by the department was condemned at the national level. The attempts in the department to drive out the non-jurors were reversed by the Minister of the Interior.[2] Their return to Bayeux was the occasion of a hostile demonstration organized by the *société populaire* but the municipal council, made confident by its recent success, turned out the National Guard and restored order.

The municipal authority had won the first round against the bishop but the second victory was Fauchet's beyond any shadow of doubt. The quarrel with the municipal council had come at an unfortunate time for the politically ambitious bishop. To secure a place in the Legislative Assembly he needed the backing of Bayeux. He had been forbidden to undertake any political manœuvring himself. The elections were to demonstrate the electioneering qualities of the group of episcopal vicars Fauchet had so carefully chosen. Throughout August they were hard at work organizing the three sections of the city. This, coupled with the political support he knew he possessed in the *société populaire*, Fauchet deemed sufficient to secure his victory in the primary elections. His calculation proved correct, though the counter activities of the municipal council made the victory narrower than it might otherwise have been, and Fauchet was sent to the final election to be held in Caen. In the larger city he was on far more sympathetic territory: 402 out of 536 voters chose Fauchet as deputy to the Assembly.[3] On 28 September 1791 he left Caen never to return to his diocese. His departure did not mean political peace for Bayeux. The bishop had engulfed the small town in bitter dissensions, which were intensified over the ensuing months by the activities of the episcopal vicars in the sections and the *société populaire* of Bayeux, in their attempt to ensure that henceforth

[1] A.N. BB¹⁶. *Division dite civile*, 107.
[2] A.N. F¹⁹ 410. Letter of 10 October 1791.
[3] Charrier, op. cit., vol. ii, pp. 7–21.

all positions of influence in the town should go to Fauchet's
supporters. Anyone with political aspirations willing to adhere to
the bishop could count upon the backing of the club and the votes
of the sections. The first indication of the success of this political
manœuvring on the part of the episcopal vicars was given at the
municipal elections of November 1791. None of the old officials
who had opposed Fauchet was returned. The council was still
composed of men of the courts, but they were men who were
ready to identify themselves with the bishop's party in order to
gain office. The new mayor, Duhamel de Vailly, a former notary,
had written to Fauchet formally seeking his support and Fauchet
agreed to nominate him. The new *procureur* of the town and the
municipal officials secured election in the same way. Fauchet was
pleased with the result. He wrote to De Vailly:

S'il m'était possible d'oublier jamais les trahisons, les perfidies et les
noirceurs de la minorité aristocratique et infâme qui a eu l'impudence
de m'y faire les plus insolents outrages, je me retrouverais heureux
d'habiter une cité dont la municipalité serait composée de mes meilleurs
amis; mais je rencontrerais encore, dans l'administration du district,
les ronces de la haine et les épines de la mauvaise foi; dans le tribunal,
des hommes éhontés qui mettent leur honneur dans la persécution des
bons citoyens et leur bonheur dans les plus sanglantes et les plus
atroces injustices envers les zélés défenseurs de la patrie. Quand on a
du sang dans les veines et le feu sacré de la liberté dans l'âme, on ne
se remet pas à la merci de pareils monstres. Il n'est pas jusqu'au receveur
du district qui épuise toutes les chicanes les plus malhonnêtes pour
retenir encore mon traitement.[1]

But it was only a matter of months before other elections fell due.
One by one Fauchet's opponents lost office. Genas Duhomme,
judge of the tribunal, resigned when he saw how office was
obtained. De Vailly passed from being mayor of Bayeux to the
district and then the departmental assembly in the short space of
eighteen months. Throughout 1792 those prepared to use Fauchet
to gain power gradually monopolized the administrative positions
of the town and district. It also meant that they could in turn be
used by the bishop. This was an alliance which was ultimately to
prove disastrous to both parties, but for those desirous of office
in 1792 there was no surer way to the top.

It might have been expected that the first issues on which

---

[1] Bibl. Chanoine Deslandes, cited by Charrier, op. cit., vol. ii, p. 84.

Fauchet would make himself heard in the Assembly would be religious. In February 1792 he undertook a scathing denunciation of the religious policy of the Minister of the Interior, De Lessart, whom he directly accused of leniency toward traitors and complicity in the plots of non-jurors in the department of the Calvados. He cited the names of the moderate elements in the departmental *directoire*, the *procureur syndic*, and Maheust and de la Croix as the agents through whom he worked. In Paris the speech was virtually ignored, but it was printed by the Jacobins and a copy circulated to affiliated clubs including that of Caen where it was to have serious repercussions. Led by Chaix d'Est Ange and Le Gros, two of the episcopal vicars, the *clubistes* of Caen demanded the resignation of the *procureur syndic*.[1] But the Legislative Assembly issued a warning and the matter had to be dropped. The survival of a moderate element was still a barrier to Fauchet's plans for the expulsion of the non-juring clergy. On the issue of the withdrawal of tolerance for the non-jurors, he drew only a blank. On the other hand, on the question of the withdrawal of payment for non-jurors he had greater success. By October 1791 the government was aware of the enormity of the payment it owed to the clergy of France and the relative impossibility of ever fully acquitting its debts to the two churches. The financial implementation of the civil constitution was an early topic of discussion for the new Assembly because payment for the last quarter of 1791 was long due. Indeed, those who could theoretically claim payment in advance were clamouring outside the district office in Bayeux.

Fauchet was quick to point out the uneconomic nature of a system which used the nation's money in the payment of men who were not even obedient to the will of the country. His speech on this issue, on 26 October 1791, declared:

> Tolérons-les, mais ne les payons pas — la nation permet tous les cultes; mais elle n'en paie qu'un ... pourquoi payerions-nous d'anciens fonctionnaires qui ont volontairement abandonné la patrie? Pourquoi nourririons-nous une horde de chanoines qui n'ont jamais fait rien d'utile et qui travaillent à renverser l'édifice des lois?[2]

He was ready with a comprehensive plan to insist upon an oath for all pensioners who received state assistance. Failure to comply would mean complete deprivation of pension. Faced with the

---

[1] A.D.C. L. *Registre de correspondance du directoire du département.* 19 February 1792.
[2] *Moniteur.* 26 October 1791.

debts of 1791 and the vision of an identical 1792, the Assembly passed the measure on 29 November; but the royal sanction was refused and so the measure could not pass into law. Fauchet's assertions were, however, quite correct. By late 1791 the maintenance of two churches was an economic impossibility. The department of the Calvados sent in its estimates but Paris never met them. The districts had to decide who to pay first. Obviously those who had taken the oath had to have first claim. Pathetic letters arrived almost daily from aged nuns whose families had long since died and who had no resources other than the pension. Some of them were too feeble to find alternative employment. In fact the measure of 29 November, which had not received royal sanction, was notwithstanding partially put into practice by the district of Bayeux, which paid the constitutional clergy and the nuns as far as it could and the rest if there was anything left. The district treasurer, Varin, complained continually of crowds of ecclesiastics thronging about his door awaiting payment.[1]

At the same time, the conflict between the two churches was clearly intensifying. Parishes which had both a juror and a non-juror were regaled with the spectacle of two men fighting bitterly for the adherence of the faithful of the parish. Theoretically the non-juror was not prevented from saying mass but the hours at which he did so were regulated by the juror. They had to share the same ornaments, the same vestments, the same keys to the same church. Sometimes the constitutional clergy of Bayeux observed the letter of the law, but rarely its spirit. All sorts of petty difficulties were raised which made arrangements for the masses of non-jurors so complicated as to make them virtually impossible. The hours when they were permitted to say mass were suddenly changed; candles were locked up; chalices disappeared; and baptismal fonts were hidden. In the town the non-jurors were afraid to complain since Fauchet's men were entrenched everywhere. Indeed the position of those who had not taken the oath in the town became increasingly untenable and non-juring leaders in Normandy accepted that the decree of 29 November, even though it did not pass into law, was the beginning of a general persecution. The townspeople do not appear to have taken sides in the dispute. The most striking feature of their attitude is that some time between December and Lent of 1792 they simply ceased

[1] A.D.C. Lv. *Pensions ecclésiastiques. Bayeux.*

to attend mass. The women from whom chairs were hired complained of the lack of attendance even at the cathedral. Sometimes,
they said, less than a dozen were present.[1] The townspeople
obviously tired of the rival claims of juror and non-juror and
preferred to let them argue it out alone. In the country districts
the situation was different. The country people were equally indifferent to the theological implications of the oath, but they
clung to their priest, whether juror or non-juror, simply because
he was their man, familiar to them, and had shared their hardships.
Where the priest opted to refuse the oath, the juror who replaced
him was treated with hostility. The new-comer to Bernières sur
Mer found himself confined to his presbytery: he dared not go
out lest his parishioners kill him. At Noyers the incoming priest
received letters threatening his life. At Litteau even the municipal
officials took the side of the non-juror. Again, at Troarn the
municipal officials tried to retard the installation of the new priest
and then refused to attend his masses.[2] Wherever juror and non-
juror met friction was apt to ensue.

Fauchet grew increasingly impatient over the continued official
policy of tolerance for non-jurors. This more than any other
consideration moved him into a position of constant opposition
to the king and his ministers in company with that group of
politicians—Roland, Brissot, Pétion amongst others—who were
urging the government to declare war in an attempt to force the
hand of the king and his ministers to make them define their
position *vis-à-vis* the Revolution.[3] In January 1792 he spoke in the
Assembly for a limited offensive against Austria.[4] In April the
government was forced into war and the war party assumed office.
Finally when the *journée* of 10 August proved beyond doubt that
the king was in contact with the enemies of France and the power
of the suspensive veto was taken from the monarchy, Fauchet's
hopes were realized. The non-jurors lost their main support and
a harsher attitude was immediately adopted. Failure to take the
oath was equated with lack of patriotism and all priests, whether
they held a position or not, were required to take an oath of
adherence to the constitution or lose their pension.[5] Then on 23
August 1792 came the decree which decided the fate of the non-

---

[1] Latreille, op. cit., p. 108.   [2] Charrier, op. cit., vol. ii, pp. 43–44.
[3] M. Sydenham, *The Girondins* (London, 1961), p. 124.
[4] Ibid., p. 103.   [5] *Procès Verbal* ..., vol. xiii. 11 August 1792.

jurors of Bayeux. All those who had refused to take the oath or had retracted it were ordered to leave French territory within a fortnight.[1] The non-juring priests of Bayeux all applied for passports within the week.[2] Even the capitular clergy who were not theoretically subject to deportation since they were not included in the provisions of July 1790 went into hiding.

These extreme measures of the summer of 1792 were in part the product of panic engendered by a war which was in its early phases totally unsuccessful. Popular panic during these months found an outlet in the persecution of non-juring priests who were suspected, because they belonged to the old régime, of treachery and sympathy with the royalists who were menacing France's frontiers. The non-juring priests of Normandy made their way to the coast hoping to take a boat to England or Jersey. The large numbers of ecclesiastics on the roads caused concern in many rural communities. Whereas many villages were prepared to hide their own non-juring priest and menace his constitutional successor, they viewed these strangers with alarm. Perhaps they were royalist spies with a rendezvous in mind where they would congregate and descend *en masse* upon the innocent populace. The coastal area a few miles north of Bayeux proved most accessible to this kind of rumour. In August some twenty priests and curates of Bayeux took passports and prepared to leave the country. They congregated with others, estimated at about a hundred, at Port en Bessin to await a vessel bound for England and due the following day. At Port en Bessin in time of war there was always fear of bombardment by the English. The fact that France was not yet at war with Great Britain made no difference. The English were the enemy. They had destroyed the port twice in the past fifty years. Nor was it an area over-sympathetic to the church. The bishop had been *seigneur*, and an unpopular one, of Port en Bessin. The large number of ecclesiastics caused some alarm. The rumour spread that three hundred English troops had descended on the port and were about to burn it. News of the arrival of the non-existent English brought rushing to the town the peasantry of the surrounding area. They were reported back to Bayeux as numbering anything between 3,000 and 4,000, armed with pitch-

[1] Ibid., 23 August 1792.
[2] E. Sévèstre, *La Déportation du clergé orthodoxe pendant la Révolution* (Paris, 1915), p. 192.

8214   O

forks and farm tools and intent upon preventing the enemy from
destroying the port and ravaging the countryside. The boat
designed to carry the priests into exile was pointed out as an
English vessel and the cry was raised that it must be grounded
and destroyed. The captain decided to sail there and then without waiting for his passengers to embark. The crowd was left,
irritated, roused for nothing and with only a hundred priests as an
outlet for its fury. They were stripped of their clothes and their
money and several were roughly handled. The arrival of the
National Guard from Bayeux saved them from a worse fate.
The crowd only turned them over to the soldiers with great
reluctance. They were ushered back to Bayeux, penniless and
in rags. The next day they addressed a letter to the municipal
council stipulating their anxiety to leave and begging protection.
It was accorded and they were conveyed to the nearby port of
Bernières and from thence to England and exile.[1]

The proximity to the coast made flight fairly easy for the clerics
of the area. They were more fortunate than others who lived in
central France and who came increasingly under attack as France's
difficulties increased. Many even of the district of Bayeux, provided
they had sufficient contacts and could depend on their families in
the more remote rural areas, did not judge flight necessary. But
those of the town were well advised to shake the dust of France
from their heels and accept such hospitality as the British afforded.
Contrary to Fauchet's expectation, the expulsion of the non-jurors
during the summer of 1792 did not inflate the power of the
constitutional church. The rejection of the old was not out of
any love for the new. An unsuccessful war brought increased
financial problems: the government could not meet the estimates
sent in by the districts. Throughout 1792 payment to the constitutional clergy of Bayeux was at least three months in arrears. The
new church was also cracking from within. Irregular payment, a
possible knife in the back in the countryside, jibes or indifference
in the towns, these were not inducements to enter the service of
the state church. Never had the seminary of Bayeux had so few
ordinands. In November 1791 it contained a mere twenty-four,
in December twenty-six, in January twenty-nine. In his anxiety
to ensure a steady flow, Fauchet sanctioned a course lasting no

---

[1] Uzureau, 'La Déportation ecclésiastique dans le Calvados, 1792', *Revue Catholique de Normandie*, 1931.

longer than six weeks. Moreover, the quality of those leaving the seminary was the subject of much criticism. Thomas Lindet, bishop of the Eure, remarked to his brother in a letter of 18 May 1792:

Je viens d'ordonner vingt prêtres. MM. de Calvados sont toujours aux aguets des mes ordinations et ont une pépinière inépuisable. Il est vrai que ces messieurs en ramassent de toutes les extrémités du monde. Ils avaient amené de Bayeux un homme qui, il y a trois semaines, était comédien à Bayeux: il était de Perpignan. J'ai dit que je croyais qu'un comédien pouvait être actuellement un bon citoyen, mais que je ne croyais pas qu'il pût être actuellement un bon prêtre, surtout dans le lieu où il a développé ses talents.[1]

As defections increased the training decreased. Candidates were rushed through the preliminary stages of tonsured clerk, minor orders, subdeaconate to deaconate in two days. Probably about two hundred priests were ordained in the Calvados during Fauchet's tenure of office, but still there were not enough. By mid 1792 even the episcopal vicars had to serve rural cures in order to remedy the deficit.[2]

More and more during the autumn of 1792 Fauchet was pushed into a defensive position. The picture of the bishop at this time is of a man fulminating in vain over issues in which other men had clearly lost interest. The political support he had engineered for himself in the Calvados secured his re-election to the Convention, but he was now a lonely figure without political affiliations who was continually in opposition. His attack on Roland on the issue of clerical marriage received only a cold reception.[3] The church meant little when the defence of France was at stake. Finally, in January 1793, Fauchet took to print and created a weekly paper, the *Journal des Amis*, to express his personal views on issues on which he was condemned to silence in the Assembly. The clerical policy of the Convention came under fire. The king's execution received his unqualified disapproval. An issue of the *Journal des Amis* was devoted to an examination of the illegality of the proceedings at the trial.[4] The paper became one of the organs by which the Jacobin hold on the sections of Paris came under attack. Fauchet held that the views of provincial France were

[1] Montier, *Correspondance de Robert Lindet . . .*, pp. 348–9. Lindet performed the ordinations since Fauchet was in Paris.
[2] Charrier, op. cit., vol. ii, p. 70.   [3] Ibid., p. 212.   [4] Ibid.

stifled. The tone of his writings became increasingly bitter as he went virtually unheard in the Assembly, but his very considerable literary talents were sufficient to make the Jacobins regard him as an enemy with which to be reckoned. In June 1793 he was among the members of the Convention proscribed by the Mountain. At his trial he pointed out, with justification, his opposition to the anti-clerical views of Roland and his associates with whom he was now numbered. All that could be brought against him were his political writings and his attendance at meetings with the deputies of the Calvados to discuss how the Jacobin hold on the sections of Paris could be undermined. He was able to deny any direct association with the federalist movement of the summer of 1793, since during those months when several of the departments of France were in insurrection he had been in prison awaiting trial. The truth of this had to be admitted; yet in the Calvados, the federalist movement was to be in very large part directed by those men who had used Fauchet to gain power and whose positions depended upon Fauchet's continuance in office.

The federalist movement in the Calvados assumed important proportions because the department was chosen as the place for the last stand by the fleeing 'Girondins'. The struggle for supremacy in the Convention had been won by the Jacobins not because they were in the majority but because they were a small, determined nucleus with the backing of the capital. The federalist movement has been described as an attempt by a part of provincial France to assert that Paris was not the whole country and that the provinces had a right to an opinion in political matters and the government of the country. There is some truth in this. All the Calvados deputies had been either arrested or in some way compromised and the department could feel justifiable anger. Also by mid 1793 much of the sympathy previously shown towards events in Paris had evaporated. During the summer months of 1793, when parts of the Calvados were suffering from acute food shortage, the two government representatives who arrived in June in Caen, Prieur de la Côte d'Or, and Romme, had been asked to assist the departmental administration in solving the food problem of the area. They replied that there was nothing they could do;[1] their concern, it seemed, was to ensure that supplies to Paris were

[1] A. Goodwin, 'The Federalist Movement in Caen during the French Revolution', *Bulletin of the John Rylands Library*, no. 42 (1960), p. 341.

not checked. On 11 June Caen resolved that the transport of all foodstuffs from the Calvados to the Paris market should be immediately suspended. The roads leading from the Calvados to the capital, in particular the Cherbourg to Paris road along which dairy produce was carried, were blocked.[1] Moreover, as has already been said, Fauchet had been assiduous in building up his influence in the Calvados, and in his episcopal vicars his influence remained. The Carabot society in Caen would have risen for Fauchet's cause alone. Now his vicar general, Chaix d'Est Ange, on 1 July called the general assembly of the Calvados and projected a grand march on Paris to reinstate the banished members.[2] In Bayeux the municipal council, the district assembly, and the district tribunal had all been staffed by men appointed through the bishop's influence. The *société populaire* of the town had been organized by another episcopal vicar, Prudent Gasnier, and the priest, de Beaudre.

However, the faction in the *société populaire* headed by de Beaudre was challenged throughout 1793 by a small but influential party led by the leading surgeon of the town, Jean Le Tual. It was in the nature of things that Le Tual would oppose any faction composed of ecclesiastics, whether jurors or non-jurors. His anti-clericalism was founded on a long struggle with the nursing sisters of the *hôtel Dieu*, who had continually crushed his projects for the formation of a surgical school and had gone so far as to prevent him doing post-mortem examinations on the dead of the hospital on the grounds that this showed a lack of respect for the dead. To Le Tual, to be a juror was almost worse than being a non-juror, for at Bayeux at least it meant being a political churchman. On at least three occasions he had delivered an onslaught on the clerics in the *société populaire*.[3] Whatever their current position, he urged, they should be remembered as the former puppets of despotism. On one occasion so pointed was his attack that de Beaudre undertook a personal apology for the errors of his youth which had caused him to enter the old church. Le Tual was strongly backed in his opposition by a notary named Vautier, who had long conducted a bitter feud with de Vailly, who was now

[1] H. Wallon, *La Révolution du 31 mai et le fédéralisme en 1793* (Paris, 1886), vol. i, p. 447.
[2] Goodwin, op. cit., p. 329.
[3] E. Anquétil, 'La Société Populaire de Bayeux et J.C.C. Le Tual, Maire', *Mémoires de la Société des Sciences, Arts et Belles Lettres de Bayeux* (1924), pp. 6–7.

in the departmental assembly and one of Fauchet's supporters. Vautier had worked for de Vailly as a notary for many years. He had been an employee receiving a pittance compared with the proceeds which had entered de Vailly's hands. He spoke of de Vailly as an egoist, bent on nothing but personal political preferment. No matter what point at issue, it was said, if de Vailly had opted for one side, Vautier would quickly choose the other.[1]

This small knot of opposition was extremely energetic. Le Tual was a man both well known and highly respected in Bayeux and his attention for the sick, often free of charge, was widely appreciated. In comparison the episcopal vicars were outsiders and in any case the new church was not quite like the old. It did not dispense charity, it did not employ a host of servants and bell ringers and odd-job men, nor did it spend as freely. The municipal councillors who in 1791 had used the backing of the club to gain office had thought it safely under the control of their supporters and had neglected to ensure that it remained so. They seldom attended the meetings of the club. But suddenly they became uncomfortably aware that all was not well when, in February 1793, Le Tual was elected president.[2] The spring of 1793 saw the *société populaire* sharply divided between the supporters of Fauchet and those of Le Tual. The anti-clerical policy of the Convention which Fauchet had striven so hard to resist was urged upon the municipal government by the Le Tual faction, who criticized the local administrations for their recalcitrance in implementing government policy. It was not until June, however, that the strength of Le Tual's opposition was fully appreciated. On 8 June the administration of the department embraced the federalist cause and announced the insurrection of Caen. A day later the town officials of Bayeux announced that their town too would rally to the side of the federalists. Throughout June the proscribed deputies fled from Paris for Caen. Louvet, Pétion, Guadet, Meilhan, Salles, Gorsas, La Rivière, Buzot, and Barbaroux arrived within a matter of days to make a last stand.[3] In their final bid for power they were to join with a totally different ally, the royalist

---

[1] *Rapports des agents du Ministre de l'Intérieur dans les départements 1793–an 11,* publiés par P. *Caron* (Paris, 1951); *Rapports de Heudier,* pp. 17, 20–21.

[2] Anquétil, op. cit., p. 7.

[3] F. Vaultier, *Souvenirs de l'insurrection normande dite du fédéralisme, en 1793* (Caen, 1858), p. 275.

de Wimpffen. De Wimpffen, the popular noble military leader sent to the Estates General in 1789, had been one of the first nobles to read the writing on the wall and join the third estate in the National Assembly. His political career had revealed his basic conservatism but there was no denying his ability as a military leader. He had held Thionville for a month in August 1792 against sustained Prussian attack and had indeed stemmed their advance. After Valmy he was offered the Ministry of War but refused it and accepted instead the position of general of the *armée des côtes de Cherbourg*. As such, the defence of Normandy was in his hands after the declaration of war on Great Britain in February 1793. De Wimpffen was no republican. His belief in the old social order had been made patent time and again since the elections of 1789. The king's execution removed any shadow of allegiance he had ever had to the régime and he hovered for months on the brink of open defection to the royalist cause.[1] He could not, however, forget his past record. He could not admit to himself that somewhere he had been wrong, and that somewhere he and the Revolution had parted company. In June the administration of Bayeux and that of the department began to put pressure upon him to join the opposition to the Jacobins of Paris. They spoke of their disapprobation of the death of the king and current policy. De Wimpffen was reluctant to commit himself but after a week of pressure he promised to bring the army over to their side.[2] On 26 June the Convention heard of his defection. Barère denounced him to the Assembly as yet another Lafayette and Dumouriez.[3] He was formally relieved of his command. Now the federalist movement in Bayeux could count all the administrative bodies and the National Guard as its supporters, but little else. The episcopal vicars undertook to organize the sections of the town but without success because a rival force was at work, Le Tual and his faction in the *société populaire*. Small though his supporters were in number, they were able to meet the exhortations of the episcopal vicars in the sections. Le Tual toured the town reading an address from the *société populaire* of Cherbourg condemning any split within the republic.[4] To make sure it was well known, the address was printed and circulated to the sections. Delegates were sent out into the countryside to dis-

[1] *Biographie Universelle*, t. xliv, p. 669.   [2] Pezet, op. cit., p. 284.
[3] Ibid.   [4] Anquétil, op. cit., p. 23.

courage the peasants from active participation in the revolt. The local authorities decided to make an example of Le Tual and Vautier. The first had already been beaten up by the servants of the municipal councillors in early June. Vautier was left to the National Guard of which he had been a member. His epaulettes were torn off: he was rolled in the dust and publicly humiliated.[1] With Le Tual stronger tactics were required. He was arrested along with eight of his associates, tied up in a cart and driven off to Caen where he was incarcerated in the *château* until the insurrection was under way. The *société populaire* of Bayeux was closed by force.[2]

But whatever the council might do, federalism was never a popular movement. The struggle of one group of politicians against another in Paris or in Caen, or of the lawyers and officials and episcopal vicars against the town surgeon, were hardly live issues for the townsfolk. The district tribunal called a rally of all prepared to fight for the federalist cause in the cathedral and found themselves virtually alone except for the town council.[3] The movement was really damned from its inception. The only troops at its disposal were de Wimpffen's men and volunteers from Brittany. The Girondin leaders were suspicious of de Wimpffen.[4] Louvet accused him openly of being a traitor. De Wimpffen did nothing to disillusion them in this trend of thought. He offered to ship them all off to England and to take his men to join the royalists of Brittany.[5] This was hardly the intention of the men gathered in Caen. De Wimpffen, it has been alleged, admitted to his officers the strong likelihood of local failure but urged on them the possibility of salvation in the *chouan* camp with British payment.[6] Be this as it may, his troops gathered in Caen were obviously recalcitrant. Counter revolutionary forces arriving from Brittany were indignant that the Calvados had not produced more to aid them. Moreover, in the light of the general unwillingness on the part of the Bayeusains to volunteer, the local officials began to panic. Reports of the assembled *armée de la municipalité de Paris* to crush the provincial insurgents caused daily defections amongst the troops. By late July the federalist movement in the Calvados peacefully folded up. The administration of the department had

[1] *Rapports de Heudier*, p. 17.   [2] Ibid., p. 35.
[3] A. Montier, *Robert Lindet* (Paris, 1899), p. 203.   [4] Ibid., p. 155.
[5] Ibid.   [6] Vaultier, op. cit., p. 272.

sent news to Paris of its decision to terminate the state of insurrection.[1] Its members had in fact appreciated that they had no chance
of success and that the best thing to do was to beat a hasty retreat
lest they should further compromise themselves. The deputies
were abandoned. Fauchet was tried and executed in Paris along
with the Girondin leaders. De Wimpffen went into hiding at
Bayeux and his troops either returned to duty or made for the
chouans of Brittany.

The collapse of the federalist movement meant a complete
reorganization of the administrative bodies of the town, district,
and department. The central government took a direct part in the
choice of the new officials. Its greatest support against the spread
of federalism had been elements in the *sociétés populaires* and the
government tried to collect as precise information as possible
about these bodies. It used its *représentants en mission* and semi-
official spies like Heudier, the wine-merchant of Tournay sur
Odon, who in 1793 found his way to the district of Bayeux, to
report on the most likely local patriots. The *société populaire* had
been reopened by government order and Heudier was soon in
contact with Le Tual and Vautier, of whose patriotism and
loyalty there could be no doubt.[2]

That the federalist municipal council and district assembly must
go there could be no question. Nor could there really be any
hesitation about who would be the government nominee for
mayor. The determined nucleus of opposition had been Le Tual's.
He possessed the backing of the *société populaire* and the blessing
of Paris. Nominated to office in September, the new council
to which he belonged represented the only really revolutionary
change in the composition of the municipal authority at Bayeux
in the course of the Revolution. The clique of lawyers and men of
the courts who had been solidly in control since 1790 were now
temporarily displaced.

Heudier strongly advised that these men should be disqualified
from holding office in the light of their past record. He reported
to Paris:

C'est pourquoi je demanderais que, par un décret, aucun prêtre,
aucun ex-noble, aucun homme de loi, soit de l'ancien, soit du nouveau
régime, ne pût être éligible dans les prochaines élections. On ne peut
disconvenir cependant qu'il n'y ait de bons patriotes parmi les hommes

[1] Montier, op. cit., p. 157.   [2] *Rapports de Heudier*, p. 17.

de loi; mais ils sont en si petit nombre qu'il serait à désirer . . . que ceux qui pourraient être élus ne pussent profiter de leur élection qu'après qu'elle aurait été confirmée par la société populaire.[1]

The Convention accepted this last piece of advice. The new municipal council included only four men of the courts as opposed to ten *échevins* and fifteen *notables* in the previous one and those chosen were all tried members of the *société populaire*. All the members of the district tribunal were also relieved of office by an act of 17 October 1793 and were replaced by erstwhile less notable figures who had remained loyal to the club and had not been deeply involved in federalism.

The churchmen who had so actively espoused Fauchet's cause were arrested : some of the episcopal vicars were imprisoned in Caen. Their brief period of power was over. On the eve of their arrest a last struggle had occurred between the jurors of Bayeux and Fauchet's episcopal vicars, which revealed the impotence of the constitutional church. Long before September 1793 the people of Bayeux had ceased to worship and a pathetic struggle ensued for the few who had not completely stopped attending mass. Lecuyer, priest of St. Jean, stated that on 5 September 1793 his congregation contained no more than the three curates of the parish. The question as to which parishes should be suppressed had at last been resolved and the priests whose parishes had ceased to exist saw the possibility that they might become episcopal vicars in the place of the supporters of Fauchet who held these positions. To stake out their claim, and when one of their former parishioners asked for a service such as the baptism of a child (a practice which continued after attendance at mass had completely ceased in the town), they endeavoured to officiate at the cathedral. Fauchet's episcopal vicars retaliated by locking up the baptismal font, claiming a monopoly of all services within the cathedral.[2] During the late summer, when federalism had completely collapsed, many of those men whom Fauchet had chosen repudiated his influence and tried to ingratiate themselves with the new Jacobin municipality. Two of them declared their intention to leave the church and married amidst the jeers of the townsfolk, but even this did not save them from arrest.[3]

The creation of 1790, the constitutional church, died in Bayeux

[1] *Rapports de Heudier,* pp. 19–20.　　[2] Charrier, op. cit., vol. ii, pp. 81–84.
[3] Ibid., p. 292.

in the autumn of 1793 with the discredit of Fauchet's men and the anxiety of the mayor to urge the town in the direction of a dechristianization campaign like that pursued by the sections of Paris. In December the government proclaimed freedom of worship and in April officially suspended payment to the constitutional church, though effective payment ceased in the summer of 1793. Overnight the church from which Fauchet and Moulland and the other priests of the town who had defied the bishop in 1790 had expected so much lost the right to call itself either civil or constitutional, 'Catholic it had never been'.[1]

[1] Edington, op. cit., p. 295.

IV

POLITICS AND ECONOMIC PROBLEMS

SEPTEMBER 1793–AUGUST 1795

I

THE choice of Le Tual as mayor was incontestably that of the strongest character local politics at Bayeux had so far produced. But his very strength made him the object of criticism by the politically ambitious who resented the apparent completeness of his control; while his intransigent attitude towards those former officials even remotely implicated in federalism and his bitter hatred of both clerics and former clerics excited the fear of those partially compromised by their previous political records or careers. Bayeux was too small and the influence of Fauchet and his supporters had been too pervasive to enable most of the politically conscious to escape completely untarnished from the events of summer 1793. The municipal council and the *notables* were drawn almost exclusively from *journaliers*, masons, joiners, and small shopkeepers ready to give Le Tual unqualified support, and he enjoyed the friendship and encouragement of the *représentant en mission*, Lindet. But in the *société populaire*, where his influence had been most extensive, he was, during the autumn and winter after he had assumed office, challenged increasingly.

His presence as mayor of the town was from the outset regarded by a substantial section of the *société populaire* with some apprehension. His supporters were numerous but he was not omnipotent; in particular, a faction under de Beaudre, a former priest, did not hesitate to oppose his policy and set themselves up as spokesmen for a quieter and more conciliatory policy than the one Le Tual was prepared to pursue.

In the autumn of 1793 the machinery of the Terror was set up in Bayeux to punish traitors and counter revolutionaries whose presence menaced the life of the republic. The burning issue in the town was obviously the treatment of those involved in federalism,

whose actions in the summer of 1793 had proved beyond doubt
that they were disloyal to the republic. The attitude of the mayor
to this question was to sever him from the majority in the
société populaire who were unwilling to commit themselves to his
policy. The first indication of this was seen in the choice of the
société populaire of members of the *comité de surveillance* set up
on 27 September 1793 with the purpose of denouncing the enemies
of the people. Its composition did not meet with Le Tual's
approval, for it included two former priests, one of whom was de
Beaudre, a former supporter of Chaix d'Est Ange and who had
only narrowly escaped a close association with the federalist rising
by a last minute denunciation and withdrawal. He and Le Tual
had often clashed in debate and the ex-cleric, a former teacher of
rhetoric in the *collège* of Bayeux, had a fluent and persuasive tongue.
The other members were two bailiffs, two *canonniers* and a former
ingénieur des ponts et chaussées. Without exception, de Beaudre was
the most active member of the new *comité* and the most ready
to counteract the suggestions of the mayor. A week later, the
représentants en mission chose the members of the *comité de salut
public*; de Beaudre's name again appeared together with those of a
surgeon, a former *procureur*, a *canonnier*, an infantry captain, two
bailiffs, three joiners, and an apothecary.[1] Only in Philibert the
surgeon and Hardouin le Jeune, the former *procureur*, could
Le Tual command any firm support. At the first session of the
comité de salut public, held almost immediately, Le Tual addressed
the twelve assembled and outlined what he considered was their
first duty: he asserted that the employees of the *directoire du district*,
many of whom had been implicated in federalism, were still not
in prison and that their liberty was a direct contravention of the
law. The *comité*, however, far from rushing into a series of
immediate arrests, merely promised that it would consider the
mayor's suggestions. Le Tual, disturbed by the delay, compiled a
speedy letter to Lindet, by which he hoped to force the *comité*'s
hand. 'Mandez-moi promptement si la situation de notre ancienne
municipalité rend suspectes les personnes qui la composaient;
votre réponse m'éclaircira beaucoup dans ma marche. Plus de
grâce, plus de modérantisme; il faut vaincre ou mourir; mon parti
est pris.'[2] Armed with the reply that the members of the municipal
council were indeed culpable, he confronted the *comité de salut*

---

[1] Anquétil, 'La Société Populaire de Bayeux...', op. cit., pp. 41–42.   [2] Ibid., p. 42.

public with their failure to imprison immediately all the secretaries, employees, and petty clerks associated with the former municipal authority; in so doing, he urged upon them a step which Lindet had not in fact sanctioned.

De Beaudre replied to the mayor that the *comité de salut public* did not expect the mayor to dictate its policy: that the members of the former council itself were already in prison and that a further examination was necessary to find out the degree of involvement of minor employees. The mayor accused him of recalcitrance and of sympathy with enemies of the republic, but met only with silence; he left the assembly but did not let the issue drop. On *16 brumaire* (6 November 1793) he addressed a letter to the *comité de salut public* in which he referred to its lack of devotion to duty and included a letter from Paris which, he claimed, gave him powers beyond those of the *comité de salut public*. Certainly the tenor of the letter he included seem to indicate this:

Convention Nationale — Comité général de sûreté et de surveillance. Nous Coulonghon et Féneaux, commissaires de sûreté générale de la Convention Nationale, autorisons le citoyen Le Tual, fils, maire de Bayeux, conformément à la loi du 17 septembre dernier, de faire arrêter et incarcérer les personnes suspectes dont il aura la certitude de leurs principes contre révolutionnaires, tels que ceux qui ont leurs parents émigrés et qui sont en correspondance avec eux, tous ceux qui troublent l'ordre social, tous ceux enfin qui n'ont manifesté aucun attachement pour la Révolution. . . . Autorisons en outre ledit Le Tual à choisir à cet effet tous les citoyens qui lui semblent les plus convenables, à requérir les autorités constituées et la force armée pour l'exécution du présent ordre.[1]

The *comité de salut public* were alarmed not only by the contents of the letter, which gave Le Tual powers which by right belonged to them, but by the way he had got this letter. They reached the conclusion that Le Tual had in some way accused them of slackness to the Convention and that they must, in all haste, counteract the mayor's activities. De Beaudre volunteered personally to go to Paris, defend the actions of the *comité de salut public* of Bayeux, and obtain an explanation for such a letter. His journey was wholly successful. He returned with a letter from Coulonghon and Féneaux which was calculated to crush the mayor's pretensions by clearly stating that the Convention did not intend in the earlier

[1] Anquétil, 'La Société Populaire de Bayeux . . .', op. cit., p. 50.

letter to endow the mayor with powers to 'former un comité dans sa personne individuelle' but merely to 'agir d'après les déclarations du comité existant et de concert avec lui'.[1]

But whilst the mayor had lost one round in the struggle, the *comité de surveillance*, lest there should appear to be any justification for Le Tual's criticism, certainly speeded up the number of arrests, particularly of those previously engaged in federalist activities; at the same time, however, they made it clear that the arrests, in many cases, would be of a purely temporary nature, whilst they discovered the truly guilty.[2]

Le Tual had good reasons for feeling defeat, for signs in the *société populaire* indicated that the *comité de surveillance* commanded support from the majority of its members. On *28 brumaire* (18 November 1793) Willame, also a former cleric, urged upon the *société* a recognition of the principle that whilst there doubtless existed many citizens in the commune tainted with federalism, notwithstanding, the bulk of these must be regarded as having been temporarily deluded rather than as irrevocably criminal and that the *société populaire* should express this to the *comité de surveillance*.[3] Neither the *société populaire* nor the *comité de surveillance* needed overmuch persuasion: too many had, at one time or another, been on the side of the episcopal vicars as opposed to that of Le Tual and were reluctant to be held guilty for their actions. Le Tual spoke out against the proposal but was defeated. More and more convinced of the laxness of the *comité de surveillance*, on *5 frimaire* (25 November 1793), in the middle of a meeting held to consider the case of Le Brisoys Surmont, a member of the compromised municipal council, he entered and delivered an impassioned speech. Stripped of its rhetoric, this was largely an assertion that the *comité de surveillance* had overstepped its powers in liberating from prison men whom everyone in the town knew had been involved in federalism. The *comité* did not hesitate to reply in a letter delivered to the mayor's house: 'Le citoyen Le Tual est invité et même interpellé par le présent, au nom de la République, de déclarer les noms des personnes qu'il croit avoir été légèrement mises en liberté, et de communiquer tout présentement au comité.'[4]

---

[1] Ibid., p. 50.

[2] A.D.C. Lm. *Comité de Surveillance. État dressé par le Comité de Surveillance de Bayeux, le 19 brumaire an II.*

[3] A.M.B. no. 61. *Registres de la société populaire, le 28 brumaire an II.*

[4] Anquétil, 'La Société Populaire de Bayeux . . .', op. cit., p. 50.

Le Tual apologized by saying that he only wished to act in concert with the *comité de surveillance* and had no intention of usurping its powers. In spite of this assertion, however, the criticism had been made and the *comité* knew Le Tual too well to doubt that he would write to Paris. The incident was followed by over a hundred arrests within forty-eight hours, which filled the two prisons of the town with suspects: ex-federalists, priests, relations of *emigrés*, whether noble or clerical, friends and servants of de Wimpffen, and employees of de Cheylus. In under a month, about five hundred people were under lock and key.[1]

The Terror at Bayeux was singularly bloodless; only half a dozen inhabitants of the town found their way to Paris and the guillotine and those mostly for obvious reasons. De Marguerie, *seigneur* of Vierville and *colonel de la 3e division de la garde constitutionnelle de Louis XVI*, was found guilty of attempting to defend the king on the night of 10 August and executed; Francastel, former servant of the bishop, was accused of subversive correspondence with de Cheylus and met the same fate; so did the immediate families of the Comte d'Albignac and de Faudoas who had attempted to flee.[2] On the other hand, the large numbers arrested in November to January 1794 caused many to fear for their lives; and not the least apprehensive were the innumerable petty officials, clerks, and secretaries who had done the purely routine work connected with the compromised municipal and district authority and whose imprisonment was constantly pressed upon an unwilling *comité de surveillance* and *société populaire* by the mayor.

The punishment of political offenders was only one issue on which Le Tual's attitude was markedly more intransigent than that of the majority in the *société populaire*. The process of dechristianization and the implementation of repressive measures against the church was also accelerated by his actions. From October 1793, when official government policy was one of tolerance for all cults and only the sections of Paris had embarked upon destroying the vestiges of Christian worship, Le Tual, in active correspondence with Lindet on the subject, set out to inculcate the old episcopal town with the principles of dechristiani-

---

[1] A.D.C. Lm. *Comité de Surveillance. Listes des Suspects, le 7 frimaire an II*; A.M.B. *Prisons.*

[2] Pezet, op. cit., p. 352.

zation. In so doing, he went far beyond anything the *société populaire* wanted or seemed at first completely to understand.

On 20 October 1793 a deputation from the *société populaire* presented the municipal council with a project to celebrate the introduction of the revolutionary calendar:

Le vœu de la société était que le lendemain, jour de repos, une fête civique fut célébrée, qu'une messe soit chantée en l'église Notre Dame où tous les corps constitués civils et militaires, y soient présents, que chaque membre soit armé d'une pique, qu'à la suite de cette messe tous les corps réunissent leurs piques en faisceau et qu'elles soient liées avec un ruban tricolore, en signe de fraternité, d'union et de force.[1]

The council agreed, but when the question was put to the mayor he refused to accept the proposition and hurried down to the *société populaire* to explain his opposition. He stressed that the fête in question was essentially non-religious and that to inaugurate it with a Catholic ceremony would be clearly against the will of the government, which was now opposed to the *'grimaces sacerdotales'* of the old church. He promised the *société* that to omit a mass from the celebrations of the next day would not mean the sacrifice of pomp and splendour. His proposals were accepted in spite of criticism from Willame.

Ten days later the *représentants en mission*, Lindet and Oudot, visited Bayeux and the townspeople were urged by Lindet to beware of the *fanatisme des prêtres*. The clique of ex-priests, in particular de Beaudre and Willame, were silent on this occasion, but Le Tual was far from so: he indulged in a lengthy eulogy of Lindet and an even longer one of anti-clericalism in general. The news in late November that Paris had closed its churches was followed in Bayeux by exhortations from the mayor to emulate such an example. Le Tual was in a particularly strong position to urge his points home: the opposition faction did not dare to speak because although de Beaudre had renounced his priestly state he remained peculiarly susceptible on this subject. If he attempted to counter the mayor's policy, then Le Tual could denounce his attachment to the old creed and his inherent fanaticism; he was also well aware—Le Tual took care to see that all the members of the *société populaire* were—of the actions of the sections of Paris. The mayor enjoyed substantial support in his

[1] A.M.B. no. 61. *Registres de la société populaire, le 20 octobre 1793.*

measures to stamp out Catholic worship from the soldiers garrisoned in the town. They were always prepared to stage anti-clerical demonstrations, to urge the smashing of statues and of relics savouring of the despised faith, and even went so far as to erect scaffolding to remove the crosses from the cathedral spires, one of their number undertaking a perilous ascent to this end. De Beaudre was moved during the last week of December to make a denunciation of Catholicism; in the first week of January he married—perhaps over-anxious to prove his emancipation from the past—and indeed by early 1794 he and the other ex-priests of the *société populaire* were the most outspoken in their condemnation of any worship other than that of the *patrie*.

On *12 pluviôse* (31 January 1794) the cathedral of Bayeux was sacked by the *société populaire* and the soldiers of the garrison. Every statue was destroyed; every relic was burnt; the pulpit was placed in the central aisle and put at the disposal of any orator making a patriotic speech on fête days; the figure of the Virgin carved on the side was repainted and the *tricolore* substituted for the cross in her hand; this done, she was renamed goddess of Reason. The highlight of the occasion, and a spectacle which must have afforded Le Tual great pleasure, was an hysterical speech by de Beaudre in which he decried the misguided views of his youth which had caused him to enter the church. The same day, the *société populaire* organized search-parties to go from house to house to discover hidden priests, altar vessels, catechisms, or any vestiges of Catholic worship.[1] Le Tual himself acted as leader of these expeditions the following week, ignorant of the fact that his days as mayor were numbered.

On *19 pluviôse an II* (7 February 1794) the *représentants en mission*, Bourret and Frémanger, arrived in the Calvados; their first act at Bayeux was to ask the *société populaire* to elect a commission of seven men to prepare a report on the administration of the town, preparatory to a purge designed to remove the inefficient and those insufficiently devoted to duty. The most able of those chosen was Willame, a friend of de Beaudre and one who had already clashed with Le Tual over the question of the arrest of those involved in federalism. Willame succeeded in impressing upon Bourret, with whom, it is claimed, he struck up a close friendship, the desirability of removing from public office all

---

[1] Bisson, *Histoire Ecclésiastique du diocèse de Bayeux pendant la Révolution*, p. 20.

those who simultaneously engaged in some other occupation and who could not therefore wholly occupy themselves with their public duties. The move was directed largely against Le Tual, who had never abandoned his surgery. Willame went further: he condemned the mayor's intervention in the meetings of the *comité de surveillance* and his attempts to assume powers which did not belong to him. There was plenty of evidence to support Willame's assertions. Bourret was indeed critical of Le Tual's actions when he wrote to Paris. He accused the mayor of inadequately fulfilling his duties: the cathedral had perhaps been sacked, but there were still priests in the town who urged the people not to use the revolutionary calendar and the *représentant en mission* claimed that he had in his possession a register of births and deaths kept according to the old calendar by a reactionary priest named Moulland. Bourret suggested that hysterical demonstrations took the place of careful attempts to implement the intentions of the central government.[1] On *20 pluviôse an II* (8 February 1794), a mere five months after assuming office, Le Tual heard that he had been dropped from the new list of municipal officials and was offered no new position. Guérin de la Houssaye, former *lieutenant général civil du bailliage*, an *échevin* of the old régime, was chosen in his stead. Two soldiers of the *société populaire* tried to draw up a petition to the government demanding the reinstallation of the mayor but they could not command sufficient support and Le Tual was forced to retire. He attributed his defeat to the work of ex-priests and others who were the enemies of the people in disguise, but it availed him nothing. He did not cease to attend the meetings of the *société populaire*, but his loss of office came as a severe shock and the continued presence of de Beaudre in the *comité de surveillance* and the influence of Willame on the *représentant en mission* perhaps made him aware of the need to act cautiously. He spoke rarely in discussion and occupied himself during the early summer with a project for forming a school of surgery at his own expense now that the restricting influence of the Sisters of Charity had been removed.

The fall of Le Tual brought one major change to the tone of political life at Bayeux: the question of the punishment of those implicated in federalism was quietly dropped and though few were released from prison, arrests for this reason stopped.

[1] A.N. C290.

The new mayor was an administrator not a politician, a timid man who had tried hitherto to avoid involvement in politics—one of the few men of the courts of Bayeux of whom this could be said—and he was completely the tool of the *société populaire*. After the defeat of Le Tual the latter was less divided in its debates. De Beaudre and his clique were less on the defensive on account of their past conduct and the *société* could present a united front to a threat far more formidable to the town than the federalist traitors had seemed but which was to the *société populaire* no less a force of the counter revolution. The new menace was posed by the peasant farmers of the Bessin and the pressing question of food supplies, an issue which was to throw into relief the whole relationship, past and present, of the town and country and to define with unprecedented clarity the complete dichotomy of interests of the two.

II

By the spring of 1794 it was possible to assess some of the changes, both anticipated and unexpected, the Revolution had brought to the lives of the people of the district of Bayeux. In 1789 everyone had imagined that financial benefits and certainly financial rearrangements would follow the political changes. The old system of indirect taxation was undermined from the outset: the townspeople anticipated the abolition of the *aides* and the *gabelle* by simply ceasing to pay them. For some, however, the Revolution during its early months brought with it a threat to their existence by threatening the complicated edifice upon which their livelihood was based. The night of 4 August had struck a blow not only at the owners of seigneurial rights but at the proliferation of middlemen and officials concerned in their collection. The customs officials were forced to flee; officials of the *intendance* and the *subdélégation* found themselves unemployed; the keepers of feudal records, the highly specialized lawyers whom the large landowners had employed to manipulate the law to extort more rent, were faced with a lack of clientele. Administrative reform also rendered hazardous the future of the old courts. Before any other section of the population, with the exception of the clerics, those previously concerned in the old administrative system in France were faced with change. The law of 16–24 August 1790 organized the new judicial framework of France as far as civil justice was concerned. It was followed on 16 September 1790 by laws on criminal justice. All the old courts were immediately abolished. Some, like the *grenier à sel*, had no longer any justification for existence; others like the *bailliage* and the *élection* now had their functions transferred to new tribunals, of which there was to be one in each district. Under the new procedure an attempt was made to cut down work in the courts by the introduction of processes of reconciliation and arbitration before justices of the peace; only affairs involving national questions and public order were exempt from this procedure.[1]

These measures obviously involved a marked diminution of the numbers employed in the administration of justice. All the officials of the minor courts lost their posts. Five former high officials of the *bailliage* became judges of the tribunal but the judges of the other courts were redundant. In addition, the attempt to keep matters out of the courts by the process of reconciliation and arbitration meant a decrease in business. Costs had indeed been reduced for the clients, but these costs had been someone's livelihood. The Assembly tried to be fair: nor were its members going to cut their own throats. Any office holder, or his ancestors, would have a substantial sum paid for his office. That compensation must be paid was not questioned. How much was paid is less clear. It is not easy to estimate the exact amount payable to each office holder at Bayeux. Where figures do exist they are given for the court as a whole and not for the individual offices. What evidence does remain suggests that in the light of the assessments made on the *vingtième* lists of 1782 the compensation made to the office holders of Bayeux was not generous. For the *bailliage* court the sums were well below market prices current in 1788.[2] On the other hand, business in the *grenier à sel* and the *élection* had long been so slack that offices had been up for sale and had long lain empty. There was little immediate criticism of government assessments for several reasons. First, many of the offices had only been purchased for reasons of social prestige and the administrative arrangements of 1790, by increasing the number of personnel in the departmental and district assemblies, afforded an outlet for anyone interested in the prestige conferred by public service. Secondly, several holders of offices, such as the *procureurs* of the

[1] Godechot, op. cit., pp. 116–19.
[2] A.N. F¹ᵇ 11. *Calvados 10*. Letters of *20, 25 nivôse an IV*.

bailliage and of the *élection* courts, whose offices had provided the basis of their income, were employed in the *tribunal de district* without having to purchase their new positions, and so still had their job plus the promise of compensation for its loss. Thirdly, and perhaps most important, a whole series of minor bureaucratic posts were created which offered opportunities to men with experience such as the most numerous and least important of these officials possessed. The clerical work for the assessment and sale of national property, the drawing up of inventories of silver and furniture from the religious houses, paper-work for the reorganization of parish boundaries, all fell into their hands. In fact, this class of minor officials was able to make ends meet in a way not dissimilar from that which it had employed before the Revolution. By the possession of one of these small posts, an investment in the house of a canon or cleric, or more rarely a piece of land, the host of minor officials of the *ancien régime* made the transition to a new economy. True, many of the new posts were temporary, but stability was not something to which they were accustomed. Le Tual revealed in 1793 that some landowners in isolated areas were still attempting to collect seigneurial dues, aided and abetted by collectors and bailiffs who had performed such tasks under the old régime and who submitted in their defence that this was their only livelihood.[1] On the whole, however, the immediate problem of employment for these groups had been solved in 1790 even if there was no guarantee for the future.

For the artisan and the tradespeople of the town even the immediate prospect was gloomier. There could be no doubt that the reduction of the clergy to salaried officials had cut off many of Bayeux's resources. The district assembly, in one of its least generous estimates, claimed that the bishop and chapter alone had dispensed some 400,000 *livres* per year as wages, in return for consumer goods, and as charity.[2] Each canon had had at least one servant: most had had two. The bishop had maintained a staff of footmen, cooks, and valets. Each religious house had employed several odd-job men and domestics, often for low wages but none the less it had provided for their upkeep. The Assembly had promised compensation for the loss of employment, but it materialized slowly, and in any case the employees were expected

[1] *Rapports de Heudier*, p. 37.
[2] A.D.C. Lx. *Assistance. Bayeux*.

to find alternative work. When once a lump sum had been paid for the debts owed by religious establishments to butchers, bakers, grocers, and candlemakers, the truth was only too apparent: trade had been lost. The problem was more serious in a town such as Bayeux in that there was no obvious replacement for this source of supply. The Revolution did not create any new openings for the artisan and the tradesman. Indeed, they might well have asked by 1793 if anyone had profited less from the Revolution than they.

The sale of clerical property in 1791 aroused the expectations of many sections of French society, but hardly those of the small tradesman and artisan. In no way could such a sale be to their benefit. The sale of the property was not an act of philanthropy on the part of the government. The government wanted money as quickly as possible. Suggestions made in the Assembly that the state should see that the property on the market was split into lots large enough for the maintenance of a family and no larger were to evaporate in the light of the need to sell to the highest bidder irrespective of who he might be. Even in the event of the lots being small there was nothing to prevent one buyer uniting several of them providing that he was prepared to pay. The sales were to be rapidly followed by marked disenchantment. The rural area around Bayeux was grossly overpopulated. The large estates of the bishop and chapter of Bayeux had been jealously coveted by the small peasantry as a solution to the acute land shortage, and a possible means to the making easier of a precarious existence. But if the landless and small landowning peasantry had hoped that the land on the market would pass into their hands they were to be bitterly disappointed. The auctions of the property took place in the town. The personnel of the district assemblies were well placed to gain or engineer a small investment. At least one syndicate trying to corner ecclesiastical property was later discovered.[1] Officials of the *bureaux* granted land to themselves without putting up the notice of sale the law demanded and some attempts were made to rig the bidding at auctions. For the most part, although the officials made small purchases, the buyers in the town were the same sort of people as had been active property speculators before the Revolution: the apothecary Troplong, the lace-merchant Tardif, the grocer de la Mare, made extensive investments. So did the rich *noblesse*. As for the buyers of the

[1] A.M.B. *Registres des délibérations du corps municipal, floréal an II.*

country areas, they were the wealthiest sections of the landowning peasantry, who thus added to their existing properties.[1]

Both the small peasant and the artisan had in fact been economically disappointed by the Revolution. The difference was in the degree of the deception. The peasant had expected much more profit than he in fact got. He had expected the church lands to solve his very real problems. Instead he was back where he started. The abolition of the *gabelle* and the tithe had on the whole been to the benefit of the landowning peasant. But here, advantage ended. The new direct taxes were as heavy as the old ones even if they were more evenly distributed. Even the abolition of the tithe had proved a very mixed blessing for it meant a reduction of the amount of grain, and more especially hay, in circulation.[2] Whereas the large tithe-owners had put the goods on the market, the farmers now held on to their hay for the consumption of their own cattle. The first two years of the Revolution were, for the small peasant, a period of intense disillusionment. Gradually he moved into an attitude of sullen if passive hostility to the Revolution and towards the townspeople who implemented government measures. The first to feel the effects of that hostility were the poorer sections of the town.

The struggle between the townspeople and the peasants of the district began shortly after the introduction of the *assignat*. The suspicion felt by the peasant for paper money was as marked in the Bessin as elsewhere. As early as September 1791 the municipal council of Bayeux complained that the country people would only accept payment in *assignats* for the corn they brought into the market with reluctance and always accorded preference to those who could pay in coin.[3] They possessed an effective weapon. The commodity in universal demand was bread: if the *assignat* would not purchase this essential then as a currency it became meaningless. As early as January 1792 the printers of government decrees in Bayeux refused to work unless paid in the old coinage.[4] The dilemma was obvious. The *assignats* had been issued in anticipation of the sale of church property. The delays involved in the realiza-

---

[1] A.D.C. Q. *Biens nationaux. District de Bayeux.* Information relating to sales of clerical property is very incomplete.

[2] A.N. F[ic] III. *Calvados 7.*

[3] A.M.B. *Registres des délibérations du corps municipal.* September 1791. There are striking parallels at Orléans. G. Lefebvre, *Études Orléanaises*, vol. ii, pp. 53–55.

[4] A.M.B. *Registres des délibérations du corps municipal.* January 1792.

tion of the proceeds from the property, which in any case was rarely paid for in ready cash, the new expenditure of the government on clerical pensions and on compensation to office-holders and at the same time the impossibility of raising taxes in 1790, had placed the government in severe financial difficulties. Local authorities had no other source of money at their disposal. By February 1792 the municipal government was condemning the peasants of the surrounding district for causing unnecessary hardship to the people of the town through this refusal to accept their currency or at the least to surrender their goods only against a far larger sum in *assignats* than they would take in coin.[1] Their refusal meant an almost immediate devaluation of the paper money. According to the tables drawn up in the year V, the *assignat* in the Calvados had fallen by May 1791 to about 91 per cent. of its original value. Up to January 1792 the decline was gradual: it then stood at 84 per cent. of the original. Then rumours of war accelerated the pace and it descended rapidly to 74 per cent., which it maintained until February 1793.[2] The decline of the *assignat* as a means of exchange was accompanied after June 1791 by a rapid increase in prices. The harvest was compromised by the heavy storms of that month. When gathered in, it fell well below that of 1790 in quantity but was by no means poor. Even fear of shortage, however, was sufficient to cause some withholding of supplies to the town and an increase in price. This, coupled with the instability of the value of the *assignat*, meant that as early as the winter of 1792 the town was facing severe economic distress. The pattern of distress was familiar. As well as the perpetually indigent, the day-labourers, artisans of the building and manual trades, and the landless of the countryside all stood in need of relief, and the old sources for the distribution of charity had evaporated. The government in its search for money to pay for the war put out a new issue of *assignats*, this time backed by the property of *émigrés*. But the new paper money commanded no more confidence than the old. Ugly scenes occurred in December 1792 when women in the market at Bayeux tried to force the *assignat* upon the peasants in exchange for corn. It is perhaps indicative of the prevailing temper of townsfolk that during this month the only substantial goldsmith of the town,

[1] Ibid.
[2] P. Caron, *Tableaux de dépréciation du papier-monnaie* (Paris, 1909), p. 71.

who possessed the metal the peasant trusted, found his premises
looted and fled for his life.[1] The constant fear in the Bessin of
invasion by the royalists of Jersey and the English increased the
tension. In February 1793, when war was finally declared on
England and Holland, the *assignat* in the Calvados fell virtually
overnight from 74 per cent. to 62 per cent. of its original value
and by August 1793 to a mere 42 per cent.[2]

The declaration of war brought problems both of recruitment
and of feeding and clothing the armies of France. The French
economy was put on a war basis and a maximum imposed upon
the prices of essential goods, first on grain in May 1793 and
secondly on all commodities by the law of the general maximum
of September 1793. This policy of economic control was to meet
the unconcealed hostility of the peasant. He was prepared to sell
nothing for a price fixed by the government in *assignats*. His
refusal took the form of ignoring the maximum and either of
selling on the black market or of withholding the goods completely. The results of either practice hit the townspeople directly.
Failure to provide the tanners with hides meant the cessation of
the tanning industry and placed the shoemakers and saddlers in
difficulties; failure to provide fat meant that the candlemakers
and soap-manufacturers were hit and the lack of candles made
evening work impossible. The town workers were not well placed
for evading the maximum; they were forced to put their goods on
the market at the regulated price. On the other hand, they could
not afford to pay black-market prices for leather and fat and accept
payment for their work at the scale of prices stipulated by the
government. Over the next few months many of them had to shut
up shop in the face of bankruptcy.[3] In other occupations the same
consequence followed. Candlemakers and grocers closed down
when they found they had nothing to sell.

But it was the refusal of the peasant to surrender his grain which
was to be the determining factor in paralysing the economic
policy of the government and causing immeasurable hardship to
the people of the towns. Even without the *assignat* and the
maximum, the troop movements in France and the need to keep
the armies provisioned radically altered the traditional *carte de
ravitaillement* of France. The government had two preoccupations,

---

[1] Dastignac's property heads the *biens des émigrés*. A.D.C. Q.

[2] Caron, op. cit., p. 71.   [3] Pezet, op. cit., p. 396.

the feeding of the troops and the feeding of the capital. A hungry mob in Paris spelt more than danger for any régime: it was its epitaph. The people of Paris could feel assured that the government was striving its utmost to supply them with their daily pound and a half of bread per head. No other region of France could feel the same assurance, or hope for anything which approached the same treatment. Indeed they could expect to have their supplies reduced still further in order to keep some semblance of order in the capital. The zone which supplied Paris stretched from the channel ports to the Saône, from the plateau of Langres to the cornlands of the Brie. Moreover, all the larger ports were depots of imported foreign corn and American rice destined to help out supplies in the capital. Northern France especially, or that part that lay between the ports of the Seine and Paris, could see grain in transit for the capital. Into Le Havre, Rouen, and Honfleur came imported sacks of Baltic and English corn intended for Paris. Government policy aimed at securing the maximum amount for the city but it recognized one factor: that the towns *en route* to the capital must also receive sufficient to ensure that the supplies for the city escaped pillaging. Towns were well or ill supplied according to the extent to which they jeopardized the provisioning of Paris.[1]

The position of Bayeux was not such as to command favoured area treatment. On the other hand, it was exposed with full force to the problem of provisioning. Distant from a port of any size, and situated in a predominantly pastoral area, it had always found it difficult to feed its citizens. Bayeux and its district never expected, even given the most abundant harvest, to be able to feed its population from local resources for more than eight months of the year. To fill the deficit before the Revolution it had depended on supplies from the plain of Caen and the area around Thorigny and Périers now included in the new department of the Manche. The war, however, had changed this whole pattern. To feed the republican armies in the Vendée, corn was sent from the Beauce which had previously been a source of supply for Paris. To remedy the deficit in the capital, the government drew on the supplies of the department of the Eure which had previously supplied Rouen.

[1] R. Cobb, 'Problèmes de subsistance de l'an II et de l'an III. L'exemple d'un petit port normand. Honfleur, 1794–5', *Actes du 81ᵉ Congrès des Société Savantes* (Rouen–Caen, 1956), pp. 296–9.

Rouen in turn sought supplies in the Eure, which had previously supplied part of the district of Caen and the area around Pont l'Evêque and Lisieux. The corn of the plain of Caen was now required by Caen itself, whilst Pont l'Evêque and Lisieux looked to other districts in the Calvados and the Manche. Bayeux found itself not only cut off from supplies it had hitherto enjoyed but at the same time expected to help out Pont l'Evêque and Lisieux,[1] and to send provisions to the army of the *côtes de Cherbourg*. Bayeux was neither large enough nor well enough placed strategically to make itself felt. A riot within the old town would cause no government to fall: at the worst it might lead to a change of municipal officials. The administrators of the department, like the central government in Paris, concerned themselves primarily with the supplying of the city which constituted the gravest threat to its peace, in this case Caen. Bayeux was left to fend for itself and to resort to whatever expedient it could find in order to feed its populace of some 80,000 people, of whom some 10,000 were in the city itself. The district authority and the municipal councils were for the next three years to be occupied almost exclusively with this problem.

Even given good harvests, minimum demands from the army and other districts, and the full co-operation of the peasant, the situation would have been difficult enough. The new municipal council of September 1793 was, however, hopeful that the district might get from September to June, eight months, without substantial crisis. The administrators were prepared to draw in their belts, send out scouts to other areas, or lay hands on foreign grain at Le Havre, which would allow them to build up a surplus and carry them through the difficult months of June to September 1794. They planned in September 1793 a comprehensive three-fold policy, introducing ration cards indicating the size of the household, laying in a small supply purchased outside the district in November, and sending out surveyors into the district to estimate how much each rural canton produced for general consumption.[2] Though food was partially rationed from September, the quantities allowed were generous. The local administrative bodies had to take account of public opinion. An outbreak of panic on the part of the populace might so easily lead to riots,

---

[1] Cobb, 'Problèmes de subsistance . . .', op. cit., p. 309, and A.N. F1b II. *Calvados 1. 23 brumaire an IV.*

[2] A.M.B. *Registres des délibérations du corps municipal.* 20 September 1793.

pillaging of existing stocks, and spread the general fear of shortage, which would aggravate the situation by causing the peasant farmers to withhold their grain. No one with any experience of government under the old régime was ignorant of the consequences attendant upon popular fear nor of the methods which had to be used to counter rumours of famine. At nearby Caen the municipal officials exposed sacks of grain on the wharves for days to create an atmosphere of confidence. Popular fears thus dispelled, they packed up the grain and dispatched it else-where.[1] In Bayeux the municipal government undertook a propaganda campaign, glorifying the work of the central govern-ment, stressing the magnitude of France's resources and explain-ing to the people that there was no need for disquiet, and that a government interested in the maintenance of liberty and equality would not see them deprived of food.[2] For about a month, as long as grain supplies were not interrupted, the propaganda worked.

Unfortunately, there was little real prospect that adequate supplies would continue to be forthcoming. The administration of Bayeux and its district had failed to reckon with the extent of the opposition of the peasant farmers of the Bessin to the sale of produce under the enforced maximum. Their attitude is readily explicable. Why should they sell their grain for a fixed price and in *assignats* of rapidly declining value and risk going short of food and seed themselves? All the astuteness of the Normandy peasant was applied to the struggle against the application of the maximum. He had several weapons: he could conceal his grain for his own consumption or sell it on the black market; or he could, though not at once, change over from arable to pasture. In the mean-time he hid his grain in his attic, under the floor, in disused buildings or, more commonly, he opened up the earth and buried it in trenches, so that he might be arbiter of its fate. His immediate victims were the landless labourers of the countryside and the townspeople. Several months before real shortage came an artificial shortage had been created.

As early as December 1793 peasant opposition to the sale of corn and agricultural produce at the maximum was fully apparent. The town's immediate grain supplies were adequate and there was

[1] This had been the expedient of the *intendants* of the *généralité* of Caen to combat popular fears. J. C. Perrot cited by Cobb, op. cit., p. 303.
[2] A.M.B. *Compte Rendu.* 18 September 1793.

as yet no question of real shortage, but the markets of the last weeks of December contained no butter. Complaints were also made of the failure to supply milk to the town.[1] Neither of these commodities was lacking, it was simply that the peasants who produced them refused to deliver them. Bitter indictments were made against the *cultivateurs* in the *société populaire* and a document was handed to the municipal council to urge if necessary the use of force to see that the town received the food it needed.[2] The municipal council noted the complaint but was not stirred to action until February, when the supplies of grain were interrupted not only to the market of Bayeux but to the markets of the other cantons of the district. Throughout January and February the district assembly sent out missives stipulating the amount of grain to be surrendered monthly by the farmers of each canton according to their means as estimated in the previous November, and urging the prompt delivery of the corn. But the failure of mere words to impress the peasant farmers was only too obvious. By late February the district assembly had resorted to the threat of force. The monthly statement was accompanied by the warning that failure to supply the necessary grain would result in its seizure by armed force. Nor did they stop here. When the farmers paid no heed to the admonition, a commission, usually of two representatives of the town and some twenty armed troops, descended on the village in default to implement the threats. They were charged at all costs to lay hands on the amount of corn the particular area had failed to submit. If necessary they were authorized to use force and in any case they had to be housed and fed by the village and were not to leave until the required amount of corn had been collected.[3]

It was expected that the officials of the villages would co-operate in forcing the peasant farmers to surrender their corn. But the district assembly soon learnt its mistake. These men were not men of the government or of the town but mostly came from the better-off peasantry and owed their positions to election by them. They were prepared to connive at and join in the schemes of the farmers. Exposure meant deposition from their offices but first they had to be caught.[4]

[1] A.M.B. no. 61. *Registres de la société populaire, 30 frimaire an II.*

[2] Ibid. '*Cultivateur*' embraced alike large landowner and large tenant farmer.

[3] A.D.C. L. *Registres des délibérations du directoire du district de Bayeux, 25 pluviôse an II.*   [4] A.M.B. no. 61. *Registres de la société populaire, 24 floréal an II.*

The commissions were at first conducted by officials of the district assembly; but when it became apparent that it was not going to be a temporary problem, the leadership of the expeditions was turned over, from April 1794, to a group of men experienced in dealing roughly with offenders, the bailiffs of the old régime. Throughout 1794–5 their occupation was a regular one and well paid. They were backed up by troops, housed free, and detested with an intensity even greater than in the pre-Revolutionary days. Most of them were leading members of the *société populaire* and these were used by preference, for as such they could doubtless inculcate the peasants with better sentiments and greater patriotism.[1]

Against the troops of the districts and the exhortations of the *société populaire* the country put up further resistance. The peasant farmers denied that they had any corn: they declared that their barns were empty and that they could not give what they had not got. Even if they were eventually exposed, such practices were time consuming and time was a commodity which the district authorities did not possess.

The town limped through May. The market never contained at any one time more than barely sufficient for immediate use and that had only been gained by intimidating the peasantry and indeed literally forcing them to sell their grain at the maximum. Indeed, but for the arrival, long solicited from the government, of some fifteen hundredweight of potatoes, at least one market might have ended in riot.[2] The potatoes arrived before the bill, but so hard pressed were the municipal council that they distributed them free of charge, merely taking note of who took them and fully aware that the money would never be recovered. By June the experience of the previous three months had impressed itself indelibly upon the minds of the administrators. They were convinced, and with sufficient proof, that the farmers were self-interested hoarders, ready to profit from public hardship, and that their stubborn self-interest could only be overcome by armed force. By this time the town and local authorities had virtually declared war on the farmers of the country. They refused to believe even when the men in question had genuinely sold all they possessed in the way of grain. By crying wolf before the wolf appeared the peasant

[1] Ibid.
[2] A.M.B. *Compte Rendu, floréal an II.*

farmers had lost irrevocably the support of the town and government.

At a meeting on *3 prairial an II* (22 May 1794) the district assembly was informed that the canton of Crépon had not paid the quota it owed to Bayeux and that moreover the communes of that canton had not received any supplies for a week. Drastic measures, it was suggested, were needed in this area. Working on previous estimates, and even before the opposition of the peasant farmers was taken into consideration, it was believed that the entire district had only sufficient to feed itself for a fortnight and no longer.[1] The district decided that an appeal should be sent in all haste to Bourret and Frémanger, the *représentants en mission* in the area. They must be made to help. The town administration could not afford to wait for a reply. It urged that within the district supplies must still lie hidden and that a large force headed by good *sans-culottes* should leave Bayeux immediately to search in the district. Three days after the request had been granted they were able to report that they had met with no success.[2] No matter what methods they used to force corn from the peasants, they failed. Frémanger replied on *13 prairial* (1 June 1794) that he could afford some help from supplies in the Manche and some of the military provisions.[3] The maize which arrived lasted until the end of June, when the council reported that of the 2,400 people likely to present themselves at the next market, less than half would be served.[4] They begged extra relief from the military supplies. It came two days later and consisted of 150 hundredweight of rice from the military stocks at Granville.[5] Even distributed at a pound per head per week it could only last a month. By *13 thermidor* (31 July 1794) the 150 hundredweight were exhausted.[6] Cantons which had not paid their estimated quota of grain were raided and searched but it availed Bayeux nothing.

The search parties sent by the district and the *société populaire* had no doubt by spring of 1794 that the peasant was under the influence of counter revolutionary forces intent upon impeding the government's policy, such as treacherous clerics in whose interest it was to starve the town and so contribute to the over-

[1] A.D.C. L. *Registres des délibérations du directoire du district de Bayeux, 3 prairial an II.*
[2] Ibid., *8 prairial an II.*   [3] Ibid., *13 prairial an II.*
[4] Ibid., *9 messidor an II.*   [5] Ibid., *11 messidor an II.*
[6] Ibid., *13 thermidor an II.*

throw of the central government. In *ventôse, germinal, floréal,* and *prairial,* the spring and early summer of 1794, frequent expeditions of *sans-culottes* were sent into the villages to propagate sound revolutionary principles and emancipate them from the evil influence of the parish priest. Le Tual led one such expedition and such enterprises became noteworthy for the intensity of their anti-clericalism. Several communities, Crépon and Lingèvres for example, were singled out for their lack of patriotism and their stubborn adherence to superstition. The expedition returned from Crépon with copies of catechisms printed in Oxford for the traitor de Cheylus and circulated by his emissaries. Faced with such evidence of the work of royalists and traitors the *société populaire* found it fully credible that Crépon had not supplied its quota of grain to the market of Bayeux; nor, as long as priests lay hidden in the district secretly encouraging their flock to starve the town and thus overthrow the government, would the situation improve.[1] Intensive hunts for hidden clerics revealed little, but those caught were roughly handled. Indeed whether jurors or non-jurors, the priests interned at Bayeux for failure to surrender the certificates conferring priesthood upon them were the most harshly treated of all the prisoners.

On *5 thermidor* (23 July 1794) the *société populaire* had once again decided to send out its good *sans-culottes* to make an urgent appeal to the farmers to get their new harvest in as soon as possible. They returned on *29 thermidor* and submitted an extensive report. The leader of the commission, the notary Vautier, made a bitter indictment of the farmers. He claimed that in order to retard the harvest and escape surrender of their goods to the town, they were refusing to pay labourers even the wage of 10 *sols* a day to get in the harvest, and that it was only due to a peasantry interested in prolonging shortage that each citizen was not receiving an adequate ration of new grain.[2] The district and municipality, he urged, must take immediate steps to get in the harvest. It was easy enough to say, but less easy to realize, the more so because of the weather. A hard winter had been followed by a wet spring; the corn was late in ripening and when it did the wetness had produced plenty of stalk for straw but the ears were relatively small.[3] Supplies of vegetables increased during August and did much to

---

[1] A.M.B. no. 61. *Registres de la société populaire, floréal an II.*
[2] Ibid. [3] A.N. F¹ᶜ III. *Calvados 7.*

relieve the situation. An appeal to the government for bread realized in early September 112 hundredweight of salt cod. The public claimed that it was too old to eat and that it was already bad, but by the end of the month they had laid their scruples aside and the rotten fish was distributed in the markets.

Throughout September hopes of relief from the incoming harvest were poured out to the people by the local authorities. It was only a matter of time, they were told, before plenty was restored; the authorities were doing all in their power to see to a speedy distribution of grain before autumn descended. But the townspeople could look back over a fearful year, a year when supplies had been so intermittent that they had scarcely known where to turn. True, something had always materialized—maize, rice, potatoes, swedes, salt fish—something to keep them from famine, but their nerves had been kept continually on edge wondering where the next supplies would come from. Industries which were dependent upon raw materials supplied by the peasants had come to a standstill; the smaller shopkeepers had gone out of business at a rate unprecedented since the crisis of the 1740s. In addition, deprivation of candles meant a cessation of evening work—a severe blow to a lacemaker with small children who had to work late hours to obtain a wage sufficient to provide for them. The municipal council and the *société populaire* had done all in their power to impose price regulations and to ensure supplies, and they had not hesitated to use force to keep the townspeople supplied. But they had encountered an enemy far more formidable than *émigré*, priest, or English—one who belonged to what was described in the *société populaire* as the 'nouvelle aristocratie meurtrière du cultivateur'. He it was who was withholding the benefits of the Revolution from the townspeople by the creation of an artificial food shortage. This sort of propaganda was impressed upon the townspeople by *société populaire*, municipal government, and *représentants en mission* alike and cogently demonstrated at every empty market. The disloyalty and lack of patriotism of the large farmers were to the townspeople evidence that they were ringed by enemies and traitors, aiding the royalists by destroying the government's policy of economic controls.

The changes of *thermidor* (July–August 1794) which modified the Jacobin government of France had an almost immediate repercussion on Bayeux. On *26 thermidor* (14 August) the *société populaire* excluded from the club Le Tual, Hardouin le Jeune, and Le Fort as the leading figures of the Terror at Bayeux. This nominal gesture in the direction of a purge hardly represented a drastic change in the composition of the club; but during the same month many of the men of the courts who had been members of the municipal council, *bureau de district*, and the *tribunal* during the federalist rising were released from prison and many of them re-entered political life. The former personnel of the machinery of the Terror, though not formally excluded from the *société populaire*, nevertheless, perhaps made anxious by the turn of events in Paris, slipped as far as possible into obscurity. The mayor, who was more than ready to retire from political life, though there was no pressure on him so to do, abandoned office. His successor was Jehanne, former *avocat en parlement*, who had not been associated with the Terror and had not been in Bayeux at the time of the federalist rising but who now came forward to head a municipal council once more composed of men of the courts, some of them tenuously associated with federalism. Only a handful of lawyers and officials immediately rejoined the *société populaire*, but the club that emerged from the thermidorean reaction was a body very unsure of itself and its allegiances. Its sessions degenerated into denunciations of one member against another and attendance dropped steeply from over a hundred stalwarts in the spring of 1794 to under a dozen during the heavy winter of 1795.

The problem that faced the new administration was the one that had faced the old—that of food supplies. For the incoming harvest the authorities were determined to be on the spot from the start. They had no confidence in any figures that the peasant farmers might submit of their harvest returns, and they suspected with good reason that the local authorities of the communes were much too sympathetic towards the large landowners to be honest. Moreover, these local authorities might well spend such a long time in the calculation of the crop of each farmer that to arrive at any general conclusion would be impossible without a long delay, during which time the communes could be starving. In late September the town sent commissioners to be kept at the expense of the individual communes until they had arrived at an estimate.[1] In October sterner measures were deemed necessary

[1] A.D.C. L. *Registres des délibérations du directoire du district de Bayeux, 6 vendémiaire an III.*

by the district assembly and it was arranged that gangs of labourers should be sent out by the town to cut down all the grain of any farmer who had not yet done so and who was seeking in this way to avoid its requisitioning. Their wages were to be paid by the farmers themselves. Moreover, any mayor or official suspected of complicity with peasants withholding grain would have to lodge soldiers in his house until the survey was completed.[1] No authority was prepared to hazard a repetition of the previous year's experience. By the beginning of November their estimates were complete and what had been only a fear became an agonizing reality. The harvest of 1794 had been a 1709, a 1725, a 1739, a 1788. In panic they wrote to Paris stating that the harvest had been less by one-third than the last and that they very much doubted if it had produced sufficient grain to provide for the district for more than two months. The harvest, they complained, had yielded straw not wheat; and they were faced with the uncomfortable choice of sowing grain for next year or consuming their small stock immediately. The document terminated with a plea to the government to send 10,000 bushels of corn for use as seed.[2]

This time there was no possibility of disguising the plain truth. The country people, proprietors, and labourers, anyone who had come into contact with the harvest, were only too well aware of its penury. Anyone who had any grain took steps to hold on to it. Nothing could be got from the country people without force. The commissioners and their troops had never treated the country people softly; now their ways were conditioned by their panic. They maltreated the country people and their actions served to worsen the situation. In several villages of the district violent scenes took place. Perhaps the worst were at Martragny where peasants were beaten and their property wrecked.[3] The news circulated. Stories of the brutalities of the commissioners and their troops, and their arbitrary treatment of those who were sometimes innocent, were repeated, exaggerated, passed on from village to village, market to market, farm to farm. Panic spread; determination to conserve what remained to them intensified amongst the peasants. By November it was fully apparent that 1795 would be even more difficult than the preceding year.

[1] A.M.B. no. 61. *Registres de la société populaire, 26 vendémiaire an III.*
[2] A.M.B. *Registres des délibérations du directoire du district de Bayeux, 11 brumaire an III.*
[3] Pezet, op. cit., p. 401.

The problem was enhanced by the activities of groups of women in the country districts and in the town who attacked the convoys of grain. The women were usually mothers with hungry families, often fully prepared to pay a fair price for the grain. They were not stealing: they pressed payment upon the carters. They merely wanted food for their children and were prepared to go to all lengths to get it. Scenes like this took place at Lingèvres, at St. Vigor, at St. Sulpice, at Crépon.[1] If caught and delivered to the urban or municipal authorities they usually escaped with a very short term in prison, since it was often discovered that they had children who were dependent upon them or even babies at the breast. It was not easy for the authorities to condemn women fighting for the lives of their infants. In November and early December the number of gatherings of women imploring the council for help became daily more frequent. They carried their children in their arms and declared they were robbed of nourishment. In their distress they did not stop short of violence. Indeed, on *27 brumaire an III* (17 November 1794) the *société populaire* urged upon the district assembly the passing of a decree which would allow the immediate arrest of any woman found carrying a club or suspicious weapon.[2]

Three days before this the district had claimed that 1,500 people at the market of Bayeux had not received any grain. The market was 986 bushels to the bad.[3] It was an alarming state to be in as soon after the harvest as November. It was the sort of situation which might be expected in the late spring and early summer, when the old supplies were running out and the new ones had not yet come in, but to be in this state before winter was a frightening prospect. Moreover, from the late autumn the municipal council was clearly afraid of what the townspeople might do if their wants were not satisfied. For all food supplies it was necessary to join an interminable queue and every queue was a nucleus of discontent and potential danger. No food of any sort, bread, milk, vegetables, butter, went unrationed. The authorities did everything in their power to see that everyone was treated alike and that the poor did not receive any less than the rich, but however

[1] A.D.C. L. *Registres des délibérations du directoire du district de Bayeux, 11 brumaire an III.*

[2] A.M.B. No. 61. *Registres de la société populaire, 27 brumaire an III.*

[3] A.D.C. L. *Registres des délibérations du directoire du district de Bayeux, 24 brumaire an III.*

well intentioned their policy, they were far from successful. The shortage did not affect all alike: those who owned even a little land staved off the worst of the hardship. The sessions of the municipal council and district assembly were continuous, but only as long as daylight lasted, for by now it was impossible to obtain candles. The councils met as early as possible in the mornings and went on until dusk.[1] The rooms in which they deliberated were unheated because of the fuel shortage. Almost daily they sent representatives on long journeys to try to procure grain—to the Manche, to Le Havre, and to Paris—before the season advanced still further. Government officials in the department were besieged by men sent by the district authority to get some sort of help before the worst happened and the town was faced with famine. The usual expeditions were sent into the country districts to get something out of the landowning peasantry; those suspected of having something hidden were led to Bayeux and imprisoned. The commissioners refused to believe, even when the farmer was telling the truth, that he had not got produce hidden away for his own use. They believed him to be ill intentioned, deliberately starving the people of the towns for his own selfish ends.

On 4 *nivôse an III* (24 December 1794) the relics of the Convention abolished the maximum. In so doing the government admitted the defeat of its attempt to control prices. It was in fact selling out to the peasant. He could now demand any price he saw fit. True, the *assignat* was doubtful exchange, but the peasant could make his own terms. A year previously, when the peasants really had some corn, the abolition of the restriction might have constituted a substantial victory for them in their struggle against the maximum, but the same situation no longer existed. On *17 nivôse an III* (6 January 1795) the district once again embarked upon an extensive propaganda programme designed to counteract fear. It stressed that now the maximum had been abolished there was nothing to prevent the free circulation of corn. Proclamations of this nature, however, did not carry conviction when on 17 and on *24 nivôse an III* (6, 13 January 1795), between 400 and 500 people got nothing at the market at Bayeux.[2] The bailiffs were

---

[1] Pezet, op. cit., p. 398.

[2] A.D.C. L. *Registres des délibérations du directoire du district de Bayeux, 17 nivôse an III.*

sent off to the country districts, carrying addresses from loyal citizens of Bayeux condemning the peasants' recalcitrance now that the maximum no longer existed, and accompanied by bands of troops. A little grain was realized but not sufficient to prevent a repetition of the expedition in February and March. Moreover, the central government had embarked on an underhand policy as far as the districts were concerned. Besieged on all sides for help, it gave rash promises and accorded to their demands, even though it knew that it lacked the means to implement them. Thus Bayeux in January was solemnly promised 34,000 bushels of wheat. Counting on them to remedy the situation in February, the municipal government made further promises to the townsfolk, once again reiterating the generosity of the government and its tender care for the people, but the supply never came.[1] In mid April a proclamation was issued by the municipality admitting the difficulties before the town. It was concluded with a severe warning: 'Citoyens, il ne faut pas vivre pour le moment, il faut envisager l'avenir. Celui qui ne fixe que le pain qu'il mange aujourd'hui sans s'occuper de celui qu'il doit avoir le lendemain, court à une famine évidente et par conséquent à sa propre destruction.'[2] At the same time the municipal officials announced that the bread ration would be 12 oz. per head for each adult male—a promise they had no means of carrying out, and the townspeople by this time knew only too well that they were unlikely to realize more than half of any official estimate. The printed announcement, posted throughout the town for all to read, was to be the occasion of a popular rising in the town similar in character to those of *germinal* in Paris, the towns of the Seine valley, particularly Rouen, and in towns not far distant from Bayeux like Honfleur and Port en Bessin and later Caen.

On the morning of 2 *floréal* (21 April) a crowd of townsfolk gathered outside the town hall shouting: 'Nous voulons du pain, il nous faut du pain.'[3] Municipal officials who appeared cautiously at windows were hissed at and threatened with the vengeance of the people if they did not there and then produce the demanded grain. Then the crowd moved off in the direction of the cathedral and no municipal official was ignorant of where it was going. The people were after the military grain supplies stored there.

[1] Ibid., *17, 24 nivôse an III.*   [2] Pezet, op. cit., p. 401.
[3] A.M.B. *Registres des délibérations du corps municipal, 2–3 floréal an III.*

There were 4,000 bushels reserved by government orders and intended for the army. The high oak doors were forced; the corn was divided; everything was pillaged. But the crowd did not disappear with its booty immediately. The next day found the municipal council still confined to the town hall by a crowd demanding cheaper food. A decision was made to send two representatives to impress upon the people the folly of their conduct, and to warn them of the dangers of a clash with the soldiers over the military grain supplies. The unfortunate couple chosen for this mission left the room but never addressed the people and returned in fear saying that the gathering must be threatened with armed force. In the meantime the crowd had repaired once more to the cathedral. A group of hysterical women tore down the altar of liberty and the trappings of the goddess of Reason. They then turned their attention to Jean Jacques. A bust of Rousseau was shattered to the cry of: 'A bas putain. Quand le bon Dieu était là, nous avions du pain.'[1] Others fell to their knees and prayed for forgiveness. A district official was seized by a group of angry women, dragged before the erstwhile altar, made to prostrate himself and demand pardon of an offended Christ.

The rising of *floréal* was essentially one of hunger and protest against rising prices. It took place at a time when deprivation had never been more apparent or costs greater. When the crowd was satisfied that there was no more food to be found it went home, its ends accomplished, and peace was restored without any action at all on the part of the municipal council. The cries of the women and their gestures against dechristianization were perhaps the most cogent expression that could be made against the thermidorean government, which must have appeared to them largely responsible for the shortage and increased costs, rather than indication of a movement inspired by hidden clerics or royalist sympathizers. In the year II it had been possible to believe that an ill-intentioned peasantry and a counter revolutionary priesthood were responsible for the hardship, but in the year III the government alone had to shoulder the blame. Perhaps the news of revolts in Paris and the provincial capital and nearby towns gave some encouragement, but it is difficult to estimate how much. The officials of Bayeux represented the riot to the central government as the work of the enemies of the people. Seven women were

[1] A.M.B. *Registres des délibérations du corps municipal, 2–3 floréal an III.*

arrested and found guilty of shattering Rousseau's bust.[1] They pleaded drunkenness and escaped with a month in prison. The confidence of the municipal government could not be easily restored, however. When the 4,000 bushels pillaged from the cathedral had been consumed more would have to be found. An immediate application was made for a state loan in the lean hope that somewhere some foodstuff might be purchased. The local officials prepared themselves for one ultimate effort. The next harvest was five months away and the events of April alone had been sufficient indication of public unrest. All that remained for them was a further search of the district, a further embassy to Caen, a further entreaty to Paris in the hope, which might indeed be in vain, that something would emerge. On *23 floréal an III* (12 May 1795) the district decreed that yet one more commission should be sent into the countryside to lay hands on whatever grain they could find. The central government ordered the district to turn over 6,000 hundredweight of grain for the provisioning of Bayeux, but none of the administrators looked upon this as realistic.[2] They knew that nothing would produce such results. As if matters were not already sufficiently difficult, a new fear now presented itself that the hungry people of the country might rise *en masse* and cut down the unripened corn in the fields. Already in April there were isolated cases of this and further attempts might jeopardize the next harvest.[3] When the requisitioning realized very little the district assembly decided to imprison all those farmers who had not fully paid the amount of corn they owed according to the estimates of the previous November.[4] One hundred and thirty-four men were immediately imprisoned. The district also ordered the arrest of any woman caught pillaging convoys, but without success. A day later it was reported that a group of women had seized 16 hundredweight of corn intended for Bayeux in the village of Asnières without the authorities of the area taking action.[5] The administrators of Asnières were ordered to make good the theft, but grain could not be got out of them nor out of the imprisoned farmers, simply because it was not there to be got. Desperate attempts were made by those im-

[1] Ibid.
[2] A.D.C. *Registres des délibérations du directoire du district de Bayeux, 23 floréal an III.*
[3] Ibid., *3 floréal an III.*
[4] Ibid., *5 prairial an III.*
[5] Ibid., *6 prairial an III.*

prisoned to lay hold of grain; some managed to buy on the black market at an exorbitant price, but many had to be released without payment.

On *6 prairial an III* (25 May 1795) the mayor of Bayeux himself set off to Le Havre to purchase grain or some foodstuff at whatever cost. He reported back six days later that he had found rice at Le Havre, but at 18 *livres* a pound. The district was not prepared to quibble over the price:

> Dans l'état de pénurie et même de disette extrême dans lequel se trouve ce district, il ne faut négliger aucun des moyens capables de nous préserver des horreurs de la famine. Que depuis longtemps les campagnes épuisées n'apportent rien au marché de la commune de Bayeux ... Que les maisons d'arrêt ont été remplies de cultivateurs désolés, qui pour sortir de prison, n'ayant aucuns grains chez eux, n'ont pu parvenir à s'en procurer dans les districts étrangers qu'avec dépenses énormes et à des prix qui les ruinent ... l'un d'eux a payé un sac de blé 2,100 livres ... qu'il en est de même qui ont donné jusqu'à leur semence réservée.[1]

The money would be raised by a government loan of 100,000 *livres* and a forced loan payable by the community of Bayeux of 200,000 *livres* repayable at an interest rate of $2\frac{1}{2}$ per cent. when the *contribution foncière* was realized.

Up to the harvest the town had no other resources than the rice from Le Havre. A pound was distributed to each citizen each week. At first it was sold at 8 *livres* a pound but in early August it had to be reduced to 5 *livres* 10 *sous*. Even this was too dear. The municipality found itself confronted with mothers trailing young children and crying that they had exhausted all their resources, sold their household linen, their cooking pots, and the clothes from their backs in an attempt to keep their children fed.[2] Rice of poor quality was reduced to 1 *livre* a pound. Moreover, as food rice was suspect. Some did not know how to cook it: others did not have the fuel needed for boiling it and had to be content to soak it in water.

The years 1793 and 1794 had been hard, but the hardship was nothing in comparison with what Bayeux and much of northern France were subjected to in 1795 and 1796. The sufferings of Bayeux were perhaps little in comparison with those of a large

---

[1] A.D.C. *Registres des délibérations du directoire du district de Bayeux, 13 prairial an III.*
[2] A.M.B. *Registres des délibérations du corps municipal, 17 thermidor an III.*

city like Rouen. Even so, living on the bare minimum affected the spirits of the townspeople. If they did not die of hunger, many were weakened by malnutrition. An observer spoke of the swollen stomachs and eyes that seemed disproportionately large in the shrunken faces of the children.[1] Mortality rates increased during the winter months, for unrelieved malnutrition meant a lowering of resistance to even minor complaints.[2] The lack of fuel in the cold winter of 1794, endless standing in food queues, the selling of clothes in an attempt to raise a little money, all made the hardship worse. The plight of the landless of the surrounding rural area cannot have been any better, though it is not so well recorded; but the town had limped along through the efforts of its administrators, while the poor of the countryside had no one so actively concerned to protect them. Only the rich, the *cultivateur aisé* and the large urban landlord had been spared from the crisis. The cries of the poor had given no peace to those concerned in local administration and the officials were virtually worn out. It is not surprising that the food crisis marked the end of any attempt at Bayeux to pursue a nationally orientated policy. With over half of the town reduced to paupers, forced to queue for municipal food supplies, many who had once been proud and independent were virtual beggars whose spirits were crushed, and those who governed them, exhausted by constant effort, were after the year III concerned only with the purely parochial interests of a small provincial town.

[1] A.N. F¹ᶜ III. *Calvados 7. Bayeux, 20 brumaire an IV.*

[2] The unit studied is too small to permit any further conclusions to be drawn from mortality rates. The average number of deaths annually in the town was *c.* 210, rising in the year IV to 275 and in the year V to 277. A.D.C. *État Civil, Bayeux, Registres 32 & 33.* The effects of the crisis are strikingly demonstrated in R. Cobb, 'Disette et Mortalité. La crise de l'an III et de l'an IV à Rouen', *Annales de Normandie* (1956), pp. 267–91, and in his *Terreur et Subsistances* (Paris, 1965), pp. 307–42.

V

THE RESPONSE TO THE PROBLEM OF THE POOR

SOCIAL LEGISLATION, 1790–1796

B Y the beginning of the year IV the disillusioned and the discontented could find more than one instance in which high-sounding promises had been made and hope held out by the government without anything having been effectively accomplished. Without doubt, the most striking of these was the question of the poor. The matter had been under discussion since 1789, because the annexation of church property and the abolition of tithes and dues affected not merely the country's ecclesiastics but also the poor, the sick, the aged, and orphaned, who for centuries had leant on the church for what little support they had. A portion of ecclesiastical revenues had, whether directly or indirectly, subsidized the poorest strata of society. The withdrawal of that support threatened immediately the economically most vulnerable sections of the population. The question was a particularly burning one at Bayeux because the church had contributed so largely to the support of the many indigent, and the municipal authorities waited anxiously throughout 1789 and 1790 to see what the central government would do. The latter was well versed in progressive thought on social legislation, on the demoralizing effects of almsgiving and the need for the creation of work for the poor. Indeed, in 1790 the Assembly was optimistic that the annexation of church property and the abolition of tithes would inaugurate a new period in the history of poor relief in France, that the whole system would be reorganized; almsgiving would cease and the paupers of France would become useful citizens by honest employment. On 2 November 1789, when ecclesiastical property was placed at the disposal of the nation, the Assembly did not hesitate to undertake on behalf of the nation as well as the upkeep of religion the succouring of the poor. The immediate concern was, of course, the assumption by the state of the wealth of the church. Until that happened no new project could be financed. Moreover, a comprehensive plan would have to be worked out which would take time. Anxious that no one should suffer whilst the new arrangements were under consideration, the Assembly decreed that the old *hôpitaux* and *hôtels Dieu* should keep their property, which would be exempted from the rules applying to other church lands, and that any losses these establishments suffered from the abolition of tithes would be made good by the state. As for the unemployed, the Assembly promised that during the winter period they would provide funds for *ateliers de charité*.[1] Further than this they would not go for the moment but left the drawing up of plans to a *comité de mendicité* and waited for the necessary funds from the sale of church lands. To ensure that the facilities existing in 1789 were not diminished, the legislation which aimed to destroy the power of the church was tempered to assure the continuance of some help for the poor. When, on 13 February 1790, the law no longer recognized religious vows, attempts were made to dissuade the nuns engaged in charitable work from leaving.[2] Whereas on 3 October 1790 any member of a religious order was released from vows made upon entry, an exception was made for the nursing sisters and those who ran the poor institutions.[3] They were expected to give at least six months' notice of their intention to leave their congregation and it was hoped they would not do so at all. The Assembly may have opposed the church of the old régime, but it was reluctant to sacrifice the benefits the church had bestowed. Unfortunately the efforts of the Assembly to ensure that the measures affecting the church in no way hurt the poorer members of society were a dismal failure.

The Assembly was prepared to reimburse the hospitals for their losses from the abolition of tithes, of seigneurial rights or of *rentes*. What it was not prepared to meet out of public funds was the sums the church of the old régime had accorded as charity to families who could not make ends meet: sums bishops and chapters and religious orders had distributed to the poor out of the superfluity of their revenues, which had sustained many a poor family in towns like Bayeux and which were far more important to those

[1] *Archives Parlementaires*, t. xxxi, p. 375.
[2] A. Aulard, *La Révolution française et les congrégations* (Paris, 1903), p. 171.   [3] Ibid.

towns than the hospitals themselves. The policy of the Assembly aimed merely at bridging the gap between the old and the new. It could not compromise itself on the issue of almsgiving which it condemned out of hand.

In late 1790 the municipality of Bayeux drew up, at the request of the government, an official list of its poor which put in black and white the biggest problem: the large number of children who needed some sort of subsidy since their families were too poor to support them.[1] Of the town's 10,320 inhabitants, 1,884 were estimated in need of relief, and of these 622 were children. Altogether, Bayeux estimated almost 20 per cent. of the townspeople and 15 per cent. of the rural population to be in need of relief. Of these 33 per cent. of the first and 63 per cent. of the second were children. A mere 34–35 per cent. of the paupers living in the town were fit for work. Only the sick and the crippled were catered for by the hospitals: what was going to happen to the rest?

The local authorities appreciated immediately that the losses from the cessation of ecclesiastical alms were far more serious to the town than the direct loss to the hospital of the tithes it owned. The revenues of the *hôtel Dieu* went down in 1790 by some 2,717 *livres*, the greatest loss being the proceeds from the tax levied on corn as it entered the market, which had generally been suppressed. Those of the *hôpital général* were reduced by some 4,720 *livres*, the deficit being largely due to the abolition of the tax on cider entering the town.[2] At least, however, the government had offered compensation for such losses, though as ever with government money, a long wait was unhappily implicit.

Bayeux was informed in September 1790 that the responsibility for the financial management of the hospitals should be taken away from the religious orders and placed for the time being in the hands of the municipality, which also had the task of arranging for *ateliers de charité* temporarily at its own expense. Provisionally, the treasury would not be responsible for the poor except for the upkeep of the orphan babies and the provision of compensation to the hospitals for losses from tithe. Other needs must be met out of municipal funds. The central government was anxious to restrict at all costs the large deficit in the treasury on the eve of a new issue of *assignats* and wanted to cut expendi-

[1] A.D.C. Lx. *États d'assistance, Bayeux.* See Appendix V.   [2] Ibid.

ture to a minimum.[1] It left Bayeux, however, in an unenviable position. New legislation and compensation had been promised but in the meanwhile the sick, the old, and the indigent had to be kept alive and all this without apparent means. Late 1790 saw only the beginning of a long correspondence between Bayeux and the government—a correspondence to which the government did not always reply. A representative example is the following letter sent in December 1790 to Paris by the municipal government:

La ville de Bayeux est absolument sans commerce, sans manufacture et sans industrie. C'est une ville de chapitre et comme le corps ecclésiastique de cette ville était dans le cas d'y dépenser 400,000 à 500,000 livres tous les ans, cette somme distribuée et répandue dans la main des fournisseurs faisait la masse de la fortune publique de cette ville . . . les pauvres avaient des secours au moyen des quêtes qui se faisaient et où le chapitre et l'évêque fournissaient de leurs moyens. Depuis la révolution les ressources se tarissent, la misère augmente et celui qui n'était que pauvre est actuellement misérable. . . .[2]

The municipal council went on to suggest that many of the townspeople regretted the end of the institution which had kept them alive, a threat they often used to try to impress upon the government that unless something was done to replace the alms, largely in kind, distributed amongst the townsfolk by the church, the government must expect the discontented to take sides with the non-jurors. In fact, this was extremely unlikely: the poor of the town, the old, and the children, scarcely understood the issues at stake in 1790 sufficiently to undertake any demonstration on behalf of the former ecclesiastical authorities.

The problem of the municipality was essentially the same as that of the government, the lack of available money. The *aides* were no longer collected. The abolition of *octrois* in May 1791 cut off an important source of municipal income: the *aides* had long ago disappeared. Losses, it was expected, would be made good ultimately out of a sixteenth of the total proceeds accruing from the sale of national property; but the slowness of assessment and the complicated negotiations involved made immediate relief from this source unlikely. In January 1791, 2,000 *livres* from the government came to help the town set up an *atelier de charité*

[1] M. Bouchet, *L'Assistance en France pendant la Révolution* (Paris, 1908), p. 256.
[2] A.D.C. Lx. *États d'assistance, Bayeux*.

during the winter months.[1] This was a much smaller sum than was really needed. The task was, as usual, demolition work on the *château*. The number of workmen employed was limited to forty and funds only permitted the continuance of work until the late spring. Nevertheless, in late March a further twenty men turned up to work who were not included amongst the original forty. They took up shovels and started to dig. The municipality agreed that they should be paid for the work they had done at the rate of 15 *sols* a day but warned them that they must not come again; if they did so, their work would be unpaid and they would be treated as rebels.[2]

The compensation promised by the government for the losses to the hospitals in 1790 had not materialized by March 1791. The nuns told the district that since they could not pay their food and heating bills and the tradesmen were refusing to deliver supplies, their tending of the old and the sick was becoming totally in-effective. They threatened that unless something was done quickly they would walk out.[3] The district assembly promised the nuns that their demands would be met as soon as possible and that it could only be a matter of weeks before the money came. The district was very anxious to prove its worth. It entered into the spirit of the *comité de mendicité*, proclaimed that work was the only effective remedy for the paupers of France and set about planning extensive work projects for the poor of the area. In July 1791 it sent to the department a *mémoire* outlining the project of a canal to link Port en Bessin with Bayeux.[4] The plan was not new and it represented an old ambition of the town. Such a scheme, the *directoire* claimed, would employ the poor of both town and country and people of all ages could be given work. It sought permission to levy an extra *sol* per *livre* on the *contribution foncière* to meet the initial cost of such a plan, and hoped, ultimately, to secure some government aid for the scheme. The department accorded a tentative sanction, subject to government approval. The plan was, after all, in full accordance with the Assembly's theoretical projects for the useful employment of the able-bodied poor. The temporary acceptance was sufficient to give hope to the

---

1 A.D.C. *Registres des délibérations du directoire de département.*
2 A.M.B. Q72. 11 April 1791.
3 A.D.C. Lx. *Hospices de Bayeux.*
4 A.M.B. *Registres des délibérations du corps municipal.* 11 July 1791.

district authority. It seemed as if after initial difficulties the long-promised changes were coming and better days were ahead. The president of the district assembly spoke cautiously of the danger of pinning too much faith upon the project. Everything depended, he said, upon stability in the upper branches of the administration, so that Bayeux might count upon a continual stream of support for work which would obviously take many years to complete. Moreover, he pointed out in October 1791, the initial work would be heavy and it would be some time before it would relieve the unemployment situation to any considerable extent. He urged that in addition to the canal, the town should try to open an *atelier de charité* specifically designed for day-labourers with families who were unemployed during the winter months. Something too must be done for the widowed women and old people of the town. The same letter, addressed to Paris, stressed that the hospitals were still in a pitiful condition. The meat bill for 1790 and the first ten months of 1791 had not been paid and tradesmen were refusing to deliver more. The lace school owed several merchants of the town money for thread.[1] By December, when no reply had materialized from Paris where the Legislative Assembly was still organizing itself, the municipal council wrote to the district to say that since nothing had been received from Paris they had been forced to hold a door-to-door collection, though they knew that this method of raising funds for relief was no longer approved in Paris. They pointed out that without immediate help they would be forced to open the doors of the hospitals and expel the old and the sick. The collection which the council had hoped would afford them some help was a severe disappointment. Under the old régime such an appeal realized a minimum of 3,000 *livres*; this time the figure was under 500 *livres* since there was no help from the church.[2]

On 17 January the problem of the poor and the fate of the hospitals was raised in the Assembly. No one was prepared, as yet, to face the problems which would arise from the assumption by the state of hospital property and complete responsibility for their provision. Accordingly the only legislation passed was a decree giving the hospitals permission to enjoy the rents from their property until 15 January 1793.[3] Moreover, in the same

---

[1] A.D.C. Lx. *Hospices de Bayeux.* October 1791.
[2] Ibid. 5 December 1791.   [3] Bouchet, op. cit., p. 289.

month a subsidy of 4,100,000 *livres* was voted to sustain the poor of France during 1792, of which 2,500,000 *livres* was to be spent on creating useful work for the able-bodied poor. The sum was to be distributed among the departments, but before they could receive it they must justify their need of it and prove that it was to be spent not on almsgiving but on work.[1]

The opportunity was the one for which Bayeux had been waiting. The town was one of the few of the *département* of the Calvados which had a work project on paper and approved. By April 1792 eighty men were at work on the canal and 65,000 *livres* had not only been promised, but was arriving in instalments.[2] At least the able-bodied men of the town who lacked resources could be employed. The work, however, could only be paid for at the rate of 15 *sous* a day. One of the conditions for the setting afoot of such projects was that remuneration for the employees should be sufficient to maintain the individual concerned, but slightly lower than that afforded to day-labourers elsewhere employed. The provision was necessary because the government feared that if state work was more highly paid than other jobs then the employees would have no incentive to look elsewhere. State work was meant to be provisional, not permanent; the employee as soon as possible must become self-supporting.[3]

This did not provide for wife and children: there were, as yet, no opportunities for the widowed and the weak, but the commencement of work upon the canal de Soucy meant that at least one sort of pauper need no longer concern the local council. Not every town was as fortunate; few could think of public works to employ their poor; in some areas obviously the type of pauper who needed care was something other than an unemployed day-labourer. In any case, the wage restriction meant that for many the problem was unresolved, the reimbursement would not provide for a family. By July, in very special cases, the Assembly relaxed some of its stipulations and accorded sums to areas which could not justify their expenditure in useful works.[4]

At the advent of war, the first signs of relief for the poor of the area were visible; but the alleviation was to be of short duration. Against the stark reality of inflation the government's promises of

[1] Bouchet, op. cit., p. 289.
[2] A.M.B. *Registres des délibérations du corps municipal.* 15 April 1792.
[3] Bouchet, op. cit., p. 294.
[4] Ibid.

poor relief in early 1792 were to evaporate. The realization of estimates submitted by the municipalities became increasingly unlikely and, moreover, the fate of the hospital personnel was linked with the question of tolerance and payment for non-jurors. The decree of August 1792 suppressing religious communities did not exempt the nuns engaged in charitable works. It was, however, decreed that in hospitals the same people should continue to look after the sick and the needy but as individuals, not as a congregation. The religious rule binding the congregation together was broken.[1]

The tending of the sick, the aged, the cripples, and the babies of the *hôtel Dieu* was not enviable work. Doctoring was primitive and funds limited to a minimum. The most any nurse could hope to do was to see that the internees were kept clean and fed whilst awaiting death. To find anyone other than the nuns to care for syphilitic infants or the mentally insane from any respectable level of society was not easy. The Sisters of Charity who ran the hospital at Bayeux had sustained themselves through periods of economic stress and deprivation largely by the strength and moral fervour obtained from the communal religious life: dissolve the religious tie and all that remained to them was a thankless struggle against poverty and sickness. The nuns were aware of their scarcity value. Their chaplain had been a non-juror; and they had counteracted efforts to replace him by organizing measures to sabotage the masses of his successor. A non-juror could always be found to administer the viaticum.[2] The municipal government, anxious above all to retain their services, had reproved them but was prepared to meet them half-way. It hesitated before implementing the decree of 18 August, then announced to the nuns that the decree would not make any effective difference except that they must don secular clothes and cease to carry out any communal offices; they would, however, still be able to participate together with the internees of their hospitals in worship. The municipal council agreed to pay for a full outfit for each nun and promised that their labours would, from henceforth, be reimbursed by the state.[3] The nuns were not pressed for an immediate decision and it was April 1793 before the municipal council demanded an answer. The nuns gave their consent and received appropriate

[1] Ibid., p. 325.   [2] A.M.B. Q71. *Hospices.*
[3] Ibid.

clothes. They did so, they said, because of the state of misery currently existing in the town.[1]

The difficulties to which they referred, and of which the municipal council was only too well aware, arose from the scanty harvest of 1792. The municipal council claimed that there were within the town over 2,000 needy and these mostly members of large families, often with an unemployed bread-winner. They had had recourse to a door-to-door collection which had realized little and were on the point of making a further appeal to the townspeople in the name of humanity and religion.[2]

Humanity and religion were high-sounding words. They were the slogan which accompanied the collection of 1793 but to small avail. Funds for the canal materialized; so did, in April 1793, the repayment of losses to the hospitals for October 1792. But nothing else came; nothing to subsidize the fathers of large families or those whose wages were only sufficient for themselves and who had dependent relatives. In November the department had received 80,000 *livres*, but of this Caen would only let Bayeux have 9,000 *livres*, since the town had had money for the canal and other areas did not have this outlet.[3] Indeed, the government refused any subsidy which would be used for almsgiving. It would, at the same time, do nothing to raise the wages in the *ateliers de charité* to make them more attractive places to work and support oneself and one's family. In fact, the town was trapped by the government's attitude to poverty—an attitude which it showed no signs of abandoning.

The nurses at the hospital, and the municipal council, did not know where to turn to raise funds. They cut down the meals of the internees at the hospital to one a day, ceased to heat the buildings, made door-to-door collections and still they could not raise enough to keep these establishments running. By summer the hospital only functioned at all because the surgeon, Le Tual, undertook to supply drugs free of cost, the wages of the nuns were unpaid, and the diet of the patients was clearly inadequate.[4] The municipal officials tried to turn away all newcomers demanding entry unless they were dangerously ill and had no shelter of their

---

[1] A.M.B. Q71. *Hospices.*
[2] A.M.B. *Registres des délibérations du corps municipal.* 21 March 1793.
[3] Ibid., May 1793.
[4] Ibid., *11 germinal an II.*

own. The lace school and the *manufactures* of the children at the *hôpital général* closed since there was nothing with which to buy raw material. In the autumn, after the collapse of federalism, La Planche, the *représentant en mission* in the Calvados, attempted to start a soup kitchen in Bayeux to relieve the obvious distress of the town.[1] But the ingredients had to be bought and the questions were with what and whence. By this time the Sisters of Charity who had been the traditional organizers and distributors of such projects were in prison and the municipal council claimed they could not find a sufficient number of women whom they could trust to undertake such an enterprise. At a time of crisis, unless they had full confidence in those responsible for soup distributions, they feared the food would be stolen by the distributors. By the end of 1793 the paupers of Bayeux, both inside and outside the hospitals, did not know where to turn for relief.

Le Tual had his own visionary projects for the care of the sick and the aged. One of these was to get rid of the nuns, as an obvious handicap to medical progress in the hospital at Bayeux. His struggle with them had been long. He knew they were ignorant in their methods of treating the sick and he wasted no time in dismissing them. At the beginning of 1794 the Sisters of Charity of Bayeux were imprisoned as non-jurors. His action did not help the situation. The nuns had worked without wages: the new nurses expected payment. When this failed to come they took the sheets and utensils, robbed the hospital of its property, and one of them tried to take the municipal councillors, as directors, to court. Many of the new nurses walked out.[2]

By March 1794, after the hardest winter in living memory, the local administration was forced reluctantly to suspend work on the canal de Soucy. The ground had been frozen solid for months, and work had been very intermittent, but even with the spring and the softening of the earth, the working teams were told they must be disbanded. The district *directoire* could not guarantee them the food they needed to carry out such hard manual labour.[3] The abandoning of the project meant the end of the one positive attempt at the employment of the poor of Bayeux since 1789. In the same

[1] Laffetay, op. cit., p. 387.
[2] C. Garnier, 'Les Hospices de Bayeux', *Mémoires de la Société des Sciences, Arts et Belles Lettres de Bayeux* (1908), p. 39.
[3] A.D.C. *Registres des délibérations du directoire de district, ventôse an II.*

month, a few days after the notice served to the workmen of the canal de Soucy, the town was asked to supply the government with a list of *indigents patriotes*, with their names, ages, profession, and number and age of their children so that the government could consider ways to help the paupers of France out of the property of the enemies of the Revolution.[1]

Another list, further promises; the district was tired and disillusioned and did not trouble to send a reply. Instead it beseeched Lozeau, the *représentant en mission*, throughout March and April 1794 for funds to open an *atelier de charité* and 12,000 *livres* to be used as a fortnightly subsidy for poor families until the harvest brought relief.[2] It was all very well, the *directoire de district* pointed out, for the government to proclaim the right of the individual to a living wage and adequate food but the means to supply these were simply not to hand.

The central government was in fact faced with a situation for which it possessed no solution. It could not retract its high-sounding principles, but war expenditure, the depreciation of the *assignat*, the pressing problem of getting food supplies, all these had clouded the vision of a welfare state and made it unrealizable in the existing conditions. It made promises and did not cease to make them, but it could not surmount the lack of money and food. Moreover, by now the war had to come first and funds had to be found for it. It was this necessity which delivered the final blow.

On *23 messidor an II* (11 July 1794) the property of the hospitals was annexed by the state: annexed not because the government had worked out a comprehensive plan for the support of the poor but because the government needed the money from the sale of the land. The needs of national defence perforce overrode any other consideration and to that end the patrimony of the poor was dissolved.[3]

The local authorities of Bayeux did not know what to do. Part of the property might be withheld, but only temporarily. The government was demanding funds and promising the provision of work but the local authority was not deceived. The municipal council addressed an immediate appeal to the *société populaire* to levy a tax on each member in an attempt to keep the hospital

---

[1] A.D.C. *Registres des délibérations du directoire de district, ventôse an II*.
[2] Ibid.
[3] L. Lallemand, *La Révolution et les Pauvres* (Paris, 1898), p. 69.

going. They warned the townsfolk that no one who was not sick could expect any help. Small loans were made to the hospital out of the pockets of the councillors to ensure its continuance. Commodities in short supply, such as soap and candles, were auctioned to the highest bidder in order to afford some slender resources to the hospital.[1] At the peak of the food crisis, in the years II, III, and IV, the town was without any relief at all for its able-bodied poor. The aged who had previously been sheltered by the hospital and who had nowhere to go, remained within its precincts, huddled together for warmth, because there was no fuel, covered in lice because there was no soap or change of linen, and not seeing food on at least three days of the week. The fate of the children who had lived at the hospital and of the foundlings was as bad, for payments could not be made to foster-parents who were themselves feeling the pinch of food shortage and inflation and who duly dispatched the children back into the town in an effort to force the municipal government into payment.[2] Other wetnurses claimed that since they themselves were without adequate food, they did not have sufficient milk to feed a child and that until the municipal council made provision for regular bread supplies and payment, they were physically incapable of taking in a foundling.[3] Children without foster-homes wandered about the town crying for bread, shelter, and attention. Nameless children deposited in the doorway of the hospital died, in some cases without being taken inside.[4] A description of the material condition of the poor of the *hospices* of the town during the years 1794 and 1795 is perforce partial in the silence of official documents. No regular day-to-day accounts or register of entries and deaths were kept by nurse or doctor or administrator to indicate what was done for the poor, infirm, aged, and orphaned of the town. The only informants of the municipal government were the two surgeons, Le Tual and Philibert, who, without payment or any means at their disposal to remedy the material condition of the hospital, notwithstanding put in a daily attendance and addressed wretched letters to the municipality appealing for help: 'J'ai visité aujourd'hui les salles . . . j'ai vu des malheureux expirant étendus sur du fumier, sans avoir qui les soigne, sans aucun des

[1] A.M.B. *Registres des délibérations du corps municipal, 8 ventôse an III.*
[2] A.N. F15 267. *Hospices de Bayeux.*   [3] Garnier, op. cit., p. 40.
[4] A.M.B. Q72. *Hospices.*

secours indispensables à leur état. . . .'[1] Le Tual supplied medicaments out of his own purse but the root of the trouble, he claimed, was the *pénurie des subsistances*, continual malnutrition, and food of dubious quality which together sapped the strength of the aged and lowered the resistance even of the young to disease.[2] Without food and fresh linen, Le Tual could do very little to alleviate the plight of the sick.

The breakdown of provisions for the poor and the infirm were associated in the minds of the townspeople with the disappearance of the old church. The cry for a resumption of the charitable activities of the Sisters of Providence and the *bureau de charité* became more and more vocal after the revolt of *floréal an III*. The following month a crowd of angry women surrounded the prison demanding the release of the Sisters of Providence and the re-opening of the lace schools.[3] A similar incident was repeated two weeks later. The town council tried to gloss over the events in its records by presenting them as the work of the disloyal and drunken few; but it was forced to concede that the works of charity of the old régime were missed and that the republican government had abandoned the weakest of the town's citizens and that they themselves could do nothing to help them.

Large-scale unemployment, food shortage, the breakdown of such provisions for social welfare as the town possessed were the most apparent results of the Revolution to the bulk of the townspeople. The aged were uncared for, the children untaught, for the laicization of education, like the laicization of poor relief, meant its disappearance. The teaching orders had been suspended when the first religious houses were closed. The Christian brothers had agreed to lay aside their habits and continue their work but they too ceased to function in 1793. Early government projects for an educational system freed from religious superstition, where the recital of the Declaration of the Rights of Man took the place of the catechism, simply collapsed in the general breakdown of 1794–6. Wherever one looked in Bayeux, the Revolution had caused a dislocation of the lives of the townspeople and with that dislocation, Bayeux moved into an attitude of resentment and opposition to the central government.

[1] A.M.B. Q72. *Hospices.*   [2] Ibid.   [3] Garnier, op. cit., p. 40.

VI

THE COUNTER REVOLUTION
SEPTEMBER 1795–1798

By the beginning of the year IV (September 1795) Bayeux was entering upon its third year of acute hardship and there was no sign of alleviation. The difficulties of the preceding three years are sufficient in themselves to explain popular attitudes in Bayeux and its district towards government policy and the changes of the Revolution by the end of that period. The Directory, though bent on appeasement and reconstruction, had to contend with a solid wall of hostility and mistrust built up over the preceding years which did much to frustrate its attempts to govern effectively. It was not merely that the relationship between town and country during the food crisis had degenerated into open hatred, or that schism between rich and poor in both country and town can rarely have been more marked, but that rich and poor alike were tired. By the year IV even those who during the first years of the Revolution had demonstrated some enthusiasm were demoralized. A large section of the population, many of whom before the Revolution had been able to manage fairly well, had been forced to join the municipal bread queues and was reduced to pauperism.

The situation was if anything worse in the country than in Bayeux itself. The agricultural labourer felt the pinch no less than the people of the towns. Indeed perhaps he felt it more, because the officials of the town were intent upon keeping the townspeople fed in order to maintain civil order even at the expense of the rural areas. There had also been a degree of brutalization of the countryside which could not fail to have its effect. It was the product of savage requisitioning and marauding expeditions which had thrown small and large landowner alike into an attitude of hostility. The bailiffs of Bayeux and the troops who accompanied them had taken all they could find. The peasants' property had not been held sacred. Now that every provision for the relief of the destitute had broken down and there was not even a *curé* to share his miserable pittance with the paupers of his parish and address wretched letters of complaint to his bishop, no possible buffer remained for the poor man who had exhausted all his resources. If he took to the roads now what could he anticipate but a life given over to more violence?

It was not that the inhabitants of the area were whitewashing the old régime or wanted to return to it. Nor did they deny that from the abolition of indirect taxes they had derived a very positive benefit; but the benefits were not as apparent as the failures. By the year IV nothing attached either the peasant of the district or the townsfolk to the existing régime or aroused any enthusiasm for its continuance. 'Apathy' and 'sullen hostility' were the words used to describe the spirit prevailing in the area in an official report.[1] The Directory spoke of this attitude as part of the 'counter revolution' but it was only 'against' the Revolution in the sense that it was not 'for' it. The antipathy of the peasant towards the government was even more marked than that of the town and in its manifestation more positively dangerous. The government was faced with war in the Vendée and in the nearby Sarthe, where the *levée en masse* of 1792 had inaugurated *chouan* movements as part of the resistance to a general mobilization. Bands of peasants rose against enforced conscription: against policies imposed upon them from the town, seat of the administration and therefore the enemy: against taxation and the sale of national property to the *bourgeoisie* and large landowners.[2] This area had been constantly subjected since 1792 to intensive guerrilla warfare. The peasants rarely united for large-scale attacks but the movement harassed the government and could not be rooted out.

The Bessin had seen no such outbreaks in 1792. Here fear of invasion from England, the sight of fleeing priests, murmurs of aristocratic counterplots, alone occasioned sporadic outbursts of terrorism; but these were directed against the remnants of the old régime, not against the new. By the year IV, however, the economic crisis, the constant burden of troops concerned with defending the coast against invasion and quelling the rising in the Vendée, and the continued requisitioning of crops and horses, had brought discontent into the foreground. Even so, the peasant of the

1 A.N. F¹ CIII. *Calvados 7*. Bayeux. *20 brumaire an IV*.
2 P. Bois, *Paysans de l'Ouest* (Le Mans, 1960), pp. 640–3, 658–66.

district of Bayeux did not rush into open opposition. He did not want a restoration of the old régime. Nothing caused more alarm in the rural communes than the rumours, exaggerated out of all proportion, of nightly disembarkations of returning *émigrés*. But, on the other hand, he felt himself in no way attached to the new régime and hence was not prepared to help it against its opponents. *Chouannerie* in the district of Bayeux was not a widespread peasant movement, as it had been in the Sarthe in 1792. Thousands of peasants waging war on the town as the source of laws and taxation were not a feature of this rising. Rather was it a movement which existed with the *connivance* of the peasant. The peasant of this area continued to be negatively rather than positively hostile to the existing régime, but his attitude became increasingly dangerous to the government in that it helped to preserve the conditions of civil disorder.

The *chouan* movement in the district of Bayeux was composed largely of deserters from the army and young men fleeing military conscription.[1] The first, it would seem, were in the majority. The extensive troop movements in Lower Normandy meant that here deserters were particularly numerous. Irregularly paid and fed in the army, they fled to the forests and formed bands of outlaws loosely joined to the royalist ranks. It is impossible to get any idea of their real numbers because the royalist leader in Normandy, Frotté, grossly inflated them for the purpose of extracting more money from the English to pay them.[2] On paper they formed parish bands organized in divisions but this bore little relation to reality. Their numbers were swollen by the peasantry themselves in the same way that they had multiplied the number of brigands in the Great Fear of 1789. A handful who perpetrated a crime in one village became hundreds when reported in the next. Usually they operated in small bands of four or five: occasionally, but much more rarely, in groups of about a dozen.

For geographical reasons alone, it would have been extraordinary had the Bessin failed to experience some manifestation of the real counter revolution which royalist leaders hoped to effect. The nearby Iles St. Marcouf had fallen into the hands of the English and were the link between the royalists of northern France

---

[1] Conclusions based on A.D.C. Lm. *Police*. 18 cartons, all unclassified, of miscellaneous correspondence relating to *chouannerie*.

[2] Pezet, op. cit., pp. 426–7.

and those in exile in Jersey and in Great Britain. The Bessin with its small Channel ports became an important area of communication, constantly traversed by royalist spies and emissaries. Money came to Frotté's royalist army at Flers from England via St. Marcouf to Louvières and on to Meuvaines, both in the district of Bayeux.[1] This partly explains why the cantons near the sea like Crépon were infested with *chouans*, for here they received payment more easily. The wooded areas in the south-west of the district, the forests of Cérisy and des Liards, afforded excellent protection for small bands of men who knew the area well, and the communes which felt the presence of the *chouans* most were those of Caumont, Litteau, Balleroy, and Littry which were near the forests.

As well as the *chouans*, however, and equally significant, there was a real growth in the number of vagabonds and desperate men out to loot and kill when they knew that the forces existing to maintain civil order were weak. It was well known that most of the coin in circulation in 1789 had been accumulated and hoarded by those who had had grain to sell and that it had been hidden in progressively more obscure places as requisitioning, which so often meant taking everything, had grown more desperate and bitter. Now these wealthy *cultivateurs* were to be the victims no less of the *chouans* than of the *chauffeurs* who ranged Brittany and Normandy torturing the wealthy, who lived on isolated properties, by burning the soles of their feet to make them reveal where their money was hidden.[2] All passed as the forces of the counter revolution. Even then, the *chouans* and the *chauffeurs* were far from being the only brigands in the area. At St. Vigor des Mézerets, in the adjoining district of Vire, was the headquarters of the *armée noire*, so called because it was composed of about two hundred and fifty of Fauchet's quickly created priests.[3] With no way of supporting themselves and having fled imprisonment during the Terror, they survived by pillaging the surrounding hamlets. There were no available troops to suppress such atrocities. The local National Guard had ceased to function and the only available ammunition was sent to the troops on the frontiers. The lack of any real authority permitted a general free-for-all in which the entire area became a prey to civil disorder.

[1] Pezet, op. cit., p. 420.
[2] A.D.C. Lm. *Police*. Letters of *23 vendémiaire an IV*, *27 germinal an IV*.
[3] M. Marion, *Le Brigandage pendant la Révolution* (Paris, 1934), p. 130. M. Moulin, *Mémoires de Michelot Moulin sur la chouannerie normande* (Paris, 1893), pp. 97–99.

The offences committed by the *chouans* fell roughly into two categories. First, the sort of crime for which they are renowned—attacks on constitutional priests, revolutionary officials, and the buyers of national property, the destruction of civil registers and trees of liberty, and threats to the populace if it paid its taxes. Second, the stealing of arms, money, cattle, corn, linen, gold plate, and jewelry. This second sort of crime was by far the more common and practised too by vagabond and *chauffeur*. Attacks on individuals were usually restricted to those who possessed these commodities. *Chouannerie* in the district of Bayeux was not royalist: nor was it clerical. True, an object of attack was often the constitutional priest of a parish, who was shot and robbed if he did not recant: but how much more often was this from the sheer need to pillage than from any political or ideological reason, and the consciousness that an attack on an unpopular constitutional priest would not meet with the condemnation of the peasantry! Offences committed against municipal officials and justices of the peace had a very specific purpose. They were intended to make local government difficult and as far as possible to effect its complete collapse. Once such a policy had prevailed, then in the resultant chaos it would be easier to extend the guerrilla warfare and marauding expeditions. *Chouannerie* in the district of Bayeux was nothing finer nor more extensive than terrorism based on pillaging the undefended and isolated murders of officials and constitutional priests who had long since ceased to practise. The *chouans* in this area were not fighting *for* anything. They were fighting to avoid life in the army. It is doubtful if they ever envisaged ultimate success or indeed anything beyond a prolongation of the circumstances favourable to their new way of life and they hoped to hold out until the existing régime was changed. The amnesty offered by the government in *thermidor an IV* (August 1796) was unlikely to impress them, since it merely promised no reprisals if the men concerned returned immediately to their regiments.

The disorder which accompanied any breakdown in local administration was not necessarily to the peasant's inconvenience. In fact, it suited his purpose. Lack of officials meant a delay in the collection of taxes and the failure to implement government decisions. Unless he was known to be possessed of capital the peasant personally was unlikely to be disturbed by the *chouans*.

Hence he sheltered them and refused to give information of their whereabouts. Moreover, he was fully prepared to pass on to them details about his wealthier neighbours. A man who had sold a lot of hay or horses would be jealously watched and the information carefully passed on. He would then be the chosen victim for the next expedition. Hatred felt towards the rich or even the richer constantly manifested itself. Perhaps, too, there was an element of fear involved. If the small peasant kept quiet he would not be disturbed. If he informed, his life was in danger. The *commissaire* of the department complained bitterly that nowhere could he find a jury which would convict a brigand, for everyone dwelt in fear of reprisals. Moreover, the wealthier peasants who were the victims of the *chouans* were themselves afraid to appeal for help. The departmental administration consistently criticized their failure so to do. But they feared that if they complained, they jeopardized their lives or might have another regiment of troops billeted upon them: troops who needed feeding and who did not stop short at pillaging themselves. Better by far a handful of outlaws than a regiment of soldiers. Communes were known to bury the victims of *chouan* atrocities rather than report them and run this risk.[1] No local action could be taken to extirpate *chouannerie*. The unfortunate officials of the rural area found themselves completely without protection. They appealed to Bayeux to send the National Guard but that body had ceased to exist and there was no ammunition anyway. The government's instructions to Bayeux of *27 frimaire an IV* (18 December 1795) urging the town administration to inspire the National Guard with a love of duty and to make them take arms against the *chouans* were, in light of these facts, mere pious sentiments.[2]

The movement has been garbed in clerico-royalist colours and certainly some of the *noblesse* were involved. But they were neither the instigators nor the real leaders. True, Frotté's officers were mostly of noble families, including amongst them a handful from Bayeux; but these were not the leaders of the small marauding bands of the district of Bayeux who were indiscriminately labelled *chouan*. They were connected only by their common intention to promote civil disorder. The English who supplied Frotté with money to pay the *chouan* forces wished there were more nobles involved in the movement. Even sections of the

---

[1] A.D.C. Lm. *Police. 20 ventôse an IV.* [2] Ibid., *27 frimaire an IV.*

non-juring church condemned *chouannerie*. The bishop of Bayeux, from his exile in Jersey, wrote to one of his canons, who had newly emerged from prison, in praise of the *chouans* and heralding Frotté as the saviour of Catholicism.[1] The canon, de Boisjugon, whose brother was one of Frotté's officers, replied that he could not agree with the bishop. The *chouans* of the area were brigands intent upon personal survival and unworthy of the support of the church.[2] The bishop wrote back to say that any movement aimed at the destruction of the existing order and the restoration of the old would receive his unqualified support. One could not afford in such circumstances to be over-scrupulous. Refractory priests were instructed by their bishop to encourage *chouannerie*. One of the chief agents for smuggling money from St. Marcouf and for its distribution was the old Abbé Guérin of Vaucelles, whose brother was a fisherman. Weekly the old man made a crossing to St. Marcouf and received money and letters from the bishop. The one went into *chouan* hands and the other maintained contact between the bishop and those clerics remaining in France. The funds were carefully distributed by an intricate network of old priests and female relatives of exiled nobles who had remained behind and whom the government with good reason mistrusted.[3]

For the most part Bayeux itself escaped attack by the *chouans*. The small marauding bands steered clear of any substantial town. They were not sufficiently numerous to undertake any enterprise in the actual city. But they had several accomplices within the town. Someone in the know, for example, tipped off a group of *chouans* that a cart carrying taxes from Bayeux to Caen would be leaving the town and where and when it could be ambushed. The tree of liberty was felled three times and affixed was a warning that the people must expect reprisals if they were foolish enough to pay their taxes. All the public officials were threatened with their lives.[4]

But though *chouannerie* was not an urban movement, reports of atrocities committed in neighbouring communes had their effect on the nerves of the townsfolk. Almost daily during the

---

[1] A.N. F7 7258. Letter of 5 *prairial an V*.
[2] Sévèstre, *La Vie religieuse . . .*, p. 114.
[3] A.N. F19 9112. Correspondence of the Abbé Guerin, 23 February 1823, and A.N. F7 3027. *Correspondants des chouans dans le département du Calvados.*
[4] A.D.C. Lm. *Police.* Undated letter from Moulland to Le Forestier, *commissaire du directoire près de l'administration municipale de Bayeux.*

last months of 1795 some news was brought either of murder or larceny committed by the *chouans*. The mayor of Rubercy was shot on *13 vendémiaire an IV* (13 October 1795); so were those of Cairon and Caumont. The justices of the peace of Tours were slaughtered. A price was placed on the head of the *agent national* in the districts. Houses in the adjoining village of St. Vigor le Grand were ransacked.[1] The numbers of the *chouans* were exaggerated amongst the townspeople. Where they would next attack could not be anticipated. An attack on Bayeux itself was daily expected. The prevalence of rumour again played an important part in shaping events. In December and again in the following September, Le Forestier, *agent national* of Bayeux, wrote to Paris to express his fear of an imminent explosion in the town. Rumours had been circulated, he claimed on both occasions, that the officials of the *aides* and the *gabelle* were going to be reintroduced and that all the young men between eighteen and twenty were to be conscripted. Local officials, he said, connived at the success of the forces of counter revolution in that they did nothing to dispel these fears.[2]

There was indeed very little local officials could do. They had no arms. Their sole preoccupation was keeping the town provisioned and they were aware of the general lack of faith in the government prevailing in the town. The artisan and his wife who stood in the endless bread queues found it fully credible that the government might seek to reimpose salt and customs dues. Matters were not improved by the government's decision to make Bayeux in October 1795 a centre for a counter offensive against the *chouans* and to garrison there a further contingent of dragoons, hussars, and several companies of veterans under General Barbazan.[3] Extra troops meant a further strain on the local food supply. The forces of the republic were not welcomed in the town. Faced with the option of civil war or government protection, the inhabitants of Bayeux would have chosen the former.

Within weeks Barbazan had decreed a house to house search throughout the town and district for hidden arms and fodder for his horses. The town echoed with tales of the harsh treatment accorded to those found to possess them. In Bayeux itself, how-

---

[1] A.D.C. Lm. *Police*. Letters of *13 vendémiaire an IV*, *3 prairial an IV*, *20 ventôse an IV*, *6 ventôse an V*.   [2] Ibid., *10 frimaire an IV*, *12 fructidor an V*.
[3] Pezet, op. cit., p. 427.

THE COUNTER REVOLUTION

ever, the general had to contend with the opposition of the mayor and the municipal council. The mayor, Jehanne, was of the opinion that incidents might well occur between the troops and the townspeople if anyone in the town should be found to have hoarded arms or be accused of *chouannerie*. Relationships between the town and the troops were already strained. From the hall of the *société populaire*, Jehanne launched an attack on the policy of the general as unconstitutional and in direct violation of the principles of 1789. He cited the guarantee of the sanctity of the home as framed in the constitution of the year III.[1] He said he would support the people of Bayeux in any resistance they offered to such treatment. Barbazan appealed to Paris. He claimed that Bayeux seethed with intrigue and disloyalty. It was, he declared, a centre of *chouannerie* and royalism. The government accorded Barbazan full administrative control of the commune, including the vexed question of provisioning the town. Jehanne was dismissed on the grounds that he was the spokesman of a counter revolutionary spirit clearly visible in the town of Bayeux and head of a municipal administration which aided the enemies of the republic. He tolerated, Barbazan claimed, the criminal activities of bands of young men who had treacherously fled conscription and of deserters. He did nothing to protect the good citizens of Bayeux from the dangers of civil war.[2] As far as the government was concerned, the old mayor was readily expendable, for the Directory was intent upon making new provisions for local government.

During the next months, Barbazan made an attempt to clear up the forest regions of the district where the insurgents were most numerous and effective. By March, the bands of the forest of Cérisy had been substantially diminished and the leaders, Colin, an ex-surgeon, and the three David brothers, all of Cérisy and evaders of the *levée* of 1792, had been captured. Trapped by Barbazan whilst escaping after the murder of the constitutional priest of Tronquay on *11–14 germinal an IV* (31 March–3 April 1796) seventeen were shot by Barbazan's troops in the place St. Patrice at Bayeux. They included a Swiss and an Alsatian deserter but most of them came from the nearby Manche, Cérisy, or Crépon. What struck the silent crowd who gathered to watch their execution was their extreme youth. The youngest was

[1] Ibid., pp. 428–9. [2] Ibid., p. 431.

Charles David, aged nineteen, the eldest by far was twenty-seven. Their bravery in the face of death was to become legendary in the town.[1]

In spite of ruthless methods, Barbazan did not succeed in rooting out any of the *chouan* accomplices within the town: nor indeed at crushing *chouannerie* in the area. Temporarily the *chouans* went underground, to emerge again after the general had moved his headquarters. In May he left a town without an administration and a district superficially quiet. But the old problems remained. The movement defied such cursory rooting out. The nerves of the townspeople were still on edge and their weariness was in no way assuaged.

The constitution of *5 fructidor an III* (22 August 1795) planned a thorough reorganization of French administration. Departmental *directoires*, district assemblies, and municipal governments were suppressed. The canton, previously a subdivision of the district used only for electoral purposes, was now the unit of administration. The new assemblies were to be composed of a president, a secretary, representatives from the town and surrounding rural area, and a *commissaire* who was to be in touch with the departmental authority. This was to be reconstructed as well and the pivotal figure, the *commissaire*, was not to be a local man, but one chosen by the government.[2] The municipal councils were to be reorganized and cut in size. At the same time, an attempt was made to cut down on the large number of officials who could claim state payment in the provinces. From henceforth there would be only one *tribunal de justice* in a department and not in each district.

For Bayeux the constitution meant some drastic changes. It lost its *tribunal de justice*: that of the Calvados was to be in Caen. The lawyers, judges, and officials of the city had the painful experience of closing their offices and making provision for a new mode of existence. The incomes of those traditionally concerned in the administration of the town thus underwent a profound modification. They could justifiably claim that they must now look elsewhere for employment. But who would undertake local government? Three years of food shortage, guerrilla warfare in the rural areas, threats on the lives of officials, had scarcely made the task an enviable one. Nor was it paid employment.

[1] Pezet, op. cit., p. 439.   [2] Godechot, op. cit., pp. 411–14.

Moreover, the new cantonal governments were clearly going to have a greater burden of work than the old municipal councils. The measure was used as a general pretext to abjure participation in local government. At the elections held in November the usual men were nominated, all of them old in municipal or district office. About a fifth of those eligible to vote presented themselves and of the seven they chose, only one accepted. Those further down the list refused as well. The central government wrote to those elected to urge them in the name of the public good to take up office, but without success. Tavigny Duclos, acting *procureur de la commune*, wrote to Paris to outline the fundamental reasons for their refusal. Anyone with experience of local government over the last few years, he said, was worn out with the constant struggle administration now entailed. Many were ill or enfeebled by the lack of food and the excessive fatigue occasioned by long, arduous, and painful work. Some of them claimed, justifiably, that the burden of work had taken them from their personal business which had necessarily suffered. Others had gone into the departmental administration. Tavigny included a sheaf of about twenty letters he had received from those to whom he had offered a position in local government, in order to back up his generalizations.[1] Le Roy insisted that since he had had office from the beginning of the Revolution, he was entitled, he felt, to some rest; Le Sieur stated no less conclusively that since the closing of the tribunal at Bayeux his income had been severely cut and that all he could do was to retire to his small estate in the country as his one steady means of making a livelihood. Hardouin replied at length and in no uncertain terms that his desire for the public good was great but his need to earn a living greater and that his personal fortune was too small to support him without some additional income. Before 1789 he had made something as a *procureur* at the *bailliage* but in 1790 his office had been confiscated and his reimbursement had only been 4,500 *livres*—a small sum in comparison with the 11,000 *livres* his father had paid for the office in 1776 and less than a quarter of the market price in 1788. He had not complained and indeed, as long as the tribunal existed at Bayeux, he had had a regular income; but with the disappearance of this source of supply, he would be forced to leave the area and search for new work.[2]

[1] A.N. F1b *Calvados 10. 25 nivôse an IV.*   [2] Ibid., *20 nivôse an IV.*

Bertauld and Dozeville sent almost duplicate letters stating the debts they had incurred during the period they had worked in municipal government. Gardin de Néry declared that as long as he had held a position in the tribunal all had been well and work in municipal government possible but the tribunal no longer existed; Le Bret, erstwhile *avocat*, simply asserted that he now spent the whole of his time on the little land he possessed in the country because seven years' absence in the service of the town had meant that his land had suffered and his own health had declined and from now on all his energies must be spent in looking after the little that remained to him. Moisson de Vaux refused outright; public office had kept him, he declared, away from the academic studies he loved, and he intended to return to them.[1]

Le Septier wrote perhaps the most bitter letter. He had been, he said, a municipal official in 1789 and was re-elected in 1791 and until 1793. He had always done his best and had worked hard and long; but, since he had been compromised in the federalist movement, the only thanks he had received for his labours had been imprisonment. He had not been well treated and had emerged stone deaf. The *représentant en mission* had released him about a year later. His savings were, by then, exhausted but he still had a small piece of land. He intended to withdraw completely from town affairs to the peaceful obscurity of the countryside.[2]

The departmental authorities were well aware of the general reluctance to assume office. Throughout the year IV letters were addressed to the Directory outlining the gravity of the situation. In no canton of the *département* of the Calvados, wrote the *commissaire provisoire du directoire exécutif près de l'administration départementale du Calvados*, did there exist anything but total disorganization. Many of the rural areas were in the hands of men frankly hostile to the republican régime. Some were self interested *cultivateurs* unlikely to do anything to relieve the food shortage. Grain was hidden, or sold on the black market whilst they turned a blind eye. Prices were still rocketing. A hundredweight sack of wheat brought in anything from 1,800 to 8,000 *livres*, one of maize about 1,200 *livres*.[3] The *commissaire* could promise the government nothing but revolts if conditions did not improve.

So difficult was the situation that the *commissaire* beseeched the

1 A.N. F1b *Calvados 10. 20 nivôse an IV.*   2 Ibid.
3 A.N. F1b II. *Calvados 1.* Caen. *21 vendémiaire an IV.*

central government to allow him to continue correspondence with the old municipal authorities in order that contact with the cantons comprising the *département* should not be completely severed. Even this was not satisfactory: the old municipal bodies were everywhere disintegrating. Throughout the Calvados there were areas without any local government at all: no police, no officials to record births and deaths or receive and implement government decrees. No amount of persuasion could make people remain in office. The *commissaire* urged the government to offer sufficient remuneration to those entering office and, secondly, compensation for any losses incurred during former periods when they were in local government. He could see no other inducement possible. Wearily he described to the central government the general repugnance for any public office which characterized the area and stated that even the departmental administration was on the point of collapse and that if any member resigned there was no one to fill his place.[1] Twelve months later he could only report makeshift cantonal and municipal governments in Bayeux and Caen but nothing more, and this only at the expense of continuing communication with the previous officials.[2]

There could be no speedy solution to the social, economic, or political problems of the towns. Improved harvests after 1796, the decision of the Directory to return to the old metal currency, its promises, which were tardy in realization, to restore the property of the hospitals or find them new sources of income, could not reconstruct the shattered lives of many of the townsfolk. Throughout 1797 and 1798, though the worst of the hardship had passed, the discontent and general weariness did not lift. The town records during these years are scanty; the cantonal administration was on occasion composed of as few as two officials and their meetings were rare. They had no funds at their disposal and did not always communicate national and departmental decisions to the area nominally under their control.[3] They were not prepared to do anything which would arouse popular discontent still further. The area was left almost without control from above; and with the slackening of authority came the opportunity for the resurgence of religious conflict and more intensive guerrilla

[1] Ibid., *30 nivôse an IV*.
[2] Ibid., *24 ventôse an V*.
[3] A.N. F¹ᶜ III. *Calvados 7*. Bayeux.

warfare which a weary populace countenanced with little show of emotion.

No administrator in France could be unaware that the persecution of Catholicism had created more problems than it had solved. The church was woven into society. Even if the peasant and artisan of the Bessin were not particularly devout, their lives had for long revolved around the church and its ceremonies. For the peasant, especially in isolated communities, social intercourse was virtually restricted to his family, Sunday mass, and the customary religious rites. Each marriage, baptism, and death which were the milestones in his life had traditionally been a religious ceremony, whose loss he was bound to feel. He had often been attached to the priest who had shared his hardships. In Bayeux, popular riots during the food crisis had taken the form of demonstrations for the re-establishment of the institutions upon which the poor of the town had depended, like the lace *manufacture*. The Directory tacitly recognized in the year III that the government had failed to extirpate the traditional religion. On the other hand, whilst it ceased to persecute, it was not prepared to do anything more. It lacked the financial resources to create a state church under its own authority: nor did it have any forces to check the non-jurors emerging in the *chouan*-infested countryside. Local administrators were not prepared to do anything for the furtherance of the state cult nor did they consider that they had the means at their disposal to take steps against attempts to restore Catholic practice in the area. They preferred to turn a blind eye for the sake of peace. The cleavage between national and local interests was by the year IV apparent in Bayeux; the newly created *commissaire* of the cantonal assembly constantly heaped abuse on the narrowly parochial interests of the cantonal administration and its failure to report on matters contrary to the national interest.[1]

The decree of *3 ventôse an III* (21 February 1795) proclaimed that: 'Nul ne peut être empêché d'exercer, en se conformant aux lois, le culte qu'il a choisi. Nul ne peut être forcé de contribuer aux dépenses d'un culte. La république n'en salarie aucun.'[2] Prison doors were opened: those who had refused to surrender the certificates conferring priesthood upon them were allowed to go

---

[1] A.D.C. Lm. *Police*. Letter of *19 fructidor an IV*.

[2] R. Patry, *Le Régime et la liberté des cultes dans le département du Calvados pendant la première séparation 1795-1802* (Paris, 1921), p. 10.

home and those of the non-juring clergy not subject to former laws on deportation were released. The nuns were given their freedom. The administrators were relieved to see them go : the longer they were in prison, the longer they must be fed by the municipality. Many had suffered greatly from deprivation. They did not all immediately reconstitute themselves as a community : they had now no communal houses. Some went to their homes; others were sheltered by friends; some, like the Ursulines, managed to keep together and preserved a shred of the communal life in a poky little room in the same street as their former house.[1]

The position of the church was indeed in need of definition. The Civil Constitution of the Clergy had not so much been abolished as ceased to exist. Moreover, to distinguish only two types of clerics, non-jurors and jurors, amongst those who re-emerged in the district of Bayeux in the year IV would be grossly to over-simplify the situation. Under the word juror were gathered many different categories of priests, all equally condemned by the intransigent non-juror.[2] First, there was a group intermediate between unqualified jurors and non-jurors—those who had taken partial oaths and sworn loyalty at some time and later retracted : there were those prepared to take an oath of loyalty to the constitution of *11 prairial an III* (21 May 1795) but who were not prepared to take an oath to the schismatic church. Again, some of the former parish priests of Bayeux had renounced their priestly state during the Terror to try to save themselves from imprisonment. How could they be fitted even into the framework of a schismatic church? The jurors as a whole possessed one very positive advantage in that those non-juring clergy who had gone into exile were forbidden to return and certainly could not do so overnight. On the other hand, to be set against this was the general lack of adherence the schismatic church could command in the parishes where the constitutional priest was an outsider, and the continued demoralization of the juring clergy in the outlying areas by the *chouans*. In Bayeux itself they stood a better chance of survival. On the other hand, the schismatic church of the diocese of the Calvados was at a distinct disadvantage because it had no head. Fauchet had not been given a successor and his episcopal vicars had deemed after the collapse of federalism that

[1] Dédouit, op. cit., p. 134.
[2] M. Reinhard, *Le Département de la Sarthe sous le Directoire* (Paris, 1935), pp. 103–4.

flight or hiding was the most sensible plan. In any case the more able of them were now not intent upon a career in religion. The men to whom it was left to undertake the reconstruction of the constitutional church in the diocese were not Fauchet's political henchmen or the remnants of the *armée noire* but those urban clergy who had after long consideration and in all sincerity taken the oath in 1791 : Moulland of St. Martin and Lecuyer of St. Jean, both of them released in late 1794 after several months in prison for refusing to renounce their priestly state. Moulland was quick to act. After the declaration of *3 ventôse an III* (21 February 1795) proclaiming the virtual freedom of religious practice in conformity with the laws, he began to rally his supporters. On *19 prairial an III* (7 June 1795) he petitioned the municipal council in a document signed by seventy-four citizens of Bayeux for the use of the church of St. Jean, which had served the largest parish of the town and which was currently being used as a barn.[1] The municipal council approved the demand. Encouraged by this success, on *9 messidor an III* (27 June 1795) Moulland addressed a further petition asking for the reopening of the cathedral; and on the twenty-fourth of the same month he celebrated mass before an enormous crowd.[2] Churches dotted throughout the area began in the late summer to open under the direction of the staunchest priests of the schismatic church.[3]

But Moulland and his supporters were not to remain long untroubled in their work. The framework of the church for which he was working was extremely weak. The authorities were prepared to tolerate it as long as it caused no trouble but not to protect it in any way. And it stood in need of protection. As the law relaxed and its spirit became more difficult to define, as administration became increasingly disorganized, the non-jurors gradually came out of hiding or returned from exile. Anyone who had been deported and returned could be arrested and imprisoned, but this presupposed the co-operation of the local authorities. The return, however, took time. In 1797 many of the parish priests of the diocese of Bayeux were still on the British payroll and a large community of them were living in straitened circumstances in St. Pancras along with others from Normandy and Brittany. The first militant efforts for the restoration of the old church were not made by the exiles but by those coming out of hiding or obscurity

---

[1] Patry, op. cit., p. 52.   [2] Ibid.   [3] Ibid., p. 60.

in France—those over sixty who had not had to leave, the capitular clergy from whom no oath had been exacted, those without cure of souls to whom the early laws had not applied.[1] The basis of their justification of their activities was that since the civil constitution was no longer law it could not be exacted and that those who had not been forced by the law to emigrate might legally re-establish the old form of worship.

Their contentions did not bear close examination. On 11 *prairial an III* (21 May 1795) the central government, anxious that the religious situation should be kept under some sort of control, passed a decree demanding from every priest an oath of loyalty to the laws of the republic before he could practise in any way.[2] The oath was of a completely secular nature. It did not appear to compromise those who took it in ecclesiastical matters. The bulk of the jurors were prepared to take it as it afforded the opportunity for reconstruction. But, if pushed to its ultimate conclusions, adherence to the oath obviously meant adherence to the current legislation on divorce, clerical marriage, suppression of religious congregations, and even to the unknown evils of laws to come. A section of the emergent capitular clergy were initially prepared to accept this oath as the means to greater tolerance for their church, but their bishop in Jersey condemned it out of hand.[3] In constant correspondence with his old episcopal vicars, de Cheylus maintained an attitude of no compromise with the state on religious matters, and as head of the old church emphasized that he forbade the clerics under his authority to cede an inch on the question of any direction by an illegally constituted government. He was persuaded that in the obvious weakening of the government were the seeds of its collapse. But he had been absent for too long to appreciate the real difficulties facing the non-juring clergy. The canons who were on the spot were more aware of the problems involved in reconstructing the church. Instructions were frequently brought from Jersey, but most of them the canons failed to communicate to the diocese in light of the impossibility of their realization. De Cheylus in fact belonged to that hard core of *émigré* clergy who believed that the fate of throne and altar were indissolubly knit. He maintained that no Catholic could submit to the laws of the republic since the

---

[1] Ibid., p. 128.   [2] Ibid., p. 60.
[3] Bibl. Chanoine Deslandes. *Lettre de Monseigneur de Cheylus à de Boisjugan.*

Bourbons were the true rulers of France and their deposition was illegal. Only with the restoration of the monarchy could Catholicism be reconstituted in France. In the meantime, or rather because of this, the bishop urged his representatives to give their full support to the *chouans* and the forces of the counter revolution. The canons were not prepared to go so far. All respect was certainly due to de Cheylus as the head of the church, but many of his instructions were in the conditions of 1795–6 impossible to fulfil. The most extreme and myopic were put forward in a printed letter of 6 June 1795 written by the bishop to priests returning to France.[1] They were instructed only to exercise their priestly office in parishes which had returned to loyalty to the king. As soon as they arrived back they must report to police officials set up in the king's name. If these did not yet exist, which de Cheylus could not believe, they must go not to the republican municipal council but to that which was in office before the Revolution and from them receive the keys of the church. All babies born during the Revolution must be rebaptized: all couples married during that time remarried.

His canons could not believe their eyes. De Boisjugan, by far the most able and the most outspoken, pointed out to the bishop that the conditions he envisaged simply did not exist.[2] There were no officials set up in the king's name and any priest who returned was forced to go directly into hiding. A breach, if not an open one, soon occurred between the leaders of the chapter and de Cheylus. De Boisjugan was convinced that a more moderate policy was desirable. He withheld many of the bishop's instructions. The essential for the present, he held, was to undermine the constitutional church so that Catholicism could be presented in one form. De Cheylus's policy was so incapable of realization that it threatened to paralyse the emerging church by demanding too much. Most important for the present was to make the jurors recant—a delicate operation since their ways had obviously been gravely erroneous. Reconciliation was not in any way possible; the schismatic church must surrender. Wherever possible the flock must be won over from the juror and this would obviously be most possible in the outlying areas where government control

[1] A.N. F⁷ 7606. *Règlement provisoire donné par Monseigneur l'évêque de Bayeux aux curés, desservants, vicaires et à tous les prêtres de son diocèse.* 6 June 1795.

[2] Patry, op. cit., p. 191.

was at its weakest. Once this was truly accomplished then the task would be much easier.

At Bayeux, at Caen, and throughout the department, the authorities were aware that non-juring priests, in direct contravention of the laws enforcing residence and the obligation to take the oath, were wandering from commune to commune, hidden so effectively by the country folk that no one could know their real number, or gain precise information as to their whereabouts. Lévêque, the departmental *commissaire*, blamed these men for the continued success of *chouannerie*. He wrote in anger to Paris:

> On n'a pas idée combien ces irréconciliables et sanguinaires ennemis occasionnent de maux dans nos contrées. Il est certain que ce sont eux qui dirigent les poignards et qui sont les apôtres de la doctrine de Frotté. . . . Partout ils sont fêtés, payés et partout ils portent la désolation et l'effroi. . . . Il faut des prêtres au peuple, mais non pas de ces prêtres qui ont tant de vengeances à exercer.[1]

In the rural parishes the familiar priest was welcomed back by his flock. Exile had not made him patient. The registers of the town speak of one such scraping the tongues of those who had received communion from a schismatic priest and of whole villages being ordered to confession to be absolved for the errors of the preceding years.[2] By *29 prairial an V* (17 June 1797) the returned non-jurors considered themselves sufficiently strong to appear openly in the town. On that day they forced an entry into the old church of St. Loup and there celebrated mass. The cantonal officials ordered their arrest but when brought before a local jury they were unanimously acquitted.[3]

The government followed an ambiguous policy explicable only in terms of the political struggle which took place in Paris during the summer of 1797. On *7 fructidor an V* (24 August 1797) a law was passed abrogating all previous laws relating to the deportation or the incarceration of non-juring priests; but after the *coup d'état* of *18 fructidor an V* (4 September 1797) these conciliatory measures were revoked and the Directory claimed the right to deport any priest who troubled the peace of the republic. It decreed that any non-juring priest who remained on French soil must take an

---

[1] A.N. F7 7258. Letter of *5 prairial an V*.
[2] Bibl. Chanoine Deslandes. Instruction issued by episcopal vicars. *1 vendémiaire an VII*.
[3] A.D.C. Lm. *Comptes décadaires. 19 thermidor an V*.

oath of loyalty to the republic and declare his hatred of royalty.[1]
The non-jurors here defined were not the returned exiles but those
without cure of souls in 1790. A departmental *arrêt* of *9 frimaire an
VI* stipulated that all priests who had returned to the department
should be arrested and that no one was to exercise the priestly
office who had not taken the oath.[2] But the authorities of Bayeux
did not embark on any arrests. Most of those whom it might have
arrested were in any case too well hidden at the least rumour of
arrest. The administration of the town confined its admonitions
to the constitutional priests who had been using the cathedral and
left candles and crucifixes around at a time when the building
should have been cleared for the state cult.[3]

The most bitter struggle as it emerged during the year V was
not between the non-jurors and the government but between
the schismatic and non-schismatic churches. Not only could the
former constitutional priests not obtain any real support from the
government, but they were completely demoralized in the rural
areas by the activities of the *chouans* and the returning non-jurors.
Throughout the year VI their numbers declined rapidly. Many
recanted. It was after all the most reasonable step to take for
safety. Only in the town did they stand any real chance of survival.
Moulland was hard at work for the preservation of the church to
which he had given so much of his energies. He was the main
instigator of an attempt in 1796 to found at Bayeux a presbytery
which, since the constitutional church at Bayeux lacked a head,
would organize religious practice. The presbytery consisted of
six of the parish priests of Bayeux who had taken the oath in 1791.
Six more from the rural district were asked to attend but only three
of them would do so since the others were afraid of possible
reprisals by the *chouans* if they accepted.[4]

The act of foundation of the presbytery blamed the pitiful
condition of the church in the diocese of the Calvados on Fauchet's
death and the persecution of the Jacobins. It declared its express
purpose was to reconcile all factions within the Catholic church
by means of a national council which would discuss all differences,
open negotiations with the pope, and terminate the schism.
The tone of the document was moderate. To save Catholicism,
Moulland declared, his intention was to go out to meet the non-

---

[1] Patry, op. cit., p. 139.   [2] Ibid., p. 142.
[3] A.D.C. Lm. *Police. 22 nivôse an V.*   [4] Patry, op. cit., p. 160.

jurors half-way. He was not prepared to recant but he was prepared to discuss difficulties. The departmental authorities viewed Moulland's activities with alarm but they could not persuade the government to take steps to prevent two members of the presbytery of Bayeux from attending a council held in Paris and composed of representatives of the constitutional church from fifteen dioceses.[1] The government at this stage was intent on playing off the constitutionals against the refractories, deeming the former the lesser of two evils, but in no way prepared to accord them financial support or encouragement. In fact little could be done by the presbytery since the non-jurors refused to negotiate under any conditions other than complete surrender on the part of the jurors. Moulland's unhappy task during 1796–7 was to attempt in vain to bolster up the prestige of his church. He issued letters proclaiming the legitimacy of the church he represented and its right to nominate bishops and priests. He asserted the extreme gallican position. The civil constitution, he claimed, had not been condemned by a general council of the clergy of France but only by Pius VI, who had been blinded by a few bishops and cardinals. The church could claim infallibility but the pope could not. In short, Moulland put forward all the arguments used by the constitutional church in 1791. Throughout 1796–7 he struggled to organize the election of a bishop whose presence would lend a more weighty authority to a church whose numbers were small and daily dwindling. Lévêque, the *commissaire* of the department, on several occasions wrote to Paris for the condemnation of any elections which might take place, but Paris pronounced that they were not illegal.[2] The first choice at the elections held in July 1798, Hérault, *curé* of Touques, refused, but the second choice, Duchemin, a former episcopal vicar of the Manche, accepted.[3] He had been a month in office when he died. His death was the worst possible blow his church could have received. The non-jurors represented it as the judgement of God upon the inherent sinfulness of the schismatic church. Moulland and the presbytery were indeed in difficulties. They were dependent upon the alms of their parishioners for their livelihood whilst the non-jurors were backed by English money. A second election for another bishop

---

[1] A.N. F7 7272. [2] Patry, op. cit., p. 173.
[3] P. Pisani, *Répertoire biographique de l'épiscopat constitutionnel* (Paris, 1907), p. 172.

took place early in 1799 and the man chosen, Bisson, was in an unenviable position.[1] His main enemies were the Catholics of his diocese who refused to believe in the validity of his election. Bisson declared in vain that he hated schism and pointed out that in the face of the hostility of the state religious practice had only continued at all thanks to the activities of the juring priests. His enemies, however, were much more highly organized. The death of de Cheylus in February 1797 saw a closer organization of the non-jurors by a council of the chapter, who could claim in terms of canon law their responsibility for running the diocese during the vacancy caused by the death of the bishop. They refused to discuss anything relating to church affairs with the jurors. Thus the struggle continued. In the country districts the non-jurors won complete control but in the city a nucleus of the constitutional church clung on, commanding some respect from their former parishioners and still hoping for some ultimate reconciliation without loss of dignity.

The picture of Bayeux during 1796–9 is of a community passively hostile and defiant to the demands of national policy. Its inhabitants were bent on reconstructing as best they could some sort of livelihood. They blamed Paris for the difficulties of 1793–6. They were now indifferent to the capital's claims. The elections held in the Calvados in the year IV had been annulled by the central government as 'royalist' but they were so only by the interpretation of Paris. The people of the canton of Bayeux voted for their own *notables*: they did not care if those whom they chose were related to priests and *émigrés* and therefore ineligible for election.[2] Disillusionment and demoralization had brought the town into opposition.

[1] Pisani, op. cit., p. 173.   [2] A.N. F⁷ 3661².

VII

CONCLUSION

T HE elections of the year IV, the welcoming back of religious unsympathetic to the government, and the administrative strike represent the high-water mark of Bayeux's opposition to the government. The passing of the food crisis, or at least of the leanest years of the Revolution, lessened the violence of opposition without strengthening the attachment to the government. The people of Bayeux turned to the problem of reconstructing their means of existence. For some, it would only be possible to rebuild their shattered livelihood gradually as economic conditions slowly improved. For others, the task demanded a radical adjustment to a new mode of life. Even without the war and the food crisis it is inconceivable, given the nature of Bayeux, that the town could have passed through the Revolution without incurring substantial changes. The town was *par excellence* one which was dependent upon the institutions of the old régime and the Revolution had revealed starkly the extent of that dependence. It had laid bare its stagnant economy and the utter vulnerability of large sections of its population. It is far easier to count the losses Bayeux sustained from the Revolution than to count its positive gains.

The abolition of seigneurial rights meant not only a direct loss to the owner or renter, it also meant that no middle-men were needed for their collection. The *feudistes* were out of employment for ever. Seigneurial justices no longer existed to help a struggling *avocat* make ends meet. The work of the seigneurial courts had terminated. The bailiffs had lost the exploitation of *sergenteries*. The work of the apostolic notaries who had been needed to give attention to ecclesiastical leases and to register the *insinuations ecclésiastiques* was at an end. The division of large clerical estates had reduced the need for estate managers. The cooks and footmen and general domestics of the bishop and chapter and the religious houses were jobless. Officials of the *aides* and the *gabelle* were no longer able to deprive some unfortunate of what was rightfully his. Perhaps even more important—Bayeux certainly esteemed it so—was the removal of the wealthiest section of its population. Bayeux described itself essentially as a *ville de con-sommation*. It had profited from the spending in the town of wealth drawn from the countryside, particularly by the church. The church's income from land and tithe might almost be regarded as an annual subsidy which permitted the poorer section of the town community to make ends meet and the means by which the tradespeople of the town kept their businesses going. In large part, the country during the early years of the Revolution emancipated itself from the town. The degree of freedom was not perhaps as great as the country people would have wished. A part of the *bourgeoisie* had profited from the sale of national property; they were still the executors of government policy in the countryside; but in the main, the country had cast off its heaviest fetters and Bayeux was forced to live of its own.

The most radical adjustments were perforce those made by those who had worked in the courts or who had been involved in the administration of ecclesiastical estates. Almost to a man the lawyers and officials of the old régime had thrown themselves into the administration of department and district or had eagerly seized any new post created, such as those concerned with the sale of church property, the drawing up of new tax lists, parish boundaries, and work of that nature. The intensity with which they did so can in part be explained by political ambition but much more nearly by the need to find new employment when their offices and the means whereby they had made a living were brought to an end. The degree of their success during these early years was subject to great variation. Some handled the situation more adroitly than others. Most of them managed quite well until the financial deterioration brought about by the war, the loss of office for those compromised by the federalist agitation, and the difficulties for all local administrators resulting from the food crisis altered the picture. The rearrangements introduced by the Directory in the year III severely reduced the number of officials by abolishing the tribunal, and in any case, salaries were in arrears. By the year IV, when the administrative strike paralysed the efforts of the central government to restore order in the provinces, the lawyers and officials of the old régime could calculate with a greater degree of precision the effects of the Revolution on their careers. Prospects never seemed worse than at this moment.

The Directory struggled to give France a new form of local government but the difficulties were far too great to admit of any success in the Calvados. For five years Bayeux possessed nothing but makeshift administrations, with a composition altering from month to month, and powerless to implement the orders of the government.[1] It is difficult during this period to learn much of what was happening in the town or of the attitudes of the townspeople. Political life seemed dead. Weariness was general. Where could reconstruction begin? On the eve of the Napoleonic *coup d'état* of the *18 brumaire an VIII* (9 November 1799) the town's problems were basically those of the year V.

This situation was far from unique nor was there any quick way to remedy it. To describe the changes after *brumaire* in terms of a wand waved over chaos to transform it suddenly into peace, order, and normality would be as false as it would be over simple. It is relatively easy in Bayeux to trace the means by which, during the five years after the *coup d'état*, civil authority was restored, or the concordat was implemented, but far less easy to estimate in any way the effects of these years on the standard of living of the townspeople. There was relatively no industry in Bayeux to revive. The fluctuations of French commerce left the town almost untouched. But the return of the church, the crushing of *chouannerie* and terrorism in the countryside by a substantial military offensive between 1799 and 1804,[2] the restoration of the *tribunal de justice*, the new provisions for local administration, at least gave Bayeux the opportunity to reconstruct gradually its shattered existence as far as it could, given the irrevocable destruction of some of the means of livelihood the old régime had afforded.

Bayeux became under the new plans for local government the centre of an *arrondissement* with a sub-prefecture and a new municipal council. Its tribunal was restored. The local administrators were promised funds and guaranteed them from the taxes, and provision for the payment of their salaries was made. The new officials were not elected, they were government nominees, and they were helped, not by men who were chosen locally by

---

[1] A.N. F¹ᶜ III. *Calvados 8.* Bayeux.
[2] M. Marion, *Le Brigandage pendant la Révolution* (Paris, 1934), pp. 148–54.

election, but by a salaried bureaucracy:[1] these were engaged when they were needed and dismissed—though this seldom happened—when they were not. There was an obvious attempt to put local government, in one respect, back into the perspective of 1789, that is to make it the concern of those wealthy enough to dedicate themselves wholeheartedly to the business of government which tradition had sanctified in their eyes, men who did not have to think of their careers elsewhere. The *noblesse de cloche* was taken out of cold storage. Le Roy, former *avocat du roi* at the *bailliage*, noble and associate of de Wimpffen, was the first mayor of the town in 1803. His successor was Desjardins, a former noble, and then Genas Duhomme, former *procureur du roi* at the *bailliage*, descendant of a long line of *subdélégués*, *procureurs du roi*, and *maires nés* and last in office in 1792. At first *sous-préfet* at Coutances, he returned in 1810 to become mayor of Bayeux and before the Restoration, the *sous-préfet*.[2] The four aldermen had records almost as long. The choices were on the whole sound. They were from families with a long tradition of public service; the local *notables* had returned to their own.

With the establishment of new forms of local government came the creation of new tribunals of justice. The *arrondissement*, like the district in 1790, received a tribunal of first instance; twenty-nine courts of appeal were created, reminiscent in form, if not in spirit, of the *parlements*. All the officials of these courts were chosen by the first consul. Only the position of *avocat* remained free. For Bayeux the reconstitution of the tribunal was an important step. In the main all the old officials whose livelihood had lain in the courts were restored to office. It was to be otherwise with the petty officials; they were drastically cut in number. On the other hand, the number of men employed by the *sous-préfet* for the office work concerned with tax allocation and government correspondence was increased, and this created new jobs for petty clerks and secretaries with experience of such work. The scheme took long to complete and not all had found suitable employment by 1805.

Some made the necessary changes with such skill that it would have been difficult, viewing the situation in 1812, to imagine that the Revolution had caused any change at all.[3] Pierre Basley, for

---

[1] Godechot, op. cit., p. 520.　　　　　　　[2] A.N. F^{1b} II. *Calvados 10.*
[3] The following examples based on assessments made before 1789. A.D.C. Q.

example, had been in 1789 *procureur en élection*, secretary to Genas the *subdélégué*, a very minor receiver of dues for the bishop and he owned a little land at St. Patrice. His income was perhaps a little over 600 *livres* each year and he was about forty-two years old. His secretaryship to the *subdélégué* and his tax collecting were discontinued. He received, however, some compensation for his position at the *élection* court and he gained a new position, that of secretary to the district at a yearly salary of 600 *livres*. His position conveniently gave him the opportunity for an early investment in land though he was not rich enough to buy very much. The few *sillons* he purchased at Brécy only realized about 150 *livres* at the value of 1790. His position by 1793 was indeed a great improvement on that of 1789 but, compromised in federalism, with the whole of the district assembly, he lost office. He was about three years without paid employment. He emerged under the Directory to work briefly for the *canton* assembly and became under Napoleon secretary to the *sous-préfet*, and ultimately on retirement a member of the municipal council. Le Bret, an *avocat* at the *bailliage*, steered an even course in much the same way. He had one positive loss in 1789, that of *bailli* of a seigneurial justice, but he became a member of the *directoire de département* in 1790, a good time on the whole to have office because he had retired before real political difficulties began in 1792. He made one substantial investment in national property, a cluster of buildings: house, granaries, and outhouses—the whole valued at 75,000 *livres*, and he did not become involved in politics after 1792. He continued to plead in Bayeux. He was still one of the best-known lawyers of the tribunal established in the town and was practising in 1812 at the age of seventy-two. Le Bret was by no means a rich man but he emerged relatively unscathed from a period in which many careers were ruined. So did Le Tellier and Gosset, fellow *avocats*, employed in the tribunal in 1790.

On the other hand, the career of Duhamel De Vailly illustrates some of the disasters that could befall a man who involved himself too much in local politics. In 1789 his income fell considerably by losses sustained when the seigneurial rights of Tracy and the

Vente des biens nationaux, district de Bayeux. A.D.C. *Délibérations du directoire du district de Bayeux*, which list new personnel and salaries. A.N. F¹ᵇ II. *Calvados 10. Liste des 200 plus forts contribuables de la commune de Bayeux*, 1810, 1812. A.M.B. *États de la population, an VII*.

bishopric terminated. His position as apostolic notary to the bishopric did not qualify him for compensation, though the *notariats* of Bayeux and Rochefort which he also possessed were compensated. His only positive gain in 1790 was the position of *suppléant au tribunal*, but that was not calculated to bring him more than 1,000 *livres* income. He threw himself into politics and with Fauchet's help became mayor, member of the *directoire du département* and a prisoner during Le Tual's tenure of office. He emerged from prison a much poorer man with only a little land remaining to him at Tracy, to which he retired. The Revolution had given him a brief limelight and ruined the career he and his father had so unscrupulously built up. The fate of Richard Hardouin was similarly, though less spectacularly, hard. In 1790 he received notification of compensation for the office of *procureur* at the *bailliage* but nothing to replace the supplementary income he had owned as *receveur* for the dues owing to the *hôpital général* and the *hôtel Dieu* and as estate manager for the Dumanoir family. He claimed that the compensation he had received for his office at the *bailliage* was totally inadequate and that the removal of his other sources of income had forced him to live on his capital. He does not seem to have made any investment in land. He was, however, *procureur* at the *tribunal* until its closure, and then claimed himself to be destitute of resources and announced his intention to find work elsewhere. The name Hardouin simply disappears from the town records.

Those who were wise enough to put the compensation they received from their offices immediately into national property were the best ensured of escaping hardship. Hardouin's colleagues as *procureurs* of the *bailliage* court, Mutel and Liégard, are good examples of this. The offices of *procureur* of the *bailliage* and that of *commis à la recette des consignations* were both compensated. Their owner, Mutel, invested the money in land and after being attacked in the *société populaire* as an *accapareur* in 1792 avoided urban politics and left the town. Liégard made a substantial investment at Vaux and did not seek office after 1790 in the town. Examples of officials who improved their fortunes as a result of the Revolution are non-existent in Bayeux. Even many of those who evaded politics sustained losses. Guérin de la Houssaye, who in 1789 held the relatively important post of *lieutenant de police*, one of the four chief judges at the *bailliage* court, and paid the—very high for

Bayeux—*capitation* tax of 80 *livres*, was by 1812 reduced to a small *propriété* outside the town, his financial position substantially diminished. The same can be said of Desroziers, also a judge of the *bailliage*.

The bailiffs of the town who, during the years II and III, had found employment as a professional corps sent out to search the dwellings of those suspected of hoarding grain, lost even that employment, an obviously lucrative one, when the worst of the food crisis was over. By 1812 only three of the eight were still employed as bailiffs, one described himself as a *propriétaire*, though not a wealthy one, and at least two were dead. None showed any real increase in wealth in comparison with their earnings of 1789.

Perhaps the most substantial losers were those who had owed the entirety of their incomes to the collection of dues and taxes, the auditing of accounts or the business of a seigneurial court. Raould de la Chêsnée, who was the *fermier général* of the Abbaye Notre Dame de Longues, felt the loss less than most because he was a substantial landowner at Vaux and Nonant, but the family was significantly less rich in 1812. A relatively poor man like Guillaume Desrez was less well equipped to withstand the losses with which he was faced in 1789. He had then derived his income mostly from the positions of archivist to the bishopric (600 *livres*) and *greffier des hautes justices de l'évêché* (200 *livres*). He lost both offices without compensation. For the immediate present he had no problems because his knowledge of title deeds was deemed sufficient qualification to make him assessor of silver and objects of value belonging to religious houses, ecclesiastics, and *émigrés*. The work was temporary and only paid by the day. On the other hand, it brought him into contact with the committee responsible for the sale of national property and Desrez attended auctions for clients, presumably at a fee. He was also used as a cover by a syndicate trying to corner national property and was dismissed. He later emerged as a minor clerk.

The large unwieldy group of officials present in Bayeux in 1789 had certainly diminished by the Restoration. Many of course had died. The sort of work they had carried out was at an end. Perhaps some of the young men who sought employment in the subprefecture as secretaries and clerks would before 1789 have sought an outlet in the law, but this is speculation. Neither the tribunal nor the subprefecture employed anything which approached the numbers engaged in work for the courts in 1789. Nor was there now scope for amassing a fortune by the methods Gabriel Cahier, the joiner's son, had used as collector of dues for the Marquis of Balleroy, or Robert Douesnel as bailiff of the *élection* of Bayeux, exploiter of two *sergenteries* and tithe collector of the chapter.

Other occupations survived the Revolution with far less need for radical adjustment than the officials. Travellers continued to put up at the hotels. The apothecaries sold their cures. Trade suffered but it did not collapse entirely. The doctors and surgeons of the town emerged with their practices intact; even Le Tual continued his surgery until his death in 1802, murdered according to popular legend by the relatives of someone to whom he had caused great suffering during the Terror.[1] The lace merchants felt the hardship of the early war years but they resumed their trade. The process of reconstruction was slow, especially for the small tradesmen who had depended on an affluent clientele. The years immediately after the crisis are difficult years to describe in Bayeux. Half the population in the year VII (1797–8) was still dependent upon subsidized rations and as long as this continued the chances of any resumption of trade for the small shopkeeper were slight.[2]

The reorganization of the administrative framework of France after *brumaire* restored something to Bayeux, if not all it had possessed in 1789. It was to be the same with the religious settlement. The religious peace was an essential step in the achievement of civil order for France as a whole. For Bayeux it was something more. To give Bayeux back its bishop and chapter and its religious houses was to return to the town its essential character of a diocesan centre. Within a month of the promulgation of the concordat (18 April 1802) the priests of Bayeux vacated Somers Town and Winchester and came streaming back across the Channel to resume their duties. Economically the town gained. Those who had been involved in the religious changes of the Revolution could not expect to do other than suffer. Exile had not made the returning priests tolerant. The moot point was what would be their relationship with the former jurors, some of whom had occupied their parishes. Would they meet as equals or as enemies?

[1] Anquétil denies this assertion and states that he died from a hernia brought on by a fall. Anquétil, 'La Société populaire de Bayeux . . .', op. cit., p. 72.
[2] A.M.B. Q72. *Hospices*.

If they met as enemies who would be the victor? Secondly, and this was indeed important to the people of Bayeux, what sort of a church would emerge from the settlement?

The choice of bishop for the Calvados was M. Charles Brault, former archdeacon of the see of Poitiers, who had been a non-juror and had spent a prolonged exile in Switzerland. The choice meant that in the Calvados the church of the concordat was the instrument of the non-jurors and Brault went to no pains to conceal the fact.[1] He could scarcely have acted more blatantly. The very day of his arrival, 25 June 1802, M. de Marguerie, former dean of the cathedral and an intransigent non-juror, held a service designed to purge the cathedral and re-offer it, wholly cleansed, to God. The next day the new bishop prepared for his installation ceremony and announced his intention to refuse admission to the cathedral on this occasion to any constitutional priest. He had, apparently, examined the record of every priest of the diocese and issued cards to those he considered fit to attend. It was obvious that he had excluded all former jurors. The priests of the diocese who had taken the oath, headed by Moulland, drew up a protest and elected two of their number to visit the bishop, doubtless to point out to him the illegality of his actions. Their only reply from the bishop was that they should take steps to put their consciences in order. A further interview received the unbending reply that they must retract their oaths, choose a confessor who had been a non-juror and make a full repentance.[2]

In every way, Brault appeared to be acting completely contrary to the terms of the concordat and the spirit of its negotiators, Cardinal Caprara and Portalis. According to the terms of this agreement, the schismatic priests could only be called upon to declare their adhesion to the concordat and therefore their readiness to enter into communion with the bishop nominated by the First Consul. This the schismatic priests were fully prepared to do. But the concordat provided the means by which the new bishop, if he so chose, could create difficulties for them. It expressly stated that before anyone could administer the sacraments he must have permission from the new bishop. And Brault refused outright to grant that permission to any who would not

[1] Sévèstre, *La Vie religieuse . . .*, p. 116.
[2] Patry, op. cit., p. 188.

retract the oaths they had taken. The prefect Cafarelli, former canon of Toul, was in a difficult position but in spite of being himself a juror, appreciated too well the bitter antipathy between the two parties to intervene. He saw that the non-jurors were by far the stronger party and that in the interests of peace the best policy in the Calvados was to make an unconditional surrender to them. He advised the government to steer clear of entanglement and to leave the bishop to his business.[1] Brault was left, virtually undisturbed, to re-create the old church. In theory his grand vicars were supposed to be chosen from both parties: in reality the old canons reassumed the direction of the diocese. He was prevailed upon, though not without pressure from Cafarelli, to make Bisson, the short-lived constitutional bishop, an honorary canon of the cathedral; but he only did so on condition that Bisson went into immediate retirement and so did not offend the bishop by his presence. It was one of the very few gestures made in favour of the schismatic church.

Similarly with the new priests. Brault had a virtually fool-proof case, after the escapades of the *armée noire*, that Fauchet's men were unworthy of consideration and that the whole episode spelt shame for the church. Again, on Cafarelli's intervention, he was prepared to make an exception in the case of Moulland, to whom he did accord a grudging respect. But even here Brault took a petty revenge. Moulland was given the cure of Balleroy whose parish church lay directly next to the seventeenth-century *château* of the Marquis of Balleroy, perhaps the most splendid in the area, and in this atmosphere the energetic left-wing cleric was condemned to live out his days. This did not mean that Moulland did not fight back. To the end he irritated succeeding bishops by an intransigent refusal to retract one wit of his oaths and for some twenty-five years addressed a letter, annually, justifying his position to his wholly unsympathetic superiors.[2]

The government, in effect, abandoned the jurors. In the Calvados they were the victims of the concordat. In many respects the decision of the prefect not to intervene was a wise one and the quickest way of solving the problem. The influence of the jurors was so slight as to cause little effective trouble, even if pride would not allow them to retract. Bisson, in the rue des Chanoines, reputedly took to the bottle and refused to admit into

[1] Patry, op. cit., p. 188.   [2] Ibid.

his house anyone who was not a former juror. His house came to serve as a veritable club for the little nucleus of men who had struggled so hard with their *presbytère* for the re-establishment of Christian worship. Brault chose to ignore the activities of the house in the rue des Chanoines, which continued well into the 1820s and outlived Brault himself. Bisson's funeral caused a general scandal which kept the town talking for long after. At the ceremony one of his friends recited the orison *pro episcopo* and gathered together funds to build a small monument to stand as a last rebellious relic of a forgotten church in which Bisson and his friends had reposed so much faith and for which they had suffered so much humiliation.[1]

The church established by the concordat was no weaker than it had been in 1789 but the church that sang *Te Deums* for Napoleon's victories and to welcome back Louis XVIII worked on a much tighter budget. It could not make the same generous gestures to relieve the poor. It did not employ the same domestic staff or the horde of officials who had managed its estates, audited its accounts, and run its seigneurial courts. On the other hand, if the new church was not as wealthy, its spirit was much the same. It was ready to assume responsibility to collect alms; to organize charity; to reassume in fact that attitude of benevolent authoritarian paternalism to which a town like Bayeux under the old régime had become so accustomed. The religious orders reorganized themselves. Within a year of the concordat the Sisters of Providence were back to care for the foundlings.[2] Within five years the administration of the hospitals had been worked out anew: the nuns were fully in control and tendered accounts to an unquestioning municipality. A part of their property was restored and the remainder of their expenses met out of municipal funds. Likewise they reassumed control of primary education. The small girls of the town returned to the Ursulines, the boys to the Christian Brothers, which were both reorganized by 1808.

The restored church and a reorganized administration went a small way towards helping Bayeux to emerge from the difficulties of the early war years, but there was no easy solution to the crisis for the town. On the eve of the Revolution Bayeux had already a basic problem of under-employment and unemployment and this had been severely aggravated. What there was of industry in the

[1] Ibid., p. 189.   [2] A.N. F⁶ II. *Calvados 8*. Bayeux.

town started up again around the turn of the century; it is difficult to be more precise. The lace school was reopened after the concordat and continued to be the one successful industry the town possessed. Few towns were less well equipped than Bayeux to cope with the changes the Revolution had brought. The food crisis, the industrial slump, the breakdown of the local administration disrupted the economic life of many French towns without fundamentally altering the nature of their economy. The assumption of ecclesiastical wealth by the state and the Civil Constitution of the Clergy left Elbeuf virtually untouched.[1] Other diocesan centres like Lisieux with its woollen industry, or Angers with its more intense commercial life, were better fitted to withstand the effects of legislation on the church: even the nearby episcopal towns of Coutances or Avranches, though severely hit, had not been so accustomed to depending upon the church for subsidy since the church in these areas had never been as rich as at Bayeux. Many other erstwhile administrative centres were conscious of the reduction in business caused by the abolition of many of the old administrative institutions of the old régime. Toulouse and Dijon, for example, were quick to point out their losses from the abolition of the *parlements*[2] and the redundancy of many petty officials, an experience which Bayeux very obviously shared.

The picture of Bayeux in 1805 or 1815 or 1820 was certainly changed from that of 1789. The town had no alternative but to hark back as far as it could to the way of life it had pursued in 1789 and to rebuild its existence around the bishop and chapter, religious house, and tribunal. But these no longer offered the same solution to living within a stagnant economy. It was not possible to live off someone else in the way that so many of the townspeople had done in 1789.

The town's relationship with the country around it was also irrevocably changed. But relationships within rural society in this area had also become more clear cut. The large landowner had benefited from the abolition of the tithe but the position of the tenant farmer had not necessarily improved, for the landowners

---

[1] J. Kaplow, *Elbeuf during the Revolutionary Period* . . ., p. 243.
[2] D. Higgs, 'The Ultra-Royalist Movement at Toulouse under the Second Restoration', an unpublished doctoral thesis of the University of London, 1964, p. 14.

stepped up the rent when the tithe collector ceased to take his cut. More important than this, however, and also arising from the destruction of the territorial wealth of the church, was the speeding up of the transition from arable to pasture. The main impediment to this change in the diocese of Bayeux had been leases on clerical property which, in the interests of the tithe, forbade any change in the traditional crops grown. Those who had purchased clerical property were under no such restriction. The process of change had perhaps been accelerated by those landowners who wanted to avoid surrendering their crops during the period of the maximum. Report after report spoke uneasily about the extension of pasture in the district of Bayeux.[1] The change was already apparent by 1796 and even more plain by 1804. It was attractive to the large landholders but necessarily at the expense of the landless labourer, and for these migration to a town like Bayeux was no longer any remedy. There was less chance of employment there than before 1789 and charitable assistance, if it had reappeared, was not what it had been.

The population of Bayeux never surpassed the peak it reached in the early 1790s. Up to 1830 it declined by some 15 per cent.: after that date it fell still further and by the 1870s it was around some 7,000—a figure more in keeping with its resources.[2] Those who remained were the administrators, those engaged in the rich wholesale trade of cattle and dairy produce, small shopkeepers, repairers of farm tools, and those who did not mind scratching around for a livelihood. The artisans remained under-employed, poorly paid, and pathetically dependent on outside relief, organized by the church if no longer the product of ecclesiastical alms. Their best recourse as opportunities opened up elsewhere in the 1830s and 1840s was to leave, though many still opted for a hand-to-mouth existence, perhaps too accustomed, as the administrators of the old régime had said, to living on charity. *Les gens de Bayeux*, the saying still runs, *cherchent du travail tout en priant le bon Dieu de ne pas en trouver.*

[1] A.N. F¹ᵇ II. *Calvados 1*; F¹ᶜ III. *Calvados 7*.
[2] Michel, op. cit., vol. i, p. 13.

APPENDIX I[1]

Population of Bayeux 1774

Parish	Men	Women	Total
St. Jean	747	967	1,714
La Madeleine	216	318	534
St. Laurent	238	327	565
St. Ouen des Faubourgs	56	60	116
St. Patrice	480	852	1,332
St. Ouen du Château	11	27	38
La Pothérie	98	174	272
St. Loup	287	389	676
St. André	74	99	173
St. Malo	324	411	735
St. Martin	174	243	417
St. Vigor le Petit	171	291	462
St. Exupère	349	548	897
St. Sauveur	633	634	1,267
	3,858	5,340	9,198

[1] A.D.C. C176.

APPENDIX II[1]

Revenues of the Parish Churches of Bayeux

Benefice	Patron	Revenue (*livres*)	(*sous*)
St. André	Marquis de Castilly	150	0
St. Exupère	Chapter of Bayeux		
St. Jean	Canon of St. Germain	250	6
St. Laurent	Canon of St. Laurent	100	6
St. Loup	The Dean	300	6
La Madeleine	Canon of Cambremer	150	
St. Malo	The *Seigneur* of Argouges	100	6
St. Martin	Canon of St. Martin	100	6
St. Ouen du Château	Bishop of Bayeux	300	
St. Ouen des Faubourgs	Prior of St. Nicolas de la Chêsnée	100	
St. Patrice	Canons of Vaucelles and St. Patrice	300	
La Pothérie	Canon of St. Germain	300	
St. Sauveur	Chapter of Bayeux	400	
St. Vigor le Petit	Seminary	100	

These figures are all exclusive of *casuel*.

[1] B.V.B. MS. 27.

APPENDIX III

The complexities of the component elements of the incomes of the bailiffs, *procureurs*, and notaries of Bayeux are illustrated by the following examples.

	Livres per year
RICHARD HARDOUIN	
Procureur of the *Bailliage*	300
Property let at Bayeux	300
Receiver of the Hospital dues	(180)

+the income he gained as a drapery wholesaler and as property manager for the Dumanoir family and as a money-lender.

Paid in *capitation* 12 *livres*.

PIERRE POITEVIN	
Procureur of the *Bailliage*	300
Proprietor of the *Notariat* of Estreham	200
Property at Bayeux and Condé sur Seulles	510

Paid in *capitation* 12 *livres*.

MUTEL	
Procureur of the *Bailliage*	200
Commis à la Recette des Consignations	800
Property let	230

Paid in *capitation* 12 *livres*.

HALLOT	
Procureur of the *Élection*	250
Let 13 houses at Bayeux	600

Paid in *capitation* 6 *livres*.

PIERRE BASLEY	
Procureur of the *Élection*	250
Land at St. Patrice	200
Secretary of the *Subdélégué*	(100)
Receiver of dues for the Bishop	+

Paid in *capitation* 5 *livres*.

	Livres per year
QUESNEL	
Bailiff of the *Bailliage*	222
Rented half the *Sergenterie Royale* of Messon	100
Property Vaux sur Aure	150
Paid in *capitation* 5 *livres*.	
DELAUNAY DE FOUDRAY	
Bailiff of the *Bailliage*	220
Bailiff of the Municipal Council	75
Property in Bayeux (several houses and shops)	1,000
Paid in *capitation* 24 *livres*.	
(Incomplete)	
ROBERT DOUESNEL	
Bailiff of the *Élection*	100
Rented *Sergenterie du pled d'épée*	100
Sergenterie of Bricquevard	400
40 *vergées* vegetable plots let at Bayeux	750
Tithe of St. Patrice	1,000
Paid in *capitation* 134 *livres*.	
(Very incomplete)	
DUHAMEL DE VAILLY, *notary*	
Owned *Notariat* of Bayeux	4,000
Owned *Notariat* of Rochefort	
Agent, Receiver of Dues and *Notaire Apostolique* of the Bishop of Bayeux	
Owner of the Offices *Jurés Priseurs Vendeurs de Meubles* of Le Mans, Flèche, Falaise	
Estate Manager for the Countess of Gramont	
Property St. Loup, Subles, Tracy, St. Vigor, St. Germain	1,000
Seigneurial rights of Tracy	
Held seigneurial rights of bishopric of Bayeux on lease.	
Impossible to calculate de Vailly's income.	
Paid in *capitation* 48 *livres* 10 *sous*.	
VAUTIER, *notary*	
Owned *Notariat* of Formigny	150
Owned *Notariat* of Trevières	250
Huissier aux Traites	
(united to the *Élection*)	100
Property outside Bayeux	(300)
Mainly worked for Vailly at Bayeux.	
Paid in *capitation* 8 *livres*.	

APPENDIX IV[1]

The Poor of Bayeux, 26 January 1785

Household	Profession	Wife	Chil-dren	Other dependent relatives	Total
ST. EXUPÈRE					
Dalet	*journalier*				1
André		1	2		4
Le François (widow)	spinner		2		3
Dujardin	mason	1	5		7
Crespin	roof-builder	1	4		6
Le Véel	*journalier*	1			2
Crespin	mason	1			2
Marie Guillemar	spinner				1
Anne Baley	spinner				1
Lanci (widow)			1		2
Marie Bénard	lace-maker		1		2
Marie Adam	lace-maker			1 sister	2
Isabelle	*journalier*	1	2		4
La Régent (f)	spinner				1
Claude (widow)			2		3
Châles	*journalier*	1	3		5
Roger	carter	1	1		3
Le Prieur (widow)				1 sister	2
La Lormière (f)	spinner		1		2
Vassal	carter	1	5	aged father-in-law	8
La Guillebert (f)	spinner		4		5
La Dufourde (f)	spinner		2		3
Elisabeth Taîne	match-seller		1		2
Vallée (widow)					1
L'Honoré	weaver	1	2		4
Jacques La Haye	weaver	1		1 niece	3
Nicolas La Haye	weaver	1	3		5
Les Pauses					3
La Simone (f)	lace-maker				1
Le Ruel	*journalier*	1	2	aged mother	5
Le Bourgeois	*journalier*		1		2
La Haye (widow)	knitter				1
Le Nourrichel	*journalier*	1	4		6
3 Households of *Pauvres Honteux*					4
					106

f = female

[1] A.D.C. C955.

Household	Profession	Wife	Children	Other dependent relatives	Total
ST. JEAN					
Michel Annais	invalid				7
Cliquet (widow)			6		7
Jean Souprai	*journalier*				7
Cousin	knife-grinder				6
A. Hédiard	printer of cotton				5
Jeanne David	spinner				5
Gilles Gonfroy	*journalier*				5
Jean Chérouel	*journalier*				5
François Hélye	mason				5
Toussaint Richet	carter				5
Michel Richet	carter				5
Charles Georget	*journalier*				5
Sébire (widow)	lace-maker				5
J. Boulais	*journalier*				5
Tetrelle (widow)	washer-woman				4
Joret (widow)					4
Pierre La Haye	weaver				4
Fr. Georget l'aîné	*journalier*				4
Fr. Georget	*journalier*				4
L. Ariel	*journalier*				4
La Fleur (aged)					4
P. Le Noble	stocking-maker				4
P. Carité	mason				4
R. Thézard	*journalier*				4
P. Duval	*journalier*				4
P. Lavoine	*journalier*				3
J. Le Noble (aged)					3
N. Froment	stocking-maker				3
His wife (separated)					3
Groult (widow)	weaver				3
Jean Le Devin	wood-cutter				3
J. Blet	knitter				3
Séquet (widow)	spinner				3
J. Carabeaux	*journalier*				3
L. Cappé	mason				3
J. Chuquet	mason				3
Bion (widow)	lace-maker				3
J. Vallée					3
La Motte (widow)					3
Hamon (widow)	*journalière*				3
La Haye (widow)	*journalière*				2
J. B. Anard	knitter				2
La Haye (widow)	lace-maker				2
J. Rouget	*journalier*				2
Harivel (f)	glove-maker				2

Household	Profession	Wife	Children	Other dependent relatives	Total
L. Le François	wood-cutter				2
J. Martin	knitter				2
P. Coussey (sick)					2
Angélique Cuire					2
P. Eudine	*journalier*				2
G. Aune	knitter				2
C. Le François	weaver				2
P. Morel	*journalier*				2
N. Le Bourgeois					2
Quel (widow) (sick)					2
P. Doucet	carder				2
Marie Pavie	lace-maker				2
C. Lesseline	shoemaker				2
J. Philippe	spinner				2
Bellami (widow)	spinner				2
Marie Lavoine (sick)					1
J. Cousin (widow)	spinner				1
L'Évêque (widow)					1
Catherine Herbert	spinner				1
Jeanne Longon	lace-maker				1
Sébire (widow)					1
Poittevin (widow, paralysed)					1
Le Roy (widow)	spinner				1
Cathérine (widow)					1
Clérisse (widow, aged)					1
J. Cathérine	*journalier*				1
Louise le Cieux	lace-maker				1
Cousin (widow, aged)					1
Billard (widow, sick)					1
Panchon (widow, sick)					1
Anne (widow)					1
La Bourgoise (f)					1
Carabeux	knitter				1
J. Philippine (f)					1
Scelles (widow)	spinner				1
C. Blet (f)	spinner				1
La Haye (f) orphan					1
C. Lami (f)	lace-maker				1
G. Renouf (widow, sick)					1
Sébire (widow)	washerwoman				1
Anne Eurry	spinner				1
12 families of *Pauvres Honteux*					37
					269

Household	Profession	Wife	Children	Other dependent relatives	Total
NOTRE DAME DE LA POTHÉRIE					
N. James	*journalier*	1	2		4
Sallen (aged)		1			2
Marie Martin	spinner				2
Goudouin (widow)					1
Gainier (f)			1		2
Lagonne (sick)				granddaughter	2
Mordant					1
	weaver	1	4		6
P. Cauvin	mason	1	1		3
					21
ST. LAURENT					
Le Blanc	stocking-maker	1	4	aged father	7
Le Fèvre	*journalier*	1	1		3
J. Lesseline		1			2
Le Diacre	woodcutter	1	2		4
Philippe (f) (orphan)					1
Perrelle (f)	lace-maker				1
La Forestière (abandoned by husband)			2		3
L'Évêque (f)			1		2
Bucaille			1		2
Morant (widow)			2	4 grandchildren	6
Morant (f)			2		3
Lamoureux (f) (abandoned by husband)			1		2
J. Le Fèvre			2		3
Daniel (widow)			1		2
Le Petit					1
Babet (aged)					1
P. Le Fèvre (aged)					1
M. Le Harivel	glove-maker		1		2
G. Verel	*journalier*				1
Duval	shoemaker	1	1		3
M. Dupont (f)			1		2
P. Moront	*journalier*				1
Verel	*journalier*	1	1		3
G. Durant	shoemaker	1	2		4
G. Verdelle		1	3		5
M. Périer	*journalier*	1	2		4
Sauvage (widow)	lace-maker	1	2		4
Cliquet (widow)	spinner		1		2
J. Le Blance			2		3
Lacorte (f)		1	3		5
2 orphan children			2		3
Colibert (widow)					2
La Fremoine			3		4
P. Le Moine					1
		1	2		4

Household	Profession	Wife	Children	Other dependent relatives	Total
La Fréone	*journalier*	I	I		3
Piqueray (widow)	*journalière*		2		3
N. Lieuray	*journalier*	I	3		5
Godet (widow)	washerwoman				I
Pauvres Honteux: II					
families of:					3
					4
					7
					I
					3
					4
					4
					5
					2
					4
					5
					149
ST. LOUP					
Paucher	*journalier*	I	4		6
Belleroze	weaver	I	3		5
Masselin	weaver	I	2		4
Salen	*journalier*	I			2
Tubœuf	*journalier*	I	I		3
Tassine l'aîné	shoemaker	I	I		3
Tassine	*journalier*	I	I		3
Benoist	weaver (unemployed)	I	4		6
St. Thomas (widow) (sick)					I
James (widow)			I		2
Ouenne (widow)			4		5
Bravette	*journalier*	I	2		4
Thouroude (aged)					I
Gessine l'aîné	*journalier*	I			2
Gessine	*journalier*	I	I		3
Roger	weaver	I	I		3
Savary (f)			I		2
Grenier	*journalier*	I	3		5
De Roziers (f) (aged)	weaver				I
Liégard (f)			I		2
La Cordière (f)			I		2
Henry	*journalier*	I	3		5
Voisin	*journalier*	I	5		7
Decônes	*journalier*	I	3		5
Le Cœu (aged)					I
St. Martin (aged)					I
Soulavie	*journalier*	I	4		6
Noël	*journalier*	I	2		4
Salen	*journalier*	I	I		3

Household	Profession	Wife	Children	Other dependent relatives	Total
Pierre (widow)			1		2
Ménage	*journalier*	1	3		5
La Gassionne (f)			1		2
La Malherbe (f)			2		3
La Berge (f)			2		3
Vailland (widow)					1
La Balye			2		3
Vaillant (f) (sick)					1
Martin	carrier	1	3		5
Marie Anne Lasseline	dressmaker				1
J. Catherin	*journalier*	1	2		4
Marie Guélinel (aged)					1
M. Pipperel	*journalier*				1
Pauvres Honteux: 6 families of:					
					4
					6
					1
					4
					3
					5
					152
LA MADELEINE					
Jean Marin	*journalier*	1	3		5
Lambert Auger	*journalier*	1	3		5
Pierre Marie	*journalier*	1			2
Jean Piquot		1	1		3
Jacques le Sage	*journalier*	1	3		5
Julien Covet	*journalier*	1	2		4
Étienne le Fevre	*journalier*	1	2		4
Marguerite Fauvel	lace-maker			her niece	2
Martin Fougères	*journalier*	1	3		5
Marguerite Servot (aged)					1
Marguerite Le Due (aged)					1
Pauvres Honteux: 5 families of:					17
					54
ST. MALO					
Gisles		1			2
Bouillot					1
La Haye					1
Guérin		1	1		3
Doueslet (widow)					1
Lefebvre (f)			2		3
La Couture (widow)					1
Pierre Cotil					1
Gisles Cotil		1			2
Girette Vaudevire					1
					1

Household	Profession	Wife	Children	Other dependent relatives	Total
Guillot	carter		4		5
Voeillant (f)					1
Colleville		1	2		4
Durant (f)					1
Pauvres Honteux: 5 families of:					3
					3
					6
					3
					1
					43
ST. MARTIN					
Morin				} all sick	5
Le Boiteux (f)	lace-maker			} or aged	2
Catho (f)	knitter				1
Bouilly (f)	spinner				1
Those who worked but earned too little:					
Savary	soapmaker	1	2		4
Marie l'Ange	spinner		1		2
Masson (widow)	fruiterer		5		6
Lacourte	tinsmith	1	2		4
Adeline (widow)			2		3
Châtelet (widow)			2		3
Pauvres Honteux: 4 families of:					5
					3
					5
					4
					48
ST. OUEN DES FAUBOURGS					
Le Vaultier	companion shoemaker	1	1		3
Halley	*journalier*	1	1		3
Cliquot			2		3
Cathérine	*journalier*	1	3		5
Le Loup (widow)			1		2
Le Chevalier (widow)			1		2
Le Carpentier (f)					1
Trancy	*journalier*	1	1		3
Barbe		1	5		7
La Londe					1
Le Roy (widow)			2		3
Cliquet	spinner		1		3
Pauvres Honteux					11
					47

Household	Profession	Wife	Children	Other dependent relatives	Total
ST. OUEN DU CHÂTEAU					
R. Samson		I	7		9
F. Pain		I	2		4
Beaufils		I	2		4
P. Lozon (epileptic)					I
Pauvres Honnêtes: 2					
families					8
					26
ST. SAUVEUR					
La Porte		I	6		8
Mignon	soldier	I	2		4
Le Vaillant (paralytic)		I	2		4
La Baune (aged)					I
Le Vannier	former soldier	I	2		4
Le Ferrier		I	I		3
F. Hué (cripple)					I
Hamon	tailor	I		granddaughter	3
Pellecocq		I	I		3
Borel	soapmaker	I	2		4
Le Tellier		I			2
Cathérine Godefroy (f)	dressmaker				I
La Ferrère (sick)		I	2	granddaughter	5
Carabeux (widow)			2		3
J. Charpentier		I	I		3
Le Cavalier (aged)		I			2
C. Dumont (f) (aged)					I
Le Blond (f)	dressmaker		I		2
Guillebert (widow, aged)			I	granddaughter	3
Pauvres Honteux: 19					
families					43
					100
ST. VIGOR LE PETIT					
Truquet	*journalier*	I	2		4
Bienvenu (sick)		I	2		4
Hué (widow)			4		5
La Haye (aged)		I	2		4
Blondel (aged)		I	I		3
Trébutien (f) (abandoned by husband)			4		5
Cordier (widow)			I		2
Dupont	shoemaker		I		2
Morel (widow)	washerwoman				I
Gessine (f) (sick)					I
Le Voullant (f)					I
Malenfait	shoemaker	I	3		5

Household	Profession	Wife	Chil-dren	Other dependent relatives	Total
J. Le Cœur	soapmaker				1
J. Marel (f)	lace-maker		1		2
François	*journalier*	1	3		5
A. Morel	companion tanner	1	4		6
P. Morel	companion tanner	1	4		6
J. Morin	companion tanner	1	5		7
1 family newly arrived					2
1 family *Pauvres Honteux*		1	2		4
1 family *Pauvres Honteux*		1	4		6
1 family *Pauvres Honteux*		1	3		5
2 sisters	lace-makers				2
	plasterer	1	4		6
					89

ST. PATRICE

Household	Profession	Wife	Chil-dren	Other dependent relatives	Total
Boissel	weaver	1	4		6
J. Pavie	carpenter	1	5		7
A. Frémond	*journalier*	1	5		7
Héroult	weaver	1	3		5
Jeannette	*journalier*	1	4		6
Tanquerel	carpenter	1	4		6
Derubey (aged)		1			2
Douesnel	*journalier*	1	2		4
J. Herron (aged)					1
Pinchon	weaver	1	1		3
Vautier (aged)		1			2
Le Clerc	shoemaker				1
Martin	weaver	1	5		7
T. Detour					1
Moque	mason	1	3		5
Piquot	*journalier*	1	2		4
La Belle Germaine (f)		1	3		5
Mallet (widow)			1		2
Taillepied	*journalier*	1	1		3
La Derubée (f)			2		3
La Cordière (f)				her blind niece	2
Le Riche	*journalier*	1			2
Dubos (widow, ill)					1
Hamel	*journalier*	1	1		3
Devaux (widow)			1		2
Le Carpentier		1			2
Dupont	weaver	1	1		3
Le Coq	roof-builder	1			2
Maheust (widow)			1		2
Herbert (widow)			2	2 grandchildren	5
Cahier (aged)					1

Household	Profession	Wife	Children	Other dependent relatives	Total
Barbe					
L'Amy (widow, aged)				sister	2
La Bonnette (widow, aged)					1
Tirel (f) (aged)					1
Duval (f) (aged)					1
Liégard (f) (aged)					1
Lecolasse (aged)					1
Maladet (widow)			1	daughter-in-law, 3 grandchildren	6
Bertauld	*journalier*	1	3		5
Le Maître (f) (aged)					1
Alexandre	*journalier*	1	2		4
G. Lesseline	turner				1
La Renaude (f)			1		2
Creveuil	*journalier*	1			2
La Lunel					1
Guérard		1	2		4
Blantôt (f)					1
La Fleuve					1
Guélinel (widow)					1
Le Clerc		1	2		4
Perrée			1		2
La Haule (widow)					1
Pauvres Honteux: 4 families					11
					160
ST. ANDRÉ					
Blanchet (aged)			1		2
Pauvres Honteux					11
					13

APPENDIX V

Those needing assistance in the district of Bayeux, 1790[1]

Canton	Population	Households	No. not paying tax	Those paying less than equivalent of 2 days' work	Old	Children under 14 needing assistance	Total needing assistance	Sick	Vagabonds
Bayeux	10,320	2,767	1,584		144	622	1,884	259	2
Baynes	4,898	1,272	136	306	106	560	961	195	
Balleroy	6,229	1,670	281	271	200	519	930	179	
Caumont	8,642	2,049	230	244	189	661	945	146	
Crépon	7,320	1,840	293	540	233	752	1,281	269	300
Hottot	5,633	1,346	250	263	194	614	1,019	144	22
Isigny	6,988	1,804	1,935	433	182	739	941	182	
Juaye	5,557	1,480	276	361	159	605	789	134	
La Cambe	5,034	1,326	1,219	367	179	540	854	202	165
Magny	5,973	1,481	478	427	186	586	909	192	
Tour	4,327	1,146	214	253	112	379	564	117	31
Trévières	7,584	1,902	368	481	296	819	1,421	295	
Total	78,505	20,083	7,264	3,946	2,180	7,396	12,498	2,314	520

Parish	Population	Households	No. not paying tax	Crippled	Old	Children under 14 needing assistance	Total needing assistance	Sick	Vagabonds
Bayeux:									
St. Patrice	1,722	313	165	9	9	75	216	20	
St. Vigor	595			12	17	30	69	6	
St. Sauveur	1,381	346	109	14	20	23	285		
St. Loup	802	255	307	35	18	95	289	45	
La Pothérie	289	74	40		8	6	15	2	1
St. Malo	825	267	168	13	3	13	92		
St. André	199	52	21	3	2		7		
La Madeleine	497	142	63	7	4	65	97		
St. Jean	1,952	548	320	43	23	183	406	80	
St. Laurent	622	169		26	6	35	158	7	
St. Exupère	773	250	133	31	28	63	166	80	
St. Ouen des Faubourgs	98	24	67	10	4	22	53	12	1
St. Martin	518	157	57	5	2	12	31	7	
St. Ouen du Château	47								
Total	10,320	2,767[2]	1,584[2]	208	144	622	1,884	259	2

[1] A.D.C. Lx. *Etats d'assistance, Bayeux.*
[2] These totals include the missing entries for St. Vigor and St. Ouen du Château.

BIBLIOGRAPHY

PRIMARY SOURCES

I. MANUSCRIPT

A. The majority of the documents used for this study are to be found in the *Archives Départementales du Calvados* at Caen. Principally, they were:

Series C

Capitation des bourgeois et des arts et métiers 1781–7, C4542–7
Capitation des offices de judicature, C4645, 4647
Capitation des exempts et privilégiés, C4667
Capitation des nobles, C4629
Requêtes en décharge, C4678–80
Vingtième, 1776–9, 1783, C5309, 5310
Vingtième d'offices et droits, 1781, C5467
Vingtième d'industrie, 1776–8, C5466

Administrative Correspondence:

(a) *Industry*: C2787–94, 2796, 2806–9, 2814–21, 2824–6, 2836, 2846, 2847–54, 2861, 2936–50, 2955, 2965–71.
(b) *Agriculture*: C2591–2641, 2643, 2689–2745, 2747
(c) *Mendicity*: Maisons de Force, C451–2
　　　　　　　 Poor Houses, C590–604, 609–16, 623–30
　　　　　　　 Corvées, C3371–7, 3379, 3387–3415
　　　　　　　 Ateliers de charité, C3416–19, 3421
(d) *Town Administration*: C1075–87
(e) Register of the proceedings of the *bureau intermédiaire* of Bayeux, 6 October 1787–7 August 1790, C7655
　　　Correspondence of the *bureau intermédiaire* of Bayeux, March 1788–7 August 1790, C7657–8
(f) Registers of the *bureau de contrôle*, C9255–69

Series B

16.B.10. *Cahier du Tiers État du bailliage secondaire de Bayeux*
16.B.3. *Cahier du Clergé du grand bailliage de Caen et de ses quatre bailliages secondaires de Bayeux, Falaise, Thorigny et Vire*

Series H

This series usually comprehends matters relating to the clergy but the chapter at Bayeux has resisted the attempts to move much material to Caen.

An excellent series of records on the hospitals of Bayeux is catalogued under the Series H, but is conserved in the original buildings at Bayeux. The documents are very comprehensively catalogued in the *Inventaire Sommaire des*

Archives Départementales antérieures à 1790. Rédigé par M. Armand Benet, CALVADOS, Archives Ecclésiastiques. Tome 1ᵉʳ. Série H. Supplément.

Hôtel Dieu de Bayeux. H. Suppl. 687–1095
Hôpital Général de Bayeux. H. Suppl. 1096–1308

Series L

This series is only partially classified.

L.   *Délibérations du directoire du département du Calvados*
            Délibérations du directoire du district de Bayeux. 8 vols.
            Tribunal de Bayeux
            Tribunal de Caen: dossier de Cheylus
Lm.   *Police. Chouans.* 18 *liasses*
            Enquête des ans IV, V, VI et IX, Prêtres reclus
            Suspects
Lv.   *Liasses des serments. Bayeux*
            Collection des refus de serment
            Procès verbaux de l'assemblée électorale d'avril 1791
            Pensions ecclésiastiques 1791 à vendémiaire an IV
Lx.   *États d'assistance, Bayeux*

Series M (unclassified)

Prêtres en surveillance

Series Q (unclassified)

Information on the sale of clerical and *émigré* property in the district of Bayeux is found in the following *liasses*:

Évêché de Bayeux
Cathédrale de Bayeux
Chapitre de Bayeux
Vente des biens des émigrés, Bayeux

B. *Archives Municipales, Bayeux*

Série AA   *État des corps de la ville de Bayeux en 1789. 32 procès verbaux*
                  d'assemblées électorales tenues entre les 20 et 27 février 1789. 10
                  cahiers de doléances rédigés par corps
Série BB. III–VI *Registres de délibérations de l'Hôtel de Ville de Bayeux, 1765–*
                  1790
Série HH   *Manufactures*
Série D   *Registres des délibérations du corps municipal 1790–an III*
                  Registre de correspondance 1790–1791
                  Comptes moraux rendus novembre 1791
                                    décembre 1792
                                    septembre 1793
                                    11 floréal an III
                                    10 ventôse an IV
                                    8 germinal an V
                  Société populaire. 2 registers

Série F   *États de la population, an IV, an VII*
Série P   *Dénonciations contre de Cheylus*
     Déportations des prêtres insermentés, 1792–1793
     Pensionnaires ecclésiastiques an IV–an VII
     État-Civil des religieuses pensionnées (2 liasses)
Série Q   *Hospices*
État Civil

C. *Archives Nationales*

On Bayeux under the old régime there is little to be found in Paris. Some information on the clergy was found:

G^8 623, G^8 626, H^1 1651, S 7477

Relating to the Revolution at Bayeux:

AA 62. Correspondence of the bishop of Bayeux concerning the Civil Constitution of the Clergy
BB^{16} 107. *Tribunal de Bayeux*
C 286, 290 *Pétitions*
D IV bis 37. *État des citoyens actifs du département*
D IV bis 94. Administration
D XXIX 3. Dossier 31. *Comité des Rapports (Constituante)*
D XXIX bis 20. Ibid. *Dénonciation contre de Cheylus*
F^{1b} II. *Calvados 1–10.* Administration
F^{1c} III. *Calvados 1–12.* Public Opinion and Elections
F^2 I. 121. *Dépenses et frais des tribunaux*
F^7 3027. *Police (chouannerie)*
  3282. *Détenus pour mesure de haute police*
  3661^2. *Police (Élections an V. Calvados)*
  5645. *Statistique personnelle et morale: fonctionnaires, 1793–1815*
  7192. *Police (chouans)*
  7258. Ibid.
  7272. Ibid. *(Presbytère de Bayeux)*
  7606. Ibid. Includes *règlement provisoire donné par Monseigneur l'évêque de Bayeux aux curés, desservants, vicaires et à tous les prêtres de son diocèse, le 6 juin 1795*
F^8 38. *Police Sanitaire*
F^{15} 267. *Hospices de Bayeux*
F^{19} 410. *Fauchet*
F^{19} 911^2. *Culte*
  1380. Ibid.
W292. Dossier 204. *Tribunal Révolutionnaire. Fauchet*

D. *Bibliothèque de Bayeux*

The manuscripts in this collection were last catalogued in 1889 in the *Catalogue Général des Manuscrits des Bibliothèques Publiques de France*, vol. x. Since then, several changes in the enumeration have been made. They cover a miscellany of fields but those of use related mainly to the church and families of the town.

No. 27.   *État des officialités, archidiaconés, doyennés et paroisses du diocèse de*
               Bayeux. XVIIIᵉ siècle
No. 28.   *Pouillé de tous les bénéfices, cures simples et réguliers du diocèse de*
               Bayeux. XVIIIᵉ siècle
No. 48.   *État des bénéfices de l'ancien diocèse de Bayeux. XVIIIᵉ siècle*
No. 101.   *Comptes des recettes et dépenses de l'Hôpital Général de Bayeux,*
               années 1760, 1777 à 1793
No. 103.   *Lettres de noblesse accordées en 1746 à Louis François de Bailleul*
No. 106.   *Mémoires de la famille Bauquet. XVIIIᵉ siècle*
No. 109.   *Titres et papiers de N. de St. Vast. XVIIIᵉ siècle*
Nos. 178–9.   *Pièces relatives à la communauté des apothicaires de Bayeux. XVIIIᵉ*
               siècle
No. 180.   *Pièces relatives aux familles de Boisjugon et de la Houblonnière. XVIIIᵉ*
               siècle

E. *Bibliothèque du Chapitre de Bayeux*

   The manuscripts in this collection were also catalogued in the *Catalogue*
Général des Manuscrits des Bibliothèques Publiques de France, vol. x

17.   *Recherche des élus de la noblesse de Bayeux, 1523* (eighteenth-century
               annotations)
176.   *Recueil sur le monastère des Bénédictines de Bayeux*
182.   *Recueil sur l'Hôtel Dieu de Bayeux*
184.   *Recueil sur l'Hôpital Général de Bayeux*
185.   *Registre du bureau de charité de Bayeux, 1765 à 1791*
198.   *Catalogue des bénéfices-cures du diocèse de Bayeux et du nom des*
               patrons. XVIIIᵉ siècle
210.   *État des revenus de l'évêché de Bayeux en 1763*
217.   *Comptes divers du chapitre*
218–23.   *Registre des recettes du chapitre*
232–301.   *Insinuations ecclésiastiques*
302–3.   *Registre du secrétariat de l'évêché de Bayeux 1729–1744, 1764–1771*
304.   *5ème liasse. Administration de Monseigneur de Cheylus 1777 à 1797*
               7ème liasse. Administration de Fauchet
305.   *Collection d'actes de décès d'ecclésiastiques décédés soit à Jersey soit en*
               Angleterre

II. PRINTED SOURCES

A. *Cahiers*

E. Anquétil, *Cahier du Tiers État de Bayeux* (Bayeux, 1886)
A. Brette, 'Les Élections du clergé de Caen en 1789. Bulletins de l'Abbé
    Soulavie, 6–25 mars 1789', *La Révolution Française*, vol. xxxvii, pp. 162–9
F. Mourlot, *Le Cahier d'observations et doléances du Tiers État de la ville de Caen*
    en 1789 (Paris, 1912)
Archives Parlementaires de 1787 à 1860 (Paris, 1879), vol. ii, pp. 488–92. *Cahier*
    de la noblesse du grand bailliage de Caen et de ses quatre bailliages secondaires de
    Bayeux, Falaise, Thorigny et Vire

B. *Mémoires and Chronicles*

M. Béziers, *Mémoires pour servir à l'état historique et géographique du diocèse de Bayeux* (Rouen, 1896). 3 vols. Written in the 1760s by a parish priest of exceptional learning, these volumes offer invaluable information upon Bayeux in the eighteenth century.

Bisson, *Histoire ecclésiastique du diocèse de Bayeux pendant la Révolution*

A. Young, *Travels in France* (ed. Maxwell) (Cambridge, 1950)

C. *Collections of Documents*

A. Brette, *Recueil de documents relatifs à la convocation des États Généraux de 1789* (Paris, 1895–1905)

Isambert, Decrusy, et Taillandier, *Recueil Général des anciennes lois françaises depuis l'an 420 jusqu'à la Révolution de 1789* (Paris, 1822–8)

Recueil des Édits, déclarations, lettres patentes, arrêts et règlements du roi, registrés en la Cour du Parlement de Normandie (1643–1753) (1754–71), Rouen, 10 vols.

Rapports des agents du Ministre de l'Intérieur dans les départements 1793–an II, publiés par P. Caron (Paris, 1951), t. 11

D. *Miscellaneous*

Duhamel, *État de la magistrature en France pour l'année 1789* (1789)

J. J. Expilly, *Dictionnaire géographique, historique et politique des Gaules et de la France* (Paris, 1762–90)

C. Hippeau, *Le Gouvernement de Normandie aux XVIIe et XVIIIe siècles. Documents inédits tirés des archives du Château d'Harcourt* (Caen, 1863–9). 9 vols.

D. Houard, *Dictionnaire analytique, historique, étymologique, critique et interprétatif de la coutume de Normandie* (Rouen, 1780–2). 4 vols.

La France ecclésiastique, 1783 (Paris, 1783).

Mémoire présenté au roi par les citoyens de la ville de Bayeux pour obtenir la révocation d'une lettre de cachet (Bayeux, 1789)

E. *Dictionaries and Works of Reference*

A. Brette, *Les Constituants* (Paris, 1897)

P. Caron, *Manuel pratique pour l'étude de la Révolution Française* (Paris, 1947)

—— *Tableau de dépréciation du papier-monnaie* (Paris, 1909)

G. Chamillart, *Recherche de la noblesse en la généralité de Caen* (Caen, 1887)

A. Daumard and F. Furet, 'Les Archives notariales et la mécanographie', *Annales-Économies-Sociétés-Civilisations*, xiv (1959), pp. 676–93

G. du Boscq de Beaumont, 'Les Anoblissements et les maintenues de noblesse dans la généralité de Caen', *Annuaire du Conseil Héraldique de France, 20e année* (1907), pp. 74–164

B. Hyslop, *A Guide to the General Cahiers of 1789* (New York: Columbia University Press, 1936)

—— *Répertoire Critique des Cahiers de Doléances pour les États Généraux de 1789* (Paris: Leroux, 1933)

G. Lefebvre, 'Un colloque pour l'étude des structures sociales', *Annales Historiques de la Révolution Francaise*, no. 147 (April 1957), pp. 99–106

—— 'Recherches sur les structures sociales aux XVIIIe et XIXe siècles', *Comités des Travaux Historiques et Scientifiques, Bulletin d'Histoire Moderne et Contemporaine*, i (1956), pp. 53–61

C. Lefèvre, 'L'Ancien Droit successoral en Normandie', *Nouvelle Revue Historique de droit* (Paris, 1917)

M. Marion, *Dictionnaire des Institutions de la France au XVIIe et XVIIIe siècles* (Paris, 1923)

J. C. Perrot, 'Sources et difficultés de l'histoire des villes au XVIIIe siècle: l'exemple de la Basse Normandie', *Annales de Normandie*, viii (December, 1958), *Supplément*, pp. 25–29

P. Pisani, *Répertoire biographique de l'épiscopat constitutionnel* (Paris, 1907)

M. Reinhard, 'La Population des villes, sa mesure sous la Révolution et l'Empire', *Population*, ix (1954), pp. 279–88

—— *Étude de la population pendant la Révolution et l'Empire* (Gap, 1961)

P. de St. Jacob, 'Une source de l'histoire sociale au XVIIIe siècle; la table des contrats de mariage dans les fonds du contrôle des actes', *Actes du 84e Congrès National des Sociétés Savantes, Dijon, 1959, Section d'histoire moderne et contemporaine* (Paris, 1960), pp. 415–18

G. Vilar-Berrogain, *Guide des recherches dans les Fonds d'Enregistrement sous l'Ancien Régime* (Paris: Imprimerie Nationale, 1958)

SECONDARY WORKS

WORKS ON NORMANDY

E. Angérard, *Notes sur une famille Bayeusaine du XVIIIe siècle* (Caen, 1907)

E. Anquétil, 'La Société Populaire de Bayeux et J. C. C. Le Tual, Maire', *Mémoires de la Société des Sciences, Arts et Belles Lettres de Bayeux* (Bayeux, 1924)

P. Bernier, *Essai sur le tiers état rural ou les paysans de Basse Normandie au XVIIIe siècle* (Rouen, 1893)

J. Bidot, *Histoire de Balleroy et ses environs* (St. Lô, 1860)

M. Bouloiseau, *Cahiers de doléances du tiers état du bailliage de Rouen* (Paris, 1957)

—— *Le séquestre et la vente des biens des émigrés dans le district de Rouen, 1792–an X* (Paris, 1937)

A. J. Bourde, 'L'Agriculture à l'anglaise en Normandie au XVIIIe siècle', *Annales de Normandie* (May 1958)

Chigouesnel, *Nouvelle histoire de Bayeux* (Bayeux, 1866)

R. Cobb, 'Problèmes de subsistance de l'an II et de l'an III. L'exemple d'un petit port normand. Honfleur, 1794–1795', *Actes du 81e Congrès des Sociétés Savantes* (Rouen–Caen, 1956)

—— 'Disette et Mortalité. La crise de l'an III et de l'an IV à Rouen', *Annales de Normandie* (1956)

A. Dansin, *Le Traité de Commerce de 1786 et les intérêts de la Normandie* (Paris, 1868)

A. Dansin, *La Réforme de la justice en 1789, d'après les Vœux du Bailliage de Caen* (Paris, 1869)

A. Davies, 'The New Agriculture in Lower Normandy, 1750–1789', *Transactions of the Royal Historical Society* (1958), pp. 129–46

De Loucelles, *Histoire générale de la franc-maçonnerie en Normandie, 1739 à 1775* (Dieppe, 1875)

A. Dédouit, *Bayeux sous la Révolution, le Consulat et l'Empire* (Bellême, 1892)

G. Dubois, *Les Subsistances dans la Seine Inférieure de 1783 à 1795* (Rouen, 1936)

—— 'La Normandie économique à la fin du XVIIᵉ siècle d'après les mémoires des intendants', *Revue d'Histoire Économique et Sociale*, xxi (1933–4), pp. 337–88

L. Duchemin, 'L'Impôt sur le revenu en Normandie (Dixième et Vingtième) avant la Révolution', *Recueil des Travaux de la Société Libre d'Agriculture, Sciences, Arts et Belles Lettres de l'Eure*, 5ᵉ serie, v (1898), pp. 31–97

F. Duterque, 'Modes d'exploitation et d'amélioration du sol dans la région de Bayeux au XVIIIᵉ siècle', *Actes du 81ᵉ Congrès National des Sociétés Savantes 1956: Section d'histoire moderne et contemporaine* (1956), pp. 171–83

W. Edington, *An Administrative Study of the Implementation of the Civil Constitution of the Clergy in the Diocese of Lisieux.* (An unpublished doctoral dissertation of the University of London, 1958)

C. Gaillardon, 'L'Industrie et les industriels de Normandie en 1789', *Revue de Cherbourg*, III, pp. 22–23, 138–53, 258–69

C. Garnier, 'Les Hospices de Bayeux', *Mémoires de la Société des Sciences, Arts et Belles Lettres de Bayeux* (1908)

A. Goodwin, 'The Federalist Movement in Caen during the French Revolution', *Bulletin of the John Rylands Library*, no. 42 (1960)

P. Gouhier, *Port en Bessin* (Caen, 1960)

M. Join-Lambert, 'La Pratique religieuse dans le diocèse de Rouen de 1707 à 1789', *Annales de Normandie*, iii (1953), pp. 247–74; v (1955), pp. 37–49

J. Kaplow, *Elbeuf during the Revolutionary Period. History and Social Structure* (Baltimore, 1964)

J. Laffetay, *Histoire du diocèse de Bayeux au XVIIIᵉ siècle* (1876)

C. E. Lambert, *Les Vicomtes de Bayeux* (Bayeux, 1879)

J. Le Brethon, 'La Formation du Calvados', *Nouvelle Revue historique du droit français et étranger* (1893), pp. 146–73 and (1894), pp. 96–124, 236–77, 372–402

E. Lefebure, *Histoire de la dentelle à Bayeux de 1676 à 1900* (Bayeux, 1913)

A. Legrelle, *La Normandie sous la monarchie absolue* (Rouen, 1903)

Le Mâle, 'Départ de Monseigneur de Cheylus pour l'exil', *Baiocana* (1912), pp. 15–26

E. le Parquier, 'Les Assemblées électorales de 1789 dans les bailliages secondaires de la Haute Normandie', *La Normandie*, xiii (1906), pp. 1–12, 32–42

—— 'Une Enquête sur le paupérisme et la crise industrielle dans la région rouennaise en 1789', *Bulletin de la Société Libre d'Émulation du Commerce et de l'Industrie de la Seine Inférieure* (1935), pp. 127–97

C. Leroy, *Paysans normands au XVIIIᵉ siècle* (Rouen, 1929)

A. Létienne, *Notes sur la chouannerie normande* (Bayeux, 1924)

S. T. McCloy, 'Government aid to large families in Normandy, 1764–1786', *Social Forces*, xviii (1940), pp. 418–24

E. Michel, *Études statistiques, économiques, financières et agricoles. Un canton type.* *Bayeux* (Nancy, 1908–11). 3 vols.

M. Moulin, *Mémoires de Michelot Moulin sur la chouannerie normande* (Paris, 1893)

F. Mourlot, *La Fin de l'ancien régime et les débuts de la Révolution dans la généralité de Caen* (1911)

—— 'La Question de la mendicité en Normandie à la fin de l'ancien régime', *Bulletin Historique et Philologique* (1902)

—— 'L'Assemblée provinciale de la Basse Normandie et l'intendant', *Bulletin de la Comité des Sciences Économiques* (Paris, 1902)

P. Nicolle, *La Vente des biens nationaux à Vire et dans les communes voisines* (Paris, 1923)

G. Olphe-Galliard, *Les Industries rurales à domicile dans la Normandie Orientale* (Paris, 1913)

J. C. Perrot, 'Le commerce et l'industrie de la dentelle dans la généralité de Caen à la fin de l'ancien régime', *Actes du 81ᵉ Congrès National des Sociétés Savantes, 1956: Section d'histoire moderne et contemporaine* (Caen, 1956), pp. 215–37

M. Pezet, *Bayeux à la fin de l'ancien régime* (1856)

—— *Les Seigneurs de Ryes en Bessin*

F. Pluquet, *Notice sur les établissements littéraires et scientifiques de la ville de Bayeux* (Bayeux, 1834)

H. Prentout, 'Les Tableaux de 1790 en réponse à l'enquête du Comité de Mendicité (Calvados)', *La Révolution Française*, liii (1907), pp. 411–29

E. Sévestre, *L'Organisation du clergé paroissial à la veille de la Révolution* (Paris, 1911)

—— *Les Problèmes religieux de la Révolution et l'Empire en Normandie, 1787–1815* (Paris, 1924)

—— *Le Personnel de l'Église Constitutionnelle en Normandie, 1791–1795* (Paris, 1925)

—— *Liste critique des insermentés et assermentés (janvier-mars 1791)* (Paris, 1925)

—— *La Déportation du clergé orthodoxe pendant la Révolution* (Paris, 1915)

J. Sion, *Les Paysans de la Normandie Orientale* (Paris, 1909)

A. E. Sorel, *Pont de l'Arche pendant la Révolution* (Evreux, 1919)

Le Chanoine Uzureau, 'La Déportation ecclésiastique dans le Calvados, 1792', *Revue Catholique de Normandie*, 1931

F. Vaultier, *Souvenirs de l'insurrection normande dite du fédéralisme en 1793* (Caen, 1858)

J. Yver, 'Les Offices municipaux à Caen au XVIIIᵉ siècle', *Mémoires de l'Académie des Sciences, Arts et Belles Lettres de Caen*, vi (1931).

GENERAL WORKS

E. Alcindor, *Les Enfants assistés* (Paris, 1912)

P. Ariès, *La Vie familiale en France sous l'ancien régime* (Paris, 1959)

A. Aulard, *Histoire politique de la Révolution française* (Paris, 1926)

—— *La Révolution française et les congrégations* (Paris, 1903)

A. Babeau, *Le Village sous l'ancien régime* (5th edition, 1915)

R. Baehrel, *Une Croissance. La Basse Provence Rurale* (Paris, 1962)

C. Ballot, *L'Introduction du machinisme dans l'industrie française* (1923)

J. G. C. Blacker, 'Social Ambitions of the Bourgeoisie in 18th century France', *Population Studies*, XI (1957), pp. 46–63

C. Bloch, *Études sur l'histoire économique de la France, 1760–1789* (Paris, 1900)

—— *L'Assistance et l'état en France à la veille de la Révolution* (Paris, 1908)

P. Bois, *Paysans de l'Ouest* (Le Mans, 1960)

J. Bosher, *The Single Duty Project* (London, 1964)

M. Bouchet, *L'Assistance publique en France pendant la Révolution* (Paris, 1908)

M. Bouloiseau, 'La Répartition de l'impôt du sel à la fin de l'ancien régime', *Actes du 83e Congrès National des Sociétés Savantes, Aix-Marseille*, 1958

M. Bouvet, *Histoire de la pharmacie en France des origines à nos jours* (Paris, 1937)

L. Cahen, 'La Question du pain à Paris à la fin du XVIIIe siècle', *Cahiers de la Révolution française* (Paris, 1934)

P. Caron, *La Défense Nationale de 1792 à 1795* (Paris, 1912)

—— 'Une enquête sur les prix après la suppression du Maximum', *Commission de Recherche et de publication des documents relatifs à la vie économique de la Révolution, Bulletin Trimestriel* (1910)

—— 'La Question des prêtres insermentés en 1792', *Bulletin de la Société d'Histoire Moderne* (1951)

H. Carré, *La Noblesse de France et l'opinion publique au XVIIIe siècle* (1920)

A. Chabert, *Essai sur les mouvements des revenus et de l'activité économique en France de 1798 à 1820* (1949)

J. Charrier, *Claude Fauchet* (Paris, 1909), 2 vols.

R. Cobb, *Les Armées révolutionnaires, instrument de la Terreur dans les départements, Avril 1793–Floréal an II* (Paris, 1963)

—— *Terreur et Subsistances* (Paris, 1965)

A. Cobban, *The Myth of the French Revolution* (London, 1954)

—— 'The Vocabulary of Social History', *Political Science Quarterly*, lxxi, no. 1 (March, 1956)

—— *The Social Interpretation of the French Revolution* (Cambridge, 1964)

A. Davies, 'The Origins of the French Peasant Revolution of 1789', *History*, 1964

De Bauve, *Les Travaux publics et les ingénieurs des ponts et chaussées depuis le XVIIe siècle* (Paris, 1893)

P. Delauney, *La Vie médicale aux XVIe, XVIIe et XVIIIe siècles* (Paris, 1935)

F. Delbèke, *L'Action politique et sociale des avocats* (Louvain, 1927)

A. des Cilleuls, *Origines et développement du régime des travaux publics en France* (Paris, 1895)

P. du Puy de Clinchamps, *La Noblesse* (P.U.F. 1959)

F. Ford, *Robe and Sword. The Regrouping of the French Aristocracy after Louis XIV* (Cambridge, Mass., 1954)

R. Forster, *The Nobility of Toulouse in the Eighteenth Century* (Baltimore, 1960)

G. Friedmann, *Villes et Campagnes* (Paris, 1953)

M. Garaud, *La Révolution et la propriété foncière* (Paris, 1959)

P. Goubert, *Beauvais et le Beauvaisis de 1600 à 1730* (Paris, 1960), 2 vols.

N. Hampson, *A Social History of the French Revolution* (1963)

C. E. Labrousse, *Esquisse du mouvement des prix et des revenus en France au XVIIIe siècle* (1933)

—— *La Crise de l'économie française à la fin de l'ancien régime* (Paris, 1944)

—— 'Voies nouvelles vers une histoire de la bourgeoisie occidentale au XVIIIe et XIXe siècles (1700–1850)', *Comitato Internationale di Scienze Storiche. X Congresso Internationale di Scienze Storiche. Relazioni*, vol. iv, pp. 265–396

L. Lallemand, *Histoire des enfants abandonnés et délaissés* (Paris, 1885)

—— *La Révolution et les pauvres* (Paris, 1898)

D. S. Landes, 'The Statistical Study of French Crises', *Journal of Economic History*, x (1950), pp. 195–211

A. Latreille, *L'Église catholique et la Révolution française* (Paris, 1946)

G. Le Bras, *Introduction à l'histoire de la pratique religieuse en France* (Paris, 1942), 2 vols.

—— *Études de sociologie religieuse*, 2 vols.

M. Lecoq, *L'Assistance par le travail en France*

G. Lefebvre, *La Révolution française* (Peuples et Civilisations, ed. Halphen et Sagnac, vol. xiii, new ed. 1951)

—— *Les Paysans du Nord pendant la Révolution française* (Bari: Laterza, 1959)

—— *The Coming of the French Revolution*. Translated by R. R. Palmer (Princeton, 1947)

—— *Études sur la Révolution française* (1954)

—— 'Urban Society in the Orléanais in the late eighteenth century', *Past and Present*, no. 19, April 1961

—— 'La Révolution et l'Empire', *Revue Historique*, Avril-Juin 1955

—— 'Les recherches relatives à la répartition de la propriété et de l'exploitation foncière à la fin de l'ancien régime', *Revue d'histoire moderne*, iii (1928)

—— *La Grande Peur de 1789*

—— *Études Orléanaises* I. *Contribution à l'étude des structures sociales à la fin du XVIIIe siècle* (Paris, 1962). II. *Subsistances et maximum* (Paris, 1963)

E. le Parquier, *Ouvriers et patrons dans la seconde moitié du XVIIIe siècle* (Rouen, 1933)

P. Leuillot, 'Réflexions sur l'histoire économique et sociale à propos de la bourgeoisie de 1789', *Revue d'histoire moderne et contemporaine*, i (1954), pp. 131–44

E. Levasseur, *Histoire des classes ouvrières et de l'industrie en France avant 1789* (Paris, 1900–1)

E. Lousse, *La Société d'ancien régime* (Louvain, 1943)

H. Marion, *La Dîme ecclésiastique en France au XVIIIe siècle et sa suppression* (Bordeaux, 1912)

M. Marion, *Les Impôts directs sous l'ancien régime* (Paris, 1914)

—— 'Les Rôles de vingtième et les statistiques de la propriété territoriale sous l'ancien régime', *Revue d'histoire moderne et contemporaine*, xiv (1914)

A. Mathiez, *La Vie chère et le mouvement social sous la Terreur*

G. T. Matthews, *The Royal General Farms in 18th Century France* (New York, 1958)

J. McManners, *French Ecclesiastical Society under the Ancien Régime. A study of Angers in the eighteenth century* (Manchester, 1961)

—— 'France', in *The European Nobility in the Eighteenth Century*, ed. A. Goodwin (London, 1953)

H. Méthivier, *L'Ancien régime* (Paris, 1961)

A. Montier, *Robert Lindet* (Paris, 1899)

—— *Correspondance de Robert Lindet pendant la Constituante et la Législative (1789–1792)* (Paris, 1899)

M. Mousnier, *La Vénalité des offices sous Henri IV et Louis XIII* (Rouen, 1946)

G. Pagès, 'La Vénalité des offices dans l'ancienne France', *Revue Historique*, clxix (1932), pp. 477–95

C. Paultre, *La répression de la mendicité et du vagabondage en France sous l'ancien régime* (Paris, 1906)

M. Reinhard, 'Élite et noblesse dans la seconde moitié du XVIIIᵉ siècle', *Revue d'histoire moderne et contemporaine*, 1956, pp. 1–37

—— *Histoire de la population mondiale de 1700 à 1948* (Paris, 1949)

—— 'Sur l'histoire de la Révolution française', *Annales* (1959)

—— *Le Département de la Sarthe sous le Directoire* (Paris, 1935)

P. Renouvin, *Les Assemblées Provinciales de 1787* (Paris, 1921)

G. Rudé, *The Crowd in the French Revolution* (Oxford, 1958)

R. Schnerb, 'La Dépression économique sous le Directoire après la disparition du papier monnaie', *Annales Historiques de la Révolution Française*, 61 (1934)

H. Sée, *Economic and Social Conditions in France during the Eighteenth Century*, trans. by E. Zeydel (New York, 1935)

J. Sentou, 'Impôts et citoyens actifs à Toulouse au début de la Révolution', *Annales du Midi*, lxi (1948)

Abbé Sicard, *L'Ancien Clergé de France* (Paris, 1905), vol. i, *Les Évêques avant la Révolution*

A. Soboul, 'The French Rural Community in the 18th and 19th centuries', *Past and Present*, x (Nov. 1956), pp. 78–95

M. Sydenham, *The Girondins* (London, 1961)

E. Tarlé, *L'Industrie dans les campagnes à la fin de l'ancien régime* (1910)

A. Temple Paterson, *The Other Armada* (Manchester, 1959)

C. Tilly, *The Vendée* (London, 1964)

P. Vaissière, *Les Gentilshommes campagnards de l'ancienne France* (1904)

Vignon, *Études historiques sur l'administration des voies publiques avant 1790* (Paris, 1862)

H. Wallon, *La Révolution du 31 mai et le fédéralisme en 1793* (Paris, 1886)

INDEX

Adam family, 46, 47.

Administration, 258, 273–4; *see also* Departmental Administration, District Administration; *Intendant*; Mayor; Municipal Administration; *Subdélégué*.

Aides, 157, 212, 256, 271; officials, 67, 153.

Airel, *baronnie*, 20.

Albignac family, 51, 208.

Albignac, comte d', 42, 56.

Alsace, 95.

Amirauté, 6, 8, 59, 60, 65, 132.

Anferville, d', canon, 23.

Anfrye, sieur d', 45.

Angers, 282.

Anticlericalism, 225; *see also* Dechristianization.

Apothecaries, 58, 70–72.

Apothecary Trade, 54.

Armée de la municipalité de Paris, 200.

Armée noire, 252.

Artisans, 57, 58, 72, 73, 81, 122, 132, 133, 134, 214, 283.

Asnières, 233.

Assemblée générale des habitants, 115.

Assignat, 216–18, 230, 238, 246.

Ateliers de Charité, 106–11, 237, 238, 239–40, 241, 242, 246.

Audibert, d', canon, 23, 28.

Augustinians, 4, 30–31.

Aure, River, 4, 8.

Autin, sieur, 34–35.

Avranches, 117, 282.

Bailiffs, 58, 59, 64–65, 66–67, 76, 223, 230–1, 249, 271, 277, 287.

Bailleul, M., 55, 56.

Bailli, of seigneurial justices, 64.

Bailliage, court, 5, 7, 8, 47, 59, 60, 65, 79, 113, 114, 115, 116, 118, 122, 129, 132, 134–5, 138, 142, 213–14, 259; as electoral unit, 131, 132, 134; see also *Grand bailliage*.

Bajot, L. M., 180.

Bakers, 58, 74.

Balleroy, 178, 252, 298.

Balleroy, marquis de, 43, 77.

Banville, 44.

Barbazan, General, 256–8.

Barentan, 117.

Basley, P., 159, 274–5, 286.

Bastille, 151.

Baynes, 298.

Beaudois, de, dean, 24.

Beaudre, C. de, 197, 204, 205, 206, 209, 210, 211.

Beaumont family, 51.

Beaumont, de, canon, 23.

Beggars, 149; *see also* Poor.

Benedictines, 5, 31, 33, 50, 163.

Benefices, 285.

Bernières sur Mer, 192.

Bertauld, L., 260.

Bertin, H. L., *secrétaire d'état*, 125–7.

Bessin, 13, 19, 151, 251–2.

Béziers, M., 27, 34, 120.

Bishop, 4, 20–22, 38–39, 64, 76, 108, 111; *see also* Bisson, Brault, Cheylus, Fauchet, Luynes, Rochechouart.

Bisson, bishop, 270, 280–1.

Bobé, sieur, 63.

Bocage, 151.

Boisdelles, *baronnie*, 20, 76.

Boisgelin, de, bishop of Aix, 165.

Boisjugan, de, canon, 23, 29, 255, 266.

Boisjugan, sieur de, 53–54.

Bonneville, N., 180.

Bosq de Beaumont family, 47.

Bouche de fer, 174.

Bourgeoisie, 57–80; *see also* Third Estate.

Bourret, *représentant en mission*, 210–11, 224.

Brault, C., bishop, 279–81.

Bread riots, 150, 151, 231–3.

Briqueville family, 49.

Brissot de Warville, J. P., 192.

Brittany, 86, 95, 200–1.

Broglie, duc de, 43.

Bureau de charité, 100–1, 104–6, 111, 112, 123, 248.

Butchers, 58, 74.

Caen, 3, 16, 117, 118, 119, 124–6, 150,

PRINTED IN GREAT BRITAIN
AT THE UNIVERSITY PRESS, OXFORD
BY VIVIAN RIDLER
PRINTER TO THE UNIVERSITY